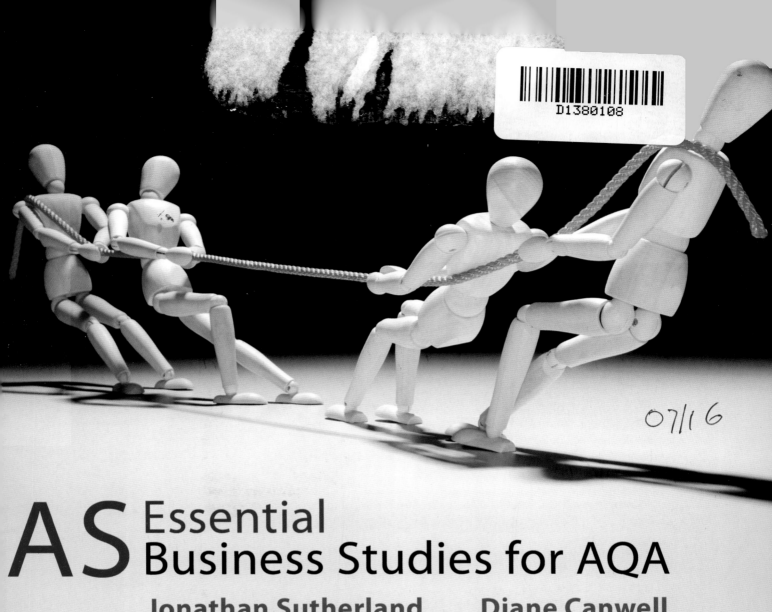

AS Essential Business Studies for AQA

Jonathan Sutherland **Diane Canwell**

United Kingdom: Folens Publishers, Waterslade House,
Thame Road, Haddenham, Buckinghamshire, HP17 8NT
Email: folens@folens.com

Ireland: Folens Publishers, Greenhills Road, Tallaght, Dublin 24
Email: info@folens.ie

Editor: Louise Wilson
Project development: Rick Jackman, Jackman Publishing Solutions Ltd
Design and layout: Patricia Briggs
Cover design: Jump to! www.jumpto.co.uk

First published 2008 by Folens Limited

British Library Cataloguing in Publication Data. A catalogue record for this
publication is available from the British Library.

ISBN 978-1-85008-360-3
Folens code: FD3603

CONTENTS

UNIT 1
PLANNING AND FINANCING A BUSINESS

Introduction

Both of the AS business studies units focus on small to medium-sized businesses operating within a national market. Unit 1 – *Planning and financing a business* – looks at all the issues involved in starting up a business, including research and planning, and other key factors that can determine success or failure.

There are two core themes in Unit 1: *Starting a business* and *Financial planning*, and these themes are further broken down into topic areas, such as *Enterprise* and *Developing business plans*. You will be expected to have a good understanding of the range of activities involved in setting up a small business. Each of the topic areas will look at one particular aspect, but it is important to remember that many of them link together and are dependent upon one another.

Throughout this AS unit you will be expected to carry out calculations; interpret and analyse data; apply your knowledge in unfamiliar situations; develop arguments; and make judgements and decisions. These are known as transferable skills, and examiners will be expecting you to demonstrate them in your answers for the examination.

The unit itself is examined in an examination of one hour and fifteen minutes. The total number of marks available to you is 60 and the examination

accounts for 20% of the overall A-level mark.

In the examination you should expect to answer short-answer questions and provide extended responses, based on a mini case study. The examination will cover *Starting a business*, which is essentially an introduction to business studies and an overview of what is involved in starting a small business. *Financial planning* looks at essential financial concepts and the relationship between finance and other functions of an organisation.

This section of the book follows the exact specification of the GCE. Each of the two core themes is examined in detail, with each topic given its own section comprising a number of double-page spreads, each of which looks at an aspect of that topic. On each spread there are either short-answer questions to test your understanding, or mini case studies with extended questions. At the end of each topic there is an opportunity for you to try out short-answer questions and extended responses based on mini case studies, as well as other activities to help you prepare for your examination.

At the end of the unit, another spread provides a checklist of the unit's key concepts and further revision aids.

Introduction

This is the first of the two core themes for *Planning and financing a business*. You will be expected to have an understanding of the range of activities that could be involved in setting up a small business.

Any new business starts with an individual or individuals having the idea and the drive to set up their new enterprise. This means coming up with a workable and potentially profitable business idea. Regardless of the type of business involved, an enterprise transforms resources, such as raw materials, stock or skills, into products and services that can be sold to customers. All businesses need to develop business plans, in order to help in their decision-making and to show that they have thought through the implications of running a business, both to owners of the business itself and also to potential sources of finance.

A new business would be foolish to think it could start without having carried out some basic market research. Market research helps to identify the types of market that may be interested in the business's products or services. It will also show the size of that market, the major competitors and whether or not the market is growing.

Businesses also need to decide what kind of legal structure is most appropriate for them. This choice can have a major impact on administration, tax, the willingness of finance providers to become involved and how the ownership of the business is divided. Most new businesses will need to obtain some form of financial assistance to set up, either in the form of the owners' savings, or perhaps bank loans, overdrafts or even the selling of shares to investors. Businesses also need to be very careful about choosing their location: some may need to be close to sources of raw materials, parts or components, whereas others may need to be close to their market or their customers. For many owners of new businesses, this will also be the first time that they will employ other people. Wages and salaries are a considerable cost to any business, and employees need to be able to bring with them the ideal blend of skills and expertise that can help ensure that the small business is successful.

Enterprise and entrepreneurs

The role of entrepreneurs

If you were to try to find a definition of the word enterprise you would probably come across a number of different meanings:

- An organisation that has been created for business ventures
- An individual's ability to take on new challenges
- An individual who is innovative and inspiring

For our purposes, enterprise is about running a business and entrepreneurship. Enterprise is about being inventive and imaginative. It also means being able to create new ideas and solve problems. These skills and drives are now commonly associated with the term entrepreneur.

Many people think that an entrepreneur is anyone who starts a business. However, there are several different types of entrepreneur, and each of them has a different role:

- There are people who take an existing business into a competitive market where they reinvent the product or service to make it different, such as Stelios Haji-Ioannou, the founder of easyJet.
- There are people who take calculated risks to start businesses because of their belief in the product or service, such as Duncan Bannatyne of the Bannatyne group of companies.
- There are those who start one or more businesses, and then use similar techniques and brand names to launch new ones, such as Sir Richard Branson and his Virgin group of companies.

INTERNET RESEARCH

Use the Internet to find out more about these three important British-based entrepreneurs. Their businesses have websites, but more interesting information can be found about them at websites such as www.independent.co.uk or www.guardian.co.uk. Try to get into the habit of visiting these websites and keeping up-to-date with business news.

Entrepreneurs are people who take risks and bring together all the resources necessary to make a business successful. Their role can be complicated. It might involve:

- developing new markets by either satisfying the needs of customers, or creating a new demand for products and services
- discovering new sources of materials, such as developing a new way of producing something
- coordinating employees, resources and money (known as the factors of production) to create products and services in an efficient and innovative way
- introducing new technologies, industries or products
- creating employment. (This is one of the many reasons why governments are very keen on entrepreneurs.)

The importance of entrepreneurs

Entrepreneurs can make major contributions to a country's economy. They are innovators, and many see that innovation is at the heart of economic progress. Entrepreneurship makes the economy more competitive. Since 1945, half of all innovations and 95% of all radical innovations have come from new and smaller businesses. Economies that have high levels of entrepreneurial activity grow faster and create more wealth.

More and more people want to start their own businesses, to have more control over their lives and careers. By 2010 it is estimated that there will be 4.5m businesses; at present there are 3.7m.

Entrepreneurship can be seen as being vital to the economy. It:

- Produces products and services
- Creates jobs, both directly and indirectly
- Generates export earnings
- Develops new products and services using modern technologies.

4

Characteristics of entrepreneurs

Jeffrey Timmons of the Massachusetts Institute of Technology identified 14 key entrepreneurial characteristics of successful owners of enterprises:

- Drive and energy
- Self-confidence
- High initiative and personal responsibility
- Internal locus of control
- Tolerance of ambiguity
- Low fear of failure
- Moderate risk taking
- Long-term involvement
- Money seen as a measure, not merely as an end
- Good use of feedback
- Continuous problem solving
- Good use of resources
- Self-imposed standards
- Clear goal setting

Few entrepreneurs will possess all the traits listed above: some will have strengths in certain areas, and weaknesses in others. Other research studies have shown that achievement, persistence and self-confidence are particularly important characteristics. Risk taking is also vital, but needs to be balanced. Many people will avoid starting their own business due to anxiety or fear of failure, while others may start businesses, suffer setbacks and then not know how to proceed.

There have been many attempts to define the characteristics of entrepreneurs. Most have focused on their leadership:

- In 1959 A Cole suggested that there were four different types of entrepreneur: the innovator, the calculating inventor, the over-optimistic promoter and the organisation builder.

KEY TERMS

Internal locus of control – placing the responsibility, choice and control of events in one's own hands.

Ambiguity – having more than one interpretation; lack of a clear meaning.

- In 1961 David McClelland believed that entrepreneurs are motivated by the need to achieve and to build.
- In 1970 J Collins and D Moore worked out that entrepreneurs are tough, sound-thinking people, driven by the desire to be independent and the desire to achieve, but that many were rebels at heart.
- By the 1990s writers such as B Bird claimed that entrepreneurs were cunning, creative and opportunistic, but at the same time resourceful and ingenious.

CASE STUDY WHAT MAKES AN ENTREPRENEUR?

Entrepreneurs are individuals who recognise that there is a need for a product or service. They can bring together resources, including materials, equipment, capital or money and employees to meet a need. There is no set profile of an entrepreneur: they can be young or old, and have small or large businesses. According to the Entrepreneur of the Year Annual Review, the list on the left shows the top ten characteristics of young, successful entrepreneurs.

1 **PASSION** They are often in a business they love, or have turned their hobby into a business.

2 **VISION** They have a clear vision both personally and for the business.

3 **UNFLAPPABLE CONFIDENCE** They are not afraid to fail, and, if they do, they pick up and start again, often starting multiple businesses.

4 **LEADERSHIP** They inspire and motivate those around them and, in doing so, build a loyal workforce.

5 **NETWORKERS** Young entrepreneurs form unusually strong business networks and rely on them heavily.

6 **APPETITE FOR RISK** They are comfortable in a high-risk environment and often thrive on it.

7 **DETACHMENT** Successful entrepreneurs can separate their passion from their business and know how to get out when timing is tight.

8 **FLEXIBILITY** They follow market desires and work in virtual teams (no 'head office'), using technology to adapt quickly.

9 **CUSTOMER-SAVVY** They're educated about fashion or trend cycles, always on the lookout for the 'next big thing' and focus on customer needs (commonly in the lifestyle/service sectors).

10 **WORLDLY** Today's young entrepreneurs are well-travelled, well-educated, well-read and often bi/tri-lingual. They think globally from day one of being in business.

Questions

1 What do you think is meant by the term 'strong business networks'?
2 What is your understanding of the term 'high-risk environment'?
3 How do these ten characteristics fit with the three entrepreneurs we looked at earlier?

Source: The True Marks of Entrepreneurship, *Entrepreneur of the Year Annual Review*, 2005

Risks and rewards

Potential risks

Managing risk is a key skill for an entrepreneur. Risk-taking is not always dangerous: there is often a reward in the form of profit. Risky business decisions have to be considered and measured against the possible returns, or rewards. Typically, the entrepreneur will ask:

- Is the return worth the risk?
- Does the situation require us to take a risk?
- What is my attitude to the risk?
- Can we afford to take the risk?
- Are we capable of dealing with the risk?

Risk management is a process that involves looking at the risks associated with the greatest possible losses and the greatest possible likelihood of them occurring. An entrepreneur will look at these risks first and then consider those where losses are lower and the chances of them occurring are less probable.

The process of managing any risk involves identifying the potential risks at the outset. Risks, if realised, will inevitably cause problems.

Once the risks have been identified and assessed, there are basically four ways of proceeding:

- Risk avoidance – not doing anything that could carry a high risk, such as not choosing to rent or buy a business property in an area that is known to flood.
- Risk reduction – reducing the severity of any losses, for instance making sure that the security systems fitted into business premises are sufficient to deter possible break-ins.
- Risk retention – deciding to accept any losses that should happen. This means accepting that some risks cannot be certainly avoided, such as theft from the business or the chance that a major customer might cease trading.
- Risk transfer – effectively transferring the risk to someone else. This can be achieved by either insuring a risk or by using a **subcontractor** to carry out the work on your behalf.

  FOCUS POINT

To what extent can the rewards gained by taking a risk outweigh the initial risk? Discuss as a group.

Risks	Rewards
The entrepreneur(s) may only be able to reward themselves with a low salary, or perhaps no salary at all, in the first months.	If the correct decisions are made at the right time then there is enormous potential for growth and wealth.
The entrepreneur may lack adequate resources to pursue ideas and opportunities.	The entrepreneur will gain a huge range of experience in different aspects of business.
It may not be possible to employ sufficient staff with adequate skills to do everything that is needed, so opportunities may be missed.	The entrepreneur will develop a broad network of partners, suppliers and customers.
The entrepreneur will not be able to give himself or herself a **job description** as such: but will have to cope with a wide variety of different tasks and responsibilities.	The entrepreneur and employees will have pride in their success and a great sense of achievement.
Start-up businesses have the highest rate of failure of all types of business.	The entrepreneur will have achieved independence and control over a business.

Potential rewards

There is usually a radical difference between an entrepreneur and an established business in their attitudes to risk. An entrepreneur will tend to view risk as a means of maximising the possible rewards of a potential success. It is on this basis that the risk will be assessed. On the other hand a more established and mature business will look at risks, and decisions related to risks, in terms of minimising the possible costs of failure.

The table on the opposite page outlines some of the key considerations relating to the risks facing start-up businesses.

Over 300 businesses close down each week. This means that around 17,000 businesses fail each year. Balancing risk means assessing the potential rewards against the ultimate fear of ruining the business and losing any hope of saving it.

Research by the Cranfield School of Management shows that entrepreneurs who are risk takers are far more likely to achieve higher sales growth. However they caution entrepreneurs that over-confidence is also a major cause of failure.

> ### KEY TERMS
>
> **Subcontractor** – an individual or a business that takes over the responsibility to perform a particular task or provide a particular service.
>
> **Job description** – an outline of the main duties and responsibilities of a particular job.

CASE STUDY BENJYS

Paul Benjamin opened the first branch of Benjys sandwich shops in 1989. The Benjamin family sold the business for around £40m in 2000. It grew into a chain of sandwich shops and van-based franchises, delivering sandwiches to offices and other venues.

In 2006 the company had a turnover of £33m and ambitions to open 250 stores. However, in July 2006 the company went into administration and was subsequently bought by the business Hamilton Bradshaw. The company ran into trouble again in February 2007, this time with debts of £22.9m. By 7 February almost all the branches were closed and the franchisees were given just two weeks to find replacement vehicles for their sandwich delivery businesses. The main reasons for the setbacks were rent rises and tough trading conditions. According to the British Sandwich Association, the British buy two billion sandwiches each year and spend about £3.5bn on them.

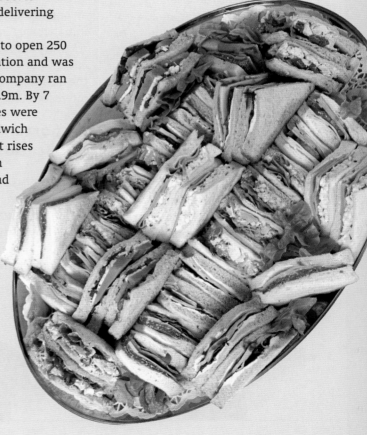

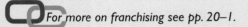

For more on franchising see pp. 20–1.

Questions

1 What might be meant by the term 'tough trading conditions'?
2 What is meant by the term 'went into administration'?
3 The operators of the mobile delivery services are franchise holders, having paid a fee to set up and trade under the name of Benjys. Why might they be particularly concerned by the closure of the business?

Opportunity cost

LEARNING OBJECTIVES
▶ What is opportunity cost?
▶ Opportunity cost implications

What is opportunity cost?

Opportunity cost is the cost of missing out on the next best alternative when making a business decision. Every choice made by an entrepreneur has an opportunity cost. This means that entrepreneurs will look at all the different alternatives before making a decision.

Deciding to make a particular investment may mean that the chance of making other potential investments has to be given up. Cash and other resources are always limited. An entrepreneur cannot make an unlimited number of investments and must usually choose one or two that offer the best possible chance of success or financial return.

Opportunity cost is the opportunity that has been lost by not choosing one of the alternative investments. If, for example, an entrepreneur considered that the most important investment was to obtain a retail outlet in a busy shopping mall, then the opportunity cost might be the opportunity to have opened two retail outlets in less popular areas.

The money that might have to be spent on paying for **stock** could be used to invest in developing a new product or service, or investing in a delivery vehicle. All the alternatives might have brought benefits to the business, but some of them have to be foregone or given up.

For new business start-ups there is another form of opportunity cost – when the business has to borrow money in order to set up or to pay for stock. There will be **interest** to pay on the overdraft or the loan. The loss of this money represents an opportunity cost, because if the initial money had not been borrowed, then any cash made by the business could be directly invested back into the business, rather than paid out as interest to the lender.

Opportunity cost implications

Opportunity cost is not just a matter of concern for entrepreneurs or, for that matter, consumers. The opportunity cost concept has more deep-rooted implications. All resources are relatively scarce:

a government, for example, may have to choose between building a new motorway or a new hospital. A business with limited production may have to decide whether to continue to supply its existing customers, or accept a new, larger contract from a new customer, knowing that it will not be able to continue supplying its existing customers.

Shortage of resources means that choices always have to be made about which alternatives can be satisfied and which have to be foregone. An entrepreneur will look for the choice that provides the greatest benefit, either in cash terms or in the longer-term interests of the business.

Even a cash-rich or resource-rich entrepreneur or business cannot possibly take advantage of every opportunity that presents itself. It will have to make choices, and each time a choice is made another opportunity is potentially lost.

Opportunity cost is not the sum of all of the available alternatives, but the benefit that the business would have had from the next best alternative.

If a business has a limited number of employees, or production capacity, it will have to decide on how many units of a particular product it produces. The business will know that producing more of one product will mean producing less of another. For example, the opportunity cost of producing a kilogram of cheese is the amount of butter that has not been produced.

Opportunity cost can also be applied at a personal level. If a premiership footballer was nearing the end of his contract at his club and chose to sign a new contract with the club for another five years, the opportunity cost to the footballer would be the success that he might have achieved if he had decided to sign for another club instead.

CASE STUDY EASYJET'S OPPORTUNITY COST

Easyjet's pricing structure is an example of opportunity cost working for both the business and for the customers. One of the major problems with airlines has been that if they did not sell all the tickets for a particular flight, they could not simply hold those seats in stock and sell them another time. The opportunity to sell them was lost once the plane took off.

Most airlines start with a high ticket price, gradually reducing it as the day of the flight gets nearer. Easyjet, on the other hand, starts with an extremely low price for the seat ticket. Every time a seat is sold and there are fewer seats available on the flight, the price increases. For Easyjet the opportunity cost is not charging the full price for all of the seats, but ensuring that most of the seats are sold as early as possible to customers looking for a bargain price.

For customers there is also an opportunity cost. Every day they do not make the decision to purchase

the ticket for a particular flight the price will increase, as other customers buy tickets for that flight. If they wait until the last minute they are likely to pay ten or twenty times the price that they could have paid when the seats for that flight were first advertised. This is their opportunity cost.

Questions

1. Easyjet rewards those who buy early. Traditionally airlines profited from those who booked early. Compare the opportunity costs of the two approaches.
2. Budget airlines sell direct to the public and usually only have one class of seat. Why might it be difficult for a more traditional airline to use Easyjet's pricing policy?

Becoming an entrepreneur

Why become an entrepreneur?

Two researchers from the San Francisco State University interviewed dozens of entrepreneurs. Most of them were under 40 years old and a large number of them were involved in hi-tech enterprises. The researchers wanted to know what motivates people to become entrepreneurs.

The most popular eight reasons for wanting to be an entrepreneur are shown in the table on the right.

The researchers also found that entrepreneurs saw the other major motivating factors as being: intellectual challenge; the possibility of career growth and satisfaction; and the ability to use their previous experience.

Becoming an entrepreneur is more than just setting up a new business. It means taking risks, coming up with new and innovative ideas, and finding solutions to problems.

There is no such thing as a typical entrepreneur; they come from all different sorts of backgrounds and can exist in any field of business. They can exist in large organisations, as Alan Sugar does, or they can be starting up and running their own businesses. Some can even be social entrepreneurs, like Richard Branson, who uses some of his business techniques to achieve positive social change.

Entrepreneurs try to take advantage of opportunities, to innovate, and to initiate change. They often get involved in areas of business that others feel are too risky.

Reason for wanting to be an entrepreneur	% of entrepreneurs mentioning this reason
Freedom to make own decisions	57
Making money and financial independence	43
Seeing a business opportunity	27
Realising a capability	23
Desire to create something new and to innovate	20
Desire to create something important and make a difference	17
Desire to grow a business from scratch	17
Excitement	3

Spotting a gap in the market

Entrepreneurs look for opportunities. They may not necessarily have any specialised knowledge or access to information that other people do not have, but they try to make more use of what they see and hear, and then identify an opportunity.

Opportunities exist where individuals want a particular product or service that is either not yet available; in short supply; of poor quality; or more expensive than they would like.

In assessing whether an opportunity has the potential to become more than just a good idea, the entrepreneur will ask a number of questions:

- Is it a real opportunity?
- Is there a market for it?
- Will it have competition?
- How long will the opportunity be likely to last?
- Has the opportunity been correctly identified?
- Is there sufficient and accurate information about the opportunity?
- Is it possible to come up with a product or service to meet the opportunity?
- Is the opportunity worth the potential risks?
- What are the most likely risks that will be faced?
- Will the potential rewards outweigh the risks?

FOR EXAMPLE

In 2005 Elizabeth Guy, a mother of three children, spotted a gap in the market and created Wensleydale Foods. She now has a successful line of food products stocked by Waitrose and Budgens. She created a range called Beth Guy's Little Pies, which are potato-topped pies without additives or preservatives that provide nutritious home-cooked style food for young children.

Developing new and innovative products and processes

Entrepreneurs need to be able to spot gaps in the market and to then develop new ideas for products or services. Sometimes they will need to think of different ways of satisfying a particular customer need.

Regardless of how clever new product or service ideas are, on average around 80% of them fail. This is mainly because entrepeneurs often do not really understand the market they are entering. Also, in a lot of cases, the entrepeneur does not understand either what their potential customers want, or the strengths and weaknesses of their competitors. Careful **market research** is important, but this can often be difficult for a new business start-up lacking in resources.

BOOK RESEARCH

Bridge, Rachel, *My big idea: 30 successful entrepreneurs reveal how they found inspiration*, Kogan Page (2006)

KEY TERMS

Motivate – to make someone want to do something to achieve a certain result.

Market research – the process of gathering information about customers, competitors and market trends.

FOR EXAMPLE

Two-and-a-half million disabled people have blue parking badges. Thousands of them are stolen from cars every year. Gowrings is a business that adapts cars for wheelchair users. They learned about the parking problem from their customers and immediately spotted a gap in the market and came up with a simple solution. The parking permit slides into a steel case, then a lockable steel cable is fed through the case and around the steering wheel of the car. A thief would have to use bolt cutters to steel the blue badge.

P Disabled badge holders only

CASE STUDY THE DYSON STORY

In 1978 James Dyson saw that powder particles clogged vacuum cleaner bags. He came up with the idea of a system that would remove the powder particles. It took five years and 5,127 prototypes for him to come up with the first bagless vacuum cleaner. The first versions were sold in Japan for $2,000 each, and with the money he set up a research centre and decided to manufacture his own model. It then took James Dyson fourteen years to get his first product into a shop. Several competitors, including Hoover in 1999, tried to copy his innovative ideas. After a legal battle that took eighteen months Dyson finally won. He continues to innovate, with a new air-blade hand drier and a two-drum washing machine now on the market.

Source: adapted from www.dyson.co.uk.

Using the case study and the Dyson website, answer the following questions on innovation.

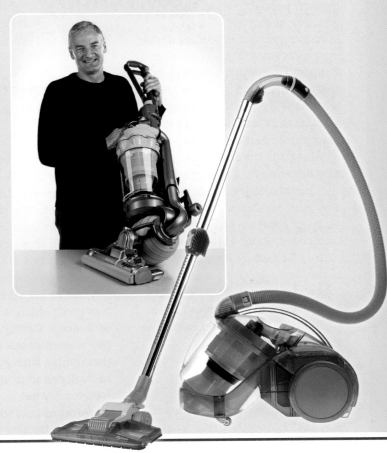

Questions

1 What were James Dyson's three innovations before the bagless vacuum cleaner?
2 Dyson patented his Root Cyclone technology. What does the term 'patent' mean?

Government support for enterprise and entrepreneurs

LEARNING OBJECTIVES

▶ Government initiatives
▶ Government departments and agencies
▶ Getting support

Government initiatives

In June 2007 Prime Minister Gordon Brown announced the creation of the Department for Business, Enterprise and Regulatory Reform (DBERR). It was to become responsible for creating the conditions for business success, and replaced the Department of Trade and Industry (DTI), which for many years had been the main government department covering business, enterprise and innovation.

The creation of the new department was seen as a major initiative and part of a wider desire by the government to create a better business framework. Company law was simplified and reformed and new laws made it easier to set up and run a business, as well as encouraging flexibility and long-term investment.

Alongside the creation of the new department, the Prime Minister also announced the creation of a new Business Council for Britain. Amongst those on the Business Council are senior entrepreneurs, such as Sir Richard Branson (founder of the Virgin Group), Sir Alan Sugar (chairman of Amstrad), Tony Haywood (chief executive of BP) and Sir Terry Leahy (the chief executive of Tesco).

Another major initiative was the creation of the Department of Innovation, Universities and Skills (DIUS). This department was specifically designed to encourage

INTERNET RESEARCH 🔍

To find out about current initiatives of the DBERR, go to www.news.bbc.co.uk. The head of the department is John Hutton.

business research and the creation of new products and services, and to help drive enterprise and efficiency.

In addition to these new initiatives, support for businesses continues, with organisations such as Business Link providing national, regional and local support, and practical advice for all types of business.

Government departments and agencies

Governments are very keen to support enterprise and entrepreneurs, but they are equally keen to control them. Businesses can provide great benefits for Britain; they develop new products and services, provide employment and pay tax. At the same time, however, certain forms of business activity can be detrimental to the country, such as causing pollution and road congestion.

Governments want businesses to make

the highest possible positive impact and minimise any negative impacts. The government will typically provide:

- Training programmes
- Development grants (particularly for regions that have high unemployment)
- Specific support for new businesses, or for businesses that export products or services

The table opposite identifies some of the main sources of government support to enterprises and entrepreneurs.

KEY TERMS

Export – one country selling products or services to another country or countries.

Mentoring – help provided by an individual to a business in relation to focussing on specific issues, developing key skills and widening the network of business contacts.

Government department or agency	Its work and role	Website
Department for Business, Enterprise and Regulatory Reform	The Department leads work to create the conditions for business success through competitive and flexible markets that create value for businesses, consumers and employees. It drives regulatory reform, and works with government and across the regions to raise levels of UK productivity. The Department will provide support to the new Business Council for Britain.	www.berr.gov.uk
Business Link	Business Link provides the information, advice and support needed to start, maintain and grow a business. It provides information and advice to help customers make the most of their opportunities. Rather than providing all the advice and help itself, it directs customers to the expert help they need. The Business Link service is a crucial part of the Government's campaign to promote enterprise and to make the UK the best place in the world in which to start and grow a business. Business Link is available locally and is quality-assured regionally to clear national standards.	www.businesslink.gov.uk
Department for Innovation, Universities and Skills (DIUS)	DIUS is responsible for driving forward the Government's long-term vision to make Britain one of the best places in the world for science, research and innovation, and for delivering the ambition of a world-class skills base.	www.dius.gov.uk
Business Council for Britain	The Council, made up of senior business leaders, will assist the Government in putting in place the right strategy to promote the long-term health of the UK economy.	
Development Agencies	RDAs have five statutory objectives: 1 To further economic development and regeneration 2 To promote business efficiency and competitiveness 3 To promote employment 4 To enhance the development and application of skills relevant to employment 5 To contribute to sustainable development	www.englandsrdas.com

Getting support

For the vast majority of new enterprises and entrepreneurs, the first thing they need is a business plan.

A business plan outlines the intentions of the business or the entrepreneur. It helps them identify the market, the products and services that will be offered, the competition and, crucially, any external advice or funding that may have to be sought. At a local level entrepreneurs can turn to various services offered by high-street banks, or they can receive impartial advice from organisations such as Business Link or the local Chamber of Commerce (www.chamberonline.co.uk).

These organisations can advise entrepreneurs on where to obtain the specialist advice and support they require. Grants, development funds and other sources of finance may be available in particular parts of the country. Banks and finance providers may be able to arrange lower-cost loans or overdraft facilities. Ongoing business advice or **mentoring** can be provided by organisations such as Business Link.

Other major sources of assistance for new enterprises and entrepreneurs include accountants, solicitors, computer services, communications services and a wide variety of financial services and advisors.

> ### Questions
> 1 What is the role of the DBERR?
> 2 Why might Business Link be a good place for a new business to seek support in the first instance?
> 3 Find out the difference between a government department and a government agency.

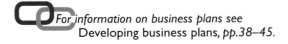 *For information on business plans see Developing business plans, pp.38–45.*

Case studies, questions and exam practice

CASE STUDY IDENTICOM

SECTOR: PRODUCT DESIGN – ELECTRONICS ● EMPLOYEES: 29 ● LOCATION: BERKSHIRE

The big idea

To develop a communicating safety device that looks like a name badge to protect the lone or isolated worker.

The companies involved

Connexion2 Limited is a company dedicated to improving the working lives and safety of lone workers.Connexion2 commissioned Triteq Limited, a leading innovator in the design, development and manufacture of electronic devices to develop its Identicom product.

The challenge

To design a communicating device for lone or isolated workers that was easier to operate than a mobile phone and more discreet to use. It should also deliver benefits to the employer as well as meet the requirements from the Police. After attending a Suzy Lamplugh Trust seminar on 'handling conflict', Craig Swallow (then Triteq's Commercial Director, now Connexion2's CEO) realised the extent of the vulnerability of some community-based workers around the world. The technology available to help protect these workers was also limited – indeed, a mobile phone was often the only device available to contact help.

An important element of the design was the need for it to be discreet. If an individual is under attack or threat, the obvious use of a phone or other alarm device might exacerbate an already difficult situation, and might even trigger a violent attack.

The solution

Craig decided to develop an alarm device to mimic the ordinary identity card worn by all community workers. Called Identicom, each unit features a discreet button on the rear of the badge. When pressed, this discretely opens a voice call to a dedicated and responsible third-party point, such as a call-monitoring centre, where it can be managed, recorded, listened to, and if necessary relayed to the emergency services.

In addition, Identicom hides a clever 'rip alarm' in the carrying strap, which automatically triggers an alarm if it is forcibly removed from the wearer. Each card incorporates GSM and battery- and power-management technologies, and helps identify the location of the wearer. The use of GSM also enables the identity card to trigger the automatic sending of text messages to colleagues. Furthermore, it allows users to pre-record useful information before going out in the field. If they do not then respond to the incorporated timer, the card will make an emergency call to initiate a response to the possible incident.

SHORT-ANSWER QUESTIONS

1 Define the word 'enterprise'.

2 What is an entrepreneur?

3 What do you understand by the term 'risk assessment'?

4 Define opportunity cost and give a simple example.

5 List **FIVE** primary motives for becoming an entrepreneur.

6 What do you understand by the term 'gap in the market'?

7 Why is innovation important as an aspect of entrepreneurship?

8 Why might James Dyson be described as both an entrepreneur and an innovator?

9 What is the role of the **DBERR**?

10 Suggest **THREE** local points of contact for support for an entrepreneur.

Issues arising

Triteq is a design and development company with a range of world-class expertise in electronic and software skills, but it has less experience of mass production or marketing of products. It's business model is to adopt a team approach to projects, to maximise its own potential in conjunction with external expertise. To this end, Connexion2 took over and developed the Identicom product. Industrial designers worked on the form of the finished product to ensure that it looked and felt exactly like a standard ID badge, and a third-party manufacturer was engaged to take the prototypes into volume production.

The outcome

Since its launch in 2005, over 25,000 Identicom units have been sold, generating revenue in excess of £3.8m. This is a great start, and the future looks very promising as these figures represent only about five per cent of the UK market, with global markets still to be explored.

Source: adapted from the Department for Business Enterprise and Regulatory Reform

Questions

1 What is meant by the term 'leading innovator'? (2 marks)

2 What might be meant by the term 'third-party manufacturer'? (2 marks)

3 If 25,000 Identicom units have been sold, what was the average sale price per unit? (4 marks)

4 Suggest sources of government support and assistance that the business could use in order both to tackle global markets, and to improve its sales in Britain. (6 marks)

5 Suggest SIX major potential users or markets for this product in Britain. (6 marks)

Sources of business ideas

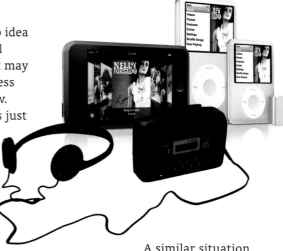

First thoughts

Many existing businesses will use research and development, either internally or externally, to come up with new ideas. Internal ideas can come from a variety of different sources, such as suggestions from employees or brainstorming sessions. Some businesses have their own research departments, which focus on either new product or service ideas, or ways in which to sell existing products or services to new markets. Ideas may come from outside the business. New ideas are registered.

For more about patents see pp.22–3, and for franchises see pp.20–1.

Some businesses might buy a franchise to produce products or provide services under the trading name of an existing business. They will have to pay the owner of the original business a fee and usually a percentage of **turnover**.

Customers can also come up with valuable business ideas. Many businesses will have customer service lines to encourage feedback, and their websites may have comment and feedback pages to encourage customers to make comment. Not only does this help the business understand what customers want, but it also gives vital clues as to what customers may want in the future.

KEY TERM

Turnover – the amount of money received by a business as sales revenue in a year.

It has been said that no idea is a bad one, but the actual chances of success of what may appear to be a great business idea are comparatively low. Coming up with the idea is just the first stage. As we will see, the ideas need to be screened, developed, tested and re-tested before they can be launched onto the market.

Innovation and invention

Many people now have iPods or MP3 players, but portable music began with the Sony Walkman. The idea for this was a bit of a fluke. Someone saw a tiny tape player and a miniature set of headphones in two different Sony research labs on the same day. The person who saw it was not just anyone – it was the chairman of Sony. Instantly he realised that it would be possible to create a product on which customers could play their own music while walking around.

A similar situation occurred when researchers were trying to create a super glue. One version that they made was completely useless; it did not even stick permanently. One of the researchers realised that this slightly sticky glue might be handy to fix bookmarks into a book. He applied the glue to one edge of a piece of paper, put it into the book and then peeled it off without marking the page of the book. Thus the Post-it note was born.

The two examples are, of course, inventions. But there is also innovation, which can involve finding new uses for an old product, or a simpler and cheaper way of

FOR EXAMPLE

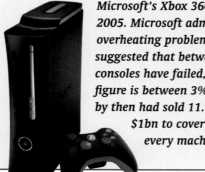

Microsoft's Xbox 360 was first launched in November 2005. Microsoft admitted that some of the systems had overheating problems. Since then various reports have suggested that between 30% and 50% of the gaming consoles have failed, although Microsoft claims that the true figure is between 3% and 5%. In July 2007 Microsoft, who by then had sold 11.6m Xbox 360s, decided to set aside over $1bn to cover the costs of extending the warranty of every machine from one to three years.

producing that product. One of the best examples is in computer technology. Businesses such as Intel are continually innovating to produce ever faster and more reliable processors. They know they need to do this in order to keep ahead of their competitors. It is usually in the technology field that innovation is essential for survival. In many other areas of business, gradually adapting to change is usually sufficient.

A new product or service does not just have to be a great idea; it needs to look right, be economical to produce and to work. Many great ideas fail due to one or more of these criteria. A great idea may not look, feel, smell or taste right. Many suggest that the relative failure of the meat substitute Quorn is on account of this (it appeals to vegetarians, but as it contains eggs is not suitable for Vegans).

Some products are clearly too expensive to manufacture, which will make them far too expensive for customers to buy. Some products cannot be made quickly and efficiently; this is why car manufacturers such as Lotus may never be in a position to sell hundreds of thousands of vehicles a year, as their vehicles have to be handmade.

Functionality is important too. Not only does the product have to work, but it also has to be reliable.

Idea to launch

Innovative new products may require a significant level of long-term investment by a business. Once a gap in the market has been identified, probably through market research, the original idea will be developed. The idea will then be turned into a

design and a brief will be prepared, outlining its major characteristics and functions. If it is a product, some initial designs will have to be drawn up, and some prototypes made. After this, working samples will have to be made and tested. These can then be passed on to groups of typical consumers to gauge their reaction to them and to deal with any faults that may only become apparent when they are being used.

Assuming that all these stages have been passed successfully, the product will then move towards manufacture. The business will need to decide how many units to produce, and where to produce and organise the raw materials and components that will be required to construct the product. Once these are in place, it can then go into full-scale production and launch the product onto the market.

CASE STUDY: HOT BUSINESS FOR THE FUTURE

Industry	Five year % growth projection
Health and fitness	59%
Life assurance	50%
Accident and health	47%
Cinema	43%
Overseas travel	41%
Personal pensions	37%
Private medical insurance	32%
Convenience foods	32%
Fast food	30%
House purchase	28%
Medicines	20%
Domestic and garden help	16%
Cleaning and laundry services	16%

Source: Mintel

Questions

1 What is the common characteristic of all these industries? (2 marks)
2 Why might these growth projections suggest that certain industries are less attractive to new businesses? (4 marks)
3 Choose one of the industries and suggest an innovative product or service that might give a new business the edge. (4 marks)

Identifying product or market niches

Niches

A niche is a segment or part of a larger market. Smaller businesses often target these niches to try to exploit an underserved part of that market.

This research involves finding out precisely what the people represented by the market would buy if they knew that a particular product or service were available. The idea is that there is a demand for a particular product or service, and that the business or the entrepreneur can recognise the fact that it is not yet being supplied.

Usually a niche market involves creating a product or service that is not being offered by mainstream or larger businesses. Potential demand is not being met by any current supply. Larger businesses may not be particularly interested, because the volume of sales to that niche market may be low in comparison to the markets they are already supplying.

Spotting that gap

There are many different ways in which a gap in the market can be identified. The following are some simple examples:

- **Timing** – any business could consider changing its opening hours. By opening later, earlier, or for longer, new customers could be attracted to the products and services offered.
- **Size** – if the business made products in a different size, would that appeal to a new market? The handmade cosmetic company Lush produces a range of small tins of solid perfume that can be carried in a pocket or a purse. This is in addition to traditional-size liquid perfumes.

- **Adapting** – an idea that may be working in another part of the country or abroad could be brought to another geographical area, or country, where it is at present not available.
- **Location** – although an increasing amount of products and services are sold over the Internet, many customers still prefer traditional forms of purchasing. In a typical high street or market town, small retailers cluster around major shops or markets.

There are other more complex ways of spotting gaps in a market, as can be seen in the table opposite.

FOR EXAMPLE

The Saga Group focuses entirely on services aimed at customers aged 50 years and over. It provides holidays, financial products, insurance and a magazine. To find out more about the Saga Group go to www.saga.co.uk.

Technique	Explanation	Example
Revamping an old idea	Some products and services may have sold well in the past, but for some reason have stopped selling. Other products may have been selling well overseas for many years, but have never done particularly well in the British market. With slight adjustment it may be possible to give an old idea a new lease of life.	The classic board game, Monopoly, used to be owned by Waddingtons. It then became part of Parker Brothers, which in turn was purchased by Hasbro. In recent years the basic Monopoly game has been transformed. It is now possible to buy a Monopoly game that features streets in Paris, towns in Cornwall, or even a Premiership football team, rather than London streets.
Using the Internet	Many of the supposed great Internet start-up ideas were not particularly unique. Many of the early ideas failed. The Internet can, however, give extra value or a competitive edge that makes a particular product or service unique.	Online employment agencies, for example, offer business clients ideas of wage rates and updates on employment law, and give applicants interview tips and other career advice.
Solving customer problems	Many larger suppliers do not really satisfy the needs of customers. They are simply too large to pay attention to individual customers. For smaller businesses this is an ideal gap in the market providing they are prepared to meet the needs of customers and match their expectations.	Smaller businesses can offer personal service and create a close relationship with the customer, providing them with a personal service rather than the standard level of service offered by larger businesses.
Creating inventions and innovations	Inventors and innovators actually often start at the opposite end of identifying the market. They come up with a product or service idea and then try to see if there is a sufficient market for it. Some may come across a particular customer problem and then try to solve it, but in many cases there may not be a need for what has been invented, no matter how clever it is.	The classic example is the 3M Post-it notes. When the Post-it was created there was no obvious market for it. But there are few office desks in the world without a pile of Post-it notes nowadays.
Marketing other peoples' ideas	Reading business magazines, periodicals and websites may give a business or an entrepreneur a basic idea for a new product or service. Although copyrights, patents or trademarks may protect some of them, others are simply broad ideas that could be adapted.	It is important to remember that many of the home-working ideas that are offered, suggesting that people can get rich quick, are in fact bogus and fraudulent. Genuine ideas are likely to have been protected before they appear in the media.
Being different	The search for something known as a USP is the goal of many businesses and entrepreneurs. A USP is a Unique Selling Proposition – something about the product or service that is unbeatable and gives the entrepreneur a competitive advantage that cannot easily be copied.	Dyson's original USP was a bagless vacuum cleaner. Amazon's USP was one-click shopping. Tom Farmer, the founder of Kwik Fit, has a USP dependent on the fact that many people have problems getting their exhaust fitted or tyres changed by regular garages. Often the estimates were wrong and the vehicles were with the garage for too long. Kwik Fit changed all that by having a set price and an almost immediate service.

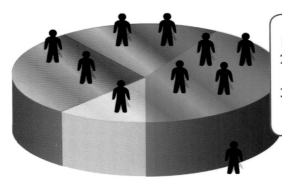

Questions

1 Define the term 'niche'. (2 marks)
2 What do you understand by the term 'USP'? (2 marks)
3 Why might it be the case that a large business chooses not to target a niche market? (4 marks)

Franchises

LEARNING OBJECTIVES

▶ What is a franchise?
▶ Advantages and disadvantages for the franchisee
▶ Do franchises always work?

What is a franchise?

Many new businesses fail in the first few years. One way in which this risk can be reduced is to effectively buy into the success of an existing business.

Franchising means using an existing company's business idea and its name. The franchisor is the business that owns the original company. It can give the right to another person or group of people (the franchisee) to run a similar business, usually in a different area.

The franchisor does not, of course, give this away for free. They charge the franchisee a fee to buy the franchise and then also take a percentage of the franchisee's profits.

There are many different franchises up and down the country, including The Body Shop, Benetton, Kentucky Fried Chicken, MacDonald's and Burger King.

In effect the franchisee is buying a licence to copy the style and the operations of the original business. Many franchises are very successful, earning money not only for the franchisee, but additional funds for the franchisor.

What the franchisor provides

The franchisor usually offers a package of services and support. This would include:

- An existing well-known company name
- Advertising that covers the area in which the franchisee operates
- Training to help the franchisee start the business
- Necessary equipment, including shop fittings
- Supplies of products and services that the franchisees will sell to their customers
- The ability to buy products and materials at lower costs, taking advantage of bulk purchasing by all franchisees
- Lists of existing or potential customers in the area that the franchisee will operate in
- Support services, such as ongoing advice, loans and insurance

A good deal for the franchisor

When a franchisee buys a franchise the franchisor is effectively expanding their business without any real financial risk to themselves. The franchisee pays the start-up costs and is responsible for the running costs of the business. This enables the chain of companies to expand much faster than if the original business was trying to expand using its own funds.

Because the franchisee has made a financial commitment, they are likely to be very motivated and keen that the business is a success. The franchisor can concentrate on providing specialist support, rather than getting the new business off the ground.

INTERNET RESEARCH

Visit the website of the British Franchise Association at www.thebfa.org and answer the following questions:

1 What is the role of the BFA?
2 How do you get in touch with a franchisor to express an interest in becoming a franchisee?
3 What is the key objective that needs to be reached by a franchisor to become a full member of the BFA?

KEY TERMS

Licence – an agreement that allows one business to have certain rights to use something that actually belongs to another.

Motivated – eager to work hard and do well in order to make the business a success.

Advantages and disadvantages for the franchisee

A tiny proportion of franchises actually fail. The failure rate is somewhere around 6%–7%. There are many reasons why the failure rate is so low, including:

- The franchisor carefully chooses who can buy a franchise
- The franchisor states precisely how much money is needed by the franchisee, both to start up the business and to run it
- Provided the franchisee follows the tested formula then the franchise should always work
- The franchisor offers ongoing support if there are difficulties

One of the other big advantages is the support from a national business and its ability to pay for national advertising and promotion. The money for this of course comes from the franchisees because they are paying a percentage of all of their profits to the franchisor.

The key drawbacks, however, are that franchises are not very flexible and the franchisor keeps a tight control over the franchisee. Franchisees are also not allowed to sell their franchises without the agreement of the franchisor.

The other key consideration is that a fixed percentage of the franchisee's turnover, rather than profit, is often paid to the franchisor.

Do franchises always work?

Many British franchises are members of the British Franchise Association. This is an organisation that checks that its members use a strict code of business practice.

In the past some franchises have failed because they are basically bad business ideas and the franchisors have misled their franchisees. Also, the franchise is only as good as the franchisee and if it is run badly then the business will fail in any case.

If the franchise is run well and the franchisor monitors the franchisee then there is less chance for the franchise to fail. A poor reputation from a franchisee would adversely affect the reputation of the whole franchise business. The franchisor would seek to avoid this.

Franchises tend to be the most common in the service sector, and include food outlets, clothing, business services, cosmetics and toiletry products.

CASE STUDY DOMINO'S PIZZAS

Domino's Pizzas was originally founded in 1960. It is one of the world leaders in pizza delivery and it is still growing today, with 8,000 stores in over 50 countries. In order to support its franchisees, the business employs over 250 people in Great Britain. Initially new franchisees take part in a three-week intensive franchise development programme. This covers everything from pizza making and people management to customer service and computer systems. At any time the business will have 20 or more new or existing stores for sale. It tends to set up new franchises with its own staff, establish them and then sell them to a franchisee.

For additional information visit the franchising section on www.dominos.uk.com

Questions

1 Find out what the initial agreement period is for each franchise. (2 marks)
2 What is the role of a franchise consultant? (2 marks)
3 What is the average net turnover of a Domino's pizza store per week? (2 marks)
4 What are the average start-up costs for a Domino's pizza store, and what is meant by liquid funds? (4 marks)

Copyright, patents and trademarks

LEARNING OBJECTIVES
- ▶ Why protect business ideas?
- ▶ Copyrights
- ▶ Patents
- ▶ Trademarks

Why protect business ideas?

The first rule with any business idea is to keep it secret or confidential until there is some form of legal protection for it. By explaining a business idea to any third party, the business or entrepreneur is effectively putting the idea into the public domain, as other people will know about it and someone may copy it.

If it is necessary to tell someone about a business idea in its early stages then the most sensible thing to do is to ask them to sign a confidentiality agreement. A confidentiality agreement binds the individual who has signed it not to disclose the business idea to a third party.

Further down the line, however, there are more successful ways of ensuring that business ideas remain the property of the innovator or inventor. The exact use of copyrights, patents or trademarks will tend to depend upon what is being protected.

INTERNET RESEARCH 🔍

The Copyright Service, at http://copyrightservice.co.uk/ provides an online registration service for copyright holders. The organisation also provides a series of useful fact sheets, which can be printed or downloaded.

Copyrights

Copyright is always automatically granted to a writer or an artist, so a picture, drawing or description of an idea automatically has copyright. It does not need to be registered and it lasts at least the lifetime of the original author.

Copyright only prevents the copying of the original work. It does not prevent the idea that is being described from actually being used by a third party. The copyright symbol is used to show that the material is protected by copyright. The copyright holder can give the right to someone to make copies.

Designers can also protect their ideas or intellectual property using design rights. These are often used instead of patents, because design rights do not have to be registered. They are automatically granted, but an unregistered design right requires the creator to show when and where they originally created the design. It is possible to register a design right with the UK Intellectual Property Office (www.ipo.gov.uk). This is a relatively straightforward procedure; the protection can last for up to twenty-five years and costs just £60.

KEY TERM

Brand image – a product's name, packaging, colouring and advertising.

Patents

A patent is used to protect a functional or technical part of a product or process – in other words, how something works, how it is made, or what it is made from. The creator can apply to the UK Intellectual Property Office with an initial patent application. If the product or process is new, then a patent is issued to protect the idea.

A British patent lasts for twenty years and it gives the patent holder the exclusive rights to use that patent for that time period. The patent holder can, of course, sell the patent so that another business can make products based on the idea. A £200 fee is payable within a year of making the original patent application in order to secure protection.

Trademarks

Trademarks can either be registered or unregistered. They tend to be used to protect a brand image or a business process. Often they are simply used to protect the name of a product or service, such as Folens or Toys R Us. This prevents another business from using these names for themselves or for any of their products or processes.

It costs around £250 to register a trademark. Many businesses do not bother to register their trademarks, but this means that they run the risk of someone else using the trademark, which is known as 'passing off'. This means trying to fool customers into believing that their products are, in fact, your products.

FOR EXAMPLE

Veteran entrepreneur and inventor, Trevor Baylis, offers wise words of advice:

'After the radio, I made an electric shoe and walked across the Namibian desert trying to raise money for anti-personnel mine detection. That didn't go anywhere, because after 9/11 anyone who was seen with a device (OK) strapped to his or her shoe would be in big trouble. But I've just seen that one of the large shoe companies has started to make an electric shoe – they stole my idea. Firstly, don't tell everyone about it. Secondly, get literature from the Patent Office and read all about how to protect your idea.

If you wish, you can approach us and we'd be delighted to look at your invention. It's important that these inventors don't get shafted. As they say, art is pleasure, invention is treasure, and this nation has got to recognise that. If it can spend a fortune on dead sheep and formaldehyde, then it can spend a bit more of that money on inventors.'

BOOK RESEARCH

Cornish, William and Llewelyn, David, *Intellectual property: Patents, copyrights, trademarks and allied rights*, 6th edition, Sweet & Maxwell (2007)

CASE STUDY SKANKY MAGGOT

Nicki Parsons devised the Skanky Maggot, a folding, reinforced tunnel that fits round a standard door frame to provide a sealed route through which building materials and debris can be moved through a home or office. They are modular, and multiple sections can be joined together to provide the required length. It can also provide a clean route through a dirty environment.

With new European Regulations being introduced relating to health and safety factors in construction areas, Skanky Maggot improves conditions in such places by isolating dust and debris.

Nicki said; 'The idea came to me of a tunnel running through the house from the front door to the back ensuring that none of the mess ended up in the house. Also, if the ends of the tunnel were airtight then no dust could get in either. I realised that the tunnel could be used for other purposes within the house.'

Source adapted from: www.trevorbaylisbrands.com

Questions

1 How might Nicki Parsons have protected her new product idea? (6 marks)
2 Skanky Maggot has just entered production and will soon be on sale. How can Nicki continue to protect the product from imitations? (4 marks)

Case studies, questions and exam practice

CASE STUDY ADS THAT CLEAN THE STREETS

Guerrilla marketing techniques have been around for years. They have a bad reputation for sometimes defacing public property. City councils do not look too kindly on adverts scrawled in spray paint on the pavement. Street Advertising Services offer a more legal way of creating images, by just using water.

The company uses high-pressure cleaning machines to wash brand names, logos and adverts onto dirty pavements. Clients provide their design, and SAS turns it into a giant stencil. Working at night, the SAS team blasts the stencil with water and steam on dirty walls, roads, pavements or even road signs. The result is a sparkling clean image in the shape of the company's logo or message. SAS uses nothing other than water and steam. It is environmentally friendly and legal.

The pricing starts at around £1,000 (plus initial set-up costs) for 15–20 adverts throughout a city. So far, new businesses (e.g. Gumtree.com) have used the service, as well as more established global brands (e.g. Vauxhall Corsa and BP).

Its founder Kristian Jeffrey launched SAS in 2006: 'I run several small online businesses, and was searching for cost-effective advertising to attract consumers to my sites. My potential customers were walking around me every day, and it was when I was walking through the dirty streets of London that the idea came to me: why not take advertising literally to the street? Having experimented with several different methods, we wanted to apply a technique that was not just eye-catching and effective but also friendly to the environment. What could be more natural than water?'

Source adapted from: www.streetadvertisingservices.com

Questions

1 What do you think might be meant by the term 'guerrilla marketing'? (2 marks)
2 Explain how Kristian Jeffrey came up with the idea of SAS. (4 marks)
3 Why might it be problematic for SAS to protect its business idea? (4 marks)
4 What kinds of target market would be most likely to respond to this type of advertising and why? (8 marks)

SHORT-ANSWER QUESTIONS

1 Give **THREE** examples of high-street franchises.

2 What is a market niche?

3 What type of business idea could be protected by copyright?

4 Distinguish between a patent and a trademark.

5 Why might a good business idea never be launched onto the market?

6 Give **TWO** advantages to a franchisee of purchasing a franchise.

7 Give **TWO** advantages to a franchisor of selling a franchise.

8 Where do patents have to be registered?

9 List **FOUR** elements of the package of services and support usually provided by a franchisor.

10 What is a licence?

CASE STUDY CHIPS

In 2007 Chips, a franchise operation, celebrated its 21st birthday. The group has eleven company-owned stores and twenty franchised outlets. The Chips outlets buy, sell and trade leading brands of consoles, games, accessories and DVDs. The British leisure software market is worth in excess of £1bn. Chips offer potential franchisees a fully stocked store for around £80,000, depending on location. The franchisor charges a management services fee of 7%, which covers the cost of providing ongoing support services. They charge a 2% marketing fee to fund marketing and promotional activity, and a 1% stock distribution contribution towards the costs of distribution and returning stock. All these charges are based on the turnover of the outlet. The average turnover for an established franchisee per year is around £300,000, with a net trading profit of £45,000. The franchisors are keen to attract those with good interpersonal skills and a high work ethic.

The company also handles franchise re-sales. The branch in Orpington, Kent, which has been open since 2004, has a turnover of £330,000 (2007–8), with a gross profit margin of 33%. The lease on the property runs until 2014 and is £16,000 per year. The price for the Orpington branch is £80,000 for goodwill, fixtures and fittings, plus an estimated stock valuation of £20,000.

Questions

1 What do you understand by the word 'turnover'? (2 marks)

2 What is meant by the term 'net trading profit'? (4 marks)

3 Potential franchisees are required to put in £30,000 of their own money. Suggest where they might obtain the balance to pay for the franchise. (6 marks)

4 What might be meant by the word 'goodwill'? (4 marks)

Inputs, outputs and transformation

Inputs

Different types of business start with a range of different inputs. Essentially they are all resources, some of them tangible, such as raw materials and some intangible, such as employees' skills and expertise.

An input is anything needed by the business to begin the process of producing a physical product, or providing a service. The types of input depend on the nature of the business and the sector in which it operates:

- Primary sector – such as farming. Inputs could be cattle feed and water for their cows in order for them to be able to produce milk.
- Secondary sector – such as car manufacturers. Inputs would include components and employee skills to construct vehicles.
- Tertiary sector – services, such as mobile phone companies. Inputs would include mobiles for customers, masts and boosters for transmission of signals, and customer service staff in call centres and high-street stores.

A combination of people, materials, machines, money and technology can all be considered as inputs. Together they will be needed to begin the process that will create outputs that can then be sold on to customers.

KEY TERMS

Tangible – in this context, an input that can be physically touched, such as a component.

Intangible – in this context, an input that cannot be physically touched, such as knowledge.

Transformation

Whatever the process involves, the idea is to combine all the inputs in such a way as to produce an output. In our three examples the outputs would be:

- Milk
- A completed car
- A working mobile phone with customer service back-up

The transformation of inputs into outputs depends on the sector and the type of industry involved. In the primary and secondary sectors the inputs tend to be primarily physical ones (components, raw materials, parts, etc) and the process of transformation is mechanical, using machinery and production processes to create physical outputs (such as televisions or cars).

In the tertiary or service sector the inputs tend to be intangible (skills, ideas, expertise and knowledge). The transformation process is a non-physical one, not necessarily relying on machinery to produce an output, as most of the outputs are services (advice or guidance, etc).

It is important to remember that the transformation of inputs can take place in a variety of different situations and locations. A farmer may transform inputs into outputs in a field or an intensive pig farm. A car manufacturer will transform components and parts using factory machinery in a plant. A bank will transform account handling and customer service in an office or branch, using experienced employees to make investments and judgements on behalf of customers, to ensure that their funds are safe and accessible to them.

Outputs

Outputs do not have to be physical products; they can be services. The business has transformed the inputs, through whatever process it uses, into something different. An output can be a mix of the tangible and intangible elements found in the input. The transformation has radically changed the value of the inputs through the process.

For a farmer, 100 newborn lambs in a field will be transformed over time into 100 saleable sheep ready for market. They are now worth considerably more than the 100 lambs, even if the farmer takes into account any costs he incurred in keeping them until he sold them.

For a car manufacturer the cost of the components, plus the employee costs and other costs, have created a car worth more than the costs incurred. For a high-street bank, the expertise of the staff and the processes used have transformed the value of the customers' investments.

In each case the output must always be of more value than the sum of the inputs plus any other expenses. If the output is not worth more, the business will soon fail, as it will never cover its costs. The whole point of the transformation is to increase value, or create added value. The added value will cover the business's expenses, provide it with funds to reinvest and provide a profit.

For more information about added value see pp.34–5.

FOR EXAMPLE

The Disotto brothers make ice cream and sell it in their ice cream parlour on the beachfront of a seaside town. They use inputs (resources), and a process (transformation), and they have outputs:

INPUTS	PROCESS	OUTPUTS
• Milk	• Ice cream making machines	• Range of ice creams for sale to customers
• Cream	• Freezer storage	• Satisfied customers and repeat sales
• Sugar	• Packaging machines	
• Flavourings	• Cleaning	
• Colourings	• Factory costs	
• Employees	• Delivery costs	
• Equipment		
• Packaging		

The Disotto brothers transform the inputs by processing them into products that can be sold at a higher price than the sum total of the inputs, the process and other expenses. This adds value and creates a profit.

CASE STUDY CHICKEN POOH

The demand for chicken waste as agricultural fertilizer has soared in recent months, largely as a result of higher natural gas costs and increased ethanol production. However, chicken farmers such as Al and Bev are not clapping their hands with joy at the prospect of making more profit from their chicken's waste:

'There's a bigger demand and people are willing to pay more, but I haven't seen a huge price coming back to the farmers,' Bev said. 'The increased prices are being absorbed by transportation costs. Much of that is going to pay for higher diesel prices.'

Al and Bev have 100,000 chickens per flock in five to six flocks per year on their farm near Ipswich, Suffolk. Their business generates a lot of chicken waste, but rising demand isn't enough to convince them to bother to even sell it.

'We will use ours to fertilise our own 540-acre cattle farm,' said Bev, 'I'd like to be able to sell the waste and pay for the bedding, but I also need the fertilizer. Using our own saves me the cost of commercial fertiliser, and we get a better product.'

The chicken sheds use bedding of sawdust, wood chips and other materials to absorb the chicken droppings. The cost of the bedding has soared faster than the farmers' litter sales prices. The result has eaten even further into the farmers' profits. Bedding costs have soared to about £1,000 per poultry house, from about £500 per house a year ago. 'There's a big push for corn to grow and be converted into ethanol,' Bev said. 'With all this pressure to plant more corn, nitrogen prices started to grow like crazy.'

Source: adapted from The Oklahoman, June 11 2007

Questions

1 Chicken waste is a by-product of Al and Bev's chicken operation, but what could it still be considered as? (2 marks)
2 If the chicks cost Al and Bev 20p each, what is the overall cost of their chicks per year? Assume five flocks per year. (5 marks)
3 If they sell all the chickens in their five flocks each year at £1 per chicken, and their other costs per chicken average out at 54p, what is their overall profit per year? (7 marks)

Primary sector

LEARNING OBJECTIVES
▶ The primary sector
▶ Primary sector's links with other industries

The primary sector

The primary sector includes agriculture, fishing, forestry, mining and quarrying. These businesses either create or recover raw materials, such as coal, that will be used by other industries, or sold directly to customers.

Many of the industries take resources from the land, so they are also known as extractive industries. The sector itself, however, is involved in a number of different areas, including:

- Growing – crops, animals, plants and trees
- Cutting down – mainly trees and plants
- Extraction – oil, gas, coal, stone and fish

Some parts of different countries are associated with different types of primary sector activity. In Britain the primary sectors use many naturally occurring resources, including:

- Coal – this is an industry in decline. Coal mines were originally located in South Wales, north-east England, the Midlands and southern Scotland.

- Minerals – these come from various different types of rock and soil formations. Materials such as chalk, limestone, clay, salt, sand, gravel and shale are all extracted. They are used for road building and construction.
- Water – there are several providers of water around the country. They are private businesses. Water involves the management of rivers, canals, lakes, streams, wells, springs, reservoirs and underground waterways.
- Gas and oil – there is still gas and oil in the North Sea and off other coastlines. The industry sets up rigs to extract the fuel and it arrives in Britain at terminals on the coast.
- Forestry – over the past few decades production of wood has doubled. The Forestry Commission controls a large amount of wood production.
- Fishing – this is important to Scotland, Northern Ireland and the south-west and east coasts of England. Fish are caught in the seas off the British coast, and fish farms have been established in Scotland.

The other most important primary sector industry is farming. Despite the huge cities, Britain is still a rural country. Different areas specialise in different types of farming:

- South-west England – sheep, cattle, potatoes and arable
- South-east England – vegetables, potatoes and arable
- Eastern England – pigs, poultry, vegetables and arable
- Midlands – arable
- Wales – sheep and cattle
- North Midlands – pigs, poultry and arable
- Borders – sheep, cattle and vegetables
- Scotland – sheep, cattle, potatoes and arable
- Northern Ireland – sheep, cattle and potatoes

In the past, workers carried out all the work on farms by hand. They also worked underground and in quarries to extract materials, such as coal or slate.

KEY TERM

Arable – a farm or a piece of land that grows crops.

In developed countries like Great Britain and America, machinery has taken over much of the hard work. This is known as mechanisation. A combine harvester can collect tons of corn from fields in a day, which would have taken workers weeks to complete.

Just as developed countries have become more hi-tech in the way they handle primary sector work, there has been a huge fall in the number of people employed in the sector. In less-developed countries work is still carried out by hand. They do not have the advantage of the machinery, nor do they have the advantage of pesticides and sprays to encourage the crops to grow, or for the livestock to avoid disease.

Once a country can produce almost enough food for itself without having to bring it in from another country, people can move away from the countryside and from the primary sector and work in cities. Less-developed countries still need large

numbers of people to work in the primary sector, but as they develop, fewer workers are needed.

Primary sector's links with other industries

The primary sector either creates or extracts the vital raw materials that are used by other businesses. A farm that grows wheat may sell the wheat to a flourmill. The flourmill is in the secondary, or manufacturing, sector. The flourmill may then sell the flour to a bakery, which will then turn the flour into bread. The bread will then be sold on to a supermarket, which is in the tertiary or service sector. At that point the wheat, transformed into a loaf of bread, can be purchased by customers and paid for at the checkout.

The primary sector has to somehow provide manufacturing with as many of the raw materials as possible. The raw materials that cannot be grown or extracted in a country will have to be brought in from somewhere else in the world.

CASE STUDY FLOWING PROFITS

The water industry in England and Wales loses about 3.5 billion litres of water through broken and leaky pipes each day. Meanwhile, households saw their water and sewerage bills rise by an average of 5.5% last April 2005.

For investors in the water industry, things could not be better. Severn Trent announced that higher bills and cost-cutting had delivered an 18% rise in yearly profits to £270m and United Utilities, which supplies customers in the North West, reported a 21% increase in profits to £481m, while Pennon in the South West announced a profit rise of 25% to £111m. Anglian Water (owned by AWG) trebled its profits to £109m. As a sector, the water industry could now produce profits of around £2bn.

Defending its profit rise and the costs to customers, the industry claimed that for every £2 earned in profit, £3 is invested in improving services – an investment of £50bn in pipes, reservoirs and water treatment works in recent years.

Every five years Ofwat reviews water companies' business plans before setting an annual price limit for each company for the next five years. The 2005–2010 review (of 4.2% above inflation) means that the average household bill will rise by £46 (18%) to £295 over the period. Investors, at the same time, will see a return on their investment of 5.1% (£105.10 for every £100 invested).

Questions

1 What is meant by the term 'return on investment'? (4 marks)
2 If inflation is running at 2.5% what would be the percentage increase in household bills in that year? (2 marks)
3 What is a business plan? (6 marks)

Secondary sector

The secondary sector

The secondary sector is also known as the manufacturing sector. It usually involves businesses that process materials provided by the primary sector. In effect, the secondary sector transforms raw materials into products and services.

The secondary sector is involved in many different types of work. A business may obtain milk from dairy farmers in the primary sector. It may transform this milk into cheese. The process has transformed one thing (milk) into another thing (cheese).

Some businesses in the secondary sector can use products that other manufacturers have already processed. By combining the products made by other businesses they can create a completely new product. A manufacturer of computers will buy various **components** from different manufacturers, including processors, memory cards and the hard case in which the computer is housed.

Britain has a wide variety of secondary sector businesses. Examples include:

- Ceramics – the making of pottery, earthenware, tableware, china and toilets
- Clothing – from wool, cloth, linen and manmade products like Nylon
- Drinks – including alcoholic beverages, such as whisky, and bottled waters
- Paint – for industry and for decorating homes, as well as artists' materials
- Printing – magazines, newspapers, books and junk mail
- Steel – for use in the car industry and in construction, as well as the manufacture of cutlery

Certain parts of the country are associated with different manufacturing industries:

- The south-west, south-east and north-west of England and Northern Ireland are involved in the **aerospace industry**
- The north, north-west and south-east of England are involved in the manufacturing of chemicals
- Clothing is centred around the north of England, the Midlands and London
- Food processing takes place in East Anglia, the North West and South East
- Merseyside is the main base for glass production
- The processing of raw materials for the clothes industry, or textile manufacturing, takes place in Northern Ireland, Scotland, the East Midlands and the north and north-west of England
- The north of England and Scotland process wool
- Northern Ireland is the centre for linen production
- The hi-tech industry of computer manufacturing is mainly based in Scotland and the southeast of England

KEY TERMS

Components – parts of a finished product. The combination of the components makes another unique product.

Aerospace industry – the construction of aircraft and anything to do with space exploration, including rocket technology.

Britain's manufacturing sector

After a long period of problems, which saw manufacturers close down and employees out of work, the British manufacturing sector is recovering. Manufacturing is making more. Working conditions are better, and modern manufacturing is hi-tech. Modern manufacturing does not need as many people to work in factories, but the ones who do so have high levels of skills and qualifications. Britain's aerospace industry is the second largest in the world. The biotechnology industry is the biggest in Europe. The chemical industry is the largest manufacturing sector in Britain. Britain is the fifth largest manufacturer of footwear. The food and drink manufacturing industry is massive, employing nearly 600,000 people.

Over the next 20 years the aerospace industry is expected to grow by at least 25%. The pharmaceutical industry will grow at a rate of 5% a year. Medical equipment will grow by 10%.

In the future there will be less repetitive low-skilled production, and employees will need to be flexible and update their knowledge. One of the most exciting areas of development is nanotechnology. The government is investing in this developing market, to help British industry be ahead of its competitors.

There are several major manufacturers in Great Britain. These include:

- 3M – manufacturs products for the home, work, school, and hospital and is best known for its Post-it notes.
- Airbus – employs over 45,000 people and builds aircraft and aerospace systems.
- Ford – primarily produces cars and employs nearly 20,000 people across the country.
- GlaxoSmithKline – employs over 42,000 people and manufactures medicines, drugs and baby products.
- ICI – owns the manufacturers Dulux, Polycell and Cuprinol. They produce a wide range of chemical products.
- Proctor and Gamble – employs over 5,000 people in Great Britain, owning Ariel, Lenor, Max Factor, Pringles and Hugo Boss.
- Unilever – employs nearly 18,000 people and owns Birds Eye Wall's, Fabergé and Ben & Jerry's. They manufacture many food products.
- Vauxhall (General Motors) – this American-owned business employs over 5,000 people in Britain. Thousands of other jobs are linked to Vauxhall as other companies supply them with components. Vauxhall's main production factories are in Luton and Cheshire.

INTERNET RESEARCH

To find out more about 3M go to www.3Mselect.co.uk. For Airbus, go to www.aerospace-technology. com. For Ford, go to www.ford.co.uk. For GlaxoSmithKline, go to www. glaxosmithkline.co.uk. For ICI, go to www.ici.com. For Proctor and Gamble, go to www.pg.com. For Unilever, go to www.unilever.co.uk. And for Vauxhall, go to www.vauxhall.co.uk.

CASE STUDY EXTREME ROAD TEST

Black cab maker Manganese Bronze signed a £53 million joint venture agreement in 2006 to make up to 20,000 of its vehicles in Shanghai, with Chinese firm Zhejiang Geely. Manganese is investing just under £20m.

A re-styled and more environmentally friendly version of London's iconic black cab called the TX4, replaced the older cabs that had been introduced in 2002. The new cabs (introduced in 2006) cost between £26,995 and £35,495. Since 1948, LTI Vehicles, a subsidiary of Manganese Bronze, has produced more than 100,000 cabs.

The vehicle was extensively tested and £5.5m has been invested to come up with the new model. The managing director of LTI Vehicles said: 'Over one million kilometres of testing has taken place, including nearly 5,000km over pave cobbled road surfaces... in real-life extreme hot and cold climates and simulated conditions.'

Source: adapted from www.lti.co.uk and www.manganese.com

Questions

1 What might be meant by the term 'joint venture'? (4 marks)
2 What is a subsidiary? (4 marks)
3 Why might it be more cost-effective to produce the cabs for the Chinese market in Shanghai? (6 marks)

Tertiary sector

The tertiary sector

For most products and services it is the tertiary sector that supplies other businesses or customers. There is a distinction to be made between the tertiary sector and the service sector. The tertiary sector includes any type of business that is not directly involved in the creation or extraction of raw materials, or their manufacturing.

This does leave an enormous number of businesses to be included in the tertiary sector. Typical tertiary sector businesses would include:

- The distribution of products (transportation businesses and delivery services)
- All types of retailing
- Communications, including land, telephones, mobile phones and internet connections
- Accommodation and food, including hotels and restaurants
- Financial services, including insurance, banks and building societies
- Transportation, including airlines, railway companies, coaches and buses and ferry companies

- Public administration, including central and local government
- Education
- Healthcare and social work
- Building, construction, servicing and repairs, from house building to car maintenance and railroad maintenance and plumbing

The tertiary sector is a significant employer. Around 76% of all British workers are employed in this sector. The main types of employer are:

- Retailing
- Tourism
- Education
- Healthcare
- Banking

The growth of the tertiary sector has coincided with other significant changes to the other two main sectors:

- The primary sector employment has dropped due to farming becoming more efficient, and the **mechanisation** and computerisation of mines, quarries and other extraction.
- The secondary sector has also reduced in numbers of employees

because certain manufacturing businesses have closed, while those that remain are more reliant on machinery and computers, and less on unskilled labour.

The tertiary sector provides a range of products and services, both to the general public, as consumers, and to other businesses. It often acts as the point of contact between a business in either the primary or secondary sector, and its customers.

As we will see, the tertiary sector does not actually transform any products, and is not involved in production in any way.

> ▶▶ **FOCUS** POINT ◀◀
>
> Why might a business such as a garden centre, which would normally be classed as being in the tertiary sector, be difficult to categorise if it has its own plant nursery? Try to come up with some other examples of businesses that do not cleanly fit into one sector only.

Services

There are many tertiary sector organisations that do not handle any physical products at all. The service sector is often referred to as the soft sector, because it provides knowledge and expertise, rather than physical products. In fact what it provides is known as intangible. This means that it provides information, services, advice, or experience, rather than a tangible, or physical product.

There is a difference, therefore, between the service sector, which would include banking and insurance, and other parts of the tertiary sector that do handle physical products, such as retailing.

The number of people employed in the tertiary sector will differ from country to country. In countries where the economy is less well developed there will be fewer job opportunities in the service sector, as the country's emphasis will be on the primary sector and manufacturing. Once a country has begun to introduce machines to replace work done by hand there will be sufficient money in the economy for a tertiary sector to begin to develop.

Great Britain has a low proportion of people working in the primary sector and in industry. The growth area for jobs is in the tertiary sector. Depending on the area, there may be jobs in tourism or in major hospitals or offices of large companies, such as insurance and banking.

The fourth sector

There is a fourth sector, known as the quaternary sector. For many years it was counted as being part of the tertiary sector, but now people recognise it as a sector in itself. It includes:

- Research
- Development
- Information services

Really the quaternary sector is linked to science, information technology and cutting edge technology. It will include scientific research, education and consultancy.

As it becomes more difficult for businesses to succeed because of the high levels of competition, new openings for ideas and innovations are always welcome. This is the purpose of the quaternary sector – to come up with new ideas, new ways of making things and ways to cut costs.

Some people believe that there is even a quinary sector, which includes health, education, culture, entertainment and research. They make this distinction because it is believed that the quaternary sector has really far more to do with information and communication technology.

> ### KEY TERMS
>
> **Mechanisation** – the process of replacing humans with machines in the production process.

CASE STUDY CHANGING FORTUNES

Britain's dominant services sector slowed sharply in the third quarter of this year (October 2007). The British Chambers of Commerce said in its quarterly survey of nearly 5,000 companies that manufacturing performed strongly in the July to September period.

The service sector accounts for more than two-thirds of the British economy. The vast majority of organisations in this sector reported that sales were higher

The survey showed, however, that the continued strength of the world economy helped British manufacturers in the services sector, even though the sector accounts for only about 15% of the economy. British manufacturers enjoyed the strongest home demand for their goods in nearly two decades in the third quarter, taking the percentage of firms working at full capacity to a 10-year high.

Source: adapted from *The Guardian*

Questions

1 Why might high interest rates affect both customers and businesses? (8 marks)
2 If the service sector accounts for around 65% of the economy, what might be the contribution of the other two sectors? (2 marks)
3 What is meant by the word 'economy'? (2 marks)

Adding value

LEARNING OBJECTIVES

▶ Adding value
▶ How a business can add value
▶ Analysing added value

Adding value

Adding value refers to the process of transforming components or raw materials into finished products, or providing specialist services using expertise and techniques.

The level of added value achieved can give a business an advantage over competitors. This advantage will arise out of how the business organises its activities, uses its resources and transforms inputs into outputs. The outputs need to be products or services that customers are prepared to buy.

The business's activities are at the heart of how it creates value. A restaurant, for example, buys in raw materials in the form of meat, vegetables and other necessities to create a menu of different dishes. Using the expertise of the catering staff and sophisticated kitchen equipment, the restaurant transforms its inputs into dishes (outputs) for its customers. Customers could purchase similar inputs themselves and create their own dishes, but are prepared to pay extra for professionals to do the work for them. This is despite the fact that the price they are paying for the dish includes a contribution to the wage bill of the restaurant, its running costs and to the business's profits.

When customers make a purchase, they often automatically compare the business's products and services with similar ones offered by competitors. Efficiency is vital in order to keep costs down, while adding the greatest value to the products and services it offers. Customers' perceptions of value change over time, with competitors gaining the upper hand on grounds of price, value for money, reliability, quality and other issues.

In this way, these characteristics of a business should also be seen as part of the value-adding process.

The restaurant can add value to its range of products in a number of different ways:

- Develop a relationship with a supplier that can ensure the highest-quality raw materials (fresh foods) at the lowest possible price.
- Automate or mass-produce popular dishes so that the time and costs involved in producing each meal are reduced.
- Invest in the restaurant, making it more attractive, creating a better atmosphere, or fitting in more tables so that more customers can be accommodated.

Value can be added at various stages of the businesses operation, as can be seen below.

Restaurant operation	Business process	Explanation	Adding value
Buying food	Inbound logistics	Logistics refer to distribution; inbound logistics cover raw materials coming into the business via suppliers. The raw materials need to be of a high, consistent quality, from a reliable supplier and at an affordable price.	Activities that are concerned with receiving, storing and distributing inputs to the product/service e.g. stock control
Cooking food	Operations	The way in which the business handles the raw materials and transforms them into finished products ready for sale. This needs to be streamlined, efficient and reliable with a consistently high quality.	Activities that transform various inputs into the final product, i.e. food production.
Serving food	Outbound logistics	How the finished products are distributed to the customer. In the restaurant this is performed by waiting staff, customers will want their products delivered in a reasonable time frame, fault free and matching their order.	The storage and distribution of finished product or service e.g. waiter service.
Customer contact	Sales and marketing	The communication process between the business and potential or existing customers. The business will inform customers of new products and services as well as constantly reminding them of the products and services that are always available.	These activities make customers aware of products/services.
Customer handling	Customer Service	Customer services, before, during and after the sales process is vital. High-quality customer service can give a business an advantage over the competition.	A range of activities which enhance or maintain the value of product/service e.g. installation or repair.

The examples given above are primary activities of the business; they are directly involved in the preparation, production and delivery of the products or services. Value can also be added by secondary or support activities, as shown in the table on the right.

Analysing added value

Businesses will look at the ways individual activities can be improved to increase the amount of added value. A business competing in a market that sells high quality products and services will focus on strategies that will continue to deliver high quality products and services. A business that competes in a market based on price will look at ways in which costs can be reduced in its primary activities.

Adding value cannot be addressed by the business alone, certainly not just in terms of its own activities. To maximise added value, suppliers, distributors and customers all need to be looked at, because they are all part of the supply chain.

A business will identify where value is added and where there is potential to add more value by changing or modifying activities. Not all activities add value, but the core activities do, and this is where potential improvements can be made. If the business finds it cannot add value from an activity, another option may be to **outsource** it to a supplier or contractor that could deliver a high level of service at a lower cost. Outsourcing has occurred in many types of business and could include customer service, distribution, cleaning services or production.

Support activity	Explanation
Procurement	Acquiring inputs (purchasing and sourcing) that will be used by primary activities.
Development and use of technology	The use of technology or improved processes to make the primary activities more efficient and faster.
Human resource management	Recruitment, training, development and a reward system for employees in the organisation, to attract, retain and reward key employees.
Infrastructure	How the business is structured and how it sets procedures and routines to ensure efficient work methods and systems, including planning, financial control and quality control.
Accountancy	Checking the difference between the total costs and the end value of the products and services sold. The difference is the margin or the added value. Accountants refer to this as the profit margin.

KEY TERM

Outsource – the contracting of an outside organisation to provide a product or service that might be too expensive, complicated or time-consuming for the business to do itself.

Questions

1 Distinguish between inbound and outbound logistics. (4 marks)
2 Give THREE examples of support activities that could add value. (6 marks)

Case studies, questions and exam practice

CASE STUDY MAPPING THE TRANSFORMATION OF RESOURCES

Suppliers provide inputs into the transformation process. They may supply raw materials or finished products or services. Customers are the users of the outputs of the transformation process.

A quarry could supply a glass factory with limestone that will be used in the transformation process to produce glass products. Customers will purchase the finished goods and can provide feedback to the business to help it improve the product range, quality and other services to the customer.

The environment: outside of the control of the organisation

Under the control of the organisation

SUPPLIERS → Transformed resources / Transforming resources → INPUTS → Transformation process → OUTPUTS → Products Services → CUSTOMERS → Feedback

Questions

1 Using the diagram as a guide, describe the transformation using an example of your choice. (12 marks)

2 Give one example of each of the following: raw materials supplied to a business to be used in the transformation process, finished products supplied to an organisation for immediate sale to customers, and a service supplied to an organisation by a specialist business. (6 marks)

SHORT-ANSWER QUESTIONS

1 Give **TWO** examples of each of the following primary sector activities:
   - **Growing**
   - **Harvesting**
   - **Extraction**

2 Briefly give an example of how a primary sector industry could link with the activities of a secondary sector business.

3 What do you understand by the word 'mechanisation'?

4 What is a component?

5 Which industry is the largest part of the manufacturing sector in Britain?

6 Which sector employs around 76% of all British workers?

7 Define the word 'intangible' in its use as a description of a product or service.

8 Distinguish between an input and an output.

9 How can human resource management contribute towards adding value?

10 Suppliers, the business, distributors and customers can all be considered to be part of what type of chain?

CASE STUDY OUTSOURCING A KEY IN-HOUSE COMPETENCY

Space specialises in the design of interiors for cruise ships, one aspect of which is to produce three-dimensional computer-aided designs and visualisations, enabling clients to 'walk through' the concept on screen.

The challenge was to maintain the quality and time-to-screen delivery of these 3-D concepts that account for only a small proportion of the company's workload, yet serve as an exciting feature for clients. Historically, specially trained members of staff carried out this 3-D work. However, there was not enough work to employ them on 3-D work full-time and so they would be seconded to other work. This compromised their availability when 3-D work was required.

Managing Director, Mark Hilferty said: 'We decided that outsourcing the 3-D work would enable us to concentrate on what we're best at. We began by drawing up a short-list of suppliers and then made our choice on the basis of technical capability, service levels and price – though price, of course was not our main consideration. What matters most in our business – to our customers – is high quality work and fast turnaround. Now we have none of the headaches of providing the service. We simply apply a margin to their work and get on with managing our business. Outsourcing has reinvigorated our approach to growing the business and we intend to use it to enter additional market sectors in the future.'

Sources: Adapted from Business Link, Department for Business Enterprise and Regulatory Reform, www.space.uk.com and Innovation Exchange.

Questions

1 What is outsourcing? Describe how Space went about finding a suitable supplier. (8 marks)
2 What does Mark mean by 'apply a margin to their work'? (4 marks)

The purpose and content of a business plan

LEARNING OBJECTIVES

▶ What is a business plan?
▶ Audience and key elements
▶ Business, markets and competitors
▶ Marketing, sales skills and financial forecasts

What is a business plan?

A business plan is essentially a document that describes a business, along with its objectives, strategies, the market in which it operates and the business's financial forecasts. It usually has two key functions:

- To act as a basis for the securing of external finance or funding
- To be used within the business, as a way of measuring actual performance to forecasted figures

The business plan should give details of how the business is going to be developed, when it will happen, and who is going to be responsible. It will also show how money will be managed. In many cases potential lenders or investors will not read much of the business plan beyond the executive summary, which covers the key points of the entire business plan, outlining the business opportunity through to financial forecasting. Ideally this part of the plan should be no more than two pages long.

Audience and key elements

A business plan is important, as there may be a wide range of different individuals or institutions that wish to have sight of the business's intentions. These could include:

- Banks
- External investors, including **venture capitalists** or **business angels**
- Providers of grants
- Someone who may wish to purchase the business
- Potential business partners

It is important that the business plan is constantly updated and changed as the business grows. The plan should ideally include the following:

- An executive summary
- A short description of the business opportunity
- The business's marketing and sales strategy
- The management team and key personnel
- The business's operations, including premises, production and use of IT
- Financial forecasts

KEY TERMS

Venture capitalists – investors who provide cash for start-up businesses and small businesses that wish to expand, in exchange for a share of the business.

Business angels – individuals who contribute an investment at an early stage of a new business, usually in a high-risk, high-potential growth area.

Overheads – unavoidable costs, such as rent or rates, which have to be paid by a business regardless of the level of sales being achieved.

INTERNET RESEARCH 🔍

For more information on venture capitalists, visit the website of the British Private Equity and Venture Capital Association at www.bvca.co.uk. For more on Business Angels visit the British Business Angels Association at www.bbaa.org.uk.

BOOK RESEARCH

Stutely, Richard, *The definitive business plan: The fast track to intelligent business planning for executives and entrepreneurs*, 2nd edition, Financial Times/ Prentice Hall (2006)

Business, markets and competitors

The business plan needs to clearly get across what the business actually does, as well as the business's vision as far as its future is concerned. This should begin with an overview:

- When the business started, or when it intends to start, and any progress made
- The sector in which the business operates and the type of business
- Any relevant business history
- The legal structure of the business

As far as the products and services offered by the business are concerned, investors will seek clarification on the following:

- What makes the business's products and services different and what benefits they offer
- Clear indication of the type of customers
- How the business plans to develop the products and services
- Whether the business holds any patents, trademarks or design rights
- Any key or relevant features about the sector in which the business operates

Investors will also want to see that the business plan shows full awareness of the market place:

- The features of the market – its size, development and current issues
- The target customer base – identifying who the customers are and how the business knows they will be interested in its products and services
- The competition – who are they, how do they operate and what market share do they have?
- Future developments – any anticipated changes in the market and how the business and the competitors are likely to react

Marketing, sales skills and financial forecasts

Marketing and sales involve promotion and sales of a business's products and services. It is important that this section is realistic and achievable:

- How will the business position its products and services in the marketplace?
- Who are the customers – what are the characteristics and how will the business attract new customers?

- What is the business's pricing policy – will different customers be charged different prices and will offers be available for bulk purchasing?
- How will the business promote its products and services – what type of marketing will be used and what type of sales methods will be adopted?
- How will the products and services reach customers – i.e. how will they be distributed?
- What sales methods will be used – using a website, face-to-face, through retailers or by telephone?

Investors will want to know how much capital is needed, what guarantees lenders may have, how the business intends to repay funding and what the business's sources of revenue and income will be. The financial forecasting should include:

- A cash-flow statement – showing the flows of cash into and out of the business for at least the first twelve to eighteen months.
- A profit and loss forecast, showing projected sales and the costs of providing products and services (as well as **overheads**).
- Sales forecast – the amount of money that the business expects to bring in from sales.

CASE STUDY BUSINESS LINK

Business Link suggests that the following should be avoided when constructing a business plan:

'Being overly ambitious – make sure you can justify any assumptions or projections. Ignoring financial difficulties – warn your bank or lender if you anticipate that you may not be able to meet a repayment. There is every chance that you will be able to come to some arrangement. Failing to devise and implement effective cash-flow arrangements, e.g. have clear procedures for chasing up any accounts receivable.'

Questions

1. What is meant by projections? (2 marks)
2. What is meant by effective cash-flow arrangements? (2 marks)
3. What is meant by accounts receivable? (2 marks)

Sources of information and guidance

LEARNING OBJECTIVES
▶ Support and advisory services
▶ Government agencies
▶ Private support services
▶ Financial services

Support and advisory services

There is plenty of help and advice available to businesses. It can be found in a variety of different forms, from trade associations related to a particular industry, to government organisations, such as Business Link.

Trade associations

Trade associations are organisations that represent the interests of their members in a particular industry. An example would be ABTA, which represents travel agents. Members pay a fee and in return receive support and services from the organisation. They will provide assistance in the application of law and dealing with problems, as well as trying to convince the government to consider the industry when it makes policies and laws.

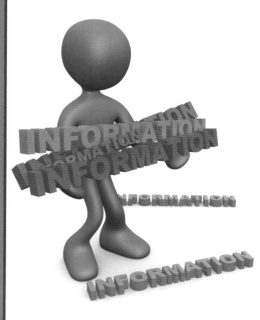

Chambers of Commerce

In each area of Great Britain there is a Chamber of Commerce. It is rather like a trade association, except that it has members involved in almost every different type of business. They represent the wishes and the needs of local businesses. The Chamber of Commerce will routinely interact with local government and central government. It can also act as a means by which businesses can receive **grants** and training from central government or the European Union.

Business Link

This is a national organisation with Business Link offices working in each area of Great Britain. They are designed to help local businesses and to provide them with services, support and advice. They provide training, assistance in writing **business plans**, exporting and importing, dealing with European regulations and improvements in the quality of products and services.

Confederation of British Industry (CBI)

This is a British organisation that works as a **pressure group** to influence the government, so that it can produce favourable policies and laws for business. The organisation also carries out research to look at how trends in the future might affect businesses.

Institute of Directors

The Institute of Directors supports business leaders, providing information, advice, training and publications. It also represents the concerns of businesses to the government.

Government agencies

The primary support for businesses comes from the government's Department for Business, Enterprise and Regulatory Reform (BERR) (formerly the Department for Trade and Industry). It has an enormous range of information, advice and support for businesses in every different industry. Specific information is available to different business sectors, such as computer games, manufacturing and telecommunications. In each subsection, the market is analysed and information provided about new opportunities and threats that could affect the industry.

INTERNET RESEARCH

To find out more about the work of BERR, visit www.berr.gov.uk.

BERR works closely with different trade associations and Business Link. It is also concerned with regional economic development, and works in partnership with Regional Development Agencies (RDAs). This is of great interest to many businesses that may wish to locate or relocate in an area suffering from high unemployment and lack of investment.

To encourage businesses to settle in these areas they can be given financial incentives. The Selective Finance for Investment project offers a minimum of £10,000 for businesses to establish, expand, modernise or relocate in particular areas that have been identified as needing assistance.

European Union

There is also assistance for businesses from the European Union. It concentrates on aiding areas where people's incomes are well below the average. Normally, European funds can be accessed via organisations such as Business Link.

KEY TERMS

Grants – financial assistance from the government or the European Union for particular businesses in particular circumstances.

Business plans – an outline of the intentions of a business in the short, medium and long-term.

Pressure group – an organisation that tries to influence the government, the European Union, other businesses and individuals to be favourable towards their members or cause.

Private support services

There is a wide range of other businesses concerned with the support or provision of services to business. These include:

- Accountants – who can help prepare financial data
- Solicitors – who can help with law, chasing of debts and business contracts
- Computer services – can provide maintenance and repair, as well as helping to organise a business's website
- Communication services – which could include telephone companies, the Post Office, courier services, Internet Service Providers, advertising agencies and mobile phone providers

Financial services

Businesses will also need assistance in handling money, and most use a bank to carry out the following:

- Dealing with cash
- Processing cheques
- Processing direct debits and standing orders
- Processing debit card and credit card transactions
- Currency exchange and transferring money to and from abroad

Insurance is also necessary for businesses to cover them against potential risks, such as fire or theft. They will also need cover if there are accidents at work. A business will pay an insurance company a premium, depending on the risk involved.

CASE STUDY ACCOUNTANCY SERVICES

Jenny Fitzpatrick set up her specialist food retailing business and coffee shop, The Fine Food Store, in Stamford, Lincolnshire straight from leaving higher education. From the start, she maximised the use of accountancy services as part of the business model.

'My business plan always included putting sound systems in place as the foundation for growth. That included managing the books. My business is open six days a week and I wanted to devote the time not spent in the shop to product development and marketing. Remembering advice from a senior lecturer, I decided to look for a bookkeeper and an auditor. It's good business practice to have your books audited separately, and I wanted to start as I meant to go on. I got the auditors to look over my business plan before I'd taken it to the bank, which was as a useful 'trial' of their services. In the end I chose a reputable local firm with experience of dealing with small companies. I was impressed by the way they had read the business plan in detail and understood what I was trying to achieve. My bookkeeper was also recommended to me and I signed her up from day one to handle invoicing, management accounts, VAT returns, PAYE for my five employees and National Insurance contributions. My bookkeeper and auditor are both established local businesses themselves.'

Source: adapted from Business Link

Questions

1 What does Jenny mean by 'managing the books'? (2 marks)
2 What do you think is meant by the word invoicing? (2 marks)
3 Why did Jenny choose the accountancy business? (4 marks)

Benefits and problems of plans and planning

LEARNING OBJECTIVES

▶ Importance of business plans
▶ Setting targets
▶ Problems with business plans

Importance of business plans

Potential investors will usually want to see a business plan before they even consider funding a business. As a result, many business plans are solely written for this purpose, but a good business plan needs to look at how the business will develop over a longer period of time.

A business can use a business plan to help allocate resources and this can also assist in attracting new funds as time goes by. The business plan will show how funds will be used. By getting into the habit of having an ongoing business plan, which is regularly updated, the business can also monitor how it is measuring up to its business objectives. In this way the business plan can be used to identify where the business is at any precise moment, and in which direction it needs to move in order for the business to grow. It can also ensure that the business meets its key targets and manages its priorities. Businesses, therefore, adopt a continuous and regular business planning cycle that ensures that the business plans are kept up-to-date. The plan can alert the business to whether it is likely to meet its objectives and to where it may be making mistakes. Usually businesses try to assess their progress every three to six months.

Target setting

Good business plans should incorporate sets of targets and objectives. Most business plans will have overall strategic goals, but these need to be broken down into specific, measurable targets. This assists the business in not only understanding what needs to be achieved, but when it needs to happen. Businesses can also use the targets to monitor the performance of employees, as well as products and services.

Usually a business will use **performance indicators**:

- Sales or profit over a given period of time
- The development of new products and services
- Productivity levels for the business and for individual teams
- **Market share**

Targets are useful, as they help individual employees to understand how they can assist a business in meeting its objectives, and how they fit into the organisation. For the business, it can use targets to monitor development. Individuals' progress can also be appraised using targets and objectives.

Many businesses use an annual plan, which is broken down into four quarterly plans. Targets can be set for each of the quarters. Businesses that are very sales-oriented may even break down their plans to include monthly or weekly targets and reviews. The whole plan does not need to be radically re-appraised on a regular basis: aspects of it need to be regularly assessed and updated, but an overall plan should be able to function for at least two years.

KEY TERMS

Performance indicators – measurable factors that can show the success or failure of a particular aspect of a business.

Market share – the percentage or proportion of the total available market that is controlled by a business.

Monopoly – a business that is the only seller of a product or service in a particular market.

BUSINESS PLAN

Problems with business plans

Some organisations feel that business plans unnecessarily restrict the activities of the business. They may be written at a time when the business is unaware of the realities of the market or the industry in which it will be operating. Then it may only be when the business is involved in delivering products and services to customers that it becomes aware of the complexities of the market. At this point, it may have to adapt more quickly and radically than the business plan had anticipated.

As far as general business plan problems are concerned, the following table outlines some of the key issues.

Problem with business plan	Explanation
Vagueness	The business plan does not have sufficient detail for potential finance providers to understand what the business is about.
Unsubstantiated statements	Broad, general statements that are not backed up by market research, facts or figures.
Over-optimism	Although business plans should be positive, investors need to know that their funds will be safe if problems occur.
Ignoring risks	It is important for finance providers to appreciate that the business has thought about what could go wrong and what could be done if that happens.
Inconsistencies	Statements in one part of the business plan do not match up with facts and figures in other parts. Finance providers will pick up on inconsistencies straight away.
Unrealistic assumptions	Figures need to reflect the real world and often do not. Overheads will not remain constant and neither will there be the likelihood of gross profits increasing year-on-year.
Sloppiness	Business plans need to be spell-checked, proofread and well presented. Calculations need to be double-checked as figures that do not add up will create a very bad impression.
Lack of market knowledge	Evidence of market research is often absent. Good market research may cost money, but it is an investment.
Lack of knowledge of competitors	Virtually no business will enjoy a monopoly. There will undoubtedly be competitors, and finance providers will want to know that the business is aware of them, as well as their strengths and weaknesses.
Dismissal of competitors	Providers of finance want to know that the business is aware of what competitors do well and how this will be countered. It is not sufficient to claim that the business's products or services are superior without qualifying the statement.
Poor focus	Providers of finance will want to know primarily how the business is going to repay the funds. Investors will want to show that the business can create a profit. Suppliers that the business wishes to become involved with will want to know that their time and effort will be well spent, and major customers will want to be sure that the business can deliver what they need, when they need it, and at a price they can afford in the long-term.

Questions

1 Why might a business plan be equally as important to an existing business as to a new business? (6 marks)

2 Why is it vital that a business plan incorporates target-setting? (6 marks)

Case studies, questions and exam practice

CASE STUDY FRACINO

Founded in 1964 to import espresso machines, Birmingham-based Fracino started manufacturing them in 1990. But it was when they developed their own machine in 2000 that the company really made an impact on the market.

Frank Maxwell, the company founder and his family had developed a new method of fresh-roasting coffee beans in a glass chamber, which was visually appealing and produced a great aroma. They saw that this machine, which they named the Roastilino, could become a dramatic centrepiece in cafes, emphasising the whole experience of coffee drinking as much as the drink itself. But how could they break into and establish a presence in a highly competitive market?

'Unless we came up with something that was clearly different from our competitors' machines, we would not be able to compete with the mass producers,' explained Commercial Director Angela Maxwell.

They put together a team of designers, engineers and marketing specialists to work from the initial business idea to its launch in the market. A three- to four-strong innovation team sees each project through from concept, prototyping and testing, to component supply and assembly. Key customers are also involved in the prototyping phase to make sure the final product meets their needs.

This approach has helped the company through the early stages of transforming from an importer to a manufacturer. Exporting their products for the first time proved to be a challenge, as Angela pointed out: 'Exporting is seriously hard work – you have to put up with many disappointments. However winning the Millennium Product Award in 2000 proved a milestone. After that, doors began to open.'

The business is continuing to grow and to introduce new products every year; the company is now one of the fastest growing inner-city enterprises, as well as a British brand leader and an exporter to over ten countries worldwide. 'To stay competitive,' said Angela, 'the company has adopted and sustained a policy of continuous improvement. We're not just focused on short-term success, we intend to keep the company ahead of the competition by generating a stream of exciting products.'

The next major decision will be whether to manufacture in countries to which the company is finding it difficult to export. However, this would mean a major change to the structure and focus of the business.

Sources: Adapted from Department for Business Enterprise and Regulatory Reform, www.fracino.com and Innovation Exchange

Questions

1 How might business planning have assisted Fracino in transforming from an importer to a manufacturer? (8 marks)
2 Suggest FOUR different external suppliers of support service that Fracino may have used, and give examples of the type of support they offer. (8 marks)

SHORT-ANSWER QUESTIONS

1 Outline the main purpose of a business plan.

2 What is an executive summary?

3 Why is it important for a business plan to address specific audiences?

4 Outline the key elements of a business plan.

5 Why is it important for a business plan to include details about the market and competitors?

6 List the principal financial forecasts that should be found in a business plan.

7 What is the role of Business Link?

8 List **FIVE** potential private support services that could be used by a business.

9 What is a government agency? Give an example of one that could assist a business in putting together a plan.

10 Give **FIVE** examples of potential problems with business plans.

CASE STUDY AKC HOME SUPPORT SERVICES

Darren Jones launched his care business, AKC Home Support Services, in 1991 with his wife Sharron. Although writing their business plan was one of the first things the couple did, Darren admits he originally saw it as a bit of a chore.

'When we started the firm I knew we needed a business plan but saw it more as a document for everyone else than something to help us. If I started another business tomorrow I would write one much more willingly as it brings a number of benefits – from helping you secure finance to keeping you focused on your goals. We got help from our local enterprise centre, looked at examples from other businesses and a template from the bank. We mixed and matched bits from these sources because not everything applied to us. We used our business plan to set out the financial and strategic goals we wanted to achieve in the short-term and long-term. We review it annually now unless there's a significant shift in our market and then we use it to immediately re-evaluate our goals. Our business plan has also helped us to avoid expanding too quickly. Early on, we were offered work in another county. This seemed great, but when we looked at our business plan – and particularly our cashflow forecasts – we realised it was important to establish a firm base in one county

before taking on work in another, otherwise we would overstretch ourselves. We purchased a residential unit four years ago and our business plan definitely helped us demonstrate why the bank should lend us the money.'

If he had to start from scratch, Darren admitted that he would do some things differently:

'I would have tried to get more assistance and perhaps made the document look a bit more professional. It's your way of gaining support for your business and is the one thing that your bank manager will remember, apart from how you were dressed. Show the plan to an independent third party – such as friends or family who have run their own businesses – who will be able to point out if anything is missing. It's much better to make mistakes on a practice run than when it really matters.'

Questions

1 Outline the reasons why Darren believes that a business plan is so important. (8 marks)

2 What does he mean by cashflow forecast? (2 marks)

3 Why is a professional approach so important in seeking financial support? (3 marks)

Methods of primary and secondary research

What is market research?

Marketing research is one of the main ways an organisation finds out about its customers and the environment in which it operates. Many companies carry out continuous investigations into trends, opportunities and threats. Market research and marketing research are sometimes confused, but they are very different. Market research tends to be narrow or focussed; marketing research is usually aimed at understanding consumer behaviour.

Marketing research is a broader term used to describe any investigation into any element of the marketing mix; the environment the organisation operates in; or any future impacts on the organisation. Marketing research is an information-gathering exercise, sometimes a continual process that attempts to uncover data, views, concerns and responses to the organisation itself, its products or services, the market in general or its customers.

We can divide marketing research into two key categories: primary research, which involves the collection or collation of fresh and new information solely for the purpose of the marketing research project. The second involves the use of existing data already collected by another organisation, or by the organisation undertaking the research, but for another purpose or reason. This is called secondary research and can make use of statistics and other information that can be bought in from another source or reused from an existing source.

Primary research

Primary research involves searching out new information for the first time by commissioning a marketing research agency, or by assigning employees of the organisation to the marketing project. Primary data is usually collected by field research. This means that the individuals carrying out the research are interacting with the subjects or **respondents** and collecting the data or information directly from them.

Primary data is not a cheap option: it can be time-consuming and easy to get wrong. Once the key objectives of the marketing research have been set, methods need to be developed or adopted in order to collect and collate that information.

Examples of primary research are given in the following table.

Primary research method	Description
Observation	Observation, or observational field research, is a method borrowed from the social sciences. It involves the researcher watching the behaviour of subjects. The most common form of observational research is to watch the shopping habits of customers using the CCTV in a department store or supermarket.
Experimentation	Experimentation research involves respondents chosen because they match the target group, testing out prototype versions of products and services. The research and development of new products and services is a costly and time-consuming affair. As prototypes become available, they are routinely 'crash-tested' by individuals representative of the types of customers that will later purchase them.
Surveys	Surveys are used by organisations (including the business itself or marketing research agencies working for a business), to collect data, responses and opinions from target groups. Surveys can be face-to-face, by telephone, email or postal.
Focus groups and panels	Focus groups involve selecting a group of individuals representative of a larger target group. These individuals could be representative of a business's customers, distributors, potential customers or those who match a typical customer's age, gender or income level. The focus groups are organised so that discussions are encouraged regarding the group's views and experiences of a product, service or topic. Panels are a variation of a focus group. Instead of choosing individuals who match the target group, panels are made up of experts in a particular field. A business that deals with retailers, for example, would bring together a focus group or panel of retailers, rather than consumers who purchase from the retailers.
Field trials	Field trials take the concept of testing new products and services one stage further. There are various ways in which a business could use field trials to gain valuable information about products and services before they are launched. The most basic form of field trial is an extension of the work carried out by focus groups.

Secondary research

Secondary research involves the collecting of existing data and manipulating it so that a summary of the findings can be used for marketing purposes. Among the most common forms of secondary research are published statistics, including the census, or published texts, including books, magazines and newspapers.

Sources of secondary research data can be broken down into internal and external types:

Internal Sources	Description
Data records	Customer records, containing information regarding the customer in terms of their name, address, purchasing habits, credit ratings and other information.
Loyalty schemes	Supermarkets, such as Tesco, run extensive loyalty schemes and programmes. They are able to match customers' purchasing habits with targeted offers to encourage them to buy more of the same product or similar products.
EPOS	Electronic Point of Sale was envisaged to link the sale of a product with the stock control system. EPOS is used in conjunction with loyalty cards to monitor customer purchases and to generate sales offers linked to their popular brands.
Website monitoring	A form of observation involving monitoring the number of clicks made by customers on an organisation's website; how long they have been on the website; and which pages they have visited. Activities on the website and the pages visited can then be compared to the purchases made by the visitor.
Accounts records	By monitoring the accounting records a business can see how long, on average, it takes a customer to pay an invoice, and which payment method they have chosen. This is only useful when a business is dealing with regular customers, as it is possible to monitor changes in payment methods.
Sales figures	These should show the accurate level of sales, and peaks and troughs in demand. Businesses can more confidently predict the level of sales in a similar future period, assuming the same conditions apply.
Product information	Production figures can be seen as a mirror of sales or orders. Many manufacturers only have a small buffer stock of products and do not over-produce and store huge levels of stock in anticipation of sales. Therefore production is very much reliant on accurate sales data or accurate orders.

External Sources	Description
Internet	Many businesses will use the Internet to trawl for information, reactions and opinions about themselves or their competitors. This kind of information can be valuable, as can constant monitoring of competitors' websites, which can reveal information about future direction, strategy, tactics and advertising.
Official Statistics	The government produces an array of statistics, from the census, different industries, marketing and trade initiatives. Much of the data is well researched and collated from wide sources.
Libraries	Businesses use dedicated business libraries, which compile data from industries by trawling magazines and newspapers, as well as the Internet, for clippings and references to specific businesses.
Trade journals	Magazines or newspapers whose readership is restricted to those in the industry. Rather like newspapers and magazines, they feature articles and information about the trade, advertisements, information about special events, and warnings about new legislation that may impact on the industry.
Agencies	Examples include Mintel, Datastream and Dun and Bradstreet, who have extensive research and information gathering potential and produce regular reports on particular industries, countries, markets and products.
Company reports	The structure of a company report is determined by law, and requires a business to outline its profit and loss, balance sheet and use of funds.
Universities	A major part of universities' work, beyond teaching, is research. They will routinely carry out research and are likely to cooperate with businesses or industry to collect and collate data.

KEY WORDS

Respondent – an individual who is the subject of a marketing research project

Prototype – an early version of a product or service

Questions

1 Distinguish between primary and secondary research. (4 marks)
2 List FOUR probable sources of internal secondary research. (4 marks)
3 List FOUR probable sources of external secondary research. (4 marks)

Benefits and drawbacks of research methods

LEARNING
OBJECTIVES
▶ Limitations of marketing research
▶ Observation
▶ Surveys
▶ Face-to-face interviews
▶ Focus groups and panels
▶ Online surveys

Limitations of marketing research

When a business decides to launch a marketing research campaign it will need to appreciate that marketing research is not necessarily capable of providing the complete set of answers to the questions being posed. Typically marketing research has the following limitations:

- The questions themselves may not necessarily be the right ones
- The methods used to choose the sample may be flawed
- A considerable number of potential respondents will either refuse to answer or not contact the researchers, which could lead to valuable data being lost
- The data collection can be flawed and vital information lost or overlooked
- In the analysis of the data, mistakes can be made and the wrong conclusions drawn
- The market research may only provide a snapshot of opinions, views or the current state of a market and will quickly become dated

Observation

Observation involves watching individuals and how they behave, and noticing and analysing their reactions. It can be carried out in controlled situations, such as an interview room, or in real-life situations, such as a supermarket. The key strengths and weaknesses of observation are shown in the following table:

Strengths	Weaknesses
Observation shows what people do rather than what people say they do.	It can be costly and time-consuming.
It can be carried out secretly without the respondent knowing.	Observing behaviour rarely answers questions.
It does not rely on the respondent telling the truth.	The researchers cannot be sure what has motivated a respondent to perform a particular act.
Researchers can observe and draw conclusions with reduced bias.	The respondents' behaviour can be misunderstood.
In secret observation there is no refusal rate by respondents.	Observation without a follow-up interview only provides part of the information necessary.

Surveys

Surveys are generally used to collect facts, opinions, attitudes and beliefs and include face-to-face, postal and telephone interviews. The table below compares the different types of survey method:

Postal surveys can give researchers a wide coverage at a low cost. The surveys can be completed at the respondents' convenience. There is no interviewer bias and no costs (such as travel expenses) involved.

The main problems with postal surveys are the low response rates and the fact that many respondents take a long time to send back the survey. Generally postal surveys are relatively short and there is a high probability that respondents may not understand the questions.

Telephone surveys offer a far quicker response rate. However the questions tend to be more limited and the respondent has less time to consider questions. Telephone surveys can also be relatively time-consuming.

	Face-to-face	Postal	Telephone	Electronic
Response rate	High	Low	Medium	Medium
Cost	High	Low	Medium	Low
Time	Slow	Slow	Fast	Fast

Face-to-face

The key weaknesses of face-to-face interviews are the high cost and the fact that they can be time-consuming. Also, if the interviewer is not very skilled then the answers given by the respondents can be misinterpreted. Their strengths include the ability for the researcher to get opinions, the fact that the interview can be flexible and that the interview can prompt the respondent and see their reactions.

Focus groups and panels

Focus groups tend to be used for qualitative information gathering, involving a moderator and up to about ten respondents. The moderator introduces topics and guides the conversation with the principal aim of finding opinions and attitudes.

Focus groups are relatively inexpensive and quick. They can discover a range of attitudes to different issues and provide detailed qualitative information. A good moderator can also encourage participation by all involved. The key weaknesses revolve around the qualities of the moderator. The moderator needs to maintain control, keep the discussion focused and build up a rapport with the respondents. Other key weaknesses of focus groups are that they can be relatively expensive, sometimes time-consuming to organise and inhibiting to some respondents.

Panels are useful, as they tend to involve the same individuals being involved in the discussions over a period of time. This can help gauge shifting attitudes and opinions. They are extremely useful for indicating trends and analysing changes. Also, as a rapport has been built up with the panel members, the questions can probe more deeply. Panels are, however, expensive. There is a high chance that the sample of respondents may not reflect the broader population and that the panellists behave differently in this environment.

Electronic surveys

Many businesses have adopted electronic or online surveys as a comparatively cheap method of collecting information from customers or visitors to their websites. The respondent can carry out the surveys very quickly, and individual elements of the questionnaire can be changed, making them the most versatile type of survey. Once electronic surveys have been created, they are relatively cheap compared to other survey methods. They are also useful in enabling the business to collect data from respondents regardless of their geographical location.

The main weaknesses are that the respondents effectively select themselves by choosing to participate in the survey. This means that the business does not have any control over the sample, and it may be completely unrepresentative.

CASE STUDY HIGHLANDS AND ISLANDS ENTERPRISE

Between August and September 2007 the Highlands and Islands Enterprise carried out a survey to assess the potential demand for air flights between Inverness and Poland. They received 2,262 responses, of which 2,077 were validated. The key findings were:

- Most respondents would make three or four return journeys over the next year
- 88% would involve air travel
- The most popular destination was Warsaw, but the demand for air services was fairly evenly spread between seven Polish airports
- The vast majority of the respondents were Polish people, resident in Scotland
- The peak demand period would be the summer, followed by the Christmas and New Year period and then the spring

Source: adapted from Highlands and Islands Enterprise

Questions

1 Based on the research survey, is there a suggestion of a demand for air services to Poland? Give reasons why. (4 marks)
2 1,312 of the respondents were Polish people, resident in Scotland. Could this large figure be considered an advantage or a disadvantage in terms of the sample and why? (4 marks)
3 Why was the phrase 'validated sample' used and why was this different from the total number of responses? (3 marks)

Qualitative and quantitative research

What is qualitative and quantitative research?

In many cases, the choice of research type is between volume and quantity; these are the two key qualities of qualitative and quantitative research respectively.

Qualitative research tends to be on a smaller scale with a great deal of in-depth information gathered from a relatively small sample of respondents or sources. It is the sheer detail of the information that is important rather than the scale of the information gathering.

Quantitative research, on the other hand, looks at far larger sets of data and considers the volume of information to be important, rather than the detail. Usually, quantitative research concerns itself with statistics rather than with opinions and ideas, which are the basis of qualitative research.

The following table illustrates the choices between qualitative and quantitative research and identifies the situations when they are appropriate:

Method	Qualitative or quantitative?	Characteristics, benefits and drawbacks
Postal survey	Quantitative	• Cost is low • Response rate can be poor • Answers may be incomplete • Responses are coded and must be simple so that people can understand them
Telephone survey 	Quantitative	• Cost-effective method of achieving robust sample • Responses are coded • Certain groups do not have access to the telephone, so may be excluded from the sample • It is difficult to ask sensitive questions over the telephone • Works well with employers
Face-to-face survey	Quantitative	• Can include both open questions and coded questions • Can achieve robust sample • Expensive and time-consuming • Ideal for gathering sensitive information or exploring complicated issues
In-depth interview 	Qualitative	• Rich and detailed information can be gathered • Interviewers are allowed more flexibility • Answers to open questions can be difficult and time-consuming to analyse • Expensive and time-consuming to administer
Focus 	Qualitative	• A group discussion with around 8–12 people • Usually lasts between 1 and 3 hours • Capitalises on interaction between participants • Participants are not representative of wider population which does not allow for generalisation • Good for gathering sensitive data • Requires careful and unbiased analysis
Case study	Qualitative	• Researcher gains understanding of a specific person's experience through an in-depth interview • Provides good quotations and rich data • Can bring alive other research, such as survey data • Findings cannot be generalised to a wider population group

Qualitative research

Qualitative research aims to understand the patterns in customers' thinking that lead them to make different choices or purchase decisions. Often these patterns are hidden, and qualitative research uses cutting-edge tools to capture both verbal and non-verbal information.

Qualitative research uses a mixture of exploration and evaluation through techniques including face-to-face interviews and focus groups.

Researchers ask customers what they were thinking and why they made a decision. The patterns involved in the decision are hidden from view, usually from both the researcher and the respondent, but the organisation undertaking the research wants to identify the patterns that drive the behaviour.

Qualitative research can be useful in identifying customer views, opinions and attitudes. The researchers can investigate respondents in-depth to understand how a purchasing decision was made. This can lead to the formation of a theory that can be later tested by broader research.

Qualitative research differs from quantitative research in the following ways:

- The data gathered is usually less structured
- The findings are more in-depth as open-ended questions are used
- It provides detail on behaviour, attitudes, and motivation
- The research is more intensive and flexible, allowing the researcher to probe since s/he has greater latitude to do so
- The research involves smaller sample sizes (though not usually representative of the population)
- The analysis of the results is more subjective
- The researchers need to be well trained to make sure that they question the respondent correctly and log the answers given

Quantitative research

Many businesses use quantitative research to guide them in their decision-making. Quantitative research techniques are used as a formal research method to measure, describe, or forecast quantity using a range of sampling methods.

Quantitative research involves measuring a market and quantifying that measurement with data. Most often the data required relates to:

- Market size
- Market share
- Market penetration
- Market growth rates

The research can also be used to measure customer attitudes, satisfaction, commitment and a range of other useful market data (and these can be tracked over a given time period).

Quantitative research can also be used to measure customer awareness and attitudes towards different manufacturers, retailers or suppliers and to understand overall customer behaviour in a market by taking a statistical sample of customers.

The techniques can be combined with segmentation analysis to provide vital information. This is because key segments can be targeted and monitored over time to ensure the best possible use of the marketing budget.

As we have seen, it is the statistical sample that is the main part of quantitative research. This needs to be selected very carefully as well as the design of the sample questionnaire and the quality of the analysis of data collected.

For many organisations, the primary focus of quantitative research is on decision-makers in businesses or major buyers and is designed to answer very specific marketing questions. The questions would tend to focus on a particular issue.

CASE STUDY CUSTOMER SATISFACTION RESEARCH

Most businesses lose 45% to 50% of their customers every five years. Winning new customers can be up to twenty times more expensive than retaining existing customers. It is essential for a business to be aware of what makes a customer choose one brand or supplier in preference to another. Successful customer research can help a business to do the following:

- Identify potential problem areas before they become significant
- Identify new products, product features and services that customers wish to be addressed
- Provide information for sales teams, products, geographic regions and distributors
- Identify issues, whether to do with product, people, or process, that the business needs to address in the short, medium and long term

Questions

1 In customer satisfaction research, which would be the more appropriate approach – quantitative or qualitative? Why? (6 marks)
2 Suggest how a business might collect information to help it identify the four sets of data that will be of use as mentioned in the case study. (8 marks)

Size and types of samples

LEARNING OBJECTIVES

▶ What is a sample?
▶ Sample size and choosing the sample
▶ Probability sampling
▶ Non-probability sampling
▶ Implications of different samples, cost and accuracy

What is a sample?

It is impossible, even for the largest organisations, to sample every single person in a target group. Not only is this beyond the scope of professional organisations, but it is also unnecessary. As we will see, it is perfectly acceptable, providing the basis of choice is correct, to pick a sample of the target group and base your assumptions on those individuals.

A census involves questioning every single individual within a target group. There are few organisations geared up to do this. Every ten years, the government carries out the only truly comprehensive census. Even then, the information provided is basic and focuses on age, gender, nationality and a handful of other considerations.

A sample can be chosen in a number of different ways, but the overriding requirement is for that sample to accurately represent the larger target group. Many surveys featured on TV have, in fact, only interviewed a sample of less than 1,000 people, yet their views are portrayed to be representative of all people in the UK with those characteristics.

Sample size and choosing the sample

There are no strict rules to follow in choosing a sample, but a degree of logic and judgement must always be applied. A small, carefully chosen sample must reflect or represent the views of the larger population. In truth, the sampling means that each member of the population has an equal chance of being selected as part of that sample. This is a truly random sample.

In terms of any research you might carry out for this course, a sample of no more than 100 is perfectly acceptable, providing you can prove that your sampling criteria have allowed you to select individuals that represent the larger target group.

Probability sampling

Sampling methods are always classified as either probability or non-probability methods. Probability samples mean that each member of the population has an equal chance of being chosen. These methods include random sampling, systematic sampling and stratified sampling (see below). More information on these types of sampling can be seen in the following table.

Sampling method	Characteristics
Random	The purest form of probability sampling. Everyone has an equal chance of being selected. It is almost impossible to track down every member of the population, so there is a slight bias.
Systematic	A variation of random sampling, also known as the 'nth name' selection technique. The required sample size is calculated and every nth record is chosen. This is straightforward as long as there is no hidden order in the names.
Stratified	Probably the most commonly used probability method. Subsets of the population are created so that each subset has a common characteristic, such as gender. Random sampling chooses a number of subjects from each subset.
Multi-stage	This is a rolling form of sampling. An initial batch of individuals is chosen, probably using random sampling, and if these are non-responsive then a new replacement batch is selected. This way the research is staggered over a period of time.
Cluster	Cluster sampling involves choosing individuals from a relatively tight geographical region. First the region is chosen in relation to the population to see if it is representative. If it is, sets of respondents are chosen.

BOOK RESEARCH

Bradley, Nigel, *Marketing research: Tools and techniques*, Oxford University Press (2006)

Non-probability sampling

Non-probability sampling means that members are selected from the population in some non-random manner. It would include convenience sampling, judgement sampling, quota sampling and what is known as snowball sampling. More information on these types of sampling can be seen in the following table.

INTERNET RESEARCH 🔍

To find out more about market research, search the pages of www.marketresearchworld.net. It is a market research portal site with useful links to current sampling techniques and examples of ongoing work.

Sampling method	Characteristics
Quota	This is the non-probability version of stratified sampling. Subsets are chosen and then either convenience or judgement sampling is used to choose people from each subset.
Convenience	The respondents are chosen on the premise that they will drive down the costs of the research project. Therefore people local to the researchers are chosen as members of the sample.
Judgement	A common non-probability method, where a particular group of individuals, usually in a small geographical area, is chosen to be representative on the basis that the researchers feel that this is the case.
Snowball sampling	In this sampling technique a few potential respondents are contacted and asked if they know any other people with the characteristics that the researcher is looking for. The initial contacts may have knowledge not only of individuals but also of groups of other people.

Implications of different samples, costs and accuracy

Having chosen a particular sampling method, the researchers will have to be aware that their choice may affect the results of the survey. For many research projects it is a trade-off between cost and accuracy. Obviously, the more random and the larger the sampling method, the higher the costs involved. This is in terms of actual time to complete the survey, and time needed by the researchers to frame the project, collect the data and deal with the results.

Some research methods are chosen for their speed rather than their accuracy. They are designed to give an immediate snapshot of opinions and views and do not necessarily profess to be truly scientific. It is important to remember that the sample should be representative of the entire target group and that the way in which the sample has been chosen should be able to be justified.

Questions

1 Briefly explain stratified sampling. (3 marks)
2 Why are samples used? (4 marks)
3 Distinguish between probability and non-probability sampling. (4 marks)

Factors influencing choice of sampling methods

LEARNING OBJECTIVES

▶ Why does a choice have to be made?
▶ Finance
▶ Nature of product or service
▶ Risk involved
▶ Target market

Why does a choice have to be made?

Most businesses have a restricted potential set of respondents, usually the total number of possible customers. This means that survey samples will tend to be small and specialised. This is not to say that small samples cannot provide meaningful strategic information. If an organisation is providing products and services to other businesses, then multiple respondents can be sought from those involved in the purchasing decision processes.

For the most part, businesses do use small samples and often have restricted budgets. It is not practical for them to mount large-scale quantitative research using complex sampling techniques.

There are a number of reasons why this is usually the case, as we will see. It must not be forgotten, however, that if the sampling techniques used are sound, and the business is cautious about the results in the light of the relatively small samples, the information can still be of considerable value.

Finance

Hiring a marketing research company can be a worthwhile investment, though even a small survey could cost in excess of £5,000. However, if the research provides the business with the quality of information it needs, this can be money well spent.

The level of investment will obviously depend on the method of data gathering, the type of product or service or the sector.

Nature of product or service

It would be pointless and expensive for the manufacturers of passenger aircraft to carry out a survey on purchasing habits that focused on people who purchased package tours. While these individuals eventually use the product, they are not the purchasers of the product.

The more specialist or sophisticated the product or service, the smaller the potential pool of respondents. Businesses that deal solely with other businesses are more likely to select respondents who have a direct interest in the product or service. Products aimed at the mass market may well require significant survey samples representing a broad spectrum of the potential purchasers of the product or service. However, the manufacturers would also wish to include bulk purchasers, such as supermarket buyers or distributors.

Risk involved

The highest risk period for products and services is during development, or certainly prior to their launch onto the market. Not only does the business need to establish that the product or service actually works, and can be either manufactured or provided, it also needs to be certain that there is a potential market.

This does mean that even at this early stage, the respondents chosen need to be able to provide insights, views and opinions on the product or service. Choosing the sample is therefore crucial in order for the business to obtain accurate information and guidance on whether to pursue the development of the product or service, or whether to delay or cancel its launch.

Target market

The target market itself may determine the choice of sampling method. Businesses that sell to a relatively limited number of customers will simply not have a broad enough choice of respondents. They may well have to sample, or attempt to sample, every customer to gauge their reactions.

The problem for businesses that provide more mass-market products or services is the complete reverse. They need to have a very clear idea of their typical customers, having identified their characteristics. They also need to know what proportion of customers exhibit the same kind of characteristics. It may mean that their sample survey is broken down into several distinct groups of respondents, each representing a proportional sample of their overall customer base. Only by doing this will they be able to ascertain the differing views of these distinctive customer sub-groups.

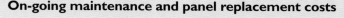

CASE STUDY CITIZEN'S PANEL

The establishment of a Citizen's Panel of about 1,000 people in Spelthorne was approved by the Council as part of an overall resolution on public consultation.

There are three elements to the costs of Citizen's Panels:

1 Initial set-up costs.
2 Annual maintenance costs.
3 Costs per consultation.

The costs quoted for recruitment of the panel are as follows:

Market Research UK	£19,000
Miller Associates	£24,662.50
MORI	£16,000
NOP	£12,900
Telephone Surveys Europe	£5,500

The MORI, NOP and Telephone Surveys Europe quotes allow for recruitment of the panel and a basic level of data such as demographic information and use of and satisfaction with Council services. The Miller Associates and Market Research quotes allow for a longer interview time in which extra information could be obtained.

NOP quote for recruitment of a panel by telephone using a methodology they have formulated that they claim overcomes the limitations of the method suggested by Telephone Surveys Europe. This method has recently been used to set up a panel of 1,000 for the London Borough of Wandsworth.

On-going maintenance and panel replacement costs

The annual costs quoted for this aspect are:

Market Research UK	£10,750
Miller Associates	£8,800
MORI	£4,000
NOP	£5,500
Telephone Surveys Europe	£950

The Miller Associates, NOP and Telephone Surveys Europe quotes allow for replacing a third of the panel each year. The Market Research UK quote is for replacement of a quarter per year and the MORI quote for a fifth.

If, as is suggested, the panel should be replaced by a third each year, then the Market Research UK and MORI quotes will need to be amended accordingly.

Costs per consultation	
Postal Survey of all 1,000 panel members	
Market Research UK	£6,250
Miller Associates	£5,670
MORI	£7,150
NOP	£7,750
Telephone Surveys Europe (by phone)	£5,500
Telephone Survey of 350 panel members	
Market Research UK	£6,200
Miller Associates (10 minutes)	£4,550
MORI (5 minutes)	£5,700
NOP (5 minutes)	£5,500
Telephone Surveys Europe (6 minutes)	£1,750

Adapted from Spelthorne Borough Council

Questions

1 Taking into account the fact that the Council had a budget of around £26,000 for this research exercise, which of the potential suppliers might be chosen and why? (8 marks)
2 Is there any significant differences between the services offered by the five potential suppliers? (4 marks)

Analysis of market research data

LEARNING OBJECTIVES

▶ Analysis and evaluation of data
▶ Presentation of findings and making recommendations
▶ Re-evaluation of marketing activities

Analysis and evaluation of data

The way in which the data can be analysed and evaluated will very much depend on how it was collected. The more complex the questionnaire, the greater the difficulty in collating, analysing and evaluating the information it will provide. Straightforward questionnaires are far easier to handle.

The complex data may need statistical data analysis and this will take time and cost money to carry out. There are a large number of highly specialised statistical analyses. Some look at factors within the information, others look for trends.

The process of collating, analysing and evaluating data has a series of key stages. These are:

- Collating the information, in other words taking the information from each questionnaire and putting it into a single document
- Constructing basic graphic representations of each question from the questionnaire, to aid the checking process
- Checking sample questionnaires for errors
- Collating again after the cross-checking and an initial presentation of the data have been completed
- Looking at links, trends and patterns, both within individual questionnaires, across questions and across questionnaires themselves
- Comparing the raw data with existing data, perhaps from a previous marketing research project
- Highlighting significant shifts, changes or errors
- Final presentation of the data in the preferred form

Presentation of findings and making recommendations

There are many different ways in which market research findings can be presented. Generally they are either oral or written reports and may be formal or informal. Usually they are supported by visual aids.

Before the findings can be presented, however, the researchers must make recommendations arising out of the data collected. Hopefully the researchers will have discovered patterns in the data, which can then be summarised. These patterns may suggest that action is required by the business in order to deal with them. Thus within the framework of the original brief and objectives, recommendations can now be made. Questions may have been posed when detailing the brief and objectives of the research. The business will now want answers to these questions and will require suggestions as to how potential problems or opportunities can be handled.

For the conclusions and recommendations of market research to be wholly accepted by an organisation and its managers and employees, it needs to prove that it has been as scientific and objective as possible.

Re-evaluation of marketing activities

A business may have decided to investigate its customer behaviour, patterns, preferences or satisfaction. Alternatively it may have looked at how aware the general population is about its brand or advertising. In some way the business would have investigated one of its activities and compared their assessment of it to the perception of the target groups for which it was originally designed. Even large organisations make major mistakes when it comes to making decisions about what they believe their customers want. A prime example is Coca Cola, who in the 1990s released a new formula of Coca Cola. It was very poorly received and the company was forced very quickly to re-release the original Coca Cola and to gradually phase out the new formula. They had underestimated their customers' brand awareness, tastes and purchasing habits.

BOOK RESEARCH

Kelly, Sean, *Customer intelligence: From data to dialogue*, John Wiley & Sons (2005)

CASE STUDY FORESIGHT PROGRAMME: six hypothetical food products

The *Foresight* programme aims to develop visions of the future, looking at possible future threats, needs and opportunities and making recommendations for what should be done now to make sure that all are ready for those challenges. It builds bridges between business, science and government, bringing together the knowledge and expertise of many people across all areas and activities in order to increase national wealth and quality of life.

Foresight provided an initial draft of a self-completion postal questionnaire, along with short versions of the product descriptions. The final questionnaires were designed from the draft, in liaison with Foresight. Foresight also selected participants; sent out the questionnaires with a Freepost return envelope; chased for responses until 100 responses were received in respect of each product; and upon receipt of the responses entered the data obtained on a database.

The group of participants was selected (from a large database of British consumers) to provide a representative cross-section of the British population.

Each participant was asked to read a description of one of the six hypothetical food products and then complete a questionnaire designed to gauge their opinion of the product described. The questionnaire consisted of a combination of open and multiple-choice questions, which were two or three pages long.

The hypothetical products were:

- Scottish banana
- Anti-cancer broccoli
- Long-life lasagne
- Zero-calorie cake
- Smart packaging
- Chicken in a bottle

A total of 3,530 questionnaires were mailed out (569 Scottish banana, 569 anti-cancer broccoli, 569 long-life lasagne, 569 zero-calorie cake, 685 smart packaging [extra 116 mailed out], and 569 chicken in a bottle). 707 completed (valid) questionnaires were returned within the survey period, which represents an overall response rate of 20%. A more detailed breakdown of response rates is below:

Product	Mailed out	Returned	Response rate
Scottish banana	569	107	18%
Anti-cancer broccoli	569	125	21%
Long-life lasagne	569	110	19%
Zero-calorie cake	569	136	23%
Smart packaging	685	107	15%
Chicken in a bottle	569	122	21%

Those with response rates above 20% were:

- Chicken in a bottle
- Anti-cancer broccoli
- Zero-calorie cake

Those with response rates below 20% were:

- Scottish banana
- Long-life lasagne
- Smart packaging

Adapted from: http://www.foresight.gov.uk

Questions

1 Why might the response rates have been so different? (4 marks)
2 What do you think is meant by the term 'combination of open and multiple-choice questions'? (6 marks)
3 What do you think was the purpose of the research, and what did the researchers learn about sampling? (4 marks)

Case studies, questions and exam practice

CASE STUDY SYBIL'S CRAFT SHOP

Sybil Thatcher runs a craft shop in the busy King's Street in Halesworth. Her shop looks quite old-fashioned, but is packed with stock. For some time she has been thinking about expanding the business. Yesterday she heard that the health food shop next door is closing when the lease runs out in six weeks' time. Sybil thinks it is a great opportunity to knock the two shops together and treble her shop space.

The problem is that she will need to persuade the bank to lend her some money to buy the lease and help pay for the shop refit. She wants to be fully prepared when she sees the business advisor and the bank manager. If she misses out on the premises next door it might be another five years before she gets a similar chance.

Sybil knows that the bank will want to see facts and figures and her research on whether the expansion is likely to work as an investment. Above all, they will want to be convinced she will be able to pay back the loan.

So far Sybil has prepared the following:

Average monthly takings	£18,000
Average monthly costs	£2,250
Average spend on stock	£4,500
Drawings	£2,250
Average monthly profit	£9,000
Average customer spend	£14.80
Average number of customers per month	1216
Cost of new lease per month	£2,400
Cost of refit	£6,800
Cost of new employee per month	£1,800
Expected new taking total (monthly)	£26,000

Questions

1 What other calculations should Sybil make to complete the set of figures? (8 marks)
2 What kind of research has Sybil undertaken so far? (2 marks)
3 What market research could Sybil undertake to back up her belief that a shop expansion would work? (8 marks)

SHORT-ANSWER QUESTIONS

1 Define the term 'marketing research'.

2 List **FOUR** types of primary research.

3 What secondary research might a supermarket use?

4 Give **TWO** strengths and **TWO** weaknesses of observation.

5 What is a focus group?

6 Distinguish between qualitative and quantitative research.

7 What are the features of telephone research?

8 What is a sample and why is it necessary?

9 What is probability sampling?

10 Why might the target market determine the size of a sample?

CASE STUDY PUT TO THE TEST

Grant and Graham Pulman have a great business idea, but between them they have only managed to save up £8,000. They are prepared to spend as much of it as necessary to commission some marketing research and then find funding for the new business.

Together they compile a marketing research brief:

Business name:	Pulman Kid Tags Ltd
Business concept:	Trackable children's ID tags
Explanation of business:	Tag your kids with a Pulman ID kit. Trendy badges, jewellery and watches, all with built-in GPS tracking devices. We track your kids, so you'll always know where they are. Instant messaging straight to the kids, warning them to leave high-risk areas or return home. You call us and we give you their exact location, any day, any time. Fully inclusive price includes ID kit of your choice, plus monthly subscription fee. Know if your kids are bunking off school or going to places you don't approve of, and achieve peace of mind that you can contact them straight away.
Price:	Set-up and ID kit: £29.99 Monthly fee (per child): £9.99

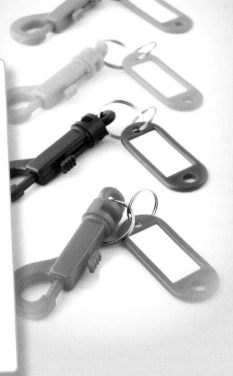

The brothers are certain that the system will work and it would appeal to many parents. The technology should work too – they have tested it on friends and family. Now they need to find out whether people would buy-in to the system.

Questions

1 Suggest appropriate primary or secondary research that the brothers could use. (10 marks)
2 How would the brothers identify the type of parents/guardians/schools that might buy into the system? (6 marks)
3 What kind of sample size should the brothers consider to collect qualitative research material? (6 marks)

The nature and types of markets

LEARNING OBJECTIVES

► What is a market?
► Local markets
► National markets
► Physical and electronic markets

What is a market?

The term 'market' is generally used to describe all actual and potential buyers of a product or service, regardless of where those individuals or businesses are located. In other words, this is the total value, or volume of products and services that satisfy a particular customer need.

In this definition of the term market, it is important to remember that a particular type of product or service is not a market in itself. A market is all of the products and services that could satisfy a particular need. A prime example would be the breakfast food market. This would include breakfast cereals, speciality foods such as croissants, and restaurants and cafes that offer breakfast menus. This definition of a market focuses primarily on the needs of the customer. The products and services provided by businesses seek to satisfy those needs. It is important to remember that it is not the products and services that define the market; it is the needs of the customer and whether those products and services satisfy their needs.

It is also important to remember that a market should not be too broadly defined. Terms such as 'the food market' or 'the entertainment market' are too broad to assist a business in defining precisely what customer needs might be in those areas.

Local markets

For many small businesses that have a physical presence on a high street or an industrial estate, their focus will be on the local market. These will be individuals and other businesses that live within the immediate area of the business. Typically, service providers, such as electricians, plumbers and hairdressers or IT technicians would cater for businesses and individuals within a fairly tight geographical area. As we will see, however, even local businesses can cater for customers that are considerably further afield, by providing online sales, mail order and intangible services.

> **▶▶ FOCUS POINT ◀◀**
>
> Think about the entertainment market and consider products and services that could provide entertainment, either at home or elsewhere. Why might considering entertainment as a single market not be very useful to a business seeking to satisfy customer needs?

National markets

Broadly speaking there are two types of businesses that cater for national markets, the first of which we will see in almost every high street and shopping mall up and down the country. Businesses such as HMV, H&M and New Look have branches that provide a similar range of products and services to customers in different geographical locations.

In many respects these businesses, although they are part of a national or international chain, cater for the local, or at least the regional market. Collectively they cater for the national market. Therefore television or media advertising allows offers, deals and special announcements to be broadcast nationwide, and customers can take advantage of these by visiting a local or regional store.

The other alternative is for a single site organisation to cater for a national market. In the case of businesses such as Harrods or Fortnum and Mason – both well-known London-based department stores – they attract customers from all over the world, but also provide mail order and online sales.

Other businesses that do not have a physical presence on the high street can also cater for a national market. These would include insurance companies, such as Norwich Union, or the AA and RAC, which provide roadside assistance, and various insurance and financial products.

Physical and electronic markets

In the two previous sections we have used a slightly different definition of the term market. In effect both are defined by geography: local businesses catering for the immediate market or demand for products and services, and national businesses catering for the overall demand for products and services across the country.

There is another way of looking at markets and this involves considering whether the products and services provided by the businesses are tangible or intangible. Tangible simply means that it is a physical product, such as a box of cereal or a television. An intangible product is any form of service from repairs through insurance to currency exchange and banking.

With improved communication, secure payment systems and enhanced transportation it is now possible for businesses, regardless of their location, to service the needs of customers. Physical products such as sofas, cars and dishwashers, can be purchased online or over the telephone, and delivered anywhere in the country.

Pure electronic services can also be provided, either using websites or automated call centres. Customers can pay bills, transfer funds, purchase insurance, make a mortgage payment or buy foreign currency without having to speak to a representative of the business.

All of these variations are markets. Clearly, electronic-based markets, whether they provide tangible or intangible products and services, are more competitive, as there are far more businesses capable of meeting customer demand than a retail outlet in a high street having to compete with similar businesses in the local area.

INTERNET RESEARCH 🔍

The organic food market is a clearly definable part of the overall food market. Use the Internet to find out how this portion of the market has grown. Useful websites are the BBC (www.bbc.co.uk) and The Soil Association (www.soilassociation.org).

CASE STUDY THE £2BN BOX

Home deliveries of boxes of organic fruit and vegetables have reached a market value of £2bn, up 53% from 2006-7. Sainsbury and Tesco have entered the market, but 40% of the sales come from farmers, who either provide box schemes themselves or contribute towards box schemes. At the same time free range and organic eggs have outstripped the sales of caged bird eggs. It is expected that during 2007 and 2008, 40% of egg farms will convert to organic status.

Questions

1 Overall organic food sales have seen a 27% annual growth since 1996. Explain what this statement means. (4 marks)
2 Home delivery of fruit and vegetables incorporates both tangible and intangible products and services. How might this be the case? (2 marks)
3 If there are approximately 26m British households, what is the average spending on home delivery of organic fruit and vegetables per household? Why might this figure be of little use for analysis? (6 marks)

The importance of demand

What is demand?

Demand is the quantity of products or services that customers are prepared to buy for the price charged by a business. Demand has to relate to the actual amount of products or services that will be sold, rather than the number of products or services desired by customers. This is an important distinction because working out demand based on actual sales is a more precise measure than simply asking people whether they would purchase the product. It is not sufficient for customers to merely want to buy the product; they must be willing and able to do so.

Obviously, there comes a point when the price will affect the demand. It will simply force too many people to reconsider whether they need that product or service. Equally, if there are not many of the products or services available and the demand remains high, the price will usually be high. The reverse of this is that if the availability of a product or service exceeds demand, the price will drop to encourage more people to purchase it.

Demand and price

There are a few products and services that customers would purchase without even considering the price. These include basic foods and necessities, such as electricity, gas and water.

More expensive products and services tend to be more affected by price, and greater consideration is given to the price before a purchase is made. This is why, for example, many expensive products are available on credit, or payments can be made for them over a period of time.

For more on the connections between supply and demand see Using break-even analysis to make decisions on pp. 112–21.

KEY TERM

Brands – a trademark, logo, image or product range that has a clearly recognisable identity compared to the competition, e.g. Cadbury's chocolate.

Demand and competition

The prices charged for products and services by competing organisations are just one factor that can affect demand. Customers increasingly look for better deals, both on price and on service, before making any purchasing decisions:

- Customers tend to be quite loyal to particular **brands**. They are loyal within reason: if the price of a particular brand is too high compared to the competitors, they will switch to another brand.
- Competition can also come from close substitutes and not just almost identical products and services. A customer may purchase a newspaper instead of a magazine, or buy tea instead of coffee, or switch from Coca-Cola to Sprite.

Demand and consumer income

When organisations recruit employees they quote their pay before any deductions. This is known as their gross income. They do not, however, receive their gross income. The government takes tax and National Insurance and the business may deduct a contribution towards an employee's pension scheme. This leaves the employee with a net income. But again this is not the amount of money that they have to freely spend each month. Regular monthly outgoings include utility bills, credit-card payments, mortgages or rent, and the community charge. What is left is called disposable income. It is the level of this disposable income that can often determine demand for products and services.

The less money that is left after all necessary expenditure has been paid out, the lower the overall demand for products and services will be. This will tend to make sellers of products and services more prepared to lower prices or offer credit terms. If disposable income increases, say as a result of a reduction in income tax, then potential customers would have a higher disposable income and could either afford to purchase a wider range of products and services or purchase the higher-priced products and services.

Demand, marketing and seasonal factors

Even if a business has the best product or service available to a market, it will fail to make any impression on that market if potential customers are unaware of its existence. Marketing aims to communicate to existing or potential customers the availability, benefits, price and features of the product or service, highlighting how it is better than the competitors.

Potential customers are exposed to literally thousands of marketing messages every day. Marketing therefore needs to be focused, effective and targeted, in order to get the message across to potential customers. Successful marketing can lead to an increase in demand. Ultimately it can lead to the willingness of customers to pay more for the product or service.

Ineffective marketing can lead to either a reduction or stagnation in demand. It should be remembered, however, that regardless of the effectiveness of the marketing of a single business, the overall demand for a product or service may not change: it is simply that the customers are buying elsewhere.

Some businesses have to cope with seasonal fluctuations in demand. The busiest period for a tour operator is during school holiday periods, particularly in the summer. This does not mean that they do not sell products and services during the rest of the year, simply that demand increases over certain weeks of the year. A manufacturer of fireworks or artificial Christmas trees will, of course, experience heightened demand at very specific times of the year. However, firework manufacturers make and sell their products at a lower level of demand all year round. Artificial Christmas tree manufacturers will be gearing up in order to match the expected demand and will have to produce enough trees by the time customer orders begin to arrive in the lead-up to Christmas.

For more information about marketing see Using the marketing mix: promotion *on pp. 290–7.*

Questions

Explain how the following factors could affect the demand for set-top digital TV boxes:

1 The knowledge that in 2012 all British television will be digital. (4 marks)
2 Increased advertising by manufacturers of the digital boxes. (2 marks)
3 A rise in unemployment. (2 marks)
4 A rise in the cost of borrowing. (2 marks)

Types of market segmentation

LEARNING OBJECTIVES
▶ What is market segmentation?
▶ Types of segmentation
▶ Problems and benefits of segmentation

What is market segmentation?

Market segmentation involves identifying particular groups that have broadly similar needs and wants within a market. Businesses will try to identify markets that have segments large enough to specifically target. For example, a manufacturer of trainers may segment its market by identifying professional and amateur athletes, leisure wearers, women and children. They will produce a range of products, and market those products to each market segment in a slightly different way. This means that the business will need to develop an appropriate marketing mix for each segment.

Market segmentation enables a business to:

- accurately define its markets;
- position products and services to match the demands of particular markets and segments;
- identify gaps in the market that it could fill;
- make more efficient use of its marketing resources.

Types of segmentation

Broadly speaking there are ten different ways of segmenting the market. These are outlined in the following table:

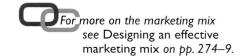 *For more on the marketing mix see Designing an effective marketing mix on pp. 274–9.*

Segmentation method	Explanation
Age	This is a basic demographic or population-based form of segmentation. It aims to identify segments of the market by age group, focusing on main age-group segments and then adjusting the product or service to attract age groups outside the core customer segments.
Gender	Some products and services are specifically aimed at a particular gender. It is important to note that all genders may use a particular product, but one gender is more likely to make the purchase.
Socio-economic group	In effect this is a mixture of occupation and income. Each socio-economic group (A-E) has broadly similar characteristics, which infer taste, lifestyle and level of disposable income.
Location	Sometimes it is appropriate to offer different products and to market them in different ways to different geographical areas. This is due to regional differences in attitude and taste.
Lifecycle of individual	This type of segmentation suggests that we all follow a predetermined lifecycle, beginning by being independent and single, then acquiring a partner, and perhaps children, and finally retiring. Products and services will be targeted at specific stages of an individual's lifecycle.
Family size and type	This links with the above, and targets single people, childless couples and families with a number of children. Pack sizes, and size or durability of products, are designed to match.
Usage rate	This is a behavioural version of segmentation, where segmentation is based on how often the customer purchases particular products or services and whether they are regular or occasional buyers.
Lifestyle	Again this links to lifecycle and family size and refers to the way in which the product or service aids the customer or fits in with their preferred ways of doing things.
Benefits	This refers to the characteristics or advantages of using a particular product or service, as identified by customers, perhaps based on taste, packaging, pack size, ease of use or peace of mind.
Psychographic	This focuses on why the customer has chosen to purchase the particular product or service. In other words, what has motivated them to make the decision to buy?

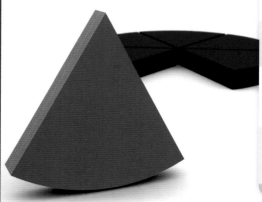

Problems and benefits of segmentation

Segmentation only really works if the segments that have been identified are accessible, in other words that the business can provide products and services to that segment. The segment also needs to be profitable, which means that any risks or investments have to provide the business with a reasonable rate of return. Also, the segment needs to be sustainable, in order to justify a long-term involvement with it.

The major problem with segmentation is the fact that a business may be convinced to produce significantly different products and services to each of the different segments. Previously it may have only produced a limited range of products, but now it will have to produce variations, which may cost more.

The key advantages are:

- It enables the business to precisely identify the requirements of specific segments
- It should allow the business to more effectively meet the demands of the groups compared to the competitors
- It means that all marketing can be targeted at segments, and resources will not be wasted

Example

Innocent smoothies are targeted at adult age groups. However, a kids' version in a bottle has been designed.

Specific toys are aimed at females, such as Barbie dolls. However, packaging of certain products is aimed at female buyers, even though they may be consumed by the whole family, e.g. washing powders.

Newspapers use socio-economic groups to target potential readers. Newspapers such as *The Times* target socio-economic groups A and B, whereas *The Sun* targets groups C to E.

National breweries offer different brands of beer to different geographical areas, matching the specific tastes of each region.

The housing market caters for first-time buyers, those moving to bigger housing, and those seeking retirement homes.

Typically, supermarkets or manufacturers will offer family-sized products. Car manufacturers produce vehicles with a range of seating capacities.

On-pack offers, such as money-off vouchers for next purchase, encourage increased usage rates.

Convenience foods are primarily designed to provide microwaveable meals for young working people and busy families.

Toothpaste can provide different benefits to customers who may vary in focussing more on taste, fresh breath or cleaning power.

Luxury products are often bought for the purpose of rewarding oneself, or to pamper a loved one.

KEY TERM

Marketing mix – the appropriate application of product design, pricing, type of promotion and method of distribution to cater for the demands of a particular market or segment.

INTERNET RESEARCH

For more information on socio-economic classifications visit www.statistics.gov.uk and type in 'socio-economic' in the search box.

Questions

1 Suggest the key market segments targeted by McDonalds. (4 marks)
2 How might a supermarket use socio-economic groups for market segmentation? (6 marks)
3 Suggest SIX products or services specifically aimed at families with young children. (6 marks)

Market size, growth and share

LEARNING OBJECTIVES

► How to calculate market size
► How to calculate market growth
► How to calculate market share

How to calculate market size

Market size is the measurement of all the sales by businesses that supply products or services to that market. There are, however, two different ways of measuring market size:

- Market size by value – the total amount spent by customers on all the products and services involved.
- Market size by volume – the quantity of the products or services purchased (which can be a measurement of packs, cans, tons, units or any other suitable measurement).

In order to work out the price that is being paid per unit we simply have to divide the total volume by the total value, as we can see in the following example.

FOR EXAMPLE

In 2006 the total number of cars sold in Britain was 2,331,351. The value of these sales was approximately £30bn. Therefore the average price per vehicle sold was £12,868.

How to calculate market growth

Market growth is the percentage increase in the size of a market. It too can be measured by volume or value. In other words, it is the number of units sold or the revenue that was generated.

Businesses will be particularly concerned about trends in market size. They will look to see whether the market is growing or whether it is declining. A growth market should offer them better opportunities and will encourage them to launch new products and to increase distribution. They will be particularly concerned if the market is declining in size, as this will mean that there is still a high level of competition, but that the demand itself has fallen.

Most serious is the situation when the volume of products sold in a particular market is growing but the value is falling. What does this actually mean? Simply that the average price being paid by customers is dropping, which infers that there is more competition in the market and competitors are price-cutting to hold onto their share of the market.

Working out changes in market size is a relatively straightforward technique:

FOR EXAMPLE

If a market is worth £24m and this rises to £26m, the rise represents a market growth of 8.33%. If the total number of units sold in that market rises by 16,000, to 136,000, then the market growth by volume is 11.76%.

How to calculate market share

Market share is the proportion or percentage of the total market that is controlled by either a single business or a particular product or service. It too can be measured either in terms of volume or value. However, most of the time it is measured in terms of the total percentage of that market or by value alone.

Businesses see market share as a key test of their marketing strategy. While it may be difficult for marketing to increase the overall size of a market, what marketing should certainly do is to strengthen or to increase the market share of the particular business's products and services.

Economic forces usually determine the overall size of a market and its growth. These would include the disposable income of customers, the interest rate, inflation and the price of other products and services, which may directly or indirectly compete with the products and services. Market share, however, is a measurement of a business's success or failure compared to its competitors. The higher the market share the more dominant that business or its products and services are in that market.

In the snack food market Walkers has a dominant position. In confectionery, Kit Kat is considered to be market leader, as it has a significant market share.

FOR EXAMPLE

The Finnish mobile phone manufacturer, Nokia, has a 35% global market share. This is compared to its nearest competitor, Motorola, with 17.8%.

Market share can be simply calculated by either establishing the market's total value or volume, and then expressing a business's or product's volume or value as a percentage of this total figure. In other words, if the market is worth £20m and a business's sales are £4m, then the business has a 20% market share.

CASE STUDY MY TRAVEL AND THOMAS COOK

In early 2007, the German-owned Thomas Cook Group bought the holiday company My Travel. The merger cost £2.8bn. As part of the group's overall long-term plans, 150 duplicate stores and six offices were closed, costing nearly 3,000 jobs. The merger created Europe's second biggest travel company, giving it a 35% share of the British package-holiday market. The cuts, made to help make the business even more profitable, aimed to save £95m.

The merger, however, came at a difficult time, with expensive air travel taxes and higher fuel costs discouraging foreign holidays. The group also faced increased competition from Internet-based businesses, and holidaymakers planning their own holidays via the Internet.

On average, some 19m people travel with the Thomas Cook Group, including My Travel. Across the world the group employs 33,000 people, has a turnover of €12bn and operates a fleet of 97 aircraft.

In comparison, My Travel, which started in 1972, began as a travel agency operating out of two stores in Lancashire. Thomas Cook's online position in the market was fifth before the merger, and My Travel was third. The merger has now allowed it to become the leading online holiday group in Britain.

Thomas Cook continues to acquire new businesses and in September 2007 it purchased Air Berlin, which it will merge with its own airline, Condor, to create one of the leading low-fare airlines in Europe.

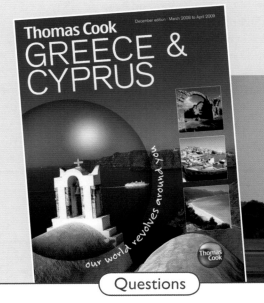

Questions

1. What do you understand by the word 'merger'? (2 marks)
2. Find out who My Travel was in talks with concerning a merger before deciding to go with Thomas Cook. (4 marks)
3. Why would Thomas Cook choose to close 150 branches after its merger with My Travel? (4 marks)
4. How has the merger affected the group's market share? (3 marks)

Case studies, questions and exam practice

CASE STUDY YAHOO v MICROSOFT v GOOGLE

In 2007, Google had a dominant market position, being the most popular Internet search engine, with a 56.5% share of the US market and a 75% market share of the British market. Lagging behind were Yahoo with 23.3% and Microsoft with 11.3%.

Both of the main rivals to Google have re-launched their products, adding new features. Microsoft's live search offered a series of new features and improved the way in which it delivered answers to questions. Yahoo primarily changed the way in which searches are requested. Another rival, Ask.com, dramatically changed the way it looked earlier in the year, offering search suggestions and thumbnail pictures of sites.

Around £2bn is spent each year on Internet advertising. This means that online advertising now accounts for over 10% of Britain's total advertising revenues. Advertising revenue is the principal source of income for businesses such as Google. Therefore Google's dominance not only affects businesses like Microsoft and Yahoo, but also other, more conventional businesses that rely on advertising revenue.

Questions

1 Using the market share figures for April 2007, and working on the assumption that online advertising revenue is £2bn, calculate the market share by value of Google, Yahoo and Ask.com. (9 marks)

2 List SIX other types of business that are reliant on advertising revenue, and that could be directly affected by Google's share of online advertising revenue. (6 marks)

3 Compared to 2006, the advertising revenue online has increased by 41.2%. What was the increase by value? (4 marks)

SHORT-ANSWER QUESTIONS

1 Define the word 'market'.

2 Distinguish between a local and a national market.

3 Distinguish between a tangible and an intangible product or service.

4 Define the word 'demand'.

5 How might competitors' activities affect demand?

6 How can marketing affect demand?

7 Define the term 'market segmentation'.

8 List SIX different types of segmentation.

9 What are the two ways in which the size of a market can be measured?

10 What is market share?

CASE STUDY CREEPING DOMINANCE

In October 2007 Universal Music bought Richard Branson's V2 label for £7m. The key artists on the label were Paul Weller and the Stereophonics. The two acts would join the Kaiser Chiefs and the Klaxons, already part of the Universal Group.

In October 2007 Universal Music was showing a 55% market share. However, the Association of Independent Music (AIM), which represents 800 smaller record labels, was concerned about the growing market dominance of Universal. AIM complained that it was seeing restricted access to the radio, TV and other outlets, and that between the 800 members its retail market share was only 20%.

Questions

1. AIM claims that Universal is trying to marginalise independence, stifle competition and limit consumer choice. What does it mean by this? (6 marks)
2. What do you think AIM means when it refers to the purchase of V2 as an example of Universal's 'creeping dominance'? (4 marks)

CASE STUDY PRIMARK FOR KIDS

The childrenswear market in Britain is worth £4.5bn. Five years ago, Primark had a 2.8% market share. By 2006 this had risen to 5.4%, and in 2007 to 6.2%. This now places Primark fourth in terms of market share.

The clothing store, Next, is the number one market shareholder, with a current market share of 10.2%. Asda is in second place with 8.5%, and Tesco has third place with 7.8% market share.

Interestingly, each of the top four increased their market share from 2006 to 2007 by at least 0.1%. Primark's growth has come at the expense of Gap, JJB Sports and BHS. BHS's market share fell from 3.2% to 2.9%. This now means that over £1 in every £3 spent is going to a 'value retailer' like Primark, Asda and Tesco.

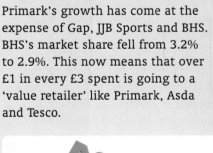

Questions

1. What do you think is meant by the term 'value retailer'? (2 marks)
2. What is Primark's share of the market worth in value terms? (4 marks)
3. What is the market worth of Next, Asda and Tesco in value terms? (6 marks)

Sole traders

What is a sole trader?

Sole traders are also called sole proprietors or the self-employed. Sole proprietors are individuals who own a business. As we will see, they have unlimited liability. In other words they are completely responsible for all the debts of the business.

A self-employed person, of course, is an individual who works for himself/herself and is not employed by a business. There are enormous numbers of sole traders in Britain today, perhaps more than three million.

Being a sole trader does not necessarily mean that the business does not have a large **turnover**, or that it does not make a high profit. Sole traders do all sorts of different things; some run shops, others are hairdressers, plumbers or electricians, others are writers or run bed and breakfast accommodation.

Usually sole traders are specialists who provide a particular service that does not have a market big enough for a large business to become involved. They often have very specialised skills, or may need to use specialist tools.

It must not be forgotten that if a business is a sole trader it does not necessarily mean that only one person is employed or directly involved in the business. In fact many sole traders employ a large number of people.

Many people set up their own businesses so that they can be their own bosses. They often see a business opportunity and usually start quite small. They must be prepared to work long hours, take risks and take all of the responsibility.

Since 2000 the number of businesses in Great Britain has increased by 600,000, but the number of employers has only increased by 50,000. The balance is sole trader business.

When a sole trader starts up they will need some **start-up capital**. This is used to sort out the business premises and to buy stock or materials and perhaps tools and transport. As many small businesses start in a tiny way, these expenses may be quite low. Many sole traders finance this with their savings and, perhaps, an overdraft from the bank.

As a business gets going it also needs to cover its day-to-day running costs, such as:

- Replacing stock that has been sold
- Paying the owner some money to live on
- Covering the costs of rent, rates, wages, lighting and other essential bills

This money is known as operating capital, as it is cash required to cover the running costs.

Eventually the business should get itself into a position where it is making enough money to pay its running costs.

Liability

As far as the law is concerned there is no difference between a sole trader's business funds and that sole trader's private money. If the business does not earn enough to repay a loan then the sole proprietor of the business will have to find the money. They are still liable for the repayments. This is called unlimited liability, and means that there is no limit to the amount that the sole proprietor might owe if the business is in debt.

Legal issues

The main legal requirements of a sole trader are to keep appropriate business accounts and records. These will be necessary in order to supply a tax return to the Inland Revenue, who will collect tax on the profits of the sole trader.

Also, as with all businesses, sole traders are required to comply with legal requirements concerning consumer protection. As the sole trader has unlimited liability there is no distinction between the sole trader's business and their private financial affairs. The sole trader will be ultimately liable for any debts that the business incurs, and legally obliged to sell off any of their own personal assets in order to pay creditors if the business should fail. This is often a major reason why people are reluctant to become sole traders, and why they may consider other forms of legal business structures as an alternative.

KEY TERMS

Turnover – the amount of money received by a business as sales revenue in a year.

Start-up capital – money that is needed to begin a business.

INTERNET RESEARCH 🔍

Business Link, at www.businesslink.gov. uk, has useful background information on becoming a sole trader, along with links to Revenue and Customs and other sources of information.

CASE STUDY BABY SALON BOUTIQUE

Carol McKeown runs a clothes boutique in London as a sole trader. She sells around £250,000 worth of goods each year. She is paying 40% tax on most of her earnings because she is personally taxed. If she were to create a limited company she would only be taxed on her profits. This would mean that the tax would be limited to the salary paid to her by the business.

Carol has unlimited liability, so she is financially liable for everything. If she were to become a limited company then she would need to find another director. She could bring in someone who knows about retailing or fashion. Carol knows that she needs to grow her business. Currently she designs all her clothes and accessories and has them made in a factory in East London.

There are many decisions ahead of Carol if she wants to expand from a single retail store in Portobello Road

to become a more obvious force in the high street. If things went wrong then everything she owns is at risk. It is difficult for her to raise money. If Carol was to make Baby Salon a private company then she would become a shareholder in the business, and she would have limited liability. She would no longer have to be responsible for the debts of the business.

Questions

1 How does limited liability differ from unlimited liability? (4 marks)
2 What is Business Link, and how might Carol get advice and assistance from this organisation? (6 marks)

Partnerships

What is a partnership?

One option open to sole traders who want to grow their businesses is to take on a partner. Partners are joint owners of the business. There have to be between two and twenty partners.

Each partner takes a role in the running of the business. In most ordinary partnerships the partners have unlimited liability, just like sole traders. Most partnerships are ordinary partnerships. As far as the law is concerned, there is an assumption that responsibility, profit and capital are equally shared by the partners.

If the situation is different then, as we will see, they will draw up what is called a deed of partnership.

Sole traders sometimes enter into partnerships because their own resources are limited, and they can bring in new funds to the business in this way.

Many businesses actually start as partnerships. It is easier to borrow money from banks because several people are involved in the borrowing. This means that the bank can draw on the **assets** of several people if the loan is not repaid.

In addition to bringing in new finance, forming a partnership can also be a way of introducing new skills and expertise into a business. Partners will take responsibility for different aspects of the business, perhaps one focusing on financial matters and another on marketing. It also gives the partners a chance to share the responsibilities of running the business. In this way if one of the partners is unavailable due to illness or holidays then the others can take up their work and responsibilities.

The law assumes that the partners are equal, but in practice this is rarely the case. However, regardless of how much work a partner does, or the amount of money each has put into the business, they have equal responsibility for the debts.

The deed of partnership deals with the fact that partners work different hours and put in unequal amounts of money. The legal contract covers:

- The names of the partners and the purpose of the partnership
- How much money or capital each partner has put into the partnership
- How profits and losses should be divided (this is usually in the same proportion as the amount of capital put in by each partner)
- How many votes each partner has at partnership meetings
- How disputes between partners are handled
- Arrangements for any of the partners wanting to leave the partnership, or for a new partner to join
- How the partnership can be **wound up** if necessary
- What happens if a partner dies
- How the partners can withdraw their share of the profits

If there is not a deed of partnership, it is assumed that all partners are equal, regardless of how much money each has put into the business.

"I'm here to wind up the company."

Liability

There are two other types of partnership apart from ordinary partnerships. These can have more than twenty partners:

- Limited partnerships can have some partners who do not take a role in running the business, but own part of it. They are called sleeping partners. The sleeping partners in limited partnerships have limited liability, but one member of the partnership has to have unlimited liability.
- The second type of partnership is known as a limited liability partnership. In this version of the partnership all the partners have limited liability.

KEY TERMS

Assets – items of value, such as property and vehicles, which can be seized or sold in order to pay off an outstanding debt.

Wind up – to close a business, dispose of its assets, and pay off any of its debts.

Auditor – an accounts specialist who makes an independent assessment of a business's account, to check for accuracy and whether the company has followed the law.

Legal issues

Partnerships, just like sole proprietorships, are easy to set up. A few legal documents, such as a deed of partnership, need to be completed, and only two people are needed.

Ordinary partnerships do not need solicitors or accountants to be involved. In practice, solicitors are often used to draw up deeds of partnership, and accountants are used to sort out the tax liabilities.

It is slightly more complicated with limited liability partnerships because these can be as complicated as a limited company. They have to have their accounts checked by an **auditor**, and the accounts need to be sent to the Registrar of Companies.

In most partnerships each partner has an equal say in how the business should be run. Some partners, however, are given more power and responsibility. The exact power and responsibility is spelled out in the deed of partnership. Together the partners should be able to make the right decisions, as they will have a good mix of skills and expertise. This gives them an advantage over a sole trader.

It is also easier to raise money because banks and other lenders of finance are more inclined to lend money to partnerships than to sole traders.

If the partnership has limited liability, then it can attract other investors to put money into the business.

When a partner leaves the partnership, the partnership automatically ends. A new partnership needs to be formed and often the remaining partners will disagree about what should be done. If a partner with vital skills leaves, then the business could suffer.

In an ideal situation, the weakest partner would leave and then the partnership could find a better partner, with a wider range of skills. Family partnerships often break up because the children do not want to take over the business. This would mean the partnership closing when the parents retire.

It is relatively difficult and complicated to leave a partnership. For one thing there is the question of getting back the money that was originally invested in the business by the partner. This could seriously undermine the partnership at what might be an important time.

A partner cannot pass on their share of the partnership or sell their share of the partnership to another person without the agreement of the other partners.

Questions

1 Distinguish between a limited partnership and a limited liability partnership. (4 marks)
2 Briefly outline the purpose of a deed of partnership. (4 marks)

Private limited companies

What is a private limited company?

There are, of course, two different types of limited company. The first is known as a private limited company. Its shares are not traded on the **Stock Exchange**. It is easy to identify a limited company as it will have Ltd. at the end of its name.

Public limited companies do have their shares available for sale or purchase on the Stock Exchange. They have the letters Plc after their company name.

'Ltd.' or 'Plc' only tells you about a business ownership type. Both types are limited liability businesses. It is not even true to say that Plc companies are bigger than Ltd. ones. No assumptions can be made about sales revenue, profit or number of people employed.

Liability

As we have seen, sole traders and partnerships find it quite difficult to raise money and to expand. This is because potential investors are worried about unlimited liability. When limited liability comes into it, more people are happier to invest in the business. All owners of limited companies have limited liability. The company itself is separate from its owners. Remember that there is no difference between an owner of a sole proprietorship or ordinary partnership and the proprietorship or partnership itself. This is where companies are different.

Companies have shareholders who are the owners. The limited liability means that they cannot be forced to pay the debts of the company. They only stand to lose the value of the shares they have in the company.

If a company ceases trading then the assets of that business are used to pay off what is owed by the company. If there is anything else left then the shareholders will receive their share of it.

Legal issues

Although shareholders legally control a limited company, they rarely take day-to-day control of the business, particularly when there might be thousands of shareholders in a public limited company. Each year the shareholders elect directors at the **Annual General Meeting**. They are there to represent the wishes of the shareholders.

The directors cannot, of course, do everything in a business, so they use managers to run the company for them. The Board of Directors begins by appointing a Managing Director. Directors on the Board of Directors with day-to-day responsibilities are called Executive Directors because they execute, or carry out, the wishes of the Board of Directors.

For smaller businesses it is often the case that the same people are the shareholders, the managers and the directors of the company. As far as the law is concerned they are shareholders and directors, but

because they are involved in the day-to-day running of the business they are also managers.

Because limited companies have a separate legal existence from the owners of the company, all limited companies have to be incorporated. This sets the business up as a limited company.

Incorporation means that the company can enter into agreements using its own name, rather than the names of its owners. If the company breaks the law in any way the company can be fined, rather than the owners.

Limited liability partnerships have to register with Companies House. All British limited companies also have to register with the Registrar General, or the Registrar of Companies. This means that the company, before it can even start trading, has to complete a number of very important documents and submit them to the Registrar. Only after this has happened will the

limited company officially exist. After that it can engage in business as a separate, legal entity.

There is a choice at this stage as to whether the business will be a private limited company or a public limited company. Both types of limited company have limited liability, but both types have their advantages and disadvantages.

There are several key documents that need to be created before incorporation can take place. The first is the memorandum of association. This includes:

- The company name and whether it is a private limited or public limited company
- The registered office of the company
- A statement that says the shareholders will have limited liability
- The amount of each type of share the company can issue, which is known as authorised capital

- The main activities of the company

In most cases the company will state that its authorised capital is greater than its actual needs. This will allow the company at a later date to raise more money by selling shares without having to change its memorandum of association.

The last point is also important because legally the business should not do things that are not covered by the 'objects' clause, which is the description of its activities.

The articles of association show how the company will be run. It will include the following:

- The voting rights of shareholders
- How often annual general meetings will be held and their procedures
- How profits will be shared
- The number, rights and duties of the directors of the company

---

KEY TERMS

Stock Exchange – an electronic market that allows investors to buy and sell the shares of public limited companies.

Annual general meeting (AGM) – a meeting of ordinary shareholders that is held once a year, at the end of the financial year.

Authorised capital – the total amount of money a company can raise by issuing shares.

Questions

Use the Internet to find out the answers to the following questions:

1 What is Form 10? (2 marks)
2 What is Form 12? (2 marks)
3 What are the two other documents that need to be completed before incorporation? (2 marks)
4 What must be filed annually with Companies House if a company has limited liability? (2 marks)

Public limited companies

What is a public limited company?

In order to begin trading, a business must have a minimum capital of £50,000. Although only two people are needed to sign the Memorandum of Association there need to be at least seven shareholders.

Their shares are traded on the Stock Exchange. British companies are traded on the London Stock Exchange, while American businesses will use the American Stock Exchange.

The business must hold an Annual General Meeting. At this meeting the directors of the company present the Annual Report and accounts to the shareholders. The shareholders then approve the accounts and appoint directors for the following year. The public limited company needs to send a copy of the Annual Report and accounts to Companies House. These are housed with the Registrar of Companies so that they can be inspected by anyone with an interest in the business.

New, smaller Plcs have some major differences from normal public limited companies. They are listed not on the London Stock Exchange, but on the Alternative Investment Market. This system is designed to attract investors to new businesses that do not have the same kind of track record as more established public limited companies.

Although public limited companies need to have at least £50,000 of share capital to begin, the London Stock Exchange does not tend to allow new public limited companies to trade their shares unless their share capital is worth several million pounds. This is why the Alternative Investment Market is so important to smaller public limited companies which do not have millions of pounds of share capital.

In very large businesses the directors and the managers will probably own very few shares, and shareholders outside of the business will own most of them. The decisions made by the Board of Directors are still carried out by Executive Directors, but there are often Non-Executive Directors on the Board.

Non-Executive Directors are directors who may only work for the company on a part-time basis. They are not managers of the company, but are brought in for their particular expertise or knowledge.

There are often difficulties when businesses make decisions at Board level, caused by directors and managers who do not own many shares making decisions that the shareholders do not like.

The shareholders do not have any real power in controlling the business on a day-to-day basis. They could confront the directors at the Annual General Meeting (AGM), or call an Emergency General Meeting (EGM). Here they can demand that the directors give them an explanation and, in extreme cases, they could vote the directors off the Board. Ultimately the only real power or option that shareholders have if they do not like the policy of the company, is to sell their shares.

INTERNET RESEARCH

To find out more about incorporating a company and the rules regarding the running of companies, visit www.companieshouse.gov.uk.

The website, www.annualreports.co.uk, is a free service that allows you to review annual reports from a huge variety of public limited companies. Searches can be carried out using either an industry search, a sector search or an alphabetical listing. Many of the major Plcs are present, including British Telecom, Rolls Royce and Alan Sugar's company, Amstrad Plc.

THE STOCK EXCHANGE

Liability

Like private limited companies, investors in public limited companies have only limited liability. They stand to lose only the money that they have invested in purchasing the shares. This is seen to be an encouragement to potential shareholders and investors, as they know that they can only lose what they have invested if the company should fail.

If an individual or another business has a claim against the company, limited liability means that they can only recover money from the assets of the business itself. They cannot turn to the managers or the shareholders to recover any money owed to them by the company.

Legal issues

Just like a private limited company, a public limited company needs to be registered with the Registrar of Companies at Companies House. In addition to this the following legal obligations are required:

- The company's name needs to be clearly displayed outside all its offices and places of business.
- The company's name must be included on all its stationery.
- On all stationery, including electronic business communications, the company's place of registration, registration number and registered office address have to be shown.

- All necessary registration documents need to be sent to the Registrar, completed and signed.
- HM Revenue and Customs must be contacted for tax and possibly for VAT purposes.

KEY TERMS

Capital – the amount of money that the business has immediate access to.

Annual Report – a summary of the activities of the business in the previous financial year.

CASE STUDY FIONA'S BIG PLANS

Fiona now runs her father's organic vegetable business. Her father set up the business in the 1970s, first as a sole trader and then in partnership with his brother. Ten years ago David decided to make the partnership a private limited company. Nearly all the family members work for the business, but Fiona, as the eldest and the one with the most business sense, is the managing director. Her father still owns some shares, but only takes a minor interest in the business these days. For many years they have been working with a chain of health food stores that are also a private limited company. Fiona is seriously considering merging with them to form a public limited company, although not all of her family are so keen.

Questions

1 Why might members of the family be reluctant to create a public limited company? (6 marks)

2 What do you think is meant by the term 'merging'? (2 marks)

3 What documents would Fiona have to prepare if the public limited company was to be created? (4 marks)

Benefits and drawbacks of legal structures

Advantages and disadvantages of sole traders

Becoming a sole trader is very straightforward and for many people it gives them a level of independence, where no one else is involved and the individual can make decisions alone. Drawbacks include the unlimited liability and the relatively long working hours. Raising cash can also be a difficulty, and sole traders need to develop a range of skills in a variety of different areas, including accounts and possibly the management of employees.

Advantages and disadvantages of setting up as a sole trader

Advantages	Disadvantages
• There are no particular legal formalities to complete before commencing to trade.	• Capital is limited to the owner's savings or profits or any other money he or she can borrow.
• There are no particular legal requirements governing the layout of their accounts.	• The owner has sole responsibility for debts – if the owner does fall into financial difficulties it may be necessary to sell his or her own personal possessions to meet the business's debts.
• The annual accounts do not have to be audited.	• Responsibility for a range of activities falls upon the shoulders of the one person who runs the business. In other words, the owner is entirely responsible for running the business – dealing with paperwork, customers, filling in tax returns and dealing with day-to-day contact with any employees or sub-contractors.
• The owner has the freedom to run the business in his or her own way.	• The success of the business is always dependent on how hard the sole trader wishes to work.
	• Any unforeseen accident or illness could seriously affect the business since all responsibilities rest on the shoulders of that one person.

Advantages and disadvantages of partnerships

Partners share profits, so there is always a link between the amount of hard work and effort put in and the rewards. It is important to remember that the share of the profits may not be equal, particularly if there is a deed of partnership. For most partnerships liability is also a concern; risks taken by one partner can have a direct impact on the other partners, so partnerships need to be built on trust. Raising cash is slightly more difficult than for limited companies, but each new partner can bring in additional funds.

Advantages and disadvantages in setting up a partnership

Advantages	Disadvantages
• It is easier for partners than sole traders to raise capital because all the partners can pool their resources, giving access to more capital than one person could raise.	• A partner is personally liable for all the firm's debts.
• Partners can share their expertise and their workload.	• Disagreements can arise between partners about the amount of effort that each of them puts in.
• Partners can arrange to cover one another at times of illness or holidays, or even during lunch breaks.	• Partnerships can only raise limited amounts of capital as compared with businesses like limited companies.
• A partnership, like a sole trader, does not have to publish its accounts or have them audited.	• Decision-making can be slow since all partners have to be consulted.
• Additional capital can be raised by introducing more partners into the partnership.	• The death or retirement of a member can bring a partnership to an end if such a rule is written into the deed of partnership.
	• All profits must be shared.

Advantages and disadvantages of limited companies

Many private limited companies are family-run and limited liability does take away all the financial dangers. This type of company can effectively choose its own shareholders, as the sale of shares has to be approved by existing shareholders and offered to them first. Private limited companies are often seen as a halfway house between a partnership and a public limited company.

A plc's shares are openly traded through a stock exchange. This means that they can raise capital by the issuing of shares. It is easy for Plcs to raise money, particularly if they have a large amount of share capital.

The key disadvantage is often the vast number of shares that have been issued, meaning that smaller shareholders cannot exert a great deal of influence. Many shareholders of Plcs are criticised for appearing to be interested only in short-term profits.

Advantages and disadvantages of setting up a limited company	
Advantages	*Disadvantages*
• Shareholders have limited liability.	• The formation and running costs of a limited company can be expensive.
• It is easier to raise capital through shares.	• Decisions tend to be slow since there are a number of people involved.
• It is often easier to raise finance through banks.	• Employees and shareholders are distanced from each another.
• It becomes possible to operate on a larger scale since, when additional capital is required, additional shares are offered to the public.	• All the affairs of the company are public, through the audited accounts and annual returns that the company makes.
• It is possible to employ specialists.	• Legal restrictions under the various Companies Acts are fairly tight and there are very heavy penalties for companies that break the rules.
• Suppliers tend to feel a bit more comfortable in trading with legally established organisations.	
• Directors are not liable for the debts of the company, provided they follow the rules, and it is easy to pass shares in a company down from one generation to another; in this way control may be kept by the same families.	• Large companies are often accused of being impersonal to work for and to deal with.
• The company name is protected by law.	• Rates of tax on profits are often higher than those that sole traders and partnerships have to pay.
• There are tax advantages attached to giving shares to employees.	
• A company pension scheme can give better benefits than those available for the self-employed.	
• The ill-health or death of shareholders does not affect the running of the business.	

Questions

1 What do you think is meant by the fact that in a Plc there is separation of ownership and control? (4 marks)

2 Large institutional shareholders effectively own many large Plcs. What does this mean? (4 marks)

Not-for-profit businesses

What is a not-for-profit business?

Charities and voluntary organisations share many features. Generally they are:

- set up for charitable, social, philanthropic (good works), religious, political or similar purposes;
- required to use any profit or surplus only for the organisation's purposes;
- not a part of any governing department, local authority or other statutory body.

Voluntary organisations have a legal structure or status, being unincorporated associations, trusts or companies limited by guarantee. The constitution or governing document and the governing body depend on the legal structure:

1 If the organisation is a registered company, the governing document will be a Memorandum and Articles of Association and the governing body will consist of company directors.
2 If the organisation is a trust, a Trust Deed or Declaration of Trust will be the governing document and a board of trustees will govern.
3 If the organisation is an association set up exclusively for charitable purposes, it will be governed by a constitution or rules, and members of the governing body have all the duties of charity trustees.
4 If the organisation is charitable and also a company, the voting members can be directors and also trustees.

The number of registered charities is growing. At the end of 2003 there were 162,104 main charities registered with the Charity Commission in England and Wales; by the beginning of 2007 there were 168,617. According to the Charity Commission, in 2006 the total annual income for all the registered charities was £41,263,255,021 or just over £41bn.

Charities

Charities have distinct legal formats and also a special tax status. They can be unincorporated, trusts, or companies limited by guarantee.

To register as a charity the organisation must have purposes that are defined by law as charitable. These could include:

- Relieving financial hardship
- Advancement of education
- Advancement of religion
- Something that is of direct benefit to the community

Registered charities are not allowed to have political objectives or even take part in political lobbying. This means that they:

- have to be primarily set up for a charitable purpose;
- do not make a profit, but any surplus money has to be used to further the organisation's purposes;
- need to be independent and not part of a government department, local authority or other organisation.

Pressure groups

Unlike charities, pressure groups are set up primarily to influence political decisions. They have specific aims and interests and will be involved in research, lobbying, providing expertise, increasing public awareness and attempting to influence decision-makers.

Sometimes pressure groups are known as lobby groups because they are trying to change opinions of decision-makers in their favour, or to further their cause. Pressure groups are not political parties: they work outside government, but some, such as the British Medical Association or the Confederation of British Industry work closely with government.

Pressure groups try to exert their influence on British businesses. Many are concerned with businesses' impacts on the environment or local community; some are concerned about the types of products and services offered by businesses. Other pressure groups are linked to customers and seek to force businesses to offer better value for money and improved customer services. Some pressure groups are far broader-based, including Greenpeace (www.greenpeace.org.uk)

INTERNET RESEARCH

The Charity Commission for England and Wales is the regulator and registrar of charities. For more information on its work and registered charities, visit www.charity-commission.gov.uk.

INTERNET RESEARCH

The British Medical Association (www.bma.org.uk) has nearly 140,000 members and represents practising doctors. The Confederation of British Industry (www.cbi.org.uk) represents over 200,000 businesses based in Britain.

and Friends of the Earth (www.foe.co.uk), which seek to minimise the impact of business and industry on the environment.

Societies

A society is an organisation set up for one of the following purposes:

- For charity
- To enable participation in or to support sport, athletics or cultural activities
- Any other non-commercial purpose that does not involve private gain

Key examples include the Royal Society for the Prevention of Cruelty to Animals (RSPCA) or, on a business basis, the Cooperative Wholesale Society (the Co op).

Cooperatives are incorporated organisations with limited liability and a separate legal existence from their members. Members buy shares and provide capital to the business. The shares are not sold on the Stock Exchange and have to be sold back to the cooperative if a member wants to cease involvement.

The profits of the cooperative are shared in the form of **dividends**. Cooperatives have Annual General Meetings and are like those run by limited companies. The major difference is that each member has one vote, regardless of how many shares they have.

Consumer cooperatives have merged together to form regional societies. They stick to their original plan to sell food at fair prices, honestly measured and weighed and not just for profit. These cooperatives are not just the retail supermarkets. They include the Cooperative Insurance Society and the Cooperative Bank.

The members buy shares in order to provide the capital for the business. Decisions are taken at meetings. This means that the individuals who will actually be affected by the decisions are the ones who make the decisions.

Successful worker cooperatives tend to be sold to limited companies. Usually cooperatives set the upper limits on pay, and many of them believe that everyone should be paid the same if they do the same amount of work.

Many cooperatives are directly concerned with reducing the impact their work methods have on the environment. Others give a proportion of their profits to charity.

The key drawbacks, however, are that it is difficult for them to raise money and that they have problems with how to deal with new members joining the business. The question is always whether the new employees should put in their own capital before they get a share of the profits. If the business gets larger and more complicated it is often harder for these cooperatives to agree and make decisions.

KEY TERM

Dividend – a share of profits in a cooperative.

Questions

1 In terms of a cooperative, define the word 'dividend'. (2 marks)
2 Using the Internet, find out where the first consumer cooperative opened and in which year. (4 marks)

Case studies, questions and exam practice

CASE STUDY SEVERN TRENT WATER

Severn Trent Water supplies nearly 2bn litres of water every day through 46,000km of pipes. The company also has 54,000km of sewers to take wastewater away and process it through 1,000 sewage works. The following table shows that the public limited company has an enormous number of shareholders. These figures are correct as at 6 October 2006.

Shareholdings	Number of shareholders	% of total shareholders	Number of ordinary shares (m)	% of ordinary shares
1–499	51,680	60.48	10,076,646	2.88
500–999	19,408	22.71	13,254,461	3.79
1,000–4,999	13,012	15.23	20,339,231	5.82
5,000–9,999	471	0.55	3,114,064	0.89
10,000–49,999	421	0.49	9,562,013	2.74
50,000–99,999	141	0.16	10,010,466	2.86
100,000–HIGHEST	328	0.38	283,174,358	81.02

Source: Severn Trent Water

Questions

1 How many shareholders owned less than 50,000 shares, according to the table? (2 marks)
2 How many shares did these individuals or businesses own? (2 marks)
3 What is the total number of shareholders of Severn Trent Water? (2 marks)
4 How many ordinary shares has Severn Trent Water issued? (2 marks)

SHORT-ANSWER QUESTIONS

1 What is meant by the term 'unlimited liability'?

2 Who actually owns a limited liability company?

3 What are the two groups or organisations that are entitled to see a limited company's set of accounts?

4 What is a board of directors?

5 Define the word 'shareholder'.

6 Why might there be a limit to the number of partners in a partnership?

7 Why might unlimited liability be more of a risk to a partner in a partnership than a sole trader?

8 Who owns a partnership?

9 What are the two key documents required to be completed before incorporation can take place?

10 What is the Registrar General?

CASE STUDY KEVIN'S DILEMMA

Kevin is a window cleaner. He used to work for Molly Mops domestic and commercial cleaning business, but he decided to start his own business. He bought himself a van and a set of ladders and had a friend paint his name and telephone number on the side of the van. He had to borrow the £3,000 to buy the van, as he had no savings. Kevin is very nervous about trying to get new customers and avoids knocking on doors to ask people if they want their windows cleaned. Instead he waits for them to approach him when he is doing someone else's windows. He also subcontracts to Molly Mops, and does pretty much the same work, but only gets paid half of what he was earning before. Kevin is now getting threatening letters from the bank, telling him he must repay his loan for the van, as he has missed half-a-dozen payments.

Questions

1 What are the implications of unlimited liability for Kevin? (4 marks)
2 What do you think is meant by subcontract? (3 marks)
3 Suggest TWO ways in which Kevin could deal with the problems he is currently experiencing. (4 marks)

CASE STUDY ROB, BETSY, SARAH AND MILES

Four friends have decided to set up a partnership. From the outset they decide to share the profits out according to how much each of them invests in the partnership. Rob puts in £10,000, Sarah finds £15,000 to invest, Betsy puts in £45,000, and Miles uses an inheritance from his grandfather to invest £30,000. In the first year the business makes a profit of £62,000; in the second the partners decide to invite a fifth person to become a partner, as they need someone who has marketing expertise. Joe joins the partnership and invests £25,000. At the end of the second year the business makes £87,000 profit.

Questions

1 What is the total share capital at the end of the first year? (4 marks)
2 What is the total share capital at the end of the second year? (4 marks)
3 What is Sarah's entitlement to the share of the profits at the end of the first year? (2 marks)
4 What is Sarah's entitlement to the share of the profits at the end of the second year? (2 marks)

Sources of finance

LEARNING OBJECTIVES

▶ Where does finance come from?
▶ Ordinary share capital
▶ Loan capital (bank loans and overdrafts)
▶ Venture capital
▶ Personal sources

Where does finance come from?

Businesses need money in order to invest in equipment, stock and premises. They also need money to pay regular bills. This is known as working capital.

It is only once a business becomes established that income filters into the company from purchases made by customers.

The sources of finance depend on the stage of development of a business, the type of business, the current state of the economy and, in the case of an existing business, how successful it has been to date.

Sole traders will have limited access to sources of finance, and will usually be limited to their own funds and any money that they are personally able to borrow. Partnerships can rely on the resources of all of the partners. Limited companies will be able to raise share capital. It is unlikely that a new business will immediately become a Plc, as it needs to be of a certain size and have a proven track record.

New businesses tend to find it more difficult to raise capital. Once the business has developed, it is far easier to attract investors and to obtain loans because the business will have its own assets.

The state of the economy is also important. When the economy is doing well it is easy to raise finance from borrowing, and investors are keener to become involved. If the economy is not doing well, and potential investors are unsure of a business's long-term prospects, they are likely to chose to put their money in more secure investments.

Once a business has a track record of success it will attract investors and lenders. Both will have confidence in the fact that the business will be able to either pay back a loan or provide them with a share of future profits.

Ordinary share capital

One of the main ways in which a business, such as a limited company, can raise money is by issuing shares to potential investors. The business has what is called a flotation, where the shares are made available for sale.

There are two different types of share, these are:

- An ordinary share – where the owner is entitled to receive a share of the profits in the form of a dividend. The dividend changes from year to year, depending on how the business is doing.
- A preference share – this has a fixed dividend and is still paid out even if the business is not performing very well. Preference shareholders always receive the first payment before ordinary shareholders.

KEY TERMS

Working capital – money used to finance wages and bills and other day-to-day costs.

Economy – the current status of production, distribution and consumption of products and services in a country.

Flotation – the sale of shares to investors when a business becomes a public limited company.

Collateral – assets used to guarantee the repayment of a loan.

Loan capital (bank loans and overdrafts)

Banks can usually provide two different types of finance. The first is a loan. The business will borrow an amount of money and pay it back on a regular basis, in instalments. The bank will charge interest on the money that has been borrowed. Often banks will demand security on the loan.

Security is often in the form of assets owned by the sole trader, partners or shareholders of a business. The bank can seize these if the business fails to pay back the loan. Sole traders often have to offer their own homes as security, or collateral.

Loans can be given over an extended period of time. Obviously the longer the period for which the money is borrowed, the more interest will be paid.

Banks also offer overdrafts. This means that a business can write cheques or make payments in excess of the amount of money that it actually has in its account. The bank will set an overdraft limit, which is the maximum amount that the business can go 'into the red'. If a business has a £1,000 overdraft facility this means that it can write cheques to the value of £1,000 even if its bank account is empty.

Venture capital

In Britain there are a number of venture capital businesses and 'business angels' (private investors). Venture capital provides a business with long-term share capital. Venture capitalists usually make an investment in a start-up business, or to help an existing business expand.

Venture capital is invested in exchange for a share of the business, and the return on the investment is dependent on the growth and the profitability of the business. Usually a venture capitalist will leave the business by selling their shareholding once they have obtained a sufficient return on their original investment. Venture capitalists usually stay with a business for between three and seven years.

"Where I come from it's called collateral."

Personal sources

As already mentioned, smaller businesses may have to rely on the owners either providing funds from their own savings or sale of assets, or by the owners themselves obtaining personal loans, which they can then invest in the business.

For a new business, borrowing money is often difficult, if not impossible. The government, however, has a guarantee loan scheme, which can allow a business to borrow between £5,000 and £250,000 for a period of two to ten years. The government guarantees a proportion of each loan and for this security a premium of 2% is payable to the government.

INTERNET RESEARCH

For more information on the government's Loan Guarantee Schemes visit the Department for Business Enterprise and Regulatory Reform at www.berr.gov.uk.

> ### Questions
> 1 What is meant by the term 'overdraft'? (2 marks)
> 2 Why might a provider of a loan wish a business to provide collateral? (2 marks)
> 3 What is a venture capitalist? (2 marks)

Advantages and disadvantages of different sources of finance

LEARNING OBJECTIVES
- Finance as a problem
- Ordinary share capital
- Loan capital (bank loans and overdrafts)
- Venture capital
- Personal sources

Finance as a problem

Finance or money is a scarce resource. For any business to obtain it from a third party, such as a bank, they will have to compete to get it. This means showing that they are less of a risk than other businesses, and that the lender (or the investor) has a reasonable chance that they will see their money again and receive a reasonable rate of return (profit) from the investment.

When we look at loans, the implication is that the bank or building society is only lending the money for the short term. They will expect the business to pay interest on the loan, and at the end of the loan period to pay back the capital sum (the amount that was originally loaned). Investment, on the other hand, infers a longer-term relationship between the investor and the business. A shareholder, as a part owner of the business, will expect it to provide them with cash dividends on their shares, and for the value of the shares to gradually increase.

Once a business is trading and more established, one of the major sources of finance is from the retained profit it keeps as a result of selling products and services to its customers. However, if a business is just starting up, or it needs extra finance to expand, then it will have to find money from a different source.

The key questions a business should ask itself are:

- How long will we need the money? (Duration of loan needed.)
- How much will it cost to borrow the money? (Rate of interest and perhaps payment protection insurance.)
- How much will we have to pay on a regular (monthly) basis? (What is the repayment schedule?)

In effect, a business will obtain finance from either:

- Internal sources – such as the owner's capital (in the case of new businesses) or **retained profits** (in the case of existing businesses).
- External sources – overdrafts (both new and existing businesses), **hire purchase**, loans and mortgages.

KEY WORDS

Retained profits – money that has been obtained as a result of adding value to the sale of a product or service to a customer and which is not made available as a payment to shareholders.

Hire purchase – Under an (HP) agreement, the business pays an initial deposit followed by monthly payments over an agreed period. At the end of this period, the business has the option of owning the item outright.

Ordinary share capital

The main problem with issuing shares in order to raise finance is the fact that the business owners are diluting their ownership of the business. As investors buy shares, they become part owners in the business and, to some extent, the original owners of the business lose ownership and some control over the business. Investors may want different things from the business, such as improved profits, more cautious expansion, and a lower reliance on borrowing. They may have fundamental criticisms of the way in which the originators of the business run the operation.

Providing the original owners retain at least 51% of the shares, they will always have the final say over decision-making, even at the AGM. However, if they sell more than a 50% stake in the business, then they run the risk of losing control over the business that they created.

Loan capital (bank loans and overdrafts)

Overdrafts in particular can be seen as an extremely expensive way of borrowing money. Overdrafts not only have to be agreed with the bank or building society (in terms of the amount that the business can be overdrawn), but attract a relatively high level of interest.

Bank loans tend to be for a fixed term, with interest payments due on a monthly basis (they either include a contribution to the capital amount rather like an endowment mortgage or the capital sum is due at the end of the loan period). The longer the period of the loan, the more interest will have been paid over the term of the loan.

In the case of loans, the business needs to make sure that it can afford to pay the monthly instalments and that these repayments do not eat into its working capital affecting its ability to pay other current liabilities.

Venture capital

Rather like the sale of shares, the involvement of venture capitalists inevitably means some loss of ownership of the business. Unlike smaller shareholders who may own relatively few shares, a venture capital business will tend to own a substantial block of shares or be a partner in the business. This means that it will want to exert an influence on the day-to-day running of the business and be involved in key decisions.

Usually a specified cash sum will be invested by a venture capital company in return for a specified share of the business. The business owner needs to weigh up the comparative loss of ownership and control as well as proportionate loss of profits.

Personal sources

Like any investment made by an individual there is always a degree of risk. By investing their own money in the business, the owners are taking the ultimate risk, and could lose their money if the business fails. However, other investors and providers of finance will expect to see a degree of investment made by the owners as a sign that the owners have sufficient faith in the business to risk their own funds.

CASE STUDY 3i

3i has been operating for over 60 years as a venture capital organisation. The company works with management teams to develop businesses that have the potential for significant growth. Each year it invests over €2.7bn supporting people who start, grow, change and buy businesses.

Source adapted from: www.3i.com

Questions

Go to the 3i website and answer the following questions:

1 What are the eight main sectors the organisation operates in? (8 marks)
2 What is a 'buyout'? (4 marks)
3 What is the range of investment for their venture capital for new businesses? (4 marks)

Case studies, questions and exam practice

CASE STUDY BORROWING

A business seeking to borrow funds from banks, business angels or government agencies has to show that the money is safe in their hands. Poor management skills are the reason 80% of owner-managed firms fail. So this is the first thing lenders look at when considering a loan. Before they will lend money, lenders also want to see that the owners have:

- a good track record;
- the expertise and skills to adapt to changing financial and economic circumstances;
- a good product or a high-quality service;
- good financial controls;
- ideally, growth prospects;
- the ability to repay the money.

All lenders will want to see a business plan that explains how the business will use the money, how much it will need and when it proposes to pay it back.

The business plan needs to include cash-flow projections to show how the loan will be serviced and eventually repaid. These both need to be realistic: lenders are often suspicious of over-optimistic forecasts. The figures also need to add up, and the owners need to show that they have an understanding of the rationale behind the figures.

Adapted from Better Business

Questions

1 Why might a new business have difficulty in providing evidence for the six bullet points? (12 marks)
2 What does the phrase 'how the loan will be serviced' mean? (4 marks)
3 What is meant by the phrase 'understanding of the rationale behind the figures'? (4 marks)

SHORT-ANSWER QUESTIONS

1 What do you understand by the term 'working capital'?

2 What is flotation?

3 What is collateral? Give an example.

4 What are the two types of share? Briefly explain them.

5 What is the difference between a loan and an overdraft?

6 What is another term used to describe a venture capitalist?

7 Why would an investor in a business want a good rate of return?

8 What is retained profit?

9 What is hire purchase?

10 Why might a new business be reluctant to sell more than 50% of its shares to investors?

CASE STUDY MAKING SENSE OF LOANS

Small business loans are widely available and come in various forms. They aim to provide a flexible solution to the funding requirements of a business.

Commercial loans are available to most small businesses and start-ups, subject to status. They are offered by all the high-street banks and other lenders operating in the small business loan market. They are just like a personal loan, as the business borrows the money and then repays it over an agreed number of months or years. The loans will have either a fixed or variable interest rate.

Fixed rate loans mean that the business knows from the outset how much it will need to repay for the duration of the loan. For variable rate loans, the interest rate is tied to the Bank of England base rate. If the base rate increases, the interest rate will rise.

Some business loans are capped rate loans as far as interest is concerned. This option allows the business to benefit from any falls in the interest rate, but it means that the interest rate will not rise above the agreed level for the duration of the capped period.

Adapted from www.bytestart.co.uk

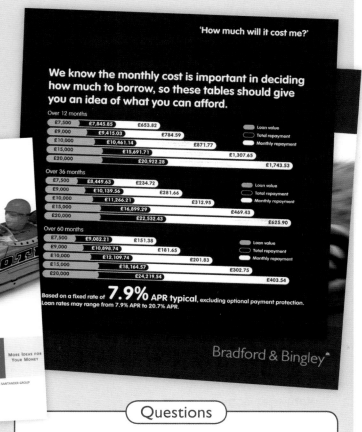

'How much will it cost me?'

We know the monthly cost is important in deciding how much to borrow, so these tables should give you an idea of what you can afford.

Over 12 months

Loan value	Total repayment	Monthly repayment
£7,500	£7,845.85	£653.82
£9,000	£9,415.03	£784.59
£10,000	£10,461.14	£871.77
£15,000	£15,691.71	£1,307.65
£20,000	£20,922.28	£1,743.53

Over 36 months

Loan value	Total repayment	Monthly repayment
£7,500	£8,449.63	£234.72
£9,000	£10,139.56	£281.66
£10,000	£11,266.21	£312.95
£15,000	£16,899.29	£469.43
£20,000	£22,532.43	£625.90

Over 60 months

Loan value	Total repayment	Monthly repayment
£7,500	£9,082.21	£151.38
£9,000	£10,898.74	£181.65
£10,000	£12,109.74	£201.83
£15,000	£18,164.57	£302.75
£20,000	£24,219.54	£403.54

Based on a fixed rate of **7.9%** APR typical, excluding optional payment protection. Loan rates may range from 7.9% APR to 20.7% APR.

Bradford & Bingley

Loans

Helping you go that extra mile

Abbey MORE IDEAS FOR YOUR MONEY PART OF THE SANTANDER GROUP

Questions

1 Distinguish between fixed and variable interest. (4 marks)
2 How might an increase in the base rate of interest affect a business with a variable interest rate loan? (4 marks)
3 What does the term 'subject to status' mean? (2 marks)

Technology, costs and infrastructure

Start-up locations

For any business, including a start-up enterprise, location can be crucial, as this may have a direct bearing on the future of the business. Ideally, a business will look for a location that offers the opportunity to maximise the revenues (income) and minimise the expenditures (costs).

A useful way of looking at the location decision is to consider what are known as push and pull factors:

- Push factors – these will include a high level of competition from other businesses in the area (or a rising level of competition); rising costs (such as rents and rates); poor communication systems (both poor road networks and issues such as the non-availability of broadband); and low or falling demand for the products and services offered by the business by local customers.
- Pull factors – government incentives to locate in an area (grants, lost-cost loans, subsidised rent etc.), low labour costs, good or improving communication systems and a healthy, growing or developing market for the products and services offered by the business.

A number of different push and pull factors can apply to new or existing businesses, as seen in the table.

Factor	Explanation and example
Closeness to the market	This is particularly relevant if the business deals with products that have a short shelf life, are perishable, or have high transport costs. A sugar factory, reliant on sugar beet deliveries, is close to areas where these are cultivated.
Communications	Transportation links can be important, but also the quality of the information technology infrastructure needs to be good for most modern businesses. Many warehousing facilities belonging to large manufacturers, and supermarkets are located close to major motorways.
Raw materials	Locating close to the source of raw materials means reduction of transportation costs and the time for deliveries to arrive is reduced. This is an important factor for businesses involved in steel-making or reliant on large quantities of fuel such as coal.
Workforce	Businesses need to have access to a reliable and trained pool of employees. Some businesses are more reliant on this than others and some look for areas with traditionally low wages (manufacturing and processing etc.).
Waste	With increased concerns and legislation regarding waste disposal and the treatment of toxic by-products from production, location can be tied to the proximity of plants capable of handling hazardous waste or dealing with recycling materials.
Power	Britain does have a comprehensive and reliable power supply, making this factor less relevant to British business, however, some businesses will locate in areas where they can negotiate discounted or favourable energy rates with power suppliers.
Land	Land is a scarce commodity on a small island such as Britain. Property prices are also high, particularly in built-up areas and areas that have a good infrastructure, useful workforce pool and proximity to markets. For smaller businesses the option of locating in central London may not be available due to the high rents and rates.
Incentives	Both central government and the European Union offer incentives to businesses if they choose to locate in particular parts of the country. These areas are usually those with higher-than-average unemployment rates or a tradition of under-investment in the infrastructure.

There are exceptions to the rule, and it is not always the case that businesses are either driven to make location choices on the basis of push and pull factors or that they are able to take advantage of the benefits by relocating:

- Footloose businesses – a term used to describe businesses that are not tied down by traditional location factors, and so can locate in any area they choose.
- Industrial inertia – when a business located in a particular area, as a result of significant benefits from that area, chooses to remain there even when the original benefts are gone, despite better options elsewhere.

INTERNET RESEARCH

To find out how your local area sells itself to businesses, begin your search by visiting the local authority website or using a post code search on the Business Link website (www.businesslink.gov.uk). Type 'grants' in the search box and select 'Grants and Support Directory' – a search box allows you to search by postcode.

Technology, costs and infrastructure

As we have seen, these three considerations can be major determinants of business location. Additional information and examples are shown in the following table:

Factor	Explanation
Technology	Some businesses need to locate close to existing technologies provided by other businesses, or enjoy the benefits of these businesses having established a reputation in the area (or indeed trained employees). The Thames Valley area is known for its high-tech enterprises.
Costs	Foremost among the costs are the potential expenditures related to securing suitable premises for the business. A second consideration is the ongoing costs of employees. In areas where there is high employment and competition from other businesses for the best employees, the wage costs will be high.
Infrastructure	Poor transportation links, support services and communications are disincentives to locate in a particular area. This can be offset by government incentives.

CASE STUDY NOTTINGHAM

The government sees urban regeneration companies as the flagship vehicles to transform the UK's towns and cities.

Chief Executive of Nottingham Regeneration Limited said of attracting businesses:

'We've never been a city to become too dependent on one industry, so if something goes wrong, it isn't disastrous. We didn't go chasing micro-chip companies when they were trendy, so we didn't suffer when that sector collapsed.'

Swales was pleased that Experian, which was founded in Nottingham in 1980, chose to remain in Nottingham. Attracting the credit card company Capital One to Nottingham in the face of European-wide competition was a major victory:

'When you're dealing with such a footloose business, it can be hard to persuade them to even consider you. We were competing with many of the leading cities in Europe. Cork, for example, offered them far more money than we could, but they came here because they liked Nottingham, and because we had the workforce they needed.'

Adapted from the Nottingham Review

Questions

1 What might be meant by 'urban regeneration', and how might the location of businesses relate to it? (6 marks)
2 Why might a business such as a financial services company be considered footloose? (4 marks)

Start-up location: market, government intervention and qualitative factors

Market

Convenience for the customer can be a location concern, particularly in cases when there is a high level of competition and not very much to choose from the businesses that offer similar products and services.

Corner shops and specialist high-street stores continue to thrive as there is still a sizeable minority of people who are either unable or disinclined to travel to do their shopping. It also means that the convenience aspect often outweighs the fact that the corner shops are more expensive.

Larger businesses also tend to locate near one of their major customers on the basis that they can better serve them and be close and convenient, making it less likely that the customer will go elsewhere to source products or services. In many cases, these suppliers will act as a form of convenient warehousing for the customer, holding onto stock until it is needed. For services, they are able to respond to the needs of the customer much faster than a similar business located further afield.

INTERNET RESEARCH 🔍

For more information on the work of the Regional Development Agencies visit their website and portal to specific RDAs at www.englandsrdas.com

Government intervention

Government policy can sometimes influence location. Government, at various levels, offers incentives to start new businesses, or relocate existing ones, in particular areas.

These areas often qualify for what is known as **regeneration**: some of the areas are called enterprise zones or assisted areas. Businesses are offered grants, interest-free loans and reduced rents if they choose to locate in these depressed areas.

Another example of government intervention in the location of business is the creation of the nine English Regional Development Agencies. Their main aims are to:

- encourage general economic development and regeneration in the regions;
- help promote business efficiency, investment and competitiveness;
- encourage and promote the creation of jobs;
- help provide training for the local workforce to improve employment levels.

LEARNING OBJECTIVES

- ▶ Market
- ▶ Government intervention
- ▶ Qualitative factors

Financial assistance is provided by both the British government and the European Union to help convince businesses to set up in areas that have high unemployment. As a more general goal, the government is also concerned with the precise location of businesses and the use of land:

- It encourages businesses to relocate or to build new premises in brownfield sites (unused land, derelict buildings, former factory sites etc.)
- It discourages the location of business and the building of new premises on greenfield sites (farmland etc.)

KEY WORD

Regeneration – economic redevelopment of a certain area as a result of under-investment and high unemployment levels.

FOR EXAMPLE

The East of England has a thriving and entrepreneurial business community, with over 430,000 businesses choosing to locate here. If the business community is to continue to prosper however, it is essential that it has access to support that is tailored to its needs.

www.eeda.org.uk

Qualitative factors

Often cost and revenue is difficult to calculate in terms of a location decision. Qualitative factors refer to location factors that do not directly relate to financial considerations, as can be seen in the following table:

Qualitative factor	Explanation
Quality of life	When business-owners make a decision about location, one of the key considerations is whether they would be happy to live in the area. They will consider the quality of the housing, shops, leisure facilities, the drive to work and a host of other lifestyle-based factors.
Safety and the environment	Potentially dangerous businesses that involve harmful processes (such as nuclear power stations) will need to be located in remote areas of the country; businesses that operate on a 24-hour basis will disrupt the local community and may be located away from housing. Environmental considerations can also affect location, such as outlet pipes from a factory entering a water system where drinking water is extracted.
Expansion	A business may seek to find suitable land or premises that can give it the option to expand at some point in the future. Moving to a highly built-up area where expansion would mean a move to an alternative location (either in the short or medium term) can be considered to be too disruptive to the business.
Local facilities	This consideration looks at the infrastructure, communications and support services that may be necessary for a business to function at full efficiency. Close or reliable transportation links are not only applicable for the business to receive and despatch products, but are also crucial for employees and visitors to the business

CASE STUDY ASSISTED AREAS

On the basis of Article 87(3)a and Article 87(3)c of the EC Treaty, State Aid granted to promote the economic development of certain disadvantaged areas within the European Union is considered compatible with the common market by the European Commission. This kind of State Aid is referred to as Regional Aid.

Regional aid consists of aid for investment granted to large companies or in certain limited circumstances operating aid which in both cases is targeted at specific regions to redress regional disparities. Increased levels of investment aid granted to SMEs located within the disadvantaged regions, over and above what is allowed in other areas, are also considered regional aid.

In Great Britain the main form of State Aid is through discretionary grant schemes:

- Selective Finance for Investment in England (SFIE) – helps fund new investment projects leading to long-term improvements in productivity, skills and employment.
- Regional Selective Assistance (RSA) – administered by RSA Scotland, part of the Scottish Executive, aimed at encouraging new investment projects, strengthening existing employment and new job creation.
- RSA Cymru Wales (Regional Selective Assistance) – delivered by the Welsh Assembly Government to help support new commercially viable capital investment projects that create or safeguard permanent jobs.

Source: www.berr.gov.uk

Questions

1 What is meant by SME? (2 marks)
2 What is meant by the term 'discretionary grant'? (2 marks)
3 What is meant by a 'capital investment project'? (3 marks)

Case studies, questions and exam practice

CASE STUDY RICS

The Royal Institution of Chartered Surveyors (RICS) has useful advice for new businesses making the difficult location decision. They suggest that the first thing to consider is making sure that the location matches the kind of business involved. If the business is concerned with manufacturing, then ease of access to raw materials, as well as to the markets, may be essential. In the case of a retail store, it needs to be where the public will notice it and find it easy to visit. For cost reasons there may have to be compromises in both cases.

A business's strategy is another major concern. Location needs to take account of the number of people to be employed; the processes used by the business; and the plant or machinery that may be required. Clearly, the type of premises will differ for a business involved in heavy manufacturing and a company developing software.

The RICS also suggests that ongoing plans are considered. Will there be space for expansion? Will the business have to think about another move in the future to larger premises? What is the quality of the working environment? How might this impact on the employees and their productivity?

The RICS recommends that a specification of the ideal premises is drawn up, and a plan provided detailing the ideal or absolute minimum requirements. From this, the business owners can work out how much floor area is needed. Alongside this, considerations such as car-parking, loading and unloading need to be brought into the equation. Other key thoughts should include power supplies, telecommunications and other services.

Finally, there is the choice of whether to buy or to lease the premises. The business needs to be able to afford to pay for the lease or to make mortgage payments, or rental charges. On top of this, there are business rates, water rates, any service charges and insurance.

Adapted from www.rics.org

Questions

1 What is meant by the term 'productivity' and how might this be affected by a poor working environment? (6 marks)
2 Why might the premises for a manufacturing business need to be different from those of a distribution centre? (4 marks)
3 Why might most new businesses have to compromise on the choice of premises? (4 marks)

SHORT-ANSWER QUESTIONS

1 What is an RDA?

2 State four qualitative factors that could influence location decisions.

3 Explain what is meant by local infrastructure.

4 Why might a small new business have less choice in terms of location than a larger more established business?

5 Distinguish between a brownfield and a greenfield site.

6 Apart from the British government, what other major international organisation is involved in regeneration?

7 Define the term regeneration.

8 Why might a manufacturer of products aimed at other businesses be more inclined to locate close to its customers than a business that makes products for the consumer?

9 What is a 'cluster' in business location terms?

10 What is a lease?

CASE STUDY BUSINESS LINK ADVICE

Choosing the right location can be something of a balancing act. Ideally, the location should be convenient for your customers, employees and suppliers – without being too expensive.

For shops and other retail businesses, location is of critical importance. Your location must attract customers.

If you rely on passing trade, you want to be in an area where enough people who want your product or service can see you. For example, key cutters are often located in or around train stations. You could also benefit from customers who are attracted by other shops in a shopping centre.

For employees, the best location will be easy to travel to. Good public transport links make it easier for employees who don't live within walking distance. Employees also tend to prefer working somewhere with good local facilities.

You may want to be near suppliers for a quick, flexible service. Deliveries may be easier if there are good road and transport links.

You may not want to be too near your competitors, though clusters of similar businesses sometimes attract more customers. Your neighbours and your location also affect your image.

Location has a major impact on cost. If you need premises in a prime location the extra costs may be justified.

Source: www.businesslink.gov.uk

Questions

1 What is meant by the term 'passing trade'? Give TWO examples of businesses that would benefit from passing trade. (4 marks)

2 Why might a cluster of similar businesses be an attraction to customers? (2 marks)

3 What is a prime location? Give TWO examples of prime locations. (4 marks)

Types of employee in small businesses

LEARNING OBJECTIVES

▶ Temporary staff
▶ Permanent staff
▶ Full-time staff
▶ Part-time staff
▶ Reasons behind the trends

Temporary staff

When an employee begins work for an employer, the **contract of employment** will state whether the job is a temporary or permanent one. If the job is temporary, the contract will state that the employee has been taken on to work for a specified period of time, such as six months or a year. Temporary contracts are given to employees to cover long-term sickness, maternity leave or the short-term needs of the employer.

In Britain there are around 1.2 million temporary workers. Attitudes to work have changed, and temporary work is often seen as a flexible way of working, offering the temporary worker **job satisfaction**. The temporary recruitment market in 2006 was worth £2.16 billion. The 1.2 million figure refers to workers operating via temporary agencies, many of whom have been temping for a considerable period of time and are registered with several different agencies. The average length of assignment with an employer is 5.7 months. Most temps are satisfied with their pay, but over half of them are actually looking for a permanent job.

Temporary workers are often supplied by temp agencies, but on a daily basis they are controlled by the employer. The employer has a contract with the agency and pays the agency directly.

In turn, the agency then pays the temporary employee. In some areas of employment, such as nursing homes, temporary staff are often used as it is difficult to find full-time permanent members of staff. One of the main advantages of using temporary workers provided by an agency is that much of the administrative work related to employing individuals is handled by the agency rather than the employer.

Permanent staff

Until relatively recently the vast majority of jobs were classed as permanent. The contract of employment between the employer and employee would not specify a particular period of time over which the employee would be expected to work for that employer. With permanent employees it is necessary for the employer to terminate the contract of employment, and when necessary, give notice to the employee that it wishes to terminate the contract. While permanent employees give the employer greater stability, certainly in terms of continuity of work, a workforce consisting entirely of permanent employees does not necessarily give the employer enough flexibility to increase or decrease the workforce according to workload.

Full-time staff

Full-time employment means that the employee is working a full working week and does this every week apart from the time allocated for leave. Typical full-time jobs include teachers, local government officers and office workers. Usually, full-time employees are paid on a monthly basis, but others, such as factory workers, might be paid on a weekly basis.

The contract of employment for full-time workers will state: the number of hours that they are expected to work; the availability and pay/time off in lieu for working overtime; and holiday entitlements. Around 60% of the British workforce is employed on a full-time basis. Not all of these jobs are standard nine-to-five patterns. There are all kinds of shift-work arrangements, from night shifts to three or four 12-hour days per week. Some employees work solely or partly from home.

KEY WORDS

Contract of employment – a legal document that sets out the rights and duties of the employer and employee.

Job satisfaction – enjoyment or pleasure derived from the work itself.

Part-time staff

Part-time employment is common in Britain and it very much ties in with the need of employees for flexible working arrangements. Obviously in the vast majority of cases it is in the interests of the employer to take on part-time staff particularly in organisations that have high proportions of employees who have other commitments beyond their work. Normally, working part-time means that the working week is restricted to less than 25 hours. The majority of part-time workers are women, accounting for well over 50% of the number of employees in part-time work. It is important to remember however, that part-time workers have the same rights as full-time workers.

Reasons behind the trends

Both employers and employees are demanding greater flexibility in work patterns in the interests of a greater work/life balance. Research suggests that this trend will continue over the next few decades. Employers have also come under increasing pressure to provide flexible working patterns. This has been both to meet the needs of employees and in order to improve their competitiveness and productivity, while delivering high-quality services and products to customers. The rapid increase in the service sector shows that there is an increasing emphasis on delivering timely services, and one of the solutions has been to increase the number of part-time rather than full-time posts. The key current trends suggest that flexible working patterns are set to gather pace. There will continue to be an employer and employee relationship as far as most work practices are concerned. While part-time working will continue to grow, there are still relatively stable trends in full-time employment.

INTERNET RESEARCH

To find out about the current levels of temporary employment in Britain visit www.statistics.gov.uk and look for the data sets for the Labour Force Survey.

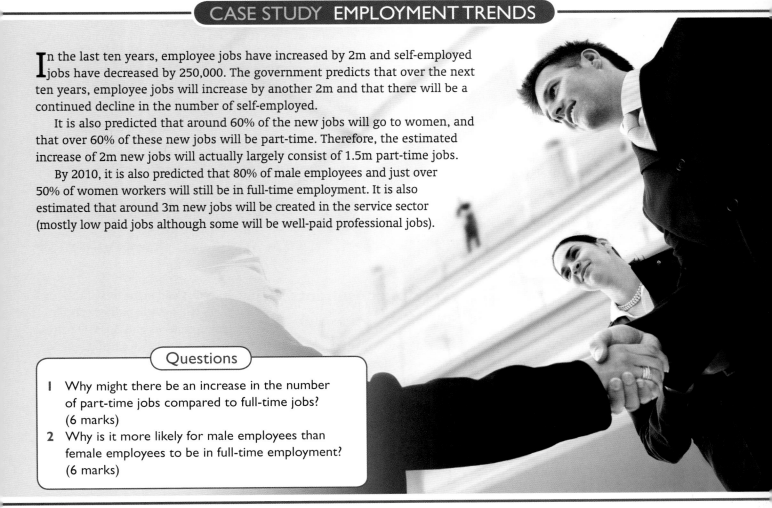

CASE STUDY EMPLOYMENT TRENDS

In the last ten years, employee jobs have increased by 2m and self-employed jobs have decreased by 250,000. The government predicts that over the next ten years, employee jobs will increase by another 2m and that there will be a continued decline in the number of self-employed.

It is also predicted that around 60% of the new jobs will go to women, and that over 60% of these new jobs will be part-time. Therefore, the estimated increase of 2m new jobs will actually largely consist of 1.5m part-time jobs.

By 2010, it is also predicted that 80% of male employees and just over 50% of women workers will still be in full-time employment. It is also estimated that around 3m new jobs will be created in the service sector (mostly low paid jobs although some will be well-paid professional jobs).

Questions

1 Why might there be an increase in the number of part-time jobs compared to full-time jobs?
(6 marks)
2 Why is it more likely for male employees than female employees to be in full-time employment?
(6 marks)

Using consultants and advisers

LEARNING
OBJECTIVES
▶ What are consultants and advisors?
▶ The work of consultants and advisors

What are consultants and advisors?

Business consultants aim to assist businesses in improving their performance. This is usually achieved by analysing any problems that the business is experiencing and developing strategies to deal with them.

There are a large number of businesses across Britain that specialise in this form of assistance. They can offer business help by identifying good practice, the use of analytical techniques, training and implementation of new technology, as well as developing new strategies and marketing.

The role of the business consultant can be specialised according to precise types of assistance – it is rare to find a business consultant who is useful in all areas of work. According to the Institute of Management Consultancy, there are several different defined roles as shown in the table.

Consultancy specialism	Assistance offered
Business strategy	Consultants in this area offer long-term planning, reorganisation, rationalisation and general business appraisal.
Manufacturing and business services	This could involve the review of the layout of a business, work on productivity, incentive schemes and offering strategies to deal with quality control issues.
Marketing	This would include assistance in conducting marketing research, forecasting, training of the sales force, the organisation of retail and warehouses.
Financial and management controls	Typically, the consultant would be used to implement new budgetary controls and work on profit planning, improving levels of working capital and increasing revenues.
Human resources	Advice on personnel policy and planning, including job enrichment, evaluation and appraisal as well as industrial relations.
Information technology	This type of management consultant is involved in the provision of software, undertaking systems analysis and design, implementing computer applications, and making computer hardware evaluations.
Environmental management	The work of an environmental management consultant involves urban and regional development planning, international economic research, cost benefit and social analysis studies, and physical, economic, ecological and sociological studies.
Quality management	Quality management involves setting policies and strategies, working on customer satisfaction, measuring performance, and people management.

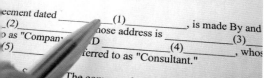

The work of consultants and advisors

When working with consultants or advisers, a business needs to clearly define the objectives. There will need to be an obvious benefit from the work carried out by the consultant, usually within a specified timescale. The business will identify key personnel to work directly with the consultant, learning techniques from them that can be used by the business over time.

Directors and managers of the business will have identified specific problems or needs and this will help them define the type of help required from a consultant. Assistance given may be system based or human-resource related. Consultants can be taken on for short periods of time, or they may be engaged for a longer period so that they can guide the business through a series of problems or decisions. A schedule can be set up with the consultant, terms of reference agreed, and the fee decided.

For most businesses it is advisable to shortlist no more than three consultants. Each should be asked to provide a written proposal outlining how they intend to provide the necessary services to the business; they should also include a written quote for the work. The business needs to make sure that the consultant is suitably qualified.

For the business to get the best possible service from the consultant, the consultant will need to be briefed properly, reporting procedures clarified, any constraints on the project identified, and the cooperation of any individuals who will be involved with the consultant secured.

It is vital that the business and the key employees are involved with the consultant throughout the time that the assistance is being provided:

- Effective use of consultants means a commitment of both time and

INTERNET RESEARCH

To find out more about the Institute of Management Consultancy visit its website at www.imc.co.uk.

money by the business.

- Consultants are cost-effective if they work to an agreed programme and timescale with regular progress meetings and briefings.
- It is often advisable for the business to involve the consultant in the actual implementation of recommendations.
- Any hold-ups caused by the business could lead to additional costs being incurred, so information and relevant staff need to be made available to the consultant.
- Most work by the consultant needs to take place on business

premises, so the business will need to provide office space and administrative support.

- It is important to involve the business's staff as they must, ultimately, feel that they have had a role in the creation of the recommendations (joint teams of staff and consultants are a good way of achieving this).

The final report by the consultant needs to be absolutely clear and usable by the business. It should be in a format that can be clearly understood and any recommendations easily implemented. The report should not really contain any great surprises or anything that is confidential or cannot be read by certain members of staff. Usually the consultant will make a presentation of the key recommendations of the report and lead the discussions of the conclusions and necessary actions.

CASE STUDY FREDDIE

'I chose management consultancy as I wanted a job where I would be challenged. Being a young graduate, I had no plans to spend the next 40 years doing the same old job in the same office. Consultancy lets me experience and learn a lot of roles in different places with a diverse mix of people.

I started off doing quite basic tasks (testing, creating documents and presentations, etc.) and then progressed to roles that gave me more ownership of particular areas of a project and leading small teams of junior consultants (analysts).

Now I am the finance manager for a large Vodafone programme. I have responsibility for a £110million budget across 17 different projects. Previously I worked on the team that trained almost 10,000 BT personnel in 18 different countries in a new Customer Relationship Management (CRM) system – the largest release of its kind at the time. Management consultancy is not about having a business background; it's about being interested and able to learn new skills. Any experience you can show of team leadership, decision-making, problem-solving and flexibility is a big bonus. It also helps to have a positive personality and be able to anticipate and deal with poorly defined problems.'

Adapted from www.prospects.ac.uk

Questions

1 Why might skills such as team leadership be important in a role as a consultant? (4 marks)
2 What are the key skills identified by Freddie and why might they be important? (8 marks)

Drawbacks of employing people and using consultants and advisers

Drawbacks and difficulties in employing people

There is a considerable risk for new or small businesses in taking on employees for the first time. Due to many small businesses' lack of experience in employing people, mistakes could often be made that would threaten the survival of the business. Standard risks could include taking on someone with whom there may be a personality clash, or indeed someone who is not quite as good as they appeared at interview or on their curriculum vitae.

Employing individuals costs money. It is often the case that small businesses reach a difficult stage when there is too much work for the sole trader, or for the partners. However, there is too great a financial risk in taking on an employee because the business needs to be sure that it has enough financial resources to support the employee.

There is a great deal of paperwork involved in employment and a business is responsible for the administration of tax (called Pay As You Earn, or PAYE), as well as National Insurance Contributions (NIC). These taxes are collected by the employer on behalf of the government. It is vital that detailed records are kept, as the Inland Revenue, for example, can demand access so that it can inspect them.

There are also other administrative burdens, such as keeping track of holiday entitlements, dealing with issues such as sick leave, maternity leave, and handling the monitoring and payment of overtime work. The business needs to be able to balance the costs and benefits of employing someone.

Most businesses recognise that by employing individuals they are able to grow and increase their turnover and profit. This is assuming that the employee can work to a greater or lesser extent on their own, without supervision and that they can contribute to the profitability of the business beyond the amount it costs to employ them.

Drawbacks of using consultants and advisers

Consultants and advisers can have an extremely important role to play in assisting even new or small businesses. They can present new ideas, which are based on their own experiences of businesses they have worked with in the past. They can provide both management and staff support, and they can encourage change and quickly train the business managers and key employees to adopt and implement changes throughout the business.

If consultants do not help businesses develop a self-sufficient means of adapting, then their impact will be superficial and short-lived.

The key drawbacks and difficulties in using consultants and advisers are:

KEY TERM

Curriculum vitae (CV) – the translation of the Latin is 'a history of oneself'; a summary of educational attainment, work experience, personal details and references.

LEARNING OBJECTIVES

▶ Drawbacks and difficulties in employing people
▶ Drawbacks and difficulties in using consultants and advisers

- **Financial costs** – consultants almost always cost a considerable amount of money. However, the costs of using external consultants may not be as great as using existing staff, who would be diverted from their normal work, affecting the productivity of the business.
- **Lack of objectivity** – many consultants are criticised for becoming involved in internal politics and simply reinforcing the views of the dominant force in the business. They are often accused of trying to find out who is in charge andt what they want, and merely recommending this in the report. Consultants may also have links with external organisations and steer the business towards particular suppliers, methods of work or potential business partners.
- **Failure to understand** – consultants cannot come to a small business and expect to implement solutions to a particular problem that have worked for large, multinational businesses. They sometimes fail to understand the organisation that they are working with, the financial constraints, the history of the business, the relationships

between owners and staff and, most importantly, financial restrictions. Most problems are solvable given time and money, and sometimes consultants are criticised for assuming that both of these resources are available, when in small businesses this is not always the case.

- **Lack of sustainability** – consultants need to leave a long-term legacy in the business. Having investigated a particular problem, made a series of recommendations and then, perhaps, helped to implement them, they need to leave the business in a stronger position, where it can carry out some of the work in the future. Consultants obviously have an interest in making the business dependent upon them, as this would ensure more work for them in the future. As a result, some businesses have consultants working for them all the time and actually learn very little from the experience. Consultants often fail to transfer skills to the business's management or employees, making the business feel abandoned once the consultants have left and the first problem arises.

- **Demotivated staff** – sometimes almost everything a consultant does could have been done by the management or employees if they had been given training, time and resources. When the management and employees see highly paid external consultants recommending and implementing ideas that they could easily have come up with themselves, they inevitably become demotivated. Consultants are rarely actually able to do the job themselves and thus sometimes suggest unworkable systems.

CASE STUDY DANGERS FOR THE SMALL BUSINESS

One of the biggest dangers for small businesses in using consultants is offloading responsibilities onto an independent third party. If the wrong consultant is taken on, bad advice could have a detrimental effect on the business. There is also the danger that much of the advice is effectively 'off-the-shelf' and not tailored to the needs of the business itself. The consultant will always be keen to sell further services, which may not be necessary for the small business. Aside from the high costs of consultants, another key problem area is that managers and employees often view consultants as a kind of executioner or threat.

Questions

1 What is meant by 'off-the-shelf' advice and why might this be a problem? (4 marks)
2 What could be done by the business to ensure that bringing in a consultant does not frighten the management or employees? (6 marks)

Case studies, questions and exam practice

CASE STUDY EMPLOYING PART-TIMERS

Employers need to consider any extra induction, training, and administration costs. They need to think about performance issues – if job-sharers do not produce the same output, it can affect the workloads of others. There can also be communication problems between job-sharers if they see little of each other, which could in turn lead to problems of continuity. Businesses need to delegate specific responsibilities to each job sharer (unclear lines of responsibility can be a problem) or make sure they have set up strong lines of communication. In many jobs, the advantages of using part-timers far outweigh any disadvantages.

The way a business manages part-timers should not differ from the way it manages full-timers. Any treatment that disadvantages part-time workers could end in a complaint to an employment tribunal, or a claim of indirect sex discrimination, because the majority of part-time workers are women.

By law, part-timers have the same rights as full-timers and must enjoy pro-rata terms and conditions including pay, holidays, sick pay, maternity/paternity leave, entitlement to company pension schemes and benefits, as well as equal access to promotion or redundancy,

It is not only rights that must be available to part-timers, but benefits also. By law, unless a business can make an objective justification for not doing so, benefits available to full-time staff, such as discounts, health insurance, company cars, annual public holidays and perks must also be made available to part-time staff.

Questions

1 What is meant by 'induction'? (2 marks)
2 What are the likely effects of poor communication? (3 marks)
3 What is a job share? (2 marks)
4 What is meant by 'pro-rata'? (3 marks)

SHORT-ANSWER QUESTIONS

1 Distinguish between a temporary and a permanent worker.

2 What is a contract of employment?

3 What do you understand by the term 'job satisfaction'?

4 Give THREE examples of typical full-time jobs.

5 What is the key role of the business consultant?

6 Outline the role of a marketing consultant.

7 Why is it important for a business to ensure that key employees work directly with a consultant?

8 Why might the business incur extra costs if it does not have information and relevant staff available for a consultant to use?

9 Suggest THREE drawbacks or difficulties in employing people for the first time.

10 Suggest THREE drawbacks or difficulties in employing consultants for the first time.

CASE STUDY WORKING WITH CONSULTANTS

Disadvantages of working with consultants

- Dependency on outside expertise, diverts budget and attention away from investing in local staff. (This is reduced if working with local consultants.)
- If working with different consultants, then project staff may need to reconcile contradictory or different views and ideas.
- If not well recruited, they may only provide a piece of the missing expertise.
- If they are not committed to the project in the long term, then this may make their suggestions unfeasible.
- If they do not have local experience, then advice or ideas may be inappropriate.
- If they work in isolation, then local capacity won't be built.
- If not living locally, then they cannot help adjust and adapt their recommendations while they are being implemented.

Advantages of working with consultants

- Can give quicker output.
- Able to stand back from the project and ask questions that staff aren't able to see.
- Bring interesting ideas from other projects.
- Can raise sensitive issues that project staff fear.
- Can provide on-the-job training if they work closely with project staff.
- May be trusted by funding agencies for the impartiality of their views.
- Can increase the professional level of an organisation.
- Can provide focused inputs that are only needed once.

Source: adapted from International Fund for Agricultural Development

Questions

1 What is meant by 'dependency'? (3 marks)
2 Why is impartiality important? (3 marks)
3 Why might working with more than one consultant be a major problem (4 marks)

Introduction

This is the second of the two core themes for *Planning and financing a business*. You will need to have an understanding of the key financial concepts essential for the planning of a small business.

Fundamental to understanding the finance of a small business is the ability to calculate costs, revenues and profits. It is also necessary to understand the relationships between costs, price, revenue and profits. One technique often used by businesses is to look at the concept of contribution, which enables them to use break-even analysis to help make decisions.

Businesses also use cash-flow forecasting and need to obtain information about their income and expenditure so they can project these costs into the future and gain a relatively accurate picture of the flow of cash into and out of the business.

Many businesses set themselves budgets and, perhaps, allocate budgets to particular parts of the organisation. They will need to look at income, expenditure and profit budgets and come up with a way to set budgets that limit spending, but that also give the business sufficient flexibility to spend money if it is absolutely required.

Finally, this section looks at how business start-ups can be assessed in terms of their risks, objectives, strengths and weaknesses, and why a large number of start-up businesses fail. Success or failure can depend on a number of internal and external factors.

Fixed, variable and total costs

LEARNING OBJECTIVES

▶ Business costs
▶ Fixed and variable costs
▶ Total and average costs
▶ Direct and indirect costs

Business costs

Businesses will use financial resources to buy or use products and services. They may have to buy raw materials and components in order to make products. They will certainly have to find funds in order to pay employees. Some costs, as we will see, are unavoidable, but others (such as advertising) can be at the discretion of a business, which may choose not to incur these costs.

Broadly speaking, costs can be broken down into two different areas. First there is money that is spent to buy **fixed assets**. Usually the funds for this come either from the owners of the business, from the shareholders, or from **retained profits**. Money that is spent on fixed assets is known as capital expenditure.

Other expenditure tends to come directly from the business's income or revenue. It consists of costs related to buying products and services that the business needs in order to generate revenue. For this reason it is called revenue expenditure and it is a term that is applied to the purchase of anything other than fixed assets.

It is also important to bear in mind that a business needs ready access to sufficient money to pay for the ongoing cost of materials, stock, utility bills and wages. This money is often referred to as working capital. Working capital is cash that a business can access immediately, or almost immediately.

Fixed and variable costs

Some business costs have to be paid out regardless of the level of business activity. These include:

- Rent or mortgage repayments
- Business rates and insurance
- Employees' wages
- Utility bills

These costs are referred to as fixed costs, although they can of course rise, particularly if the rent increases, if changes are made to rates, if the hourly rate to employees increases, or if there is a change in the tariffs from the utilities.

Businesses also incur variable costs. They are called variable costs because they change according to the level of output of the business. If a business is making or selling more, then its costs of producing or providing those additional products and services will also increase. A factory that increases its output will have to spend more money on raw materials and components, making variable costs rise. Usually variable costs increase in proportion to changes in output. In other words, as output increases, variable costs increase, and if output falls, variable costs fall.

Total and average costs

By adding fixed and variable costs together we can calculate the total costs of a business. As we will see when we consider break-even, it is also useful to work out average costs, or unit costs. This can show the business exactly how much one unit of production costs. The formula used is:

$$\frac{\text{total costs}}{\text{output}} = \text{average costs}$$

FOR EXAMPLE

A business produces 60,000 units and has fixed costs of £45,000 and variable costs of £93,000. The total costs are therefore £138,000. To work out the average or unit costs, simply divide £138,000 by 60,000 to give average costs of £2.30 per unit.

What tends to happen is that average cost per unit falls as output rises, mainly because the business can probably obtain raw materials and components more cheaply and it may be more efficient in its production. If the business doubled production to 120,000 units it may find that variable costs only increased to £162,000. Total costs are now £207,000 and unit costs have dropped to £1.72.

Direct and indirect costs

Variable costs that are linked directly to production or level of output are often referred to as direct costs. In effect this is the cost of raw materials and components, as well as direct labour costs and other direct expenses.

Fixed costs, on the other hand, can be indirect costs that are shared across the whole of the business. These would include rent, rates, administration, sales and marketing, and are often referred to as overheads. The higher the amount of overheads, the lower the amount of profit made.

Businesses will always seek to control or cut costs in all areas, whether they are fixed, variable, direct or indirect. This is because each cost cuts into the revenue that has been generated by the business and reduces profit.

> ### KEY TERMS
>
> **Fixed assets** – items such as buildings, equipment and vehicles that are used time and time again by the business.
>
> **Retained profits** – a proportion of the profit made by a business that is not distributed either to the owners or to shareholders, but held back to cover expected future expenses.

CASE STUDY CALCULATING COSTS

A business has a wage bill of £55,000 per month. Rent and rates total £3,000 per month and its utility bills average out at £2,000 per month. In order to produce 1,000 units, the company spends £6,700 on components and packaging. It also spends £800 per month on advertising.

The business discovers that if it were to double its monthly output, it could buy the necessary components for just £10,500. This would, however, mean a 20% increase in the wage bill and a 50% increase in rent, as it would need to lease an adjacent building. It has also been calculated that the utility bills would probably increase by around 25%.

Questions

1. Calculate the total costs of the business, based on 1,000 units. (4 marks)
2. Identify which of these costs are fixed, variable, direct and indirect. (4 marks)
3. Recalculate the total costs for the business if it were to double production. What is the new average cost? (6 marks)
4. Is the business significantly better off or worse off when it doubles production? (2 marks)

Price, total revenue and profit

LEARNING OBJECTIVES

▶ Calculating price
▶ Calculating revenues
▶ Calculating profits
▶ The relationship between costs, price, revenue and profits

Calculating price

Setting an initial price for a business's products or services is, perhaps, one of the most difficult tasks. It needs to take account of the costs that are incurred by the business, fixed and variable, direct and indirect. Beyond this it also needs to consider the prices charged by key competitors, as the optimum price that a business wishes to charge may not be possible if competitors are charging considerably lower prices.

Pricing policy differs from business to business and from sector to sector. Effectively, the more competitive the market in which the business operates, the tighter the pricing policies have to be in order to continue to compete and attract customers. If, for example, a key competitor were regularly offering a similar product for £10, then a business could not confidently expect to sell exactly the same product for £15. Customers would simply not buy from the higher-priced supplier unless there was a compelling reason to do so.

It is difficult for a new business to set prices, because its products and services may not be well known. Its costs may be comparatively high because it will not have the advantages of producing products or providing services on a large scale. Equally it cannot charge high prices because neither the company nor its products and services are established in the market.

Calculating revenues

The process of calculating revenue is a relatively simple task. Sales revenue or income is equal to the total number of products or services sold, multiplied by the average selling price. In other words, all a business needs to know is how many of its products or services have been sold, or might sell, and the price they will sell at. The formula is:

> sales revenue = volume of goods sold × average selling price

To increase revenue, a business either has to sell more products and services or increase the average selling price.

FOR EXAMPLE

A supermarket in a highly competitive market relies on selling a high volume of goods at a relatively low price in order to achieve high sales revenue. A pharmaceutical company that has spent an enormous amount on developing new products, will sell a relatively low volume of goods at a very high price in order to achieve high sales revenue.

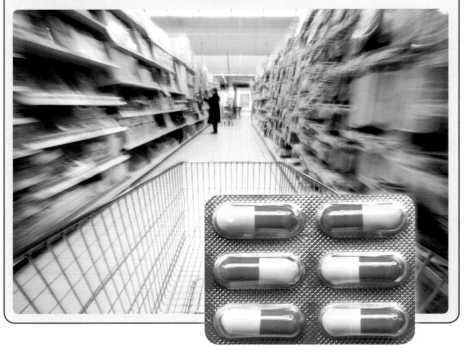

Calculating profits

We have already seen that a business incurs costs that must be paid, regardless of its level of output, as well as additional costs directly related to output. Clearly these have a direct impact on the profitability of the business.

Profit compares revenue and costs and is calculated using a simple formula:

> profit = total revenue – total costs

There are, however, different types of profit, but the most important is the profit achieved by the business after it has paid tax, since this is the amount of profit that it can choose to either pay out to shareholders or reinvest in the business.

Profits are a key measure of the success of a business. Profit means that the business can attract additional funds to invest in assets. It may also attract new shareholders. Although many businesses do borrow money, profit is the source of more than 60% of all of the finance used to help businesses grow.

Gross profit is only one calculation of profit and simply shows how much it costs a business to generate a certain amount of revenue. Businesses will also calculate their operating profit. The operating profit is the business's gross profit minus its overheads, which are all the other fixed costs that may not be directly associated with either output or the cost of achieving sales. This can often be seen as a far more accurate measure of the profitability of a business.

A business may also calculate its pre-tax profits, as it may have one-off costs, such as the restructuring of the organisation or the refurbishment of a building. These costs are deducted from the operating profit to give the pre-tax profit.

The business will then pay Corporation Tax on the remainder of its profit. It is this level of profit that is available for distribution to shareholders or earmarked for reinvestment.

The relationship between costs, price, revenue and profit

We can already see that there is a direct relationship between costs and profit. Costs cut into the revenue generated by the business and reduce its overall profitability. Adjustments can be made to the revenue generated by a business by either increasing the price of products or services sold, or by increasing production while not increasing costs by the same amount. In both cases a business would make more profit, but if costs incurred by increasing output were equal to the revenue generated, then no more profit would be made.

Businesses look for means by which they can gradually increase profit and at least sustain that level of profitability. Often the danger for small businesses is that they create an increase in profitability and then incur additional costs in order to maintain that level of profitability.

KEY TERM

Gross profit – the money that has been earned by a business, minus the costs of achieving the sales. It only includes direct costs, such as wages, raw materials and components.

FOR EXAMPLE

A business calculates that its total revenue is £128,000 and its total costs are £102,000. This means that its gross profit is £26,000.

Questions

1. A business sells 400 units of product A for £4.25 and 325 units of product B for £3.55. What is its total revenue? (4 marks)
2. In the next month the business decides that it can afford to cut its prices by 10%. This stimulates increased sales of 20%. What is the new total revenue? (6 marks)
3. Based on production of 400 units of product A and 325 units of product B, product A costs £1.56 to make and product B costs £1.24. What is the total variable cost? (6 marks)

Case studies, questions and exam practice

CASE STUDY EBBSFLEET UNITED

In May 1997, the football club transferred to the Ryman Premier Division in an effort to cut travelling distances and reduce costs. After a few seasons in mid-table, they came from nowhere under manager Andy Ford to land the Ryman League Championship in 2001–02, following a nervous and titanic struggle with Canvey Island, which saw the two meet at Stonebridge Road in April 2002 in front of an official 4,068 (but probably more like 6,000) fans.

Back in the top-flight of non-league football, The Fleet has been transformed into a fully professional club. After a few narrow brushes with relegation, manager Liam Daish's side finished in seventh place in 2006-07, its fourth consecutive Conference season. And in May 2007, 61 years after the formation of Gravesend & Northfleet, the club announced a change of name to Ebbsfleet United to take advantage of the massive regeneration of its locality.

MATCHDAY PRICES : TERRACE

Adult: £13
Concessions: £7 (senior citizens and Under 16s)
Students: £7 (on production of valid student card)

Average attendance is 993 and, excluding cup ties, the team plays 23 home fixtures each season.

Questions

1 How would you work out the average price charged to supporters for each game and what is it? (3 marks)

2 What is the club's revenue per home game and over the season? (6 marks)

3 The club also produces a programme for each home game. The cost of advertising in it for a full season is:

- Full page £1,100
- Half page £750
- Quarter page £450
- Eighth of a page £250

Assuming that the programme has 22 pages of available advertising, what is the revenue per season if all pages were taken as either full-page or half-page advertisements? (6 marks)

SHORT-ANSWER QUESTIONS

1 Distinguish between capital and revenue expenditure.

2 Give THREE examples of fixed costs.

3 What is the relationship between variable costs and output?

4 Distinguish between direct and indirect costs.

5 Give TWO ways in which a business can increase its sales revenue.

6 Why might it be difficult for a new business to establish an effective pricing policy?

7 Distinguish between gross profit and operating profit.

8 Why is profit important as a measurement of success?

9 If profit is the source of more than 60% of finance used to help businesses grow, where does the remaining 40% come from?

10 Outline the key relationships between costs, price, total revenue and profit.

CASE STUDY JACK'S FENCING

Jack has been running his small fencing business for just two years. He produces a range of natural willow fence panels and hardwood posts from sustainable forests. Jack started off by producing his fence panels from his own garden shed but has recently moved into a small industrial unit and taken on two members of staff. The table on the right outlines his annual production costs.

The average cost per unit sold, based on an output of 500 units, is £60. Jack sells each unit for £83.50.

Output	Fixed costs (£)	Variable costs (£)	Total costs (£)
0	15,000	0	15,000
500	15,000	15,000	30,000
1000	15,000	28,000	43,000
2000	15,000	52,000	67,000
3000	15,000	74,000	89,000
4000	20,000	93,000	113,000

Questions

1 Calculate the average cost per unit at the remaining four levels of output. (4 marks)
2 What would be Jack's total profit at the five different levels of output? (4 marks)
3 Why might his fixed costs increase by £5,000 if he reaches an output of 4,000 units? (2 marks)

Contribution and contribution per unit

What is contribution?

Contribution is essentially the difference between the sales revenue generated by a business and the business's variable costs. In other words it is the difference between the income that has been generated from the sales and the variable costs of producing the products in order to generate those sales.

Contribution pays for the business's **fixed overheads**. After the fixed overheads have been paid for then the remaining contribution generates profit for the business. Although contribution is important, it becomes increasingly difficult to calculate when businesses produce a wide variety of different products.

INTERNET RESEARCH 🔍

There are useful pages on break-even, contribution, costs and revenue on the www.smallbiz.uk.com website. Look under 'Help and Advice' and select 'Business Basics'.

Contribution per unit

If a business buys products from the wholesalers for £5.50 each and sells them for £8.00 each, then each product sold has made a contribution of £2.50. The £2.50, however, is not profit. The contribution first has to take care of the business's overheads. Once the business has generated enough £2.50 contributions to cover the overheads then any subsequent contributions are profit.

The contribution per unit can be modified by looking at the:

- Variable costs – whether these can be reduced by finding cheaper suppliers, reducing wastage or streamlining the production process.
- Selling price – whether this can be increased and is significantly higher than the variable costs.

The higher the contribution per unit, the quicker the business will cover its overheads and move into profit. Unfortunately it may not always be as straightforward as this.

FOR EXAMPLE

If the business were to increase the price it charges customers from £8.00 to £8.50, this would represent around a 6% price rise, with the contribution per unit rising from £2.50 to £3.00. This is a 20% increase in contribution. However, the 6% price rise might cause demand to fall, but the business would still be better off, providing demand does not drop by more than 20%.

Contribution, profit and pricing

Having established contribution per unit, total contribution is simply the number of units sold multiplied by the contribution per unit. In other words, 10 products with a £2.50 contribution per unit would give a total contribution of £25.00.

It is important to remember that variable costs, fixed costs and profit are very closely linked:

- Fixed costs – these do not vary and remain relatively unchanged. The lower the fixed costs, the quicker the contribution will cover them and move the business into profit.
- Variable costs – these are costs related directly to making or obtaining the product or service itself. Variable costs will fluctuate in proportion to **output**.
- Profit – this is generated when the sales revenue exceeds the business's total costs (fixed and variable costs).

Contribution and break-even

As long as the sales revenue from a product exceeds its variable cost, the product will be making a positive contribution. Contribution should rise as output increases, first exceeding the business's fixed overheads and then putting the business into profit.

The **break-even point** is achieved when the contributions made by each product have produced enough funds to cover the fixed costs. The break-even point can therefore be calculated using the following formula:

$$\frac{\text{fixed costs}}{\text{contribution (per unit)}} = \text{break-even point}$$

FOR EXAMPLE

Norglen Foods produces ready meals for supermarkets.

Annual production	200,000 units	
Total sales revenue (SR)	£350,000	
Total variable costs (VC)	£122,000	
Fixed costs (FC)	£104,000	
Total contribution	= £350,000 (SR) – £122,000 (VC)	= £228,000
Profit	= £228,000 (Con) – £104,000 (FC)	= £124,000

By looking at contribution, a business is able to identify whether each of the products it produces covers its own variable costs. This will then allow the business to set its prices in relation to the direct costs of production, rather than a random or inflated figure that includes fixed costs.

If a product is making a contribution per unit, it is still helping towards the business's fixed costs. It may be that a large number of units of a particular product are sold with a low contribution per unit, but collectively they contribute a high proportion of the fixed costs. Conversely, a handful of products with a high contribution per unit may make the same proportion of the fixed costs.

FOR EXAMPLE

A business has fixed costs of £120,000. Contribution per unit is £1.50.

$$\frac{£120,000}{£1.50} = 80,000 \text{ units}$$

The business would, therefore, break even once 80,000 units have been produced and sold.

CASE STUDY NORGLEN FOODS

CONTRIBUTION OF PRODUCT LINES

Each readymade meal is sold to suppliers at £1 per unit.

	Indian	Chinese	Thai	Greek	Total
Revenue	£90,000	£120,000	£70,000	£70,000	£350,000
Ingredients	£15,000	£25,000	£10,000	£10,000	£60,000
Other variable costs	£15,000	£25,000	£12,000	£10,000	£62,000
Contribution	£60,000	£70,000	£48,000	£50,000	£228,000
Fixed overheads					£104,000
Profit					£124,000

Questions

1. What is the contribution per unit for each of the four product lines? (8 marks)
2. What is the average contribution per unit across the four product lines? (2 marks)
3. Which product line produces the best and worst contribution per unit? (2 marks)

Break-even output and break-even charts

Break-even chart

A break-even chart can produce almost exactly the same information as the break-even formula, but it can reveal more. In fact it can show a business's revenues and costs at all levels of demand and output.

The three elements required are the costs, revenues and output levels. First, a suitably scaled graph is created. The main piece of information required is the total fixed costs of the business. This will always appear as a horizontal line, parallel to the X-axis. Note that these fixed costs remain the same, regardless of the level of output.

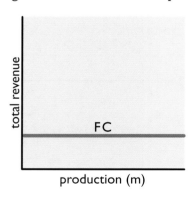

The second item to add is the variable costs. These, as seen, are in direct relation to the level of output. The variable costs, when no units of production are being created, will be zero. They will then continue upwards, again in a straight line, reflecting additional costs as the output of the business increases.

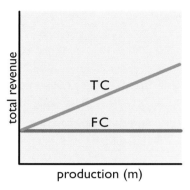

The third element to add is the total costs. Note that the total costs will include both the fixed and the variable costs, so it will be a diagonal line, just like the variable costs. The major difference is that the total costs will begin at the zero point on the units of production axis, but rise from the fixed cost line on the cost side of the graph. It should run parallel to the variable cost line.

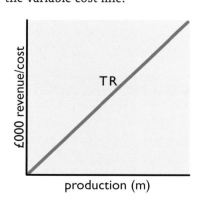

The final line to add is the total revenue. This line will begin at zero on both axes of the graph. The total revenue line will rise as the units of production increase. If we know the sale price of each unit, then we can calculate the total revenue generated by selling 100, 1,000 or 10,000 units. This will produce another straight line.

Where the total revenue line crosses the total cost line, this is the break-even point.

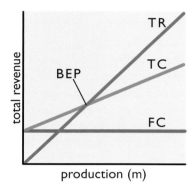

Break-even point

Let's work through an example to illustrate how the break-even point is identified.

A business has fixed costs of £5,000. The business has worked out that its total variable costs per unit produced are £5. If the business did not produce any units at all its total variable costs would be 0. If it produced 10,000 units then its variable costs would be £50,000. On the break-even chart it is possible now to place the fixed cost line at £5,000. A little calculation is required to arrive at the correct position for the variable costs line and help us work out the total costs, as can be seen in the following table:

Quantity of products produced	Fixed costs (FC)	Variable costs (VC) @ £5 per unit	Total costs (TC) – FC + VC
0	£5,000	0	£5,000
1,000	£5,000	£5,000	£10,000
5,000	£5,000	£25,000	£30,000
10,000	£5,000	£50,000	£55,000

In order to complete our calculations we now need to know how much the business sells its products for. We will set the price at £6.50. Using the same range of output figures as above we will then have the following:

Output	Total revenue
0	0
1,000	£6,500
5,000	£32,500
10,000	£65,000

It is now possible to plot all the figures on the graph. As we have seen, where the total revenue line crosses the total cost line the break-even point has been achieved.

Area of profit and area of loss

The area of profit is any level of output beyond the break-even point and between the total revenue line and the total cost line. The business can see what level of output achieves the best total revenue.

Similarly, the area of loss is below the break-even point and between the total revenue line and the total cost line. This will illustrate to the business that by having a limited output it will not achieve break-even.

Margin of safety

The business can now calculate its current margin of safety. The margin

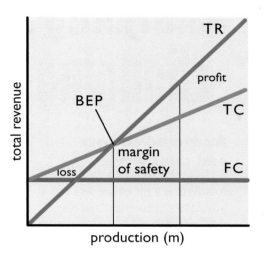

of safety represents the total current output and total revenue. In other words, it shows the current level of output at a point on the total revenue line. The difference between this point and the break-even point is the margin of safety. This means that the bigger the gap between current sales and the break-even point, the greater the margin of safety. A business needs to be aware of its margin of safety as it indicates the amount by which demand for its products or services can fall before it starts making a loss.

CASE STUDY CUSTOM PHONE COVERS LTD

The business sells fashionable and up-to-date covers for mobile phones around Europe. The phone covers are handmade and are sold to retailers at £12 each. They cost £4 to manufacture and the independent sales teams are paid 50p commission per item sold to retailers.

Distribution costs per unit are also 50p. The factory unit's fixed costs are £4,000 per month.

Questions

1 What is the variable cost of producing 1,000 mobile phone covers? (3 marks)
2 What is the contribution earned for each mobile phone cover? (3 marks)
3 Construct a break-even chart that shows the monthly level of output necessary for the business to break even and the margin of safety, assuming that the business produces 200 more units per month than is necessary to break even. (10 marks)

Analysing the effects of changing variables

LEARNING
OBJECTIVES

▶ Budgeted activity and sales
levels
▶ Numerical calculations
▶ Changing overheads
▶ Direct costs
▶ Target profit levels of activity

Budgeted activity and sales levels

A budget is a plan that sets out a business's future financial targets – in this case its level of production or activity and its sales levels. Budgets are for a defined period of time, designed to provide a focus for the business so that it can improve its control. They are agreed levels of activity or sales, not to be confused with forecasts, which are predictions of the future.

Budgeted activity levels seek to place actual output and the resulting sales further away from the break-even point, giving the business a greater margin of safety. As you can imagine, an actual change in the unit price charged by the business would have a marked effect on the total revenue. It would, therefore, also have a marked effect on the break-even point. On a graph, the total revenue line would be steeper, as more revenue is generated per unit. This means that the total revenue line would cross the total costs line at a lower level of output. Conversely, a drop in the price per unit would make the total revenue line shallower and it would cross the total cost line further along in terms of output.

What a budget seeks to do is to identify the best course of action in terms of production and sales, where for similar effort the business can cover its total costs more easily, either by increasing the sales price or by dropping the price and selling significantly more units.

Numerical calculations

Unfortunately just making the decision either to drop or raise prices is not the answer. It will depend on the demand for the product at either a lower or a higher price.

Some products are known as 'elastic'. These products are said to have price elasticity of demand. Elasticity is a measure of how much demand will change when price changes. It is not about whether demand changes or not, but the degree of change.

If a business were to cut its prices then would demand rise by 5%, 10% or 100%? Price elasticity of demand measures the responsiveness of customers' demand to a change in the price. Some products are very sensitive to price changes.

Price elasticity can be calculated using the following formula:

A business could find the net effect of price changes by experimentation. It could also try to judge the potential changes in demand if one of its competitors were to change the price of its products. If, for example, a business increased its prices by 10%, it might see a 20% fall. Using the formula, simply divide 20 by 10 to give a figure of 2. This is actually −2 expressed as a percentage, and indicates that for every 1% change in price, demand is likely to change by 2%.

Note that all these figures are negative. There is a negative relationship between price and quantity demanded. This suggests that a drop in price will boost sales and a price rise will reduce sales. There are exceptions to this, and some products rarely change in terms of demand: these are either extremely luxurious goods or absolute basics.

$$\text{price elasticity} = \frac{\text{the percentage change in quantity demand}}{\text{the percentage change in price}}$$

Changing overheads

When the costs of overheads change, this will obviously have an effect on a number of parts of a break-even chart, including:

- Movement of the fixed cost line, as either the overheads have increased (in which case the line will move up), or they have fallen (in which case it will drop).
- A change in the total cost line. If the overheads have increased, this line will be steeper, and if the overheads have dropped then it will run at a less steep angle.
- The net result of this is that the total revenue line will cross the total cost line at a different point, changing the break-even point.
- The area of profit and the area of loss will change, as will the margin of safety.

Direct costs

A similar effect will be apparent if direct costs change. Changes in the direct costs will not affect the fixed cost line but will affect the variable cost line and, therefore, the total cost line. Once again the total revenue line will cross the total cost line at a different point, with the same net effects as mentioned when we looked at changing overheads.

Target profit levels of activity

Having created a break-even chart and calculated the break-even point, the business now knows precisely how many units to produce, and at what price products need to be made and sold in order to cover their total costs. The area beyond the break-even point, where the total revenue line begins to move away from the total cost line is, as we have seen, the area of profit. A business will not be content with merely being in that area beyond the break-even point, but will want to extend the total revenue so that it exceeds the total costs by the greatest margin.

Of course in order to do this one or more of three things needs to take place. The options are:

- Reducing the fixed costs so that the total costs can be brought down
- Reducing the variable costs associated with each level of output, again bringing the total costs line down
- Increasing the price of each product sold, which will mean that fewer units have to be sold before the total cost line is crossed at the break-even point.

Questions

1 A business increases its price per unit from £5 to £6. At £5, sales were 6,000 units, and at £6, they are 5,500 units. Explain how the price change has affected demand. (6 marks)
2 If there is a 40% rise in the rent paid by a business for its factory unit, what will happen to the fixed cost line on the break-even chart? (4 marks)

Strengths and weaknesses of break-even analysis

LEARNING OBJECTIVES

▶ Limitations and assumptions
▶ Sales levels being identical to production levels
▶ Consistency of selling price
▶ Contribution and overheads behaviour
▶ External factors

Limitations and assumptions

The main limitations imposed by the business itself are its level of activity and its ability to change costs and price. Break-even analysis itself has its own limitations and sets of assumptions. It is important to remember that break-even analysis is a basic measurement of the relationship between output, revenue and costs. It cannot be the entire answer to controlling costs, setting prices or determining output levels.

Sales levels being identical to production levels

It is rare that sales levels are equal to production levels. There is always a mismatch between the two figures: either sales will exceed production capability, in which case the products will be short on supply but still highly in demand, or production levels exceed actual sales, in which case the business will have to store the additional products until they can be sold, having incurred the costs of producing them.

Break-even analysis is a crude tool for looking at the relationship between sales and production levels. Consequently, not being able to rely on selling everything that is made, leads us to believe that the break-even point is an artificial creation. The reverse of this is when production levels cannot be stepped up to the point of demand. This leaves the business losing some of its potential total revenue while still shouldering its fixed costs, despite the demand.

Consistency of selling price

The selling price that can be achieved for a product will fluctuate throughout its life. In fact the vast majority of products follow this pattern. This suggests that in order to cope with the different stages of a product's life, prices may have to differ along the path. If a product is being introduced to a crowded market with plenty of competitors, a business may have only one choice: to offer its products at a low price. This should stimulate demand and sales. The business will have to recognise that it cannot achieve its ideal profit margin while the product is being established.

As demand increases, the price can be raised. This will bring a larger profit per unit, until the point at which price reaches an unacceptable level and adversely affects demand. For a time, the price of the product may be stable, if it has a fairly regular demand and a fairly loyal set of customers. When demand drops again, the business can either retain the price, or drop it in the hope that demand will be stimulated. Eventually most products will come to the end of their useful sales life and the business will discount the selling price in order to sell off the remaining stock. None of this can be incorporated into a single break-even chart. The break-even chart makes all its assumptions based on consistency of selling price.

Contribution and overheads behaviour

The contribution required from particular products may fluctuate over a period of time. If the product becomes easier or quicker to process then there may be lower associated costs. This means that the contribution per unit can fall. A business in the first year of producing a particular product manages to process 500 units in a year and the necessary contribution is £2 a unit to net £1,000 of contribution. This could all change if production is increased: if the business managed to double production then, assuming that all other costs remain equal, the contribution per unit would be down to £1. This would have a marked effect on the profitability of every unit sold.

As far as overheads are concerned, we know that they are classed as fixed costs, payable regardless of output. Overheads, however, can change: an increase in factory floor space would probably attract more rent and a higher business rate. If a business were to move to smaller premises, the rent might be lower, but the business rate charged might also be lower. By allowing overheads to run out of control, a business is placing an enormous strain on each product made in terms of contribution.

External factors

Inflation means that working out total sales revenue in the future is notoriously difficult. There will be price changes due to suppliers passing on inflationary increases in their costs to the business. The business cannot usually absorb these costs without passing them on to its own customers. Inflation will affect the costs of the business first. Fixed costs may be higher because wages and salaries may have to be increased so that they are not adversely affected by the inflation. Variable costs will also increase because suppliers are passing on their additional costs, making raw materials and components more expensive. The net result is that the total cost line is pushed up, moving the break-even point. Assuming that the extra costs have not been passed on, the business will have to sell far more products in order to reach its new break-even point.

The inflation can be offset if the business does pass on its extra costs. This can be simply achieved by increasing the prices charged to customers. In theory this should stabilise the break-even point, but what cannot always be predicted is to what extent a price increase will adversely affect demand.

Interest rates affect the cost of borrowing, and can therefore have one of two impacts on a business. These are:

- A drop in interest rates, which will make it easier for the business to cope with its own debts, and should encourage customers to purchase more products, because borrowing money is cheaper.
- A rise in interest rates, which will make it more expensive for a business to service its own debts. This actually adds to the costs of the business. At the same time, total revenue may be driven down because demand will have been affected by the interest rate rise.

Neither of these factors is accommodated by break-even analysis.

Questions

1 Why might it be rare for sales levels to equal production levels, and what are the implications for break-even charts? (6 marks)
2 If a business chooses to cut the required contribution per unit of a product from £2 to £1, what options might the business have for this £1 of necessary contribution? (4 marks)

Case studies, questions and exam practice

CASE STUDY SANDRA'S SANDWICHES AND WRAPS

Sandra's Sandwiches and Wraps prepares and delivers sandwiches and wraps to local businesses using its own van distribution, and fulfilling regular orders, as well as one-off sales.

	Product line			
	Standard sandwich	Deluxe sandwich	Standard wrap	Deluxe wrap
Selling price per unit	£2	£3	£2.50	£3.50
Variable costs – labour	40p	45p	40p	40p
Variable costs – materials	20p	55p	30p	50p
Sales (number of units sold)	9,000	12,000	6,000	4,000

The business's fixed costs are £22,000.

Questions

1. What is the sales revenue and the total sales revenue for each product line? (5 marks)
2. What is the contribution per product line? (4 marks)
3. What is the total contribution of the product lines? (1 mark)
4. What is the level of profit or loss for the business? (2 marks)

SHORT-ANSWER QUESTIONS

1 Explain what is meant by contribution per unit.

2 Briefly outline the relationship between fixed and variable costs and profit.

3 How can establishing contribution per unit help a business with its pricing policy?

4 What is a break-even point?

5 Distinguish between areas of profit and loss on a break-even chart.

6 What is a margin of safety?

7 What is meant by price elasticity of demand?

8 What is an overhead?

9 Briefly explain how external factors can affect information contained on a break-even chart.

10 What are the effects on a break-even chart of a product's selling price remaining consistent?

CASE STUDY THERMOPLASTIC SHEETING LTD

The factory has a maximum capacity of 10,000 units. It has fixed costs of £12,000. The selling price per unit is £8 and the variable cost per unit is £4.

Questions

1 Draw a break-even chart showing the business position. (9 marks)

2 Indicate on the graph and state in words the profit or loss when 8,000 sales have been made. (4 marks)

3 Indicate on the graph and state in words the safety margin at that level of output. (4 marks)

The nature of cash flow

▶ What is a cash-flow forecast?
▶ Importance of cash-flow management
▶ What a cash-flow forecast shows

What is a cash-flow forecast?

Cash is a business's most **tangible asset**. Cash-flow forecasts and statements show the flows of cash both into and out of a business. The forecasts actually attempt to predict the flows, so that the business can identify when there might be a shortfall in cash (which may mean borrowing), or excess cash (which can then be invested).

A cash-flow statement is used as a monitoring tool and contains the actual figures as they happen, so that they can be compared to the cash-flow forecast.

KEY TERM

Tangible asset – an asset owned by a business that can easily be turned into cash in order to cover expenditure.

Importance of cash-flow management

Businesses need an adequate source of cash in order to pay bills as they become due. Delaying payment can be a major problem, particularly if suppliers are not paid, or employees do not receive their wages.

Cash-flow problems are one of the most common reasons for businesses to fail. In fact around 70% of businesses that fail in their first year have done so because of major cash-flow problems. It is important to remember that cash flow is not the same as profit. Profit is the difference between revenue and costs, but cash flow is the movement of money into and out of a business.

New businesses often suffer from cash-flow problems. They may buy new stock but may not have sold it until the bill for that new stock becomes due. They know that they can make a profit once the goods are sold, but have a cash-flow problem because the goods may not have yet been sold but the supplier wants their money.

Businesses can survive without making a profit, providing they generate enough money to cover their expenditure. However, in the long term, profit is absolutely essential.

Cash-flow forecasts can help in the following ways:

- The business can identify when a cash-flow shortage might occur and the likely extent of it
- It can arrange covering finance in advance
- It can attempt to manipulate income and expenditure in order to cover probable shortfalls

What a cash-flow forecast shows

A cash-flow forecast will, therefore, show the anticipated inflows and outflows of cash over the coming months. It outlines the money that is coming into the business and the money that is flowing out of it.

If a business's income in a given month is greater than its expenditure, then a positive cash flow will be shown. If expenditure is greater than income, a negative cash flow will be indicated. Usually a business will use an overdraft facility to deal with this, or if it appears to be a longer-term problem it may take out a loan.

The cash-flow forecast lists:

- The cash inflows (the actual money coming in from sales and other sources)
- The cash outflows (money being used to pay for bills and other expenses)
- The effect on net cash flow on the cash balance that the business holds

The closing balance on a cash flow becomes the opening balance for the next month. On a cash flow you will see figures in brackets, which represent minus figures.

A business will be able to judge how accurate its cash-flow forecasts are by comparing them with their actual cash-flow statements. This will reveal how good a prediction the business has made of the probable inflows and outflows of cash over a given period of time. Usually a business will create a cash-flow forecast covering the next six to twelve months. It will continue this process by making a projection and extending the cash-flow forecast, but as it receives more information from cash-flow statements the predictions should gradually become more accurate.

INTERNET RESEARCH

In the 'financial planning' section of the Business Link website at www.businesslink.gov.uk there is a useful series of pages on cash flow, as well as links to sample cash-flow spreadsheets and guidance from the Chartered Institute of Management Accountants.

CASE STUDY THREE STORES

CRD Ltd has three separate retail stores. In January the Birmingham store had sales of £25,000 and spent £15,000 on stock. It had an opening bank balance of £5,000. The Norwich store managed sales of £45,000, made payments of £29,000 and had an opening bank balance of £7,000. The Dorchester store had sales figures of £82,000, total payments of £74,000 and was £7,000 overdrawn at the bank.

In February, Birmingham sales were the same as January's but its total payments had risen to £18,000. Norwich had improved its sales by £12,000 but its total payments were £3,000 more than in January. Dorchester's store had increased sales by 20% but its total payments had doubled.

Questions

1 Using the format on the right, calculate the bank balances at the end of January and February for each of the three stores. (10 marks)

2 Calculate the total closing bank balance of all three stores at the end of February. (3 marks)

	January (£)	February (£)
Total receipts for the month		
Total payments for the month		
Cash flow for the month		
Opening bank balance		
Closing bank balance		

How to forecast cash flow

LEARNING
OBJECTIVES
▶ Cash inflows and cash outflows
▶ Elements of cash-flow forecasting

Cash inflows and cash outflows

Obviously the ideal situation is for a business to have more money flowing in than flowing out. If this is happening, the business will be able to build up a cash balance, which it can use to deal with any future shortfalls in cash. It could also use the cash balance to expand, or to set aside to pay off loans or make payments to investors.

For most businesses the problem is that cash inflows often lag behind cash outflows. Therefore the trick is to be able to speed up the inflows and slow down the outflows. If the business becomes short of cash it may become **illiquid** and it may have difficulties in remaining **solvent**. A cash-flow forecast, therefore, tries to estimate the expected inflows and outflows so that when a business is short of cash it can find some from

elsewhere, and if it has too much cash it can try to invest it.

The following table outlines typical cash inflows and outflows:

Cash inflows	Cash outflows
Payments received for products and services from customers	Purchases of stock, machinery, raw materials or fixed assets
Receipt of a bank loan	Payment of rent, wages and other operating expenses
Interest received on investments or savings	Payment of tax and VAT
Investments made by shareholders	**Dividend** payments to shareholders
Increased loans or bank overdrafts	Repayments of loans or reduced overdraft facilities

Some payments, such as wages, loan repayments and tax, have to be made on fixed dates. The difficulty is that the business may not be able to accurately predict exactly when it will receive payments from customers. It is important to remember that on the cash-flow forecast the actual payment date is relevant, not when the customer is invoiced or even when the customer is expected to have to pay.

Elements of cash-flow forecasting

The fluctuations of a business's cash balance can be predicted in a cash-flow forecast. Banks, for example, will usually require a forecast before they grant the business a loan. The forecast itself shows the sources and the amounts of cash that are coming into the business, as well as the amounts and destinations of cash going out of the business.

Normally a cash-flow forecast

will have two columns: one that lists the forecast and one that gives the actual amount. The business will normally forecast over a year, or perhaps three to six months. The forecast will list:

- Receipts of cash
- Payments of cash
- The balance between receipts and payments, with the negative figure shown in brackets
- The opening bank balance for the month
- The closing bank balance for the month

Sales forecasts, in particular, need to be realistic, and usually a business will look at sales revenue for a similar period and then predict a certain percentage of growth in the future. Forecasts often need adjustment to take into account changes in performance and the speed at which invoices are paid.

The top half of the cash-flow statement is either existing cash

KEY TERMS

Illiquid – assets that cannot be very quickly converted into cash.

Solvent – able to pay debts with available cash.

Dividend – payment made by a business to a shareholder.

CASHFLOW FORECAST

	START-UP F/CAST	START-UP ACTUAL	1 F/CAST	1 ACTUAL	2 F/CAST	2 ACTUAL	3 F/CAST	3 ACTUAL
Opening balance	0	0	1170	535	1750	1170	2360	1295
CASH/CHEQUES RECEIVED								
Received from cash sales	800	900	1000	1200	1000	900	1000	1200
Received from debtors	100	50	300	300	300	400	400	400
Other income								
Capital and/or loans introduced	3500	3500						
TOTAL £	4400	4450	1300	1500	1300	1300	1400	1600
EXPENDITURE								
Materials/stock/subcontractors		120		160		120		
Wages	25	25	25	25	25	25	25	25
Directors remuneration (Ltd Co.)								
Salaries – administration								
Rent and rates		180						
Heating and lighting						100		
Insurances	20	20	20	20	20	20	20	20
Postage and stationery								
Repairs and renewals	15		15		15	90	15	
Travelling and motor expenses								
Telephone	40	40	30	30		115		
Professional fees								
Advertising		200				75		
Miscellaneous expenses								
Finance charges – bank								
Finance charges – HP								
Interest								
Other payments								
VAT								
Taxation								
Personal drawings	600	600	600	600	600	600	600	600
Class 2 National Insurance	30	30	30	30	30	30	30	30
Capital expenditure	2500	2700						
TOTAL £	3230	3915	720	865	690	1175	690	675
Income less expenditure (A–B) i.e. Monthly working capital	1170	535	580	635	610	125	710	925
Cumulative working capital i.e. Closing balance	1170	535	1750	1170	2360	1295	3070	2220

held by the business, or income from trading for the period. This is totalled before turning to the expenses of the business. Each of the specific costs is detailed for each period and then these are totalled. The figure is deducted from the income or cash held by the business to produce a balance.

When the calculation has been made for each period, the balance is carried forward as the opening balance for the next period. The process is continued until the whole period in question has been looked at.

Ultimately a cash-flow forecast shows the business cycle. Income and expenditure are rarely timed to match one another. Often inflows of cash will lag behind outflows. Ideally, at some point, there should be an occasion when there is more money coming in than going out. By creating a cash-flow forecast the business can begin to try to address these imbalances.

Questions

1 What are the FIVE main elements of a cash-flow forecast? (5 marks)
2 List THREE typical cash inflows and THREE typical cash outflows. (6 marks)
3 Identify an external organisation that would insist on seeing a business's cash-flow forecast. (2 marks)

The structure of a cash-flow forecast

LEARNING OBJECTIVES

▶ Cash-flow forecasts and cash-flow statements
▶ Entering data on a cash-flow projection

Cash-flow forecasts and cash-flow statements

The cash-flow forecast is often referred to as the cash budget. It is usually set out with a column for each month, with three distinct sets of figures:

- The receipts – a totalled list of items that have been paid into the bank account, including sales, grants and loans.
- Payments – a totalled list of payments made out of the bank account, including wages, materials, stock and other expenses.
- The cash flow for the month and the bank balance at the beginning and end of each month.

Essentially cash flow is equal to the total monthly receipts minus the total monthly payments. The closing bank balance is equal to the cash flow for the month plus the opening bank balance.

A computer spreadsheet can be used to set out cash-flow forecasts. It can carry out the complex calculations automatically and can be used to create 'what if' scenarios.

KEY TERM

'What if' scenarios – cash-flow forecasts that investigate the net effect of different factors on the cash flow, such as improved or declining sales.

Some spreadsheets have a slightly different format at the bottom section of the cash flow. Instead of simply adding the cash flow for the month to the bank balance, it takes up four rows of cells on a spreadsheet instead of two. It therefore has:

- The opening bank balance
- Plus total receipts
- Minus total payments
- Equals closing bank balance

In effect this does give exactly the same set of figures.

As we have seen, there is a difference between a cash-flow forecast and a cash-flow statement. Many businesses, however, roll the two together and produce a single spreadsheet, with a forecast column and an actual column for each month. In this way, as the actual figures become available, they can be put into the spreadsheet for immediate analysis and comparison. If the cash-flow spreadsheet simply has forecast figures then it is a cash-flow forecast. Once it has actual figures on it, it assumes the role of a cash-flow statement, with real figures.

All calculations can be carried out automatically on an Excel spreadsheet with the insertion of formulae at the end of each section. All receipts and all payments can be totalled, and other calculations can be made by subtracting one cell figure from another.

Entering data on a cash-flow projection

All forecast figures relate to totals that are due to be collected or due to be paid out, not to invoices that have been sent out or received. A business will routinely adjust its forecast in line with changes.

The illustration opposite shows the structure of a cash-flow forecast, or projection, along with the necessary information that needs to be assembled in order to complete the task.

In effect the cash-flow forecast and the cash-flow statement will look exactly the same, the only difference being that the former has predicted figures and the latter has actual figures.

Cash-flow forecasts are only as good as the estimates and predictions that they are based on. Businesses will usually build in safety margins, which take into account factors such as sales being lower than they would have hoped; difficulties in getting some monies from customers; or stock being more expensive than expected.

Whenever cash-flow forecasts are considered, the following needs to be borne in mind:

- How valid are the figures and who actually constructed the forecast?
- What do the figures actually show?
- What solutions are there to possible problems?
- That there is a difference between cash flow and profitability

As we will see when we look at budgets, various different cash-flow forecasts or budgets are created by a business. See Reasons for setting budgets and problems in setting budgets on pp. 133–3, and Benefits and drawbacks of using budgets on pp. 158–9.

For how businesses deal with variances between forecast and actual figures, see Calculation and interpretation of favourable and adverse variances on pp. 160–1.

MONTHLY CASH-FLOW PROJECTION – EXPLANATION OF DATA TO ENTER

1	**CASH ON HAND**	
	[beginning of month]	Cash on hand same as (7), cash position previous month
2	**INCOME**	
a	Cash sales	All cash sales. Omit credit sales unless cash is actually received
b	Collections from credit accounts	Amount to be expected from all credit accounts
c	Loan or other cash injection	Indicate here all cash injections not shown in 2a or 2b above
3	**TOTAL CASH RECEIPTS**	
	[2a + 2b + 2c = 3]	Self-explanatory
4	**TOTAL CASH AVAILABLE**	
	[Before cash out] (1 + 3)	Self-explanatory
5	**OUTGOINGS**	
a	Purchases (merchandise)	Merchandise for resale or for use in product [paid for in current month]
b	Gross wages (excl. withdrawals)	Base pay plus overtime [if any]
c	Payroll expenses (taxes, etc.)	Include paid vacations, paid sick leave, health insurance, etc.
d	Outside services	This could include outside labour and/or materials for specialised overflow work, including subcontracting
e	Supplies (office and operating)	Items purchased for use in the business [not for resale]
f	Repairs and maintenance	Include periodic large expenditures such as painting, decorating, repair of broken equipment
g	Advertising	This amount should be adequate to maintain sales volume – include telephone book and Yellow Pages costs
h	Vehicles, delivery and travel	If personal vehicle is used, charge in this column – include parking
i	Accounting and legal	Outside services, including, for example, bookkeeping and tax return preparation
j	Rent	Property only [see 5p for other rents]
k	Telephone	Self-explanatory

l	Utilities	Water, heat, light and/or power
m	Insurance	Cover on business property and products, e.g. fire, liability; also workers' compensation, fidelity, etc. Exclude 'executive' life [include in 5w]
n	Taxes	Property taxes plus inventory tax, sales tax, excise tax, if applicable
o	Interest	Remember to add interest on loan as it is injected [see 2c above]
p	Other expenses [specify each]	Unexpected expenditures may be included here as a safety factor. Equipment expenses during the month should be included here [non-capital equipment]
q	Miscellaneous [unspecified]	Small expenditure for which separate accounts would not be practical
r	Subtotal	This subtotal indicates cash out for operating costs
s	Loan principal payment	Include payment on all loans, including vehicle and equipment purchases on time payment
t	Capital purchases [specify]	Non-expenses [depreciable] expenditures such as equipment, building, vehicle purchases, and leasehold improvements
u	Other start-up costs	Expenses incurred prior to first month projection and paid after the 'start-up' position
v	Reserve and/or Escrow [specify]	Example: insurance, tax or equipment escrow to reduce impact of large periodic payments
w	Owner's withdrawal	Should include payment for such things as owner's income tax, social security, health insurance, 'executive' life insurance premiums, etc.
6	**TOTAL CASH PAID OUT**	
	[Total 5a–5w]	Self-explanatory
7	**CASH POSITION**	
	[End of month] [4 – 6]	Enter this amount in (1) CASH ON HAND for the following month

Source: adapted from Business Link

CASE STUDY JACK'S CANINE FASHIONS

For some time Jack has been running a car boot stall, selling his own dog coat designs, which he and his sister, Sasha, manufacture in their parents' back bedroom. Demand has been relatively good and they have finally decided to set up their own business. They already have a contract with a regional chain of pet stores and sell £1,000 of dog coats to them each month. They intend to set up a permanent market stall in their local town and confidently expect sales of £1,500 per month.

Payable in March and July, they spend £3,000 on materials to make sufficient jackets for the year. In January they intend to spend £3,000 on a small van, along with £175 on road tax and insurance, estimated at £600. They expect to spend around £150 per month on petrol and maintenance for the vehicle. To begin with they will pay themselves £200 per month each. The market stall will cost £300 in rent per month. They will have £2,000 of their own money to invest immediately.

Questions

1 Create a cash-flow forecast based on the information given, covering the business's first year from January. (10 marks)
2 On the basis of the cash flow you have created, how much money do you think the business will have to borrow from the bank? (4 marks)
3 What other information do you think the bank manager might need? (4 marks)

Why businesses forecast cash flow

LEARNING
OBJECTIVES

▶ Why are cash-flow forecasts important?
▶ Profit and cash
▶ Benefits to business

Why are cash-flow forecasts important?

We have seen that many businesses fail as a result of mismanaging their cash flow. This is a particularly dangerous problem for new businesses. The flow of cash into and out of a business is all-important and it needs to be managed carefully because many problems can result from having too little cash:

- Suppliers may not be able to be paid on time – some suppliers may simply stop supplying goods, while others will demand **cash on delivery**.
- The business will lose the possibility of obtaining a discount on the prompt payment of bills. Many other businesses will simply refuse to deal with the business unless they pay in cash. In an extreme situation creditors could take the business to court in order to obtain the money that it is owed.
- The employees could be directly affected by the business not having sufficient cash: their wages or salaries will not be paid on time. Many of the better employees will leave; the business will be less efficient and the employees that do remain will have low **motivation**; there will be a higher than average **absentee rate** and a higher **labour turnover**.
- The business may also not be able to afford essential purchases, such as capital assets. This will also affect efficiency.
- Finally, tax bills may not be paid. The Revenue and Customs will pursue the business for Corporation Tax or Value Added Tax (if appropriate).

Profit and cash

One of the many mistakes that business owners and business studies students make is the assumption that a profitable business will have a surplus of cash. We have already seen that profit is not the same as cash and that a profitable business can actually run out of cash. At the same time a business that is making a loss can actually have a surplus of cash.

It may sound strange, but both sets of circumstances can occur:

- If a business is selling more of its products or services on credit than it had done in the past then it will show a healthy profit because those products and services are being recorded as sold. However, the business has not received the money, as the sale was made on credit. The period that the business has to wait for payment will leave it seriously short of cash.
- When a business makes a capital expenditure it will be shown in the **profit-and-loss account** as an expense. Only part of the additional capital spending is recorded, as **depreciation**, but the total cash payment has been made.

KEY TERMS

Cash on delivery – payment of the full invoice amount when goods or services are supplied.

Motivation – a measurement of an employee's contentment with their work, also known as job satisfaction.

Absentee rate – the number or percentage of employees not attending work due to sickness or other factors.

Labour turnover – the rate at which employees leave a business and are replaced with new employees.

Profit-and-loss account – a statement showing a business's revenue and costs over the period of a year.

Depreciation – the fall in the value of assets such as vehicles and office equipment.

Benefits to business

Cash-flow forecasts are used by businesses to head off the possibility of future liquidity problems. The information required to create a cash-flow forecast is usually taken from the budgets of a business. The cash-flow forecast will help the business anticipate any surpluses or deficits in cash. As a result, the business's bank can be warned so that arrangements can be made to cover any short-term deficit.

Providing the business has planned its financial needs, banks are usually accommodating in either extending overdrafts or offering loans. The creation of a cash-flow forecast proves to the bank that the business is aware that it needs to manage its cash flow.

There will be periods when businesses have large cash surpluses, as many businesses actually have seasonal elements to their sales. Retail outlets, for example, expect a boost in sales in the lead-up to Christmas. Tourism-related businesses will see a surge in sales over the summer; florists do well around Mother's Day and at Easter, and farmers, for example, receive the bulk of their annual income in the summer and autumn.

For more information on the causes of cash-flow problems and how to improve cash flow see pp. 166–9. For how budgets are used as a source of information for forecasts see The process of setting budgets *on pp. 136–7.*

CASE STUDY JIM MULLIGHAN

Jim Mullighan knows his antique furniture but he is not as skilful in handling his cash flow. In August he bought a table and five chairs at an auction for £110 in cash. The following day he sold each of the chairs for £40 and the table for £95. The customer paid him half in cash immediately and would pay the rest in September.

A week later, Jim bought another six chairs for £140 in total and paid in cash. He sold them to the same customer for £35 each. The customer paid the balance of the first purchase and promised to pay Jim for the six chairs in October.

Questions

1 What was the total profit made by Jim on the two deals? (4 marks)
2 How much money had Jim received by the end of September from the customer? (2 marks)
3 On average, what was the credit period Jim had extended to the customer? (2 marks)

Case studies, questions and exam practice

CASE STUDY MORE-GLENN FRANCHISES CASH FLOW

The owners have invested £100,000 in their franchise system and have also obtained a five-year loan of £150,000. If everything goes as expected, then a peak borrowing requirement of a further £199,000 will be needed. However, they have also created a worst-case scenario cash-flow forecast which reveals that their peak requirement will rise to £345,000.

The other assumptions they have made are:

- Franchisee initial fee £8,500 + VAT.
- A franchisee ongoing fee (management service fees) is 7% of turnover.
- All franchisees open at the start of each year, rather than the usual phased openings.
- Two year capital repayment holiday on five-year bank loan.
- No failures of franchisees.
- No franchisee opened in the set-up period.

Franchise sales turnover forecast:

Year	Sales turnover
1	£100k
2	£120k
3	£140k
4	£155k
5	£165k
6	£175k
7	£185k

Expected scenario	Set-up period	Year 1	Year 2	Year 3	Year 4	Year 5	Year 6	Year 7
Franchisees recruited	-	1	4	8	13	15	11	8
Total franchisees	-	1	5	13	26	41	52	60
Receipts	-	-	-	-	-	-	-	-
Franchise fees (initial)	-	£10k	£40k	£80k	£130k	£150k	£110k	£80k
Management service fees (from franchisees)	-	£7k	£36k	£99k	£208k	£348k	£476k	£591k
Owners' share capital	£100k	-	-	-	-	-	-	-
Bank loan (5-year term)	£150k	-	-	-	-	-	-	-
Total receipts (A)	£250k	£17k	£76k	£179k	£338k	£498k	£586k	£671k
Payments	-	-	-	-	-	-	-	-
Capital expenditure	£35k	-	-	-	-	-	-	-
Development expenditure	£150k	-	-	-	-	-	-	-
Franchisee recruitment costs	£3k	£20k	£24k	£39k	£45k	£33k	£24k	£24k
Loan repayments (24-month capital repayment holiday)	-	-	-	£50k	£50k	£50k	-	-
Loan interest	-	£15k	£15k	£10k	£5k	£2k	-	-
Direct costs	-	£4k	£20k	£52k	£104k	£164k	£205k	£240k
Staff costs	-	£44k	£49k	£71k	£74k	£79k	£84k	£104k
Overheads	-	£20k	£22k	£30k	£31k	£32k	£32k	£40k
ACT (Advance Corporation Tax)	-	-	-	-	-	-	-	(£20k)
VAT	-	(£26k)	£6k	£12k	£20k	£23k	£17k	£12k
Professional fees	-	£2k	£4k	£8k	£13k	£15k	£11k	£8k
Dividends	-	-	-	-	-	-	-	(£100k)
Overdraft interest	-	-	£4k	£6k	£7k	£5k	£3k	-
Total payments (B)	£188k	£131k	£144k	£278k	£349k	£403k	£376k	£548k
Net cash flow (A) – (B)	£62k	(£62k)	(£89k)	(£99k)	(£11k)	£95k	£210k	£123k
Opening balance	-	£62k	£0k	(£89k)	£188k	(£199k)	(£104k)	£106k
Bank balance credit (overdraft)	£62k	£0k	(£89k)	(£188k)	(£199k)	(£104k)	£106k	229k

Worst-case scenario	Set-up period	Year 1	Year 2	Year 3	Year 4	Year 5	Year 6	Year 7
Total receipts (C)	£250k	-	£50k	£161k	£304k	£448k	£527k	£604k
Total payments (D)	£188k	£80k	£156k	£305k	£381k	£439k	£410k	£436k
Net cash flow (C) − (D)	£62k	(£80k)	£106k)	(£144k)	(£77k)	£9k	£117k	£168k
Opening balance	-	£62k	(£18k)	(£124k)	(£268k)	(£345k)	(£336k)	(£219k)
Bank balance credit (overdraft)	£62k	(£18k)	(£124k)	(£268k)	(£345k)	(£336k)	(£219k)	(£51k)

Questions

1 Recalculate the figures, assuming that twice the number of franchisees open in the first seven years and the costs of the business remain the same. (15 marks)

2 What might be included in the professional fees? (2 marks)

3 Why would the business have created a worst-case scenario forecast? (3 marks)

SHORT-ANSWER QUESTIONS

1 Why is cash-flow management important?

2 Distinguish between a cash-flow forecast and a cash-flow statement.

3 List TWO typical cash inflows and TWO typical cash outflows.

4 On a cash-flow forecast, the opening balance of a particular month is equal to what other figure from the previous month?

5 Approximately what percentages of businesses fail as a result of cash-flow problems?

6 How can a business that appears to be highly profitable actually be short of cash?

7 How might cash shortage affect employees?

8 What is meant by the term 'labour turnover'?

9 In a cash-flow forecast what is the meaning of a figure shown in brackets?

10 How might a business use its cash surplus?

Reasons for setting budgets and problems in setting budgets

What is a budget?

A budget is an agreed pattern of income and expenditure which sets targets for revenues and costs over a given period of time in the future. Budgets are not always restricted to revenue and costs, they could include production targets, levels of profit, cash generation, investments to be made, sales targets and expenditure on marketing.

The purpose of budgeting is to:

- Define the business's goals and objectives
- Encourage analysis
- Focus on the future
- Communicate plans and instructions
- Coordinate business activities
- Provide a basis for evaluating performance against either past or expected results
- Act as a motivating tool to exceed expectations

Budgeting is simply a planning process so that the business has access to the most appropriate and accurate information. There are not any fixed time periods for a budget, but it would usually coincide with a business's financial year. It is common for businesses to split their budgets into monthly statements. Some budget on a week to four-week cycle. As we can see in the diagram below, there is a budget hierarchy in which information from various areas is brought together to create what is known as a master budget.

Only the smallest of businesses will be able to put all their financial data into one single document. It is common, therefore, for businesses

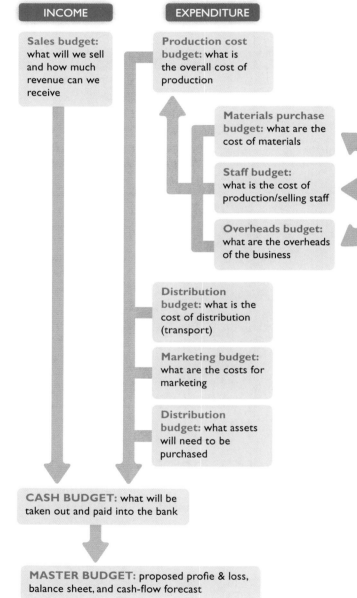

to split up their budgets into more manageable areas. The areas would typically include sales, production, purchases, debtors, creditors and cash. Once all of these budgets have been worked out then the data from them can be brought together

to compile a master budget. It is vital to remember that budgets are unique to each business and although we have mentioned all of these areas of budgets, it is not necessarily the case that all businesses will have them.

Setting a budget

For a budget to work it needs to have achievable targets. Budgets should not be imposed, but need to be agreed by all parties, particularly those directly involved in trying to achieve the budget or stay within it. Budgets also need to be coordinated across the organisation and in line with the objectives of the business. A certain amount of flexibility is also necessary, as there is always a possibility of unforeseen events or changes that will have a direct impact on the business during the budgetary period.

Many businesses also believe that budgets need to be challenging, and that the business needs to work hard in order to be more efficient. Sales budgets, in particular, need to be challenging but achievable, so that employees are motivated to strive to reach the targets.

Problems in setting a budget

Budgets tend to have six main purposes, although the major problem is that they are not always compatible or achievable. There will be different parts of the organisation that feel that the way the budgets are calculated, or prioritised, is unfair to their area of operations. The key purposes and the related problems are:

- Planning – this involves translating the objectives of the business into specific targets. The purpose is to allocate challenging but achievable targets in order to motivate employees. The major problem may be that there is not agreement about the relationship between the objectives and the targets.
- Allocation of resources – theoretically, with unlimited resources, any target can be achieved. But the business will always have limited resources and also will have to allocate those limited resources to different parts of the business. Not all parts of the business will feel that they have sufficient resources within their budgets to achieve the targets.
- Setting of targets – most businesses believe that employees and departments work much better if they have clearly defined and realisable targets to achieve. However there will always be disagreement over the fairness of targets and the resources that have been allocated in order to achieve them.
- Coordination – departmental targets are designed to encourage employees to pull together to achieve the aim. Individuals may disagree on the best steps to take, or priorities, in order to achieve those targets.
- Monitoring – regular checks need to be made to see whether budgets and targets are still achievable. The difficulties are that changes can occur that will fundamentally compromise the business's ability to either stay within budget or reach targets.
- Modifying and reviewing – if the monitoring process has identified that an objective cannot be reached then the budgets and targets should be immediately modified. It is not advisable for businesses to wait until the end of the budget period, when they will undertake a review. It is only at this point at the end of the budgetary period that it will be absolutely clear that there are differences between the budgeted results and the actual results, but by then it will be too late to have made the necessary amendments.

CASE STUDY HOWARD WHITEMORE LTD

Howard Whitemore Ltd is expecting (budgeting) the following sales revenue in the next three months.

(£000s)	January	February	March
Product A £5 per unit	500	500	600
Product B £10 per unit	600	700	600
Product C £20 per unit	400	300	300

The business buys Product A for £2 per unit, Product B for £4 per unit and Product C for £12 per unit.

Questions

1 Create an expenditure budget for the business based on the assumption that the business pays for the stock from its supply in the same month that it is sold. (9 marks)
2 The costs from the supplier have just risen by 20%. Amend the expenditure budget and the sales revue budget accordingly (Whitemores intend to increase the sales price by 20%). (12 marks)

Income, expenditure and profit budgets

LEARNING OBJECTIVES

▶ Sales budget
▶ Production budget
▶ Purchases budget
▶ Debtors and creditors budget
▶ Cash budget
▶ Department (consolidation) budget
▶ Standard costing

Sales

The sales budget is usually the first budget to be created. This is important because some of the other budgets are dependent upon it. A business will usually calculate its probable sales figures by multiplying the expected number of sales by the selling price of the product. If it has been looking at accounting data from the previous period, it will have a stronger grasp of precisely what the sales budget should be. It is important to remember that on a sales budget the business must only count sales in the month that money is received, not the month when it made the sale. For example a business that sells products to a customer in January and gives them 60 days credit will not count the revenue until it arrives in March. Usually a business will break down expected sales on a monthly or even a weekly basis, by product, product line or product type.

Production

For businesses that actually make products, 'production budget' is a suitable term. Those businesses offering services will call their production budget an operating budget. The purpose of the production budget is to make sure that the business is producing enough to meet the expected sales from the sales budget.

The budget will show the flow of stock, usually using product units rather than financial figures. Typically, each period will note the opening stock, add the units produced, deduct the units sold and then present a closing stock, which is carried forward as the opening stock for the next period. If the sales budget has predicted a marked increase or decrease in demand, the production budget can be altered accordingly.

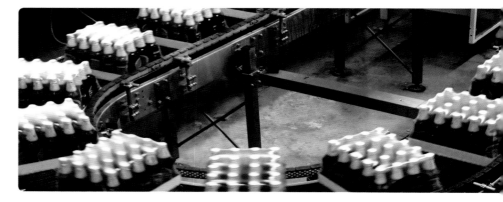

Purchases

This is often known as the materials purchase budget. Obviously it would only be prepared by an organisation involved in manufacturing. The materials budget is based on the production budget. It identifies the costs of any raw materials or components required to make the level of stock, as identified in the production budget.

Knowing their requirements for a period of time, it is possible for a business to negotiate a bulk-purchasing discount with staggered deliveries, so that they arrive only when required. It is important to remember that even though the production budget has indicated that particular purchases need to be made, the business should avoid having to pay for these until it absolutely needs them.

As part of the purchases budget there may be capital expenditure to take into account. The purchasing or hiring of equipment needs to be incorporated into the budget. For hired equipment, regular, probably monthly, payments would have to be made, whereas purchases of equipment should be noted when the business is expected to pay, either in whole or in part, for it.

Debtors and creditors

The debtors' and creditors' budgets indicate an assessment of when money owed to the business will be paid and when money owed by the business will be paid. Obviously the debtors' budget is closely linked to the sales budget. The business will probably use debtors' collection day's ratio in order to work out its current ability to retrieve cash from customers owing it money. It will also use the creditors' payment days' ratio to make an assessment of when payments fall due to suppliers or providers of finance.

Cash

The cash budget is the link between all the individual budgets and the master budget. The cash budget gives an overview of how the business's money will move into and out of its bank accounts. The cash budget can actually form the basis of a cash-flow forecast covering the budgeted period.

The information presented on the cash budget can also be used to create a projected profit-and-loss account or a projected balance sheet. The most practical way of bringing each of the budgets together is to use a computer spreadsheet such as Excel. Typically the cash budget will include:

- Income – sales, other income and total income for the month.
- Payments – creditors, other payments, the purchase or hire of fixed assets and total payments for the month.
- Bank account – opening balance at period start, a total of income

made during the period to add to the balance, a total of all payments made during the period taken from the balance and leaving a bank balance at the end of the period.

Departmental (consolidation) budget

Consolidation is designed to bring together and to check all the budgets from the different departments of a business and whether they match their appropriate partner budget. For example:

- Sales will be used to match all other budgets
- Production needs to match sales
- Purchases need to match production
- Debtors and creditors need to match sales and purchases respectively
- Cash needs to match all other budgets

Standard costing

Standard costing is a way of estimating the overall costs of

production, assuming normal operations. Having established the potential demand by creating a sales budget, and identified the necessary raw materials and components using a production budget, the purchasing department can estimate actual future costs. There are always fluctuations in the prices of raw materials, parts and components. There will also be an expectation that a number of the products will be defective and will have to be remade. Standard costing, therefore, involves looking into the future, and thus is a less-than-exact science.

Questions

1 What items might be included in a materials purchase budget? (2 marks)
2 Which budget is the link between the individual budgets and the master budget? (1 mark)
3 What is consolidation and why is it necessary? (4 marks)

Process of setting budgets

Why bother with budgets?

It is recommended that every business should budget in order to gain financial control. While senior employees or directors of the business will create the budgets, it is common for the responsibility of implementing the budget to be passed down to the lower management positions.

If a business is budgeting on a one-year cycle, it should plan the next budget at least three months prior to the end of the current one. For shorter periods, the business should begin preparing next month's budget within one to two weeks prior to the start date. The timing is crucial and the business should plan the next budget in good time so that objectives and proposed income and payments are clear for the next budgeted period.

Setting a budget

Budgets can help to meet objectives, such as minimising costs, and increasing revenue or **market share**. The first step has to be the identification of objectives, so that the budgets can be coordinated to help achieve them.

Once the objectives have been identified and the budget period determined (week, month, year etc.), the business will need to gather information to help in compiling the budget. This will include past and current performance figures (usually obtained from profit-and-loss accounts, balance sheets and cash-flow forecasts). Sometimes, a business will compile a budget without this information (known as **zero-based budgeting**).

When the business prepares the budgets, there may be figures that can be used with a degree of confidence (such as costs). However sales figures are much harder to predict as so many variables can have a direct impact on the figures (demand changes and levels of competition etc.)

KEY TERMS

Market share – the percentage of a specific market controlled by an individual business.

Zero-budgeting – a budget that is set at zero, with costs only budgeted for after they have been assessed for the benefits that they will bring.

Variances – differences between budgeted figures and actual performance.

Control measures

Budgets are used to help a business exercise control over its operations. Different managers are responsible for creating budgets and bringing them together into the master budget. Remember that the budgets are set out in numbers, so this is an ideal format for control to be exercised because it focuses on real costs and real income. By checking to see whether sales are matching budget expectations, the business can make quick decisions when it notices **variances**. Control action can include:

- Cutting down on waste
- Looking for sources of unnecessary cost
- Increasing advertising and promotions (particularly when sales are lower than expected)

As budgets are exercises in calculation, budgetary control means applying pressure to independent budget holders. By analysing what has happened, the source of the variance can be identified, and actions can be taken to limit any adverse affects.

Reliability

Most businesses understand the importance of accurate, error-free budgets. They also appreciate the fact that inaccurate assumptions about future costs and income could drastically affect the value of the budget. If budgets are correct, they are invaluable as planning tools. Simple targets can be identified in the short-term, but as we have seen, it is far more difficult to make accurate budgets covering periods further into the future.

Any final budget should not just include a profit-and-loss account, but should also incorporate a balance sheet and a cash-flow forecast. By using these, any expectations about working capital or debt requirements will show where there are likely to be cash problems. This is one way of avoiding dangerous situations.

If the budgets are inaccurate, then by breaking down the master budget to its constituent parts, the source of the inaccuracy can be identified. While it is unlikely there will be simple mathematical errors, incomplete or inaccurate figures may have been entered into one of the constituent budgets. These errors will have had a knock-on effect for the other budgets. As we know, many of the budgets rely on the completion of other budgets before they can be fully constructed.

By taking account of their known accounting data from their own financial reports, a business should be able to use this and relevant statistical information to identify trends and predict business performance. The projected figures in the budget mirror these trends and historical data.

Relationship between costs and incomes at different activity levels

There is a strong relationship between a business's costs and its income. We have also seen that costs fall into different categories: some are directly related to the production of goods or the provision of services; others are fixed and must be paid, no matter what the level of activity.

It is clear that income relies on a business's level of activity. To some extent so do costs, as we will see:

- Income is sales revenue, therefore it depends upon the production of goods or the provision of services at increased levels in order to attract additional sales revenue.
- Additional activities mean that there are additional direct costs and semi-variable costs. These

are associated precisely with the activity levels that generate sales revenue or income.
- The other area of costs is fixed costs, such as overheads. These remain static regardless of the level of activity, the direct costs or the sales revenue.

As we can see in the following example, there is a relationship between costs and income (and therefore profit), regardless of the level of activity involved.

In this example we have three different sales revenue totals, but all of them have produced the same profit level. Fixed costs have increased by £10,000 over the period, while direct costs have fluctuated between £120,000 and £140,000. We can therefore see that the close relationship between incomes at different activity levels is directly influenced by associated and non-associated costs.

Year	Fixed costs (£)	Direct costs (including semi-variable costs) (£)	Sales revenue (£)	Gross profit (£)
2006	100,000	125,000	285,000	60,000
2007	100,000	120,000	280,000	60,000
2008	110,000	140,000	310,000	60,000

Questions

1 Why are sales figures harder to predict than costs? (2 marks)
2 What are the THREE documents that should be included in a final budget? (3 marks)
3 Why might costs be related to the level of a business's activity? (4 marks)

Amending and completing budgets

Preparing and revising budgets

There are a number of budgetary techniques that can be applied to prepare and revise budgets, as well as to monitor and use them. Budgetary techniques will incorporate the control measures that will need to be taken if the budgets are at variance with actual figures. Another important technique is to ensure that the budgets are reliable. This means checking accuracy, making sure they are as error-free as possible and not making incorrect assumptions about future sales and costs.

If it appears that the budgets are in extreme variance with the actual figures, then the business will have no other choice but to prepare new ones or amend the existing budgets. Obviously the further ahead the projection; the less chance there is for them to be accurate. There will be changes to costs and to selling prices. In the first instance changes to costs will have an impact on:

- A cash budget (as more money will be spent)
- The creditor budget (as more raw materials and components are purchased)
- The purchasing budget (as this will absorb the additional costs)

Obviously if there is a favourable variance the reverse will be true.

If there is a change to the selling price, the following budgets will be affected:

- The debtors' budget (as more customers, perhaps not as a percentage but as a whole, will owe more money to the business
- The cash budget (as more money will be moving into the business's bank accounts)
- The purchases budget (as more products, raw materials and components need to be purchased)
- The creditors' budget (as more items bought by purchasing will be on credit)
- The production budget (which will need to increase its production levels and therefore place greater strain on purchasing)
- The sales budget (as this will increase assuming demand has increased)

If the sales price has come down, then the business will actually be making less money from each sale. This will place a greater strain on the cash budget.

For more on variances see Calculation and interpretation of favourable and adverse variances on pp. 160–1.

Use of budgets for short-term target setting

The natural inclination for a business is to grow and become more profitable. The creation of budgets can be used as a key tool in this endeavour.

Budgets can identify key areas of cost and income that can be manipulated to help achieve future profit targets and control of spending (costs). Budgets are more likely to be accurate in the short term rather than the longer term. By careful management of key costs and income a business can make realistic targets, which the business has all chances of achieving.

Monitoring

We have already mentioned the fact that budgets need to be constantly monitored in order to compare the budgeted costs with actual costs, as well as identifying and explaining the root cause of variances.

The monitoring process can be seen as an onerous task but many businesses insist that this is done either on a weekly or a monthly basis, in line with the periods set out within the budget plan itself. By quickly identifying changes in costs, a business can take remedial action to offset any negative impacts.

Variances can have an impact on all budgets. They force the business to revise its budgets to take greater control measures to offset negative variances, or take advantage of advantageous ones.

Cost and profit centres

A business may choose to establish a series of cost or profit centres. A cost centre is a part of a business where it is possible to identify costs that it specifically incurs. It will have its own cost budget to enable its performance to be assessed. In areas of the business where it is possible to establish the revenue it generates, the business may identify it as a profit centre.

Typically, cost or profit centres might be:

- A department – which could be either a cost or profit centre
- A geographical area – such as a sales region or outlet location
- A product or brand – within a wider product or brand range
- A specific type of equipment or piece of machinery – such as a photocopier
- An individual – perhaps a manager or a sales person

CASE STUDY FRANK'S RE-SPRAYS LTD

Frank Rogers' small business provides a service both directly to customers and to insurance companies. The business re-sprays cars that have been damaged. It can handle 100 vehicles per month. Sixty per cent of the jobs are undertaken for insurance companies, for which the business charges an average of £550 per job. The remaining 40% is for private customers, for which the charge is £720 per car. The factory's total overhead costs are £10,000. The direct costs are identified in the following table:

	Preparation	Re-spray	Finishing
Direct labour	£4,000	£5,000	£4,000
Direct materials	£2,000	£4,000	£2,000
Other direct costs	£2,000	£2,000	£2,000

Questions

1 Counting each of the three stages as separate cost centres, identify the cost per vehicle. (3 marks)
2 Would there be any advantages in treating each stage as a separate cost centre? If so, what would these be? (4 marks)
3 An insurance company has offered a flat payment of £50,000 per month for the business to undertake up to 120 re-sprays. The business would have to exclusively work for the insurance company. What are the advantages and disadvantages of accepting the contract? (8 marks)

Case studies, questions and exam practice

CASE STUDY KINGDOM TOYS

For some years Kingdom Toys has been a market leader in traditional wooden toys and craft products. The company has enjoyed steady growth due to its products being the complete opposite to hi-tech children's products, encouraging parents to look back to a time when children's toys were simple and unsophisticated.

All the toys are made in Britain from sustainable forest sources. Recently, the business has established a number of profit and cost centres and has been setting budgets and targets for the first time in its forty-year history.

The main budget reveals the following:

	1st quarter		2nd quarter		3rd quarter		4th quarter	
	Budget	Actual	Budget	Actual	Budget	Actual	Budget	Actual
Sales	£78,000	£72,000	£85,000	£92,000	£90,000	£97,000	£140,000	£165,000
Materials	£39,000	£42,000	£43,000	£46,000	£45,000	£49,000	£70,000	£82,000
Other direct costs	£12,000	£14,000	£13,000	£14,000	£14,000	£16,000	£18,000	£21,000
Overheads	£22,000	£24,000	£22,000	£24,000	£22,000	£25,000	£22,000	£27,000
Profit	£5,000	(£8,000)	£7,000	£8,000	£9,000	£7,000	£30,000	£35,000

Questions

1 What is meant by a cost centre and a profit centre? (4 marks)
2 Why were the actual figures for the first quarter so poor compared to the budget? (3 marks)
3 How might the business have set these budgets? (6 marks)
4 How does the overall yearly profit compare with the budgeted figures and how might the business amend the budget for next year after seeing these figures? (6 marks)

SHORT-ANSWER QUESTIONS

1 Distinguish between a cost and a profit centre.

2 Identify FIVE different types of budget that might be created by a business.

3 What is zero-budgeting?

4 Suggest FIVE key points that need to be taken into account when setting a budget.

5 What is a master budget?

6 Which budget might be affected if there is a change in the cost of obtaining raw materials and components?

7 How might debtors' and creditors' budgets be affected if there is a change in the selling price?

8 How might a business monitor a budget?

9 What is a variance?

10 Why are budgets used for all businesses?

CASE STUDY TWO TOO MANY COOKS?

The Timor Steakhouse and Public House is a successful joint venture run by four trained chefs. Each of them have outside interests: Tim is a regular on the BBC on a variety of cooking programmes; Franko is a consultant for a ready-meal business in a nearby town; Charlene writes cookery articles for magazines and newspapers; and Simon has recently opened his own small restaurant 60 miles away from the business.

The partnership decided to run the business on a rota basis. Tim covers Mondays and Tuesdays, Franko is in charge on Wednesdays, Thursdays and Fridays, Charlene looks after Saturdays, and Simon is duty chef on Sundays. They agreed to set the marketing budget (£40,000), which is handled by Charlene, but she always overspends by around 20%. Franko handles the purchasing budget (£124,000) which is always tight, but 15% over budget. Simon monitors the sales budget (£490,000), which is up 20% on last year, and Tim takes care of the overheads, staff and other costs through his budget (£88,000), which is overspent by 10% of budgeted figures.

They each put in 25% of the start-up costs, but now the profits are distributed on the basis of a one-seventh share for every day each covers as the duty chef. This has caused great friction between the partners and Franko is the highest paid, despite the fact that his three nights only contribute 20% of the sales revenue. Saturday nights alone bring in 45% of the sales; Mondays and Tuesdays are the quietest with 5% each; Sunday night produces the balance of sales (25%).

The partners agree to think about changing the share of the profits back to quarter shares, but Franko would want to drop down to covering just two nights. The other suggestion is to allocate profits according to the sales revenue, but Franko and Tim realise they will lose out. Everyone wants Saturday night, but Charlene won't budge on it. When they vote to change the system, it is deadlock, two for and two against. They are not sure what to do next.

Questions

1 Construct a budget showing the budgeted and actual figures, taking into account the budgeted and actual figures as given. (8 marks)
2 If the total profit were available to distribute to the partners on the basis of a one-seventh share per night, what is the share of the profit per partner? (4 marks)
3 If the total profit were distributed according to the sales revenue generated on the nights covered by the partners, what would be the new distribution of profit per partner? (8 marks)

Objectives of business start-ups

LEARNING
OBJECTIVES

▶ Does having a strategy mean success?
▶ Risk taking
▶ SWOT analysis
▶ Small business benefits

Does having a strategy mean success?

Having a good business plan does not always mean that success is guaranteed, although having objectives and a strategy can improve the success rate.

Strategies need to be correct, but they also need to be appropriate to the circumstances and well implemented. It is not always the case that businesses write down their mission statement, their aims and objectives or their strategies. For most small businesses there is not a great deal of planning, but the business owner or owners may have clear strategies in their minds.

The larger the organisation, the more formal these objectives become. As a consequence, strategy and planning become more elaborate and expensive. Added to this there is also the need to communicate these objectives, strategies, missions and aims to the organisation as a whole.

AVOIDING BANKRUPTCY

" I WAS LOOKING FOR A LITTLE STRONGER MISSION STATEMENT THAN THAT. "

Risk taking

Like any business venture, a new start-up involves a degree of risk-taking. Taking risks, certainly in business terms, should not be considered a negative or dangerous process. Taking risks can mean the difference between profit and loss. Most business decisions bring with them a degree of risk, which start-up businesses in particular need to consider very carefully and to assess in terms of their potential return.

Typically, start-up businesses will consider the initial investment as a potential risk and try to work out whether the possible returns are worth it. Business owners who are risk-averse may not be particularly successful, and there will always be occasions when risks have to be taken, regardless of the attitude of the owners.

Over 60% of businesses in Britain are owned and run by a single individual. In other words, over 2.5m people work for themselves. Not all business start-ups are single, individual organisations; they employ people, create wealth, and are vital suppliers and customers to other businesses. Their objectives may differ, from wanting freedom and independence, to looking forward to the challenges of making their own decisions and framing their own destiny rather than working as an employee.

KEY TERM

Mission statement – a short and succinct declaration by an organisation, stating its key aims, objectives and purpose.

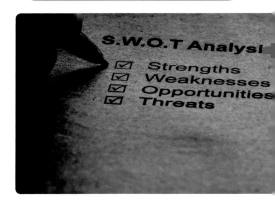

SWOT analysis

SWOT analysis is a very useful tool, not only in assessing the viability of a business start-up, but in helping frame the objectives. The start-up business will begin by looking at its own internal strengths and weaknesses, in terms of skills, knowledge, expertise, contacts, location, availability of finance, and a host of other factors. It will then address the external factors, which are known as opportunities and threats. These are factors that can influence the business and shape its future, but are out of the control of the business itself. Typical examples would include the strength and activities of competitors, the size of the customer base, demand, interest rates, levels of employment and government policy.

SWOT helps businesses understand the situation they are in and can help them frame their objectives by focusing on strengths and opportunities, while dealing with their own weaknesses and attempting to avoid external threats.

Small business benefits

A single person business start-up can easily become, in a number of years, a medium-scale or even large-scale organisation. Some businesses, however, prefer to remain small so that the original owners can cope with the volume of work, while receiving sufficient reward for their efforts.

Many small businesses have unique benefits:

- They can provide vital services to the local community – a small business is a flexible one that is able to respond quickly to change in customer needs. By staying small they can respond to gaps in the market and provide additional or complementary services, as well as gaining a good reputation in the local community for their level of service.
- They can provide a consistently high standard of customer service. By controlling who deals with customers and how those interactions take place, the small business can continue to provide personal attention to customers and gradually build up a strong and loyal customer base.
- They can control costs – by deciding not to employ people and not to take on larger than necessary premises, costs can be kept relatively low. This in turn allows a small business to keep its prices relatively low, while still providing it with sufficient profit to make a living.
- They can work with larger businesses – small businesses often fulfil a vital role for larger businesses. They can provide a range of services, work as subcontractors and provide complementary services to the larger organisation at probably a lower cost than if the larger business provided those services itself.

CASE STUDY FRANCHISES

Many new businesses opt to start a franchise, as it represents a much lower risk than starting an independent new business. A franchise often means that it is easier to obtain finance, and that the market for the product or service offered has already been established. Added to this is the fact that a business plan already exists and the marketing methods used actually work. The franchisor can offer valuable advice, as can established franchisees; they will have already encountered many of the problems and will have solutions to them.

However, some existing franchises that are up for sale may be experiencing difficulties and the potential new owner needs to understand why the franchise is being sold. The rights to a franchise or the right to sell a particular product or service is more expensive than selling other products and services. There may also be particular rules regarding the way in which the franchise has to be run that the new owners may find restrictive.

Questions

1 How might a franchise be less of a risk than another form of start-up? (3 marks)
2 Would a potential franchise-holder need to do a SWOT analysis? (3 marks)
3 How might the benefits of a small business be compromised by choosing to run a franchise? (4 marks)

Strengths and weaknesses of a business idea or plan

Why set up in the first place?

The reasons why individuals set up small businesses are numerous and varied, but usually they are driven by specific personal circumstances, which include:

- Dissatisfaction or boredom with their current job or role
- The opportunity to be able to generate profits for themselves rather than someone else
- The opportunity to develop, produce and sell a new product or service idea
- The opportunity to build a new life after having been made redundant or having taken early retirement

KEY TERMS

Patent – a document designed to protect a new invention, covering how it works, what it does and how it is made.

Marketing mix – a way of describing the use of product, place, price and promotion – the four key elements of marketing products and services.

Intellectual property – inventions, ideas, literary or artistic works, business and industrial process that have been created by an individual or a business.

Start-up process

Although there is no real blueprint for either starting up a new business or creating a business plan, there are a series of steps that are usually taken by start-up businesses. These are:

- The idea to either set up a new business or the actual business idea itself is first generated.
- The market then needs to be researched to see if it is viable.
- A business plan is then written, outlining the key costs, resource requirements, skills required and probable sales revenues and profits.
- Financial backing is then sought, either in the form of a loan, the finding of partners, or the selling of shares in the case of a private limited company.
- The products and services are then developed (or the product or service range determined).

- The business is then tested to gauge customers' response and requirements.
- The business or the business idea is then launched.
- It is then monitored and reviewed with the purpose of improving its performance and delivery.

Most ideas either come from someone's own inspiration, the adaptation of an existing idea or the purchasing of the right to sell products or services either through a **patent** or a franchise.

For more information about business ideas see Generating and protecting business ideas on pp. 16–25.

INTERNET RESEARCH

To find out about how McDonald's franchises work, go to www. mcdonalds.co.uk. Select 'contact us' and then scroll down and select 'franchising'. Two downloadable documents are available giving full information.

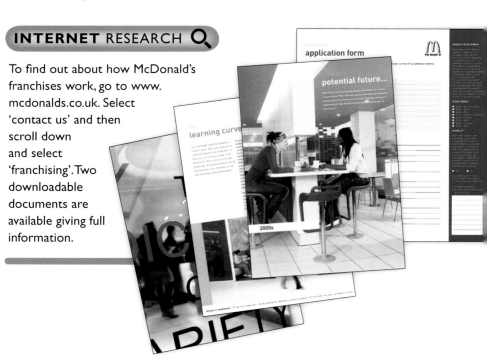

Effective planning

Without an effective business plan even the best business ideas are usually doomed to failure. A new business needs a well-researched business plan, that will give it:

- focus and direction;
- the ability to show that the business proposal is viable;
- a single document to attract potential investors;
- the ability to plan and review the business's objectives and strategies, as well as their targets and forecasts.

Typically a business plan will incorporate information about the basic business idea, the type of legal status of the business, and its overall goals. The key objectives of the business will also be identified, as will details on the products and services that will be provided, along with the key selling points. A business plan also needs to incorporate how the business will be managed and by whom, and what other key personnel are necessary.

The marketing plan is designed to show that there is a level of demand, that the customers have been identified, the key strengths and weaknesses of competitors considered and how the business intends to use the marketing mix.

If relevant, a production plan will also be used to show the methods and stages of production, equipment and premises needed and the probable levels of production.

Finally, the financial plan will show the financial needs of the business, its projected profits, a break-even analysis and a cash-flow forecast.

Making it a success

It is rare for new business start-ups to be immediately successful and provide the business owners with enormous profits and riches. Around 80% of new products actually fail.

It is necessary for the start-up business to identify an innovative product, service or business idea, and to enter a suitable market. The needs of the customer must be addressed, as well as the potential threats from the competitors.

New businesses usually begin with only a tiny budget for research and promotion, so they need to make sure that any hunches are backed up with solid facts.

It is very difficult for small businesses to protect their business ideas, particularly if they have come up with an innovative idea, product or service. It could be an extremely valuable asset and it may need to be protected from competitors and imitators. A patent will go part of the way to doing this, as it will protect a distinctive and original product for up to twenty years. Product names and logos will have to be registered as trademarks to gain full protection,

and any work created by an author, artist or composer will have to be protected by copyright. The truth of the situation is that many small businesses, while seeking to protect their intellectual property, will find it difficult to enforce that protection because court action is very expensive.

The success or failure of a business idea or plan relies largely on the individual or individuals who have set up, or intend to set up the business. It is these entrepreneurs who have to plan and manage the business, and who need a wide range of skills and abilities. They will obviously wish to succeed; they will need ideas and will often need to be creative. They will need to have good organisation and leadership skills, be hardworking and energetic, and be able to mix with a wide variety of people and motivate others.

> ## Questions
>
> 1 What qualities might be needed in an entrepreneur setting up a new business? (6 marks)
> 2 Why is planning important for any new business start-up? (4 marks)
> 3 Outline the key planning processes of a new business start-up. (5 marks)

Why start-ups can be risky

LEARNING
OBJECTIVES

▶ Start-up problems
▶ Finance
▶ Location
▶ Customers

Start-up problems

New businesses can choose their legal structure, which is largely restricted to either being sole traders, partnerships or private limited companies.

Initial considerations may have to include factors such as: the needs of other investors and whether the owners prefer limited liability or whether they consider it advisable to keep complete control of the business. For most new businesses the entrepreneurs may lack experience. An individual may have a strong set of technical skills, but lack the ability to run a business or to manage employees.

Location can often be a major issue, as the best locations are often too expensive, or existing businesses are tied to those locations and are unlikely to move. In any case location costs can often be a crippling overhead for a new business.

New businesses also find it difficult to build up a customer base, as long-term success relies on customer loyalty and repeat business. Any research that is carried out by small businesses may often be inaccurate due to the fact that extensive research is often financially impossible for a business working with a small budget.

One of the other key problems is that as soon as a start-up business has a good idea and takes the risk of testing it on the market, competitors will be quick to imitate it.

Finance

Another major practical problem for new businesses is being able to raise sufficient finance in order to launch the business onto the market. Potential providers of finance are often wary of committing too much money to a new business start-up, regardless of how good the business plan may appear, as there is a much higher level of risk. The new business will need to purchase, rent or lease premises and equipment, and will also need working capital to pay bills before having received much back in the way of sales revenue.

A small business's cash flow would be negative before the business launches itself onto the market. It would continue to be negative until such a time as the sales of products and services begin to be established and revenue begins to grow. Only at that point would cash flow be positive. At this stage the small business would find that having money to finance growth and continue trading is difficult. The business will lack the muscle to force debtors to pay on time, and the power and the trading history to stop suppliers from demanding quick payment of invoices. This could result in a cash-flow crisis, and this is often given as one of the main reasons why many small businesses fail within their first year: they have few assets that they can dispose of in the event of such a crisis; there is little chance that they can hold onto profit in order to fund a negative cash flow; and they will also find that any assets they have purchased begin to depreciate the moment that they bought them.

Overdrafts at this stage are expensive and risky, and if a provider of finance has already given them funds to start up, they may be reluctant to extend their exposure by offering additional loans.

🔗 *For the details of the legal structure including considerations of sole traders, partnerships and private limited companies, see the Starting a business section on pp. 70–83.*

Location

Although many new businesses could be considered virtual businesses, in the sense that location is not a key determinant of success or failure, many do rely on being in the right location in order to ensure success. Retailers need to be close to their customers, as do other service-based businesses. Manufacturers need to be close to their suppliers and also close to the market. New businesses can rarely find the ideal location, particularly because they need to keep their start-up costs low and maintain control over their overheads. They may find that the compromise location is simply not good enough and this just compounds their difficulties in trying to succeed.

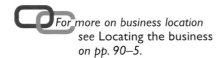
For more on business location see Locating the business on pp. 90–5.

Customers

Unless an entrepreneur has purchased an existing business, the first challenge is building up a customer base. There is often some interest in a new business when it is launched, but, as we have seen, customer loyalty and repeat purchases are vital if the business is to survive. A new business will find it difficult to convince customers that its products or services can meet their needs more successfully than already established competitors.

There may be teething problems with regard to customer care and service. It is also difficult to quickly build a reputation, regardless of how much money is spent on marketing, or whether the business is reliant upon word-of-mouth recommendation.

CASE STUDY FAILURE RATE

Research suggests that 81% of traditional new business start-ups fail within the first five years. Many argue that not enough is being done to overcome the barriers to success, especially in the case of young entrepreneurs.

In a survey carried out by high-street bank, Nat West, some 88% of franchises were seen to be profitable, and, on average, franchise holders had run their businesses for nearly ten years. The average turnover for new business start-ups is just over £30,000 per year. For new franchises, this is nearly £300,000 (with 16% achieving over £500,000). The franchising sector is worth some £10 billion to the UK economy, which is equivalent to the amount spent by the government on transport each year. Many franchisors are experiencing constraints on further growth because people fear business failure and continue to remain in paid employment.

Stephen Hemsley, Chief Executive of Domino's Pizza said: 'Franchising clearly contributes to wealth creation and to the economy, with fewer risks for the individual. The Government wants to encourage latent entrepreneurs to realise their dreams, but none of its policies and activities actually promote franchising as an alternative route to managing your own business. We are urging Government to include franchising in their enterprise policies. Franchisors and the BFA [British Franchise Association] will do what they can but we believe the Government should take a lesson from abroad in seeing what can be achieved for entrepreneurs and the economy from this tried and trusted business model.'

Source adapted from Domino's Pizza

Questions

1 Why might a franchise have a greater turnover than a similar start-up business? (6 marks)
2 What could the government do to encourage the promotion of franchises? (4 marks)
3 What is meant by the term 'tried and trusted business model'? (2 marks)

Why start-up businesses may fail

LEARNING OBJECTIVES

▶ Success or failure?
▶ Changes in demand and costs
▶ Delays and unavailability of supplies

Success or failure?

There are an enormous number of reasons why a new business start-up may fail or, indeed, why an established business finds itself losing its way after a few years. New business start-ups stand and fall on how sound the original business idea or plan was and how the plan or idea was implemented. Much of this will, of course, rely on the quality of the original research carried out by the business organisation or by a marketing company on its behalf.

Another huge burden rests on the shoulders of the founders of the business. This includes their ability to remain focused, their skills in a variety of different business areas and ultimately their drive and ambition to try to ensure that the business is a success.

Short-, medium- and long-term planning and the implementation of those plans, along with regular monitoring and review, can go a long way towards alerting any business to potential future difficulties. Corrective action can then be taken before the situation becomes too complex or terminal for the business to be able to react in any meaningful way.

A business does not just fail due to internal deficiencies, either in the business concepts, the skills of the owners or their ability to think ahead. Businesses can be undermined by external factors, which to a large extent may remain out of the control of the business and its owners. A small business that suddenly finds itself facing a national chain that can offer lower prices and better quality customer service is unlikely to survive anything beyond the short-term. There may be very little that the small business can do about this situation.

Changes in demand and costs

In looking at budgets and at cash flow we have seen that businesses need to try to plan ahead and set income, expenditure and profit budgets, as well as to forecast cash flow. This coordination and control of finances is vital. But many small businesses' cash-flow forecasts and budgets are inaccurate and at times unrealistic. They have little experience of the likely changes in demand, or whether the prices charged by suppliers, or the prices expected by customers, are static or volatile.

Changes in demand can radically affect cash flow and undermine budgets, and can mean the difference between profit and loss. Costs can be notoriously difficult to control at the early stages of a start-up business. Many factors can affect demand, many of which cannot necessarily be anticipated by a new business, as can be seen in the table on the opposite page.

KEY TERMS

USP (Unique Selling Point) – a factor or feature of a product or service that distinguishes it from competing products and services.

Factor	Implications
Price 	Price does tend to affect demand, even if it is a change in price of products or services that customers need to consume, such as electricity or gas. The effect of a price increase in these areas simply means that the customer has less to spend elsewhere. Price changes can mean customers switch brands and look for close substitutes. Complementary goods can also be affected by price changes in the main product. If car prices increased there could be a fall in the demand for petrol and diesel as there might be fewer cars on the road.
Income	Most small businesses are interested in their share of customers' disposable income. Disposable income is dependent on actual income, affected by factors such as redundancy or a pay rise, and on outgoings such as mortgage or rent payments and council tax as well as one-off commitments.
Taste, fashions and customs 	Fashion and music are just two examples of volatile markets that change almost weekly. The latest available products and services need to be made available by new businesses and they need to be aware of not overstocking on fashionable products, the demand for which may suddenly disappear.
Population change	The balance and make-up of the population of any area is constantly changing, the age distribution can affect demand, as can the ethnic background, race and culture of an area. Other population characteristics, such as a tourist town needing a wide range of catering facilities and cheap accommodation also have an effect.
Lifestyle change	One major lifestyle change is the number of women in work, which has changed the patterns of demand, as is the fact that many more people own their own homes and that most people now at least take one holiday a year.
Promotion and USP 	It is difficult for new businesses to show that their products or services are different or better than their competitors'. Customers look for products and services that satisfy their needs, and a business needs to ensure that it can predict what customers may want, what quantity they will want, and when they will want it.
Advertising 	Advertising can impact on demand, but people are still unlikely to buy things that they do not need. Advertising can be effective in helping to launch a new business, showing customers they have a wider choice.
Law 	There are laws that limit the age at which alcohol, cigarettes, car driving and a host of other activities and factors are legal. Equally the ban on smoking in the workplace and in pubs and restaurants has led to a drop in demand, as more people opt for a night in rather than a night out.

Delays and unavailability of supplies

A new business is reliant on untried suppliers, but the suppliers are likely to prioritise existing and established customers over new ones. This can put new businesses at a serious disadvantage, as they may have to obtain their supplies from alternative sources, leading to delays and higher prices.

Questions

1 State FOUR reasons why there may be a change in demand that cannot be predicted by a new business. (4 marks)
2 How might a local supermarket cope with population changes affecting demand? (6 marks)

Case studies, questions and exam practice

CASE STUDY BUYING AN EXISTING BUSINESS

There are three main advantages in buying an existing business:

- A successful existing business will already have proved its viability in the market place and have built up a trading record. The number of potential customers, number of staff required to run the business, fixed and variable costs and other factors will already have been established.
- It also means not having to build up a customer base from scratch, establish relationships with suppliers and distribution channels, or spend the time in finding suitable staff.
- As few new business start-ups are profitable at the beginning, an existing business should be generating sales revenue from the outset.

The main disadvantages are:

- If the business is a successful one, then the new owner will be expected to pay for it and the financial rewards of buying the existing business rests on whether the new owners can make improvements to it. New start-ups allow entrepreneurs to determine their own levels of achievement.
- There is always the chance that the business turns out to be less successful than the new owner expected it to be, perhaps due to external factors or unforeseen problems. Obviously the more that is paid for the business, the more could be lost.

Questions

1 Do the advantages of buying an existing business outweigh the disadvantages? Explain your view. (8 marks)
2 Why would an existing business possibly cost more than a new business start-up? (6 marks)
3 What could be done to ensure that the facts and figures supplied by the existing owner of the business are correct and reasonable before a purchasing decision is made? (6 marks)

SHORT-ANSWER QUESTIONS

1 What is **SWOT** analysis?

2 Outline the key benefits of small businesses.

3 Give **FOUR** reasons why an entrepreneur may choose to set up their own business.

4 What are the **FOUR** key alternative types of business?

5 Why might a franchise operation be potentially less risky than an independent business idea?

6 Why is cash flow often a major problem for new businesses?

7 Why is it difficult for new businesses to set up in an ideal location?

8 Why might a new business face difficulties with its suppliers?

9 Why is it important for a new business to plan effectively?

10 State **FOUR** factors which could determine whether a new business will succeed or fail.

CASE STUDY FACTS AND FIGURES

Of the four million businesses in Britain, over 99% are 'small' (0–49 employees), according to government figures. By the beginning of 2003, 46.2% of business employment was in small businesses. What is even more amazing is that 2.9 million small businesses do not have any employees at all – they are individuals or small groups of people.

The small and medium-sized enterprises (SMEs) together accounted for more than half of the employment (58.2 per cent) and turnover (52.4 per cent) in Britain.

As far as legal identity is concerned, government figures suggest that over 2.5m are sole proprietors, just under 1m are companies, and 540,000 are partnerships.

According to the banks, there has been a slowing down of the number of new businesses, but it is still growing year on year. In 2005 alone there were 388,300 new businesses established.

Questions

1 What is an SME? (2 marks)
2 How does the government define a small business? (2 marks)
3 Why might partnerships be the least attractive option as a business type? (6 marks)

CHECKLIST

Topic 1: Starting a business

- [ ] What is enterprise and what are entrepreneurs?
- [ ] Risk taking and rewards
- [ ] Opportunity cost
- [ ] Government support for new businesses
- [ ] Sources of business ideas
- [ ] Product and market niches
- [ ] Franchises
- [ ] Copyright, patents and trademarks
- [ ] Inputs, outputs and transformation
- [ ] Adding value
- [ ] Business plans and sources of guidance
- [ ] Primary and secondary market research
- [ ] Quantitative and qualitative research
- [ ] Sampling
- [ ] What is a market?
- [ ] Demand
- [ ] Market segmentation
- [ ] Market size, growth and share
- [ ] Sole traders
- [ ] Partnerships
- [ ] Private limited companies
- [ ] Public limited companies
- [ ] Not-for-profit businesses
- [ ] Sources of finance for start-up businesses
- [ ] Factors influencing location
- [ ] Employees in small businesses
- [ ] Using consultants and advisors

Topic 2: Financial planning

- [ ] Calculation of fixed, variable and total costs
- [ ] Calculation of price, total revenue and profit
- [ ] Contribution
- [ ] Calculation of break-even output
- [ ] Construction of break-even charts
- [ ] Analysing variables on break-even charts
- [ ] Nature of cash flow
- [ ] Forecasting cash flow
- [ ] Structure of a cash-flow forecast
- [ ] Why forecast cash flow?
- [ ] Income, expenditure and profit budgets
- [ ] Process of setting budgets
- [ ] Objectives of start-up businesses
- [ ] Strengths and weaknesses of plans and ideas
- [ ] Why are start-ups risky?
- [ ] Why do many start-ups fail?

MOCK EXAM

SKATE LATE LTD

Gavin hoped to compete in the 2010 Vancouver Winter Olympics, but serious long-term damage to his knee ligaments meant that this was out of the question. His sponsor, an artificial skating rink company, had gone into receivership, and Gavin and his brother, Kevin, had snapped up the business at a knockdown price by borrowing £130,000 from several members of their family.

The idea was to set up a mobile skating rink in towns and cities around the country, moving it around every week or so, like a travelling circus. The first thing to do was to put the business on the right foot and get a loan to pay back the family. The bank offered the brothers £90,000 and they raised the remaining £40,000 from personal loans and credit cards.

The rink opened in Norwich, then moved up the east coast, as far as Hull, in the first ten weeks. The trouble was that in an average week they would attract only 500 customers:

Variable costs per customer	£3.50
Weekly fixed costs	£1,900.00
Average spend per customer	£7.00

The brothers had drawn up a business plan and opted to create a private limited company, as they believed that this would offer advantages. They conducted market research in the towns they intended to visit with the rink before they set up. There was a high potential demand and little competition.

They had drawn up a cash-flow forecast and budgets before approaching the bank. Kevin had wanted to get a venture capital company on board and not take out a loan, but the best offer he had was a £100,000 investment for 40% of the business.

Living on the road, with Gavin driving a camper van that doubled as their office, kitchen and bedroom, and Kevin driving the truck with the rink, they had found it impossible to find staff willing to live on the road or work just a week in each town for them. They were putting in 16-hour days, seven days a week.

It came as a great shock that in the first ten weeks they had not even broken even. All their figures were based on a minimum of 1,000 customers a week.

Questions

1 (a) What is meant by the term 'venture capital'? (2 marks)

(b) What is meant by the term 'budget'? (2 marks)

(c) Give TWO non-financial requirements of the bank that would have to have been in their business plan before the bank would agree to the loan. (2 marks)

(d) What type of market research was carried out by Gavin and Kevin, and why did they choose this method? (4 marks)

(e) Using the information given, work out Skate Late Ltd's profit or loss for the first ten weeks. (6 marks)

(f) If, after the first ten weeks, the average number of customers rose to 700, what would be the percentage growth in customers? (4 marks)

2 (a) Give reasons why the business might have failed to reach its break-even number in the first ten weeks. (10 marks)

(b) What is the number of customers required for the business to break even, and what is its profit or loss based on 700 customers per week? (15 marks)

(c) Suggest how Gavin and Kevin could reorganise the business operations so that the pressures on them are not so great. (15 marks)

UNIT 2
MANAGING A BUSINESS

Introduction

Just as the first unit – *Planning and financing a business* – focused on small and medium-sized businesses operating within a national market, this second unit – *Managing a business* – continues this approach, looking at the ways in which a business can improve its effectiveness. It looks at specific measurements, such as profitability, labour productivity, labour turnover, unit costs and market share.

There are four core themes in Unit 2, each of which is further broken down into topic areas, such as *Improving cash flow* and *Effective marketing*. You will be expected to have a good understanding of the ways of calculating business performance and be able to interpret data that measure the effectiveness of a business. Each of the topic areas will look at one particular aspect, but it is important to remember that many of them link together and are dependent upon one another.

Throughout this AS unit you will be expected to carry out calculations; interpret and analyse data; apply your knowledge in unfamiliar situations; develop arguments; and make judgements and decisions. These are known as transferable skills, and examiners will be expecting you to demonstrate them in your answers for the examination.

The unit itself is examined in an examination of one hour and fifteen minutes. The total number of marks available to you is 80 and the examination accounts for 30% of the overall A-level mark.

In the examination you should expect to answer a series of compulsory, multi-part data response questions. The exam will include *Finance*, which looks at the financial measures that can be used to indicate how well a business is being managed. The *People in business* topic examines the issues facing managing people to make a business more effective. *Operations management* looks at operational decisions in the tertiary, secondary and primary sectors and the use of technology. Finally, *Marketing in the competitive environment* looks at the importance of marketing and issues that affect the competitiveness of a business.

This section of the book follows the exact specification of the GCE. Each of the four core themes is examined in detail, with each topic given its own section comprising a number of double-page spreads, each of which looks at an aspect of that topic. On each spread there are either short-answer questions to test your understanding, or mini case studies with extended questions. At the end of each topic there is an opportunity for you to try out short-answer questions and extended responses based on mini case studies, as well as other activities to help you prepare for your examination.

At the end of the unit, another spread provides a checklist of the unit's key concepts and further revision aids.

TOPIC 1 FINANCE

Introduction

This is the first of the four core themes for *Managing a business*. This theme introduces you to the importance of the management of finance. You will be expected to appreciate that financial measurements can be used to show how well a business is being managed and, importantly, how actions can be taken to improve that performance. You will have to carry out calculations and be able to interpret the results. This section builds on the work that you covered in *Financial planning* as part of Unit 1.

You have already been introduced to budgets. In this topic the concept is taken further and you will examine the nature of income, expenditure and profit budgets. You will not be expected to analyse budgets by price or volume, or to use flexible budgets, but it is important that you are aware of these concepts. Businesses use budgets to help them measure their predicted performance compared to their actual results, using a technique called variance analysis. This highlights the differences and tries to identify the source or reasons behind the differences.

Cash flow is another important concept that you looked at in the first unit. Here we examine cash-flow problems and what might lie behind them. Businesses are always aware that they need to have a healthy cash flow and will take steps to improve it using a number of methods, including overdrafts, factoring, loans and sale and leaseback.

Finally, this theme examines the measurement of profit and how businesses seek to improve their profits. You will not need to have an understanding of balance sheets or income statements, but you will need to be able to calculate and understand net profit margins, return on capital and how profit and profitability can be improved, for example by cost reduction or price rises. Finally you will need to appreciate and show that you understand that there is a key difference between cash and profit.

Benefits and drawbacks of using budgets

Strengths and weaknesses of budgetary techniques

LEARNING OBJECTIVES

► Strengths and weaknesses of budgetary techniques
► Historical budgeting
► Zero budgeting
► Flexible budgeting
► General benefits and drawbacks

A budget can usually be almost entirely prepared by the accounts or finance department of a business, provided they are given the correct data. This way, as the data comes in, it can be checked and cross-referenced for accuracy.

Unfortunately budgets do take a considerable amount of time to prepare, which may well leave little time to carry out analysis. It can take an enormous amount of time to collect the data, from perhaps dozens or hundreds of budget holders. They may well be using different data sources and there may be gaps in the information they provide. Most accounts departments find themselves struggling to complete the budgets on time, let alone carry out data analysis on them.

Budget data can quickly lose its significance. This is mainly due to the problem in compiling accurate and timely data. Budgets tend to be somewhat detached from normal operational activities and as a result budget holders may ignore them and the process just becomes a formality – a form-filling exercise that can be forgotten until the next memo comes around requesting the information. This can mean that the staff involved pay very little attention to the budgets, which may end up not having any bearing on the performance of the business. In any case, the budgets have to be radically revised when new business conditions arise and the existing data becomes obsolete.

The analysis of actual figures against budget figures in order to highlight variances is both a burden and a time-consuming exercise. However, it is a crucial activity for business planning.

Historical budgeting

One way of setting a budget is to use last year's figures for costs and revenue. These give an indication as to the probable costs and revenue for the forthcoming period. Usually a small increase is incorporated into the budget (perhaps to take account of **inflation**).

Historical budgeting is seen as being realistic, as it is based on what has been achieved in the past; it also speeds up the process of setting a budget. However, current circumstances may mean that last year's budget is not relevant: a new product may have been launched or a new competitor may have joined the market. Following last year's budget does not take into account any new objectives and priorities, or necessary new spending, perhaps on a new IT system or replacement vehicles. The other major drawback of historical budgeting is that it does not encourage efficiency in terms of spending: it is taken for granted that costs will be as high as they were in the previous year. In fact, they will be higher.

> ### KEY TERM
>
> **Inflation** – a fall in the value of money, which causes prices to rise.

Zero budgeting

As we have already seen, zero budgeting sets the budget as zero and only the costs that can demonstrate that they are needed and will bring benefits to the business are included. The idea is to improve cost efficiency because each individual expenditure has to be justified. In this way funds can be targeted. If resources were allocated to a project last year and are now not required, they can be reallocated.

The focus of this type of budgeting is to improve coordination across the business to meet the key objectives. Each proposal for spending is examined and the likely benefits analysed. Managers from different parts of the business will have a direct input into the budget-setting process and may have a greater commitment to ensuring the success of any proposal they have championed.

This does make budgeting more complicated and more time-consuming, because each element has to be discussed and evaluated. Zero budgeting is also seen as divisive because each of the managers has to compete for his or her share of the budget. In some cases this leads to arguments and conflict.

Flexible budgeting

As the name implies, flexible budgeting allows for figures to be amended if circumstances change. An increase in suppliers' prices would push up costs per unit, so a purchasing budget would be increased. Equally, if sales fall, then the sales figures can be revised downwards. The idea is that the budgets are kept up-to-date and realistic.

However, the business does not have a set budget nor does it have agreed targets. Managers will tend to use uncontrollable external factors as excuses for poor performance, such as lower sales or higher costs. They will also seek to reduce targets in the knowledge that the targets can be exceeded, giving the impression of having achieved a better performance.

General benefits and drawbacks

Having looked at the different types of budgeting, some general benefits and drawbacks can be identified, as summarised in the table on the left.

Benefits of budgeting	Drawbacks of budgeting
Budgets are a good way to control and monitor costs, as spending has to be approved by the budget holder.	Budgets are based on assumptions and predictions, which may not necessarily be accurate. Incorrect budgets can be frustrating and demotivating.
Budgets are a useful coordination tool, as they can bring together departmental budgets to get an instant picture of the overall business.	Many managers try to get a larger budget than they actually need. Those with influence in the business will get the bigger budgets and have more spending power. Those who lack influence may struggle to work within their budgets.
Budgets are seen as motivational. Budget holders have the authority to decide on expenditure, making them feel trusted and valued. If they meet their targets then they have a sense of achievement.	Short-term actions may have to be taken in order to stay within budget, such as demanding additional discounts or cutting back on customer service, which could damage supplier or customer relationships.

Questions

1 Distinguish between historical and zero budgeting. (6 marks)
2 Which type of budgeting would be the most appropriate for a new business and why? (4 marks)
3 Do the benefits outweigh the drawbacks of budgeting? (4 marks)

Calculation and interpretation of favourable and adverse variances

Analysis of variances

Once the budgets have been brought together into a master budget, this can then be compared to the actual figures that the business obtains. Some of the differences, which are known as variances, may be due to calculation errors or perhaps changes in plans. Some may be due to external factors, including fluctuations in demand and changes in the interest rate.

When variances are noticed it is important for the business to act upon them in a timely manner, even if they are favourable variances. If the actual figure is more favourable than the budgeted figure then the letters 'FAV' are noted. If the actual figure is worse than the budgeted figure then the letters 'ADV', meaning adverse, are noted.

A business's sales budget may, for example, show the following:

- A budgeted sales figure of £500,000
- An actual figure of £400,000
- A variance of £50,000

As the actual figure is less than the budgeted figure, this is an adverse variance.

Obviously some variances are going to be very small and will not even affect the cash flow in any great way. Businesses expect to see variances. The most significant ones need to be investigated, which will help prevent the problem occurring again in the future.

KEY TERMS

Interest rate – a percentage charge added to the amount that has been borrowed, which is paid to the lender in addition to the capital sum.

Top-down process – a management system in which all key decisions are made by senior management and then filtered down through various layers of management for implementation.

Use of accounting and statistical information

Budgetary control and investigations into budget variances are an important part of making financial decisions. Budget variances need to be monitored throughout the year and in conjunction with the performance ratios and available statistical information. From these the business can see the underlying reasons behind the budget variances.

There needs to be flexibility in the management of budgets, but the following criteria are usually applied:

- Managers responsible for budgets should be clear about their responsibilities.
- Budget holders need to be accountable and must negotiate and inform when price increases are affecting areas for which they have financial responsibility.

- If the business has made any changes in the accountability arrangements, this needs to be passed on.
- All budget holders are responsible for contributing to the budget-setting process.
- Timetables for budget monitoring need to be set and met.
- The business needs to set budget reporting timescales, either weekly or monthly.
- The monitoring of the information needs to be a top-down process, so management at all levels needs to be actively involved.
- Any budgetary reports should include statements of actual expenditure and forecasts of expenditure.

Types of variance and interpretation

Obviously the basic variances will relate to sales revenue, total costs and profits. However, this is not the full list of variances and, as we will see, many of them, directly or indirectly, affect one another:

- Sales variance – this is when sales revenue differs from the budget, which will impact on profit.
- Cost variance – the business's total costs differ from budget, perhaps because of materials, labour or overheads. This will also have an impact on profit.
- Materials variance – cost of direct materials used and obtained from suppliers, different from budgeted figures, which could affect sales and profit.
- Labour variance – cost of direct labour related to production, different from budgeted figures, which impacts on costs and profit.

- Overhead variance – costs not associated with production are different from budgeted figures, which adds to costs and impacts on profit.
- Profit variance – affected by all the other variances.

A business will begin by constructing a budget and will then monitor the results against the budget. It should be relatively easy to identify a variance and then calculate the exact variance. The next problem is to analyse and explain it and evaluate its significance. A business will then seek to attribute responsibility for the variance and take corrective action.

Variances are always caused by either:

- A price that is greater or less than the budgeted figure
- A volume that is greater or less than the budgeted figure

In some cases, variances can be caused by a combination of both factors, and the aim of variance analysis is to separate out these elements. It is important to remember that positive or favourable variances show better than expected results. In other words revenue was higher than expected, or costs were lower than expected. The net result is that profits should be higher than those expected.

An unfavourable, adverse or negative variance shows a set of results that were worse than expected. This may mean that revenue was lower than expected, or that costs were higher. The net result of this is that profits are lower than anticipated.

CASE STUDY WATERMAN AND SONS LTD

COMPANY-WIDE BUDGETS

	Budget (£)	Actual (£)	Variance (£)
Sales revenue	148,000	159,000	?
Cost of materials	62,000	68,000	?
Labour costs	29,000	31,000	?
Gross profit	57,000	60,000	?
Overheads	22,000	26,000	?
Net profit	35,000	34,000	?

DEPARTMENTAL BUDGETS

	Budget (£)	Actual (£)	Variance (£)
Sales and distribution	15,000	17,000	?
Administration	18,000	18,000	?
Production	16,000	18,000	?
Human Resource Management	2,000	3,000	?

Questions

1 Work out the missing variances from the first table, indicating whether they are favourable or adverse. (6 marks)

2 Work out the missing variances from the departmental budgets, indicating whether they are favourable or adverse, and suggest reasons for the variances. (6 marks)

Using variance analysis to inform decision-making

Sales revenue variances

When sales revenue is different from a budgeted figure it can be caused by:

- Variance in the sales volume – which means that the actual amount sold is different from the planned volume. A volume variance will measure the impact on revenue of the difference between the quantities sold.
- Sales price variance – caused by a difference in the price being paid compared to the budgeted price. A price variance will measure the difference between the planned price and the actual selling price.

> **FOR EXAMPLE**
>
> *A business budgets to sell 100,000 units, but instead sells 90,000 units. It expected that the price per unit would be £2.50 but instead it was £2.40. The sales revenue was budgeted at £250,000 but the actual sales revenue was £216,000. The sales revenue variance was caused by both a lower quantity sold and a lower actual sales price.*

It is possible to work out the precise impact of the changes on the sales revenue by using the following formula:

> Sales revenue variance
> = (AQ × AP) − (BQ × BP)

AP is actual price per unit. AQ is actual quantity sold. BP is the budgeted price per unit and BQ is the budged quantity sold.

> **FOR EXAMPLE**
>
> (90,000 × £2.40) − (100,000 × £2.50) = £216,000 − £250,000 = −£34,000

Price variance uses:

> (AP − BP) × AQ

> **FOR EXAMPLE**
>
> (£2.40 − £2.50) × 90,000 = −£9,000

The volume or quantity variance uses:

> (AQ − BQ) × BP

> **FOR EXAMPLE**
>
> (90,000 − 100,000) × £2.50 = −£25,000

In our example we can see that the volume variance was of much greater significance than the price variance, as it contributed £25,000 less sales revenue compared to £9,000.

Materials variances

Materials variances look at the way in which the cost of materials affects total costs. The first is the materials price variance, being the difference between planned costs and actual costs per unit used. The formula used is:

> (AQ × AC) − (BQ × BC)

> **FOR EXAMPLE**
>
> *A business uses 600 units at £6, giving a total of £3,600. It had budgeted to use 650 units at £5, with a total cost of £3,250. Therefore:*
>
> (£6 × 600) − (£5 × 650) = £3,600 − £3,250 = £350 adverse variance

Direct materials price variance uses:

> (AC − BC) × AQ

> **FOR EXAMPLE**
>
> (£6 − £5) × 600 = £1 × 600 = £600 (adverse variance)

The variance on materials used uses:

> (AQ − BQ) × BC

> **FOR EXAMPLE**
>
> (600 − 650) × £5 = 50 × £5 = −£250 (favourable variance)

It was the adverse cost variance being greater than the favourable usage variance that led to the overall adverse variance.

Labour variances

Three different types of labour variance can be used:

- Total labour cost variance – which is the difference between what it actually costs to employ the direct labour and what it was expected to cost. This uses (AR × AH) – (BR × BH) where AR is actual wage rate and AH is actual number of hours. BR is budgeted wage rate and BH is budgeted hours to complete the work.
- The labour rate price variance – which is where there is a variance between the wage rate that was expected to be paid and what was actually paid. This uses (AR – BR) × AH.
- Labour efficiency variance – which measures whether there was more or less labour required to produce a specific amount of units. This uses (AH – BH) × BR.

FOR EXAMPLE

	Actual	Budget
Rate per hour	£10 (AR)	£9.50 (BR)
Hours of labour needed	48,000 (AH)	46,000 (BH)
Total cost of labour	£480,000	£437,000

The total labour cost variance
= £480,000 – £437,000
= adverse variance of £43,000.

The labour rate price variance
= (£10 – £9.50) × 48,000
= £24,000 adverse

The labour efficiency variance
= (£48,000 × £46,000) × £9.50
= £19,000 adverse

The high variance on labour costs was caused by the rise in the rate paid per hour, although both factors had a similar effect.

Overheads variances

The basic formula to work out variances in fixed overheads is to subtract the actual fixed overheads from the budgeted fixed overheads, with a negative figure giving an adverse variance.

For variable overheads, the actual cost of variable overheads can be subtracted from the budgeted figures, or:

> (actual production × budgeted variable overheads per unit) – actual variable overhead cost

Variable overhead costs are usually caused by changes in utility bills or changes in activity levels, which are linked either to labour costs or to the number of hours that machines are working.

It is also possible to work out overhead volume variances, using the formula:

> (budgeted quantity of input hours for actual production – actual input hours) × variable overhead rate

If the actual output is lower than planned there will be a variance, as overheads will not be fully absorbed.

KEY TERM

Depreciate – to gradually fall in value (used in relation to a business's fixed assets).

Interdependence of variances

The cause of a particular variance may often affect another variance in either a corresponding or an opposite manner. If a business manages to achieve greater productivity, giving it a favourable labour efficiency variance, the trade-off might be an adverse variance in material usage, as the workers may waste more materials because they have speeded up and become more careless.

If a business buys new machinery it will see an adverse fixed overhead expenditure variance because it has spent money purchasing the machine, and the machine will depreciate. At the same time, however, it will see a favourable set of variances in wage efficiency and fixed overhead volume variances because the machine should give a higher production level.

If a business has problems obtaining certain materials of a particular specification for production there may be a number of interdependent variances:

- Alternative materials may actually be cheaper, giving a favourable price variance.
- The cheaper material may be harder to use, causing more wastage and giving an adverse usage variance.
- If no materials are available for a short while, production might be disrupted, causing an adverse fixed overhead volume variance.
- Customers may be disappointed, as the business cannot meet the demand because of production difficulties. This will cause an adverse sales volume variance.

Questions

1 What are the key ways in which variances related to sales can be measured? (3 marks)
2 Which FOUR sets of figures are required to work out a direct materials cost variance? (4 marks)
3 If a business lowered prices and saw increased sales, which variances might be identifiable? (4 marks)

Case studies, questions and exam practice

CASE STUDY VARIANCES

A business has recently completed a period and can now compare its budgeted figures with the actual figures:

	March (£000s)			April (£000s)			May (£000s)		
	B	A	V	B	A	V	B	A	V
Sales	120	135	15	145	133	?	160	174	?
Materials	60	71	(11)	65	75	?	80	75	?
Other costs	20	23	(3)	20	20	0	25	23	?
Overheads	20	20	0	20	20	0	20	20	0
Profit	20	21	1	?	18	?	?	?	?

Questions

1 What are the ten numbers missing from the table? (10 marks)

2 Which costs figures seem under control, and which appear to be difficult to predict? (4 marks)

3 What is the overall variance in profit over the three-month period? (2 marks)

SHORT-ANSWER QUESTIONS

1 List **THREE** benefits of using budgets.

2 List **THREE** disadvantages of using budgets.

3 Briefly explain historical budgeting.

4 Briefly explain zero budgeting.

5 What is a favourable variance?

6 If the rent of a factory increases, which variance will be affected?

7 Which variance is (AQ – BQ) × BP?

8 Which **FOUR** sets of figures are required to work out labour variances?

9 Why might increased productivity cause an adverse material usage variance?

10 Which variances might be identified if a business makes a significant investment in new production machinery?

CASE STUDY GOOD OR BAD DECISION?

A business decides to cut the selling price per unit from £10 to £9.50. Immediately, sales increase by 25,000 units to 100,000. At the same time, overheads rise marginally from 15,000 to 17,000. The cost per unit remains the same at £7.70. The business cannot understand why it is that, with the additional 25,000 sales this month, its profit has increased by only £5,500. The finance director blames the sales director and the sales director blames the administration and production departments for the increased overheads costs.

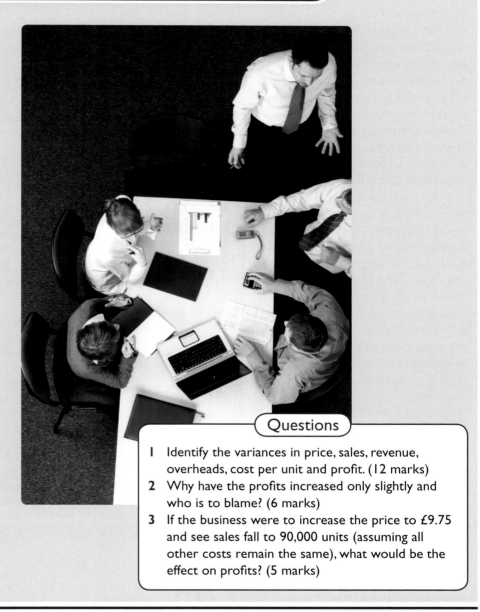

Questions

1 Identify the variances in price, sales, revenue, overheads, cost per unit and profit. (12 marks)
2 Why have the profits increased only slightly and who is to blame? (6 marks)
3 If the business were to increase the price to £9.75 and see sales fall to 90,000 units (assuming all other costs remain the same), what would be the effect on profits? (5 marks)

Causes of cash-flow problems

LEARNING OBJECTIVES
- ▶ Cash and working capital
- ▶ Reasons for cash-flow and working capital problems
- ▶ Resolving a liquidity crisis

Cash and working capital

Cash is actually a large part of what we call working capital. Working capital is the amount of money available to a business to pay for day-to-day running expenses. It is calculated by comparing what the business actually owns with what it owes. The problem is that much of what a business may own is tied up as fixed assets, such as land, buildings and machinery.

In a crisis, a business could sell some of its fixed assets, but this would take time. Therefore, as far as working capital is concerned, fixed assets are not part of the equation. The focus is therefore on current assets, which are assets that can be quickly turned into cash at short notice. This would include money in the bank; money that can be raised by selling stock; any cash at the business premises, and money owed by debtors.

To work out working capital we simply subtract the current liabilities, such as stock purchases, utility bills and wages, from the current assets. This will give us an accurate indication of the business's ability to be able to deal with its short-term debts.

A business that lacks working capital has exactly the same problems as a business that does not have enough cash. Cash, after all, is an essential part of working capital.

Reasons for cash-flow and working capital problems

There are many reasons why a business may suffer from cash-flow problems or difficulties with working capital. They are often referred to as a liquidity crisis. The major reasons are outlined in the following table:

Problem	Explanation
Too much spent on fixed assets	Expensive vehicles and machinery can tie up a business's available cash in assets that are difficult to sell. A business may be advised to lease assets to ensure that more cash is made available.
Too much stock	The business may find it difficult to sell stock fast enough to generate enough cash if it is holding too much stock in reserve.
Over-trading	This is when a business expands too quickly for the funds it has available. It may over-commit itself to additional wages, or to the purchase of assets, and if its sales do not match its forecasts, it will face a liquidity problem.
Seasonal fluctuations	Outgoings tend to remain relatively constant for most businesses. If a business is seasonal, then regular outgoings will drain working capital out of season.
Making too much credit available	Many businesses offer credit on products and services between 30 and 90 days after delivery. The longer the credit period, the longer the business has to wait for cash. It offers credit in order to attract sales, but must make sure that customers are not given a longer credit period than the credit period offered by their own suppliers.
Using too much credit	A business may find itself over-exposed to massive debt by taking advantage of long credit periods from suppliers. The business hopes that the longer it has to pay, the more likely it will be to have the cash available. But taking too much credit could lead to a major cash crisis in the future.
The unexpected	Non-payment by customers can affect cash flow, as can changes in the interest rate, levels of employment, the closure of a major supplier or customer and a host of other unexpected and unwanted events.

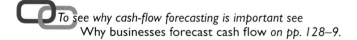

To see why cash-flow forecasting is important see Why businesses forecast cash flow *on pp. 128–9.*

Resolving liquidity problems

As we will see in the next spread, there are various ways in which the careful management of cash flow can either avoid cash-flow problems or promptly deal with them. Essentially the options are:

- Encourage debtors to pay sooner
- Cut down unnecessary expenses
- Sell debts to a debt collection agency
- Try to delay payments to suppliers
- Increase cash flow by selling off stock at a discount
- Ask the bank to extend the overdraft
- Obtain a long-term bank loan

- Sell assets and then **lease** them back
- Sell off any unused assets

It is important to recognise the fact that a problem with cash flow can be more dangerous than a drop in profits. A business needs to be aware of the impact that resolving a liquidity problem can have in the long-term. For example, selling and leasing back assets represents a long-term financial commitment for the business. The sale of unused assets may in fact inhibit the business's ability to grow in the longer-term.

> ### KEY TERM
>
> **Lease** – sometimes known as a rental plan or hire purchase agreement, an asset is made available to a business over an agreed period for a fixed, regular payment.

CASE STUDY BOO.COM

Boo.com went into receivership in May 2000. It sold branded fashionwear over the Internet. The founders spent £80m during their start-up, and their sales did not match expectations. Many of the products they did sell were returned as faulty. The business went down owing £12m to advertising agencies alone. Some 400 staff and contractors were made redundant and many of them had not been paid for months. Their cash-flow forecasts were very optimistic: they had hoped to begin by generating around £70m in sales revenue in the first year, and predicted this would increase tenfold within two years.

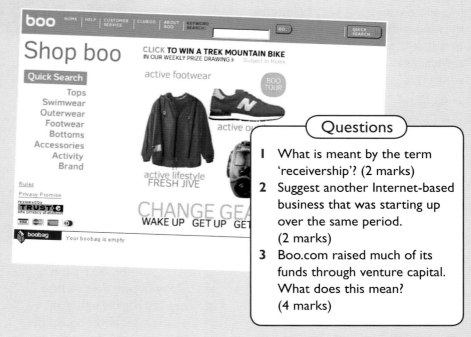

Questions

1 What is meant by the term 'receivership'? (2 marks)
2 Suggest another Internet-based business that was starting up over the same period. (2 marks)
3 Boo.com raised much of its funds through venture capital. What does this mean? (4 marks)

Methods of improving cash flow

LEARNING OBJECTIVES
▶ Speeding up inflows
▶ Delaying outflows
▶ Cutting expenditure
▶ Finding additional funding

Speeding up inflows

One of the primary techniques in helping to solve cash-flow problems is to increase the speed at which cash flows into the business. In effect there are three different ways in which this can be achieved:

- The business can negotiate shorter credit terms for customers – this is a potentially difficult and dangerous option, particularly in markets that are very competitive. The business may lose customers if it insists on reducing the period over which credit is available to their customers. In any case, larger customers demand longer credit periods. One way around this is to offer early settlement discounts to customers if they pay their invoices ahead of the due date.
- Improved credit management – by keeping a close eye on the payment of invoices by customers the business can prompt customers to make payments on invoices when they are due. This will require the business to send out reminder letters and, perhaps, make telephone calls to persuade customers to pay their invoices.
- Debt factoring – a business has the option of selling the value of an invoice to a debt factoring company. The business will receive 80% of the invoice value as soon as it is sold to the company. The factoring company then collects the full value of the invoice at the end of the credit period. It then pays the business the remaining 20% minus factoring fees. Usually this means that the business loses 5% of the total invoice value.

Delaying outflows

Just as a business can seek to improve the inflow of cash, it can also attempt to reduce the amount of money it spends. Again there are three ways in which this can be achieved:

- Negotiating better credit terms – suppliers can be approached to extend the period of credit for a range of products, services, components and raw materials used by the business. Although this only postpones payment, it can help the business over a difficult period when cash is in short supply. Suppliers will usually consider this as an option, but if they believe that the business is in difficulty they may be reluctant. Equally, new businesses with little or no credit history will find it difficult to convince suppliers to extend credit terms.
- Lease instead of buy – certainly one of most businesses' largest sets of expenditure is on fixed assets. This is particularly the case for new businesses that may need to acquire specific fixed assets in order to begin trading. Expenditure on these fixed assets represents a significant drain, but as an option the business could choose to lease the asset, rather than buy it outright. Staged payments over the lease period can help with cash flow and the business still has the option of owning the asset at the end of the lease period by making additional payments. Many businesses lease their company cars rather than purchase their own fleet of vehicles.
- Rent not buy – another significant expenditure is the purchasing of buildings, which may either be on the basis of an immediate full payment or a **commercial mortgage**. Renting the buildings rather than purchasing them will mean that the business does not have to find the capital to finance the purchase.

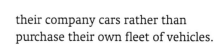

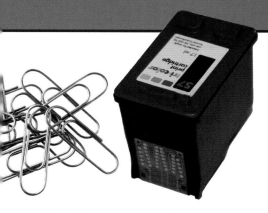

Cutting expenditure

We have already seen that it is possible to delay cash outflows, but there are more permanent ways in which a business can cut or delay expenditure:

- Decreasing levels of stock – businesses need to ensure that they have sufficient stocks of products, components, raw materials and **consumables** in order to ensure that they can fulfill customer orders and continue to run in an efficient manner. Stock levels, however, are important, as excess stock means that the stock will have to be paid for in advance of it being used or sold. By cutting down on orders to suppliers, and only placing orders when it is absolutely necessary, a business can reduce the amount of money tied up in unused stock. Businesses will usually have a re-order level for each stock item. Once the re-order level has been reached, the suppliers are contacted and an order placed. By reducing this re-order level the frequency of orders and also the level of stock held is reduced.

- Cutting costs – for many businesses the most expensive cost is their employees' wages and salaries. Businesses with cash-flow problems may not necessarily elect to reduce their workforce, but may opt not to replace employees who leave of their own accord. Businesses will also look to find other areas to cut costs, such as using in-house

employees for work usuually carried out by contractors, or finding contractors who can carry out tasks for the business at a lower cost than employing new members of staff.

- Postponing expenditure – this very much links to the delaying of cash outflows. For example, a business may choose not to replace a vehicle but to retain it for an additional period, thus delaying the costs associated with the purchasing of a new vehicle. This technique can be applied across many aspects of the business, such as computer systems or even employee training. However, the postponement of the expenditure must not adversely affect the efficiency of the business.

Finding additional funding

There are four ways in which a business can seek to find additional funding to cover any shortage of cash:

- Overdrafts – these usually have a high rate of interest, but they are flexible and the business only uses the overdraft when it really needs it. They are ideal for short-term cash shortages. However, the bank can withdraw the overdraft facility and demand immediate repayment.

- Short-term loan – this is a cheaper alternative to an overdraft, but less flexible. However, it does offer the business greater security, as the loan is for a fixed term.

- Long-term loan – a loan that is appropriate when a business needs money to cover it for a longer period of time. The overall interest payments may be relatively high.

- Sale and leaseback – a business can sell one of its fixed assets and then lease the asset back. This gives it an immediate inflow of cash. It does mean that there will be a regular ongoing cost, but the asset can be bought back at the end of the lease period.

Questions

1 Why might factoring cause problems for a business's regular customers? (3 marks)
2 Suggest at least THREE appropriate solutions to cash-flow problems for a new business. (6 marks)
3 Why might a business lose customers if it reduces its length of credit? (2 marks)

Case studies, questions and exam practice

CASE STUDY POLITICAL PARTIES' CASH-FLOW PROBLEMS

The tables below show the UK political parties' loans outstanding and donations received in 2006. The Conservatives owe £35.3m, Labour £23.4m and the Lib Democrats £1.1m. The Scottish National Party owes £525,393 and Plaid Cymru £352,000. While the Conservatives owe more, Labour loans need to be repaid sooner – £1.5m is due now, £17m by the end of next year. Labour said it was in the midst of a 'difficult financial year' and was restructuring to cut costs and to extend the repayment date of most of its loans.

LOANS OUTSTANDING

Conservatives	£35.300,000
Labour	£23.400,000
Liberal Democrats	£1.100,000
SNP	£525, 393
Plaid Cymru	£352,000
Respect	£34, 878
UKIP	£19,200

The Conservatives owe more than Labour, but almost £16m was spent on buying the freehold of the party's former headquarters in Smith Square – which it now hopes to sell. A change in the law in September 2006 means all loans of £5,000 and above to main political party offices have to be declared, bringing rules for loans into line with those for donations.

DONATIONS

Conservatives	£2,867,019
Labour	£3,227,340
Liberal Democrats	£629,903
SNP	£52,430
Plaid Cymru	£12,250
Respect	–
UKIP	£17,913
Co-operative Party	£142,036
Green Party	£138,396

Previously, any loans made with a commercial rate of interest did not have to be declared. The figures showed that in the third quarter of 2006, the Conservatives received donations worth £4m, Labour £3.2m and the Liberal Democrats £1.1m.

Adapted from the BBC and the Electoral Commission

Questions

1 What might be meant by the term 'restructuring'? (2 marks)
2 What might a lender need to know in order for an organisation to successfully negotiate an extension of a loan period? (4 marks)
3 What might be meant by the term commercial rate of interest? (2 marks)
4 Where might the donations given to a political party appear on their cash-flow forecasts and statements? (2 marks)

SHORT-ANSWER QUESTIONS

1 Why might a profitable business be short of cash?

2 What is meant by the term 'cash on delivery'?

3 Why might a supplier be unwilling to accept later payments from new businesses?

4 What is the basic formula for working capital?

5 What is meant by the term 'liquidity'?

6 What is meant by the term 'over-trading'?

7 Briefly explain what is meant by factoring.

8 What is sale and leaseback of assets and how does it work?

9 How might a business use credit management to help improve its cash flow?

10 What is a commercial mortgage?

CASE STUDY LATE PAYMENT LEGISLATION

In November 1998, the British Government introduced legislation to give businesses a statutory right to claim interest from other businesses for the late payment of commercial debt. Britain was one of the first countries in the EU to introduce late payment legislation to help promote a culture of prompt payment.

From 7 August 2002, the Late Payment of Commercial Debts (Interest) Act 1998 was amended and supplemented to incorporate the features of European Directive 2000/35/EC on combating late payment in commercial transactions.

Under the revised legislation, all business owners and managers can claim reasonable debt recovery costs and can benefit from the simplification of the calculation of Statutory Interest. Additionally, small and medium-sized enterprises can ask a representative body to challenge grossly unfair contract terms used by their customers which do not provide a substantial remedy for late payment of commercial debts.

Questions

1 How do late payments affect businesses? (5 marks)
2 Why is it necessary for there to be legislation in this area? (4 marks)
3 Compared to non-EU businesses, do you think that this legislation puts British businesses at a competitive disadvantage? (6 marks)

The calculation and understanding of net profit margins

LEARNING OBJECTIVES
- ▶ What is a net profit margin?
- ▶ Calculating net profit margins
- ▶ Understanding net profit margins

What is a net profit margin?

One of the functions of accounting is to show to stakeholders exactly how a business has performed over a given period of time. A net profit margin is one measure of performance. Simply stating that a business may have made £100,000 annual profit, does not necessarily reveal whether or not it has done well compared to the competition or the circumstances.

Obviously, if the business is small, then £100,000 profit is very healthy. However, a larger business, working on a national basis, would consider £100,000 profit to be extremely poor.

The net profit margin helps us look at just how good that level of profit actually is, and is what is known as an element of ratio analysis. The net profit margin looks at the relationship between the net profit (the profit after all overhead expenses have been taken into account) and the level of turnover, or the sales revenue, that the business generated. The formula is fairly straightforward, but it is important to remember that it is always expressed as a percentage:

$$\text{net profit margin} = \frac{\text{net profit}}{\text{turnover}} \times 100\%$$

Calculating net profit margins

There is one slight complication. Some businesses calculate net profit margin in a slightly different way. Firstly it is important to remember that net profit is always equal to a business's gross profit, minus their expenses. Some businesses just show the net profit, as we have already calculated using the formula shown above. Other businesses calculate their net profit margin using the following formula:

$$\frac{\text{profit before interest and taxation}}{\text{turnover}} \times 100$$

Those of you who have followed this so far will realise that the two formulae actually mean exactly the same thing.

Whichever version of the formula is used, it simply tells the business, a stakeholder or a potential stakeholder the amount of net profit per £ of turnover that the business has earned. This takes into account any costs of sales, administration, distribution and all other costs.

The net profit will be the profit that is left and, of course, out of this the business will have to pay interest, tax, and dividends to shareholders if appropriate.

FOR EXAMPLE

Nigel the plumber showed a net profit of £24,000 on a sales turnover of £88,000. The following calculation is used:

$$\frac{£24,000}{£88,000} \times 100 = 27.27\%$$

In the next year Nigel's net profit rose to £28,000 on a sales turnover of £98,000. His new net profit margin is 28.57%.

KEY TERMS

Stakeholders – an individual or group with a direct interest in the business, such as an employee, owner or shareholder.

Profit-and-loss account – a statement that shows a business's revenues and costs over the period of a year. It shows how much profit the business has made and where it has been spent.

Profit margins will vary from business to business and from industry to industry. The following table gives an example of the range of net profit margins earned by ten businesses based in the US, all involved in the same kind of service: the provision of Internet information:

INTERNET INFORMATION COMPANIES NET PROFIT MARGINS (US)

Company name	Net profit margin (%)
Netease.com	55.00
TheStreet.com	50.52
Baidu.com	36.82
Google Inc.	26.90
Knot Inc.	24.83
Bankrate Inc.	21.81
Global Sources Ltd.	19.17
Health Grades Inc.	18.24
Travelzoo Inc.	17.23
Sohu.com Inc.	16.44

For businesses with published accounts, such as limited companies, it is possible to work out the net profit margin by looking at the profit-and-loss account, as in the following example:

We can work out Gerry's net profit margin for each year and then compare the performance. In 2008 the turnover was £198,000 and the net profit was £87,000. This gives us £87,000/£198,000 = 0.439, or 43.9% net profit margin.

In 2009 sales were up to £235,000 but the net profit was down to £55,000. This gives us the calculation £55,000/£235,000 = 0.234, or 23.4% net profit margin. We can therefore see that although sales were up, the net profit margin was considerably down because the cost of sales rocketed by £71,000 in 2009.

Understanding net profit margins

Although the net profit margin is displayed as a percentage, a 15% net profit margin means that for every £ of sales that the business has generated it has made 15p in net profit. When we look at the earnings of a business this often does not tell the entire story. While increased earnings are a good sign, the increase does not necessarily mean that the business's profit margins

are improving. A business could have increased its earnings, but its costs may have increased at a greater rate than its sales. This would lead to a lower profit margin and should indicate to an investor and to the owners of the business that the costs need to be controlled.

If a business has a net income of £100,000 from sales of one million this would give it a profit margin of 10%. In other words it has made 10p for every £ that it has generated in sales. In the next year its net income rises to £150,000 but this time it is on sales of two million. The business has increased its sales revenue, or net income, but the cost has been a fall in the net profit margin to 7.5% or 7.5p per pound.

The net profit margin, as we will see later in this section, can be improved either by increasing sales revenue while keeping costs down, or by reducing costs and keeping sales revenue constant.

GERRY'S WINE BAR LTD – PROFIT-AND-LOSS ACCOUNT

Year ending	31 December 2008 (£000s)	31 December 2009 (£000s)
Turnover	198	235
Cost of sales	105	176
Gross profit	93	59
Expenses	22	25
Operating profit	71	34
Other income	16	21
Net profit	87	55
Interest	12	10
Tax	20	14
Net profit after tax	55	31
Dividends	33	15
Retained profit	22	16

Questions

1 Heather's small jam-making business has a turnover of £29,000 and she shows a net profit of £9,500. What is her net profit margin? (3 marks)

2 Harold the builder had a turnover of £58,000 in 2008, which rose by £19,000 the following year. In 2008 his net profit was £23,000 and this rose by 10% the following year. What were his net profit margins for the two years, and how do the two figures compare? (6 marks)

The calculation and understanding of return on capital

What is return on capital?

Before making a major decision on a substantial capital investment – such as the purchase of new production machinery, an improved computer network, new software, new premises or a replacement of a vehicle fleet – a business will want to be assured that the investment is likely to improve its profitability and efficiency.

Any major investment needs to be supported by a reasonable expectation that increased profits can be made due to the efficiencies that the capital investment will bring for the business. In other words, the business needs to measure the difference between the potential returns on its capital investment compared to current performance without the capital investment.

A business will not necessarily expect the capital investment to pay itself back by covering its costs in the short term. It will, however, look for a percentage improvement, which in this instance needs to be measured in cash or profit terms.

It is difficult for the business to judge the long-term effects on profitability of a capital investment, though it may be able to calculate the probable annual returns. It should bear in mind that any capital investment will begin to pay for itself, but will come to a point when even new investment no longer provides any benefit, as a new capital investment may need to be made.

FOR EXAMPLE

If a business purchases a new fleet of lorries, it may improve its carrying capacity and fuel efficiency in the short to medium term. However, as the vehicles age and require more maintenance and, perhaps, new legislation requires greater fuel efficiency and fewer pollutants, the business may have to reinvest by replacing the fleet again after five or six years. This means that the capital investment needs to repay itself and produce a profit within its lifetime of five to six years.

Calculating return on capital

There are two ways of calculating the net effect of an investment on efficiency and on profit. The first is to consider how much of the original investment will be paid back as a percentage each year. This will give the business an indication of how long it will take before the investment pays for itself and then begins to produce benefits to the business as pure profit. The formula is:

$$\frac{\text{annual return}}{\text{original investment}} \times 100$$

FOR EXAMPLE

A business makes an investment of £120,000 on new production machinery. It calculates that as a direct result of the investment an extra £40,000 of sales have been generated. Therefore:

$$\frac{£40,000}{£120,000} \times 100 = 33.33\%$$

This shows that in the first full year the investment has already generated in additional sales the equivalent of a third of its original purchase price. A business would then be in a position to estimate that the investment will have paid itself off after three years and then any additional contribution made by the investment would be pure profit.

One of the biggest problems in working out the return on capital of an investment is to accurately assign any increase in sales or profit to the actual investment itself. It may not be abundantly clear where the additional sales or profits were generated. A business may assume that additional sales or profit can be attributed to the capital investment and may use the following formula in order to gauge its percentage contribution to profit:

$$\frac{\text{attributed profit}}{\text{this year's profit}} \times 100$$

FOR EXAMPLE

A business shows an annual profit of £120,000 of which it attributes £22,000 as a direct consequence of the capital investment. Therefore:

$$\frac{£22,000}{£120,000} \times 100 = 18.33\%$$

The business attributes 18.33% of the additional profit generated as a direct result of the capital investment.

Understanding return on capital

As we have seen, it is difficult for a business to be absolutely sure that a capital investment, rather than other factors, has been the reason behind an increase in profits. Efficiencies may have been made in other parts of the business, or other factors, such as cheaper supplier prices, less wastage, or a host of other smaller factors, may have made the contribution.

A business can seek to isolate the generation of profit by creating a series of cost and profit centres. Each of these reports its own separate performance figures, making it easier for the business to identify where costs are being incurred and where profits are being generated. This may mean that the business can more efficiently and accurately assess the precise impact of a capital investment on profit.

CASE STUDY ANGUS FREIGHT FORWARDING

For the last two years this small business has struggled to use ageing Luton vans. It has decided to finally replace its four vans with larger, brand new trucks. Each will cost £110,000. The business's sales revenue before the investment is £960,000, of which 20% is profit. It expects to be able to increase sales revenue to £1.4m and for the percentage of profit to remain a similar figure. Without the investment the business cannot expand, neither can it hope to increase its sales revenue, and the expectation is that profits will drop, as the Luton vans become more inefficient, spend less time on the road and require far more finance due to increased maintenance costs.

Questions

1 Assuming the figures are correct, how much of the original investment on the four new trucks will be paid back as a percentage in the first year? (6 marks)

2 Again, if the figures are correct and all the additional profit can be attributed to the new vehicles, what percentage increase in profits has actually been generated by the capital investment? (6 marks)

3 What are the advantages and disadvantages of this capital investment and were there other options open to the business, which may have avoided having to invest £440,000? (8 marks)

Methods of improving profits and profitability

LEARNING OBJECTIVES
- ► Why improving profits and profitability is important
- ► Cost reductions and implications
- ► Price rises and implications

Why improving profits and profitability is important

Profit is a term that needs to be clearly understood and used in the correct manner. There are four measures of profit, these are:

- Gross profit – the profit generated by a business before expenses related to running the business have been subtracted.
- Net profit – the profit after expenses, considered either before or after tax, or before or after any interest on borrowed funds has been taken into account.
- Disposable profit – the profit that is to be made available to the owners or shareholders of a limited company. Alternatively this is the amount that sole traders or partners can take as drawings (in the case of limited companies this would be dividends).
- Retained profit – the part of the profit that the business keeps so that it has additional capital available for future investment or to use as working capital.

If a business has sufficient profit then it will have enough working capital to cover its day-to-day expenses. It should have money for growth and development (without needing to go to a finance provider for additional funding) and it can provide a reward to the owners of the business for having taken risks as a part of normal business activity.

Cost reductions and implications

There are several definitions of the term 'costs' and each of these can be specifically addressed by a business wishing to increase its profits or profitability:

- Fixed costs – this includes rent, rates, management salaries, interest charges and depreciation. Usually long-term fixed costs can alter, but in the short-term it is difficult to adjust fixed costs downwards, so this makes this aspect of costs an unlikely source of cost savings.
- Variable costs – these are costs directly related to the level of output. Costs will usually increase as output increases, as they will include the costs of labour, fuel, raw materials and components. Ways of handling variable cost reduction include sourcing cheaper raw materials or components, negotiating higher levels of productivity with employees, or seeking cheaper sources of fuel.
- Semi-variable costs – not all costs can be classified as either fixed or variable, as some costs actually have some of the attributes of both. A business that has a

delivery vehicle has a number of fixed operating costs related to it, including insurance and road tax. If output increases and the vehicle is used more often, the business would incur extra costs, such as additional fuel and more regular services. These aspects of the vehicle's costs are classed as semi-variable, as they are part fixed and part variable. Again it would be difficult for the business to be able to reduce the semi-variable costs.

One of the implications of cost reduction is the possibility that products and services will suffer in terms of quality. This can be for a number of reasons:

- The raw materials may be of poorer quality
- Components may not be as good as those previously used
- The speed of production may mean more faults and mistakes
- There may be problems with employees as new, higher targets are set without financial reward for the employees

---

KEY TERMS

Drawings – wages or salaries taken out of either a sole trader or partnership business by the owners.

Working capital – strictly, a business's current assets minus its current liabilities. It is the finance that the business uses for everyday expenses.

Market share – the percentage of total shares in a given market controlled by a particular business.

Price rises and implications

There is a strong relationship between the price that a business charges for its products and services, and the potential demand for those products and services. Price can also have a direct influence on profitability. If prices are reduced to stimulate sales, a large increase in demand is required in order to compensate for the loss of profit per unit.

In the same way, price rises can have a negative effect on demand. Increasing prices means that the business's products and services may appear to be less attractive compared to those offered by competitors. The short-term implications may be that the business will lose sales, but the loss in sales may be compensated for by the increase in profit per unit sold. In the longer term the business runs the risk of losing **market share**. Customers may switch to a competitor's products and services, causing a longer-term drop in demand for the business.

FOR EXAMPLE

The CD singles market is in decline and in fact record companies tend to lose money on singles. However they are seen as being useful marketing tools to sell CD albums, which are more profitable. Record companies use reduced prices in order to stimulate sales, and often put additional tracks onto CD singles in order to make them more attractive. The industry has discovered that customers are reluctant to pay in excess of £10 for an album with around twelve tracks when they can buy a CD single with up to four tracks for around £2.

Questions

1 Distinguish between the three different types of costs (6 marks)
2 What is the relationship between price and demand? (4 marks)
3 What is working capital? (2 marks)

The distinction between cash and profit

LEARNING OBJECTIVES
▶ What is cash?
▶ What is profit?
▶ Why does it matter?

What is cash?

Undoubtedly cash is most important for businesses. Without cash they cannot possibly survive. While a business can survive for a short period of time without making sales or making a profit, it cannot survive without cash.

In business terms cash is the ability of a business to be able to pay its bills on time. This will, of course, depend on the amounts of cash that flow in and out of the business and the timing of those receipts and payments.

In this context, cash does not just mean notes and coins. It also includes money in the business's current account; any short-term deposits it has made; its overdraft facility; its short-term loans; any foreign currency it may have, or deposits of foreign currency that can be turned into sterling.

For the most part cash is:

- Cash and cheques
- The inflow of money into a business's bank account (note: the actual money that has been received, rather than what is promised or still owed).
- The cash that flows out of the business, in order to pay suppliers' invoices (note: not all invoices are paid by cash: some of these may be on credit terms).

A business needs to build up cash reserves, in order to ensure that cash movements create a positive cash flow. This does not necessarily mean that a business that has a large amount of cash in the bank is making the right decisions. The cash may be more productive if it is being invested in order to provide a better return.

For more information on cash flow see Using cash-flow forecasting on pp.122–31 and Improving cash flow on pp.166–71.

What is profit?

Profit is obviously reliant on the inflow of cash and is measured by subtracting a business's costs from its sales revenue. Profit is different from cash because it is the actual money that has been earned by the business. It is also important to remember that sales can be made on credit terms, so that sales are not only cash: the payments may not appear immediately, and the timing of their payment will have a direct influence on cash flow.

Profit is usually calculated over a given period of trading, perhaps a month, or quarterly, six-monthly or yearly. A business can often forecast a reasonable profit for the trading period, but this does not mean that it will not face times when it is lacking in cash. This is due to the difference between cash flows and actual profit.

Profit can eventually include long-term deposits, borrowing and money owed by customers. None of these are immediately available to the business, so they do not count as cash.

Why does it matter?

It is important to distinguish cash from profit. As we have seen, profit is the difference between what a business has earned and its costs. Profit is the ultimate measure of the success of a business. It needs to show a positive difference between its costs and the sales revenue. Without showing a profit, all a business's activities are rendered ineffective, as they have not produced a surplus of funds when the costs are compared with the income received from the sales.

This is not to say that a business cannot survive for some time without making a profit. As we have seen, when we considered break-even, new businesses in particular are forced to make large investments before they even begin to offer products and services to customers. It will, therefore, take them a considerable amount of time to recoup these costs. Only once this has happened and it has broken even will a business hope to move into profit.

Many small businesses do not expect to move into immediate profit. Even established businesses

slashed as a result of a large increase in their costs.

It is also important to distinguish types of profit. Gross profit is the difference between a business's turnover and the cost of manufacturing or purchasing products and services that have then been sold. Net profit takes the gross profit and then subtracts expenses and overheads. Many believe that net profit is one of the most useful measurements of profit because a business can show a healthy gross profit, but a small net profit. This is because the business may not be controlling its overheads.

It is also important to note that business owners and potential investors look at profit quality. In other words they look to see where the profit came from. Some

profits may have arisen as a result of the sale of a major asset, perhaps for more than the expected value. A business may have sold a building that it no longer needed. This would count as income, and would boost the profits of the business, but only once, because it has sold the asset and cannot repeat the sale in the following year. This is therefore a comparatively low-quality profit.

A high-quality profit is usually a trading profit, which means the profit that the business has made directly from the sales of products and services. Investors will consider this a high-quality profit, as the expectation will be that it can be repeated year after year.

Questions

1 In 2008 a business shows a profit of £120,000. In the following year, as a result of redundancy payments made, its profits plunge to £22,000. How might the owners or potential investors view this in terms of profit quality? (4 marks)

2 A business has a positive balance in its bank account of £2,200. Six customers have as yet not paid £4,600 in outstanding invoices. The business's accountant has cheques to be paid in to the value of £3,100 and there is £468 in petty cash in the office. How much cash does the business have? (4 marks)

Case studies, questions and exam practice

CASE STUDY GOOD DEAL?

An investor purchases an off-plan two-bedroom unit close to the beach on the south coast of Spain for €250,000 plus 10% tax/costs. The investor pays a 20% deposit of €50,000 upon signing the purchase contract. Also at this point, the investor pays half the legal fees up front of €1,250, plus VAT on the deposit payment of 7% (€3,500). Total capital invested at this point is €54,750.

The second stage payment is completed six months later for a further 10% of the purchase price at €25,000 plus 7% VAT of €1,750. Total capital invested after six months is €81,500.

After year one of the investment, capital appreciation has realised at 10% for the year, meaning the property is now valued at €275,000.

The investor decides to instigate an exit strategy after 16 months (just prior to completion), with capital appreciation continuing to perform at 10% per annum. The property is now valued at €284,167.00

The investor finds a buyer for the property before proceeding to purchase contract, 14 months into the investment. At this point, to facilitate the sale, the investor settles remaining legal fees of €1,250. Total capital invested upon exit is €82,750. The sale price is €284,167.00

The investor recoups capital invested, minus the VAT and legal payments made of €7,750. Having recouped €75,000 of capital invested and seeing growth on the sale of the unit of €34,167, the total profit realised in using this short-term strategy is €26,417, a return on capital invested of 32.5% over a 16-month investment timescale.

Questions

1 What might be meant by the term 'capital appreciation'? (2 marks)
2 What is meant by the term 'exit strategy'? (2 marks)
3 Is the return on capital invested correct and what figures have been used to calculate this? (4 marks)
4 How risky might an investment of this type be to a new property developer buying their first investment property abroad? (8 marks)

SHORT-ANSWER QUESTIONS

1 What is net profit?

2 What is the formula used to calculate the net profit margin?

3 Why is net profit a better measure of a business's performance than gross profit?

4 What is return on capital?

5 What are the two ways in which return on capital can be calculated?

6 What are the differences between cash and profit?

7 Give **THREE** examples of cash.

8 What are the demand implications of cost reduction?

9 What are the demand implications of a price increase?

10 How might a business be profitable yet have no available cash?

CASE STUDY CONTACT FRAGRANCES LTD

Contact Fragrances ltd produces a new perfume suitable for both men and women. It has a sliding price structure to its distributors, dependent upon the output of bottles of perfume that it produces. The business has also worked out the likely demand for their bottles of perfume based on the sales price linked to output.

Output in bottles	Fixed costs	Variable costs	Total costs	Costs per bottle	Sales price per bottle	Estimated demand
5,000	£10,000	£10,000	?	?	£6.05	4,800
10,000	£10,000	£20,000	?	?	£5.88	9.600
20,000	£10,000	£40,000	?	?	£5.42	19,200
30,000	£10,000	£60,000	?	?	£5.13	28,800
40,000	£10,000	£80,000	?	?	£5.04	38,400
50,000	£10,000	£100,000	?	?	£4.98	48,000

Questions

1 Work out the total costs of production for the six levels of output. (6 marks)

2 Work out the cost per bottle for each of the six levels of output. (6 marks)

3 Calculate the estimated profit for each level of output based on the figures given. (6 marks)

4 Which level of output offers the business the best level of profitability? (2 marks)

Introduction

This is the second of four themes for *Managing a business*. It looks at the issues managers face in relation to the management of human resources and specifically how this is done in order to make a business more effective and efficient. Throughout, you will see how management techniques are used as part of the tactics for helping to make decisions that can directly impact on the profitability, efficiency and long-term development of the business.

Regardless of the type of industry or the sector in which a business operates, its most valuable and usually its most costly resource is its employees. Each business has its distinct organisational structure – usually several layers of management and supervision – that control and direct the activities of the bulk of the workforce. The organisational structure needs to be efficient and effective; it needs to have strong communication flows, up and down and across the organisation. Above all, each employee, supervisor or manager needs to be clear about their role.

Businesses can measure the effectiveness of their workforce using a number of different tools that look at the productivity, output and labour turnover. A truly effective workforce begins with a sound recruitment process, usually a mixture of internal promotion, redeployment and external recruitment. This is backed up by the creation of documents, such as job descriptions, that specify the requirements of a job role. In the longer term, employees are also supported and kept up-to-date through training.

In order to develop and retain an effective workforce, many businesses use techniques and ideas developed by theorists on motivation. Motivation seeks to ensure that employees are content in their work and feel adequately rewarded and valued by their employer. Businesses use a variety of methods in order to achieve these goals, including job design, empowerment and teamwork. Retaining key members of staff is vital to the long-term survival of any business. Experienced employees are difficult to replace, and even experienced replacements usually require long periods of retraining and transition before they are as effective as the individuals that they have replaced.

Key elements of organisational structure (1)

LEARNING OBJECTIVES

▶ Organisational structures
▶ Organisation trees
▶ Layers of management
▶ Hierarchies
▶ Spans of control

Organisational structures

The traditional way of visualising the organisational structure of a business is to create an organisation chart. This will show the various departments, sections or teams involved in the business and will illustrate the following:

- Each of the departments and the way that these departments are broken down.
- The levels of responsibility of managers, by showing different managers with the same level of responsibility at the same level in the chart. This can also show how the departments and their managers work with one another.
- The lines of communication within the business, showing how information passes down the organisation from senior management, and up to the senior management via the layers of management.

Organisation trees

The West Yorkshire Fire and Rescue Service organisation chart is a simplified organisation tree. It shows that there are five individuals with the same level of responsibility, answering directly to the Chief Executive. Each of these individuals is responsible for one or more management areas of the organisation, such as Human Resources or Training and Development. Obviously, underneath this senior management group there will be managers responsible for each area and fire station. Beneath them will be the fire fighters and other support staff.

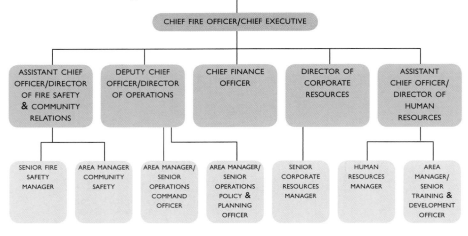

Source: www.westyorksfire.gov.uk

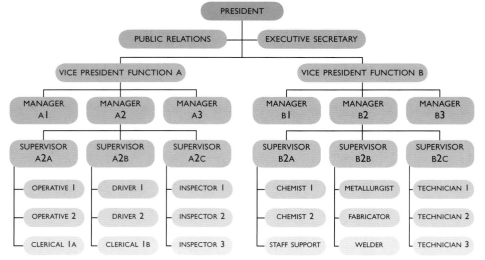

Source: www.emeraldinsight.com

As you can see from the next illustration of an organisation tree, many of the trees look like pyramids. There are only a handful of individuals at the top, but more and more managers, supervisors and employees as you move down the tree. Those employees at the bottom of the chart report, through successive layers of management, to the senior managers. This is known as a **hierarchy**.

KEY WORD

Hierarchy – the arrangement of the levels of authority in a business, with successively more authority and responsibility as you go up the organisation tree.

By organising the business more strictly it is possible to identify and place individual managers and employees in areas of specialism. Anything to do with marketing – for example, including public relations and advertising – would normally be part of the marketing and sales department. Production would have a works manager, someone with responsibility for quality, designers, and those involved in purchasing raw materials and components for the production lines. The ways in which businesses are organised will be determined by the nature of the work involved. Some departments are functional, which means they are actively involved in doing the business's work, while the rest are in support roles, such as administration.

Layers of management

Not all organisations look like tall, thin pyramids. Some are very flat. These have few layers of management between the key decision-makers and the employees. These types of organisation are called flat structures. They usually use teams of employees to carry out tasks and solve problems.

Many smaller organisations use flatter structures. This helps everyone understand the objectives of the business and learn how to work closely together. It is easy to tell just how many layers of management there are in a business by counting the number of managers or supervisors between the key decision-makers at the top of the organisation and the employees at the bottom of the structure. Obviously the more layers there are the more complicated it can become to get messages and instructions up and down the structure.

The arrangement of layers is often called the chain of command. It traces the exact lines of responsibility and communication from, for example, the managing directors to retail assistants.

Messages can easily get lost or changed in complicated structures with several layers of management. Smaller businesses find it easier to pass on information directly and ensure that it is correct. Problems can arise, however, when the business gets larger and needs more employees.

Hierarchies

Another major consideration regarding complicated pyramid structures with multiple layers of management is that they are very hierarchical. This means that each layer of management jealously hangs on to its authority and responsibility, making sure that it is always part of any decision-making process. Information must pass through each level, both up and down the organisation.

Certain managers in the structure can resist decisions that are made by senior management; perhaps ideas are watered down, ignored or deliberately misinterpreted so that they will fail. Equally, useful information coming to them from lower down the organisation can be withheld. The feeling is that information, or the possession of it, is more important than the good or bad it might do to the business as a whole.

Difficulties such as these are another good reason why many businesses have chosen to de–layer. They have cut out layers of middle management and pushed responsibility and decision-making further down the organisational structure.

Spans of control

A manager's span of control includes the number of individuals who directly report to him or her. Even the most talented and efficient manager can handle only a limited span of control. Once the span gets beyond about eight individuals, it becomes difficult for the manager or supervisor to devote enough time to each subordinate. An increased number of employees in a particular department or team will mean that more managers or supervisors will have to be created or promoted in order to manage their activities. Simply adding additional employees to an existing team or department will eventually lead to enormous inefficiencies, without additional management support.

CASE STUDY WHO'S IN CHARGE?

Three people report to Fiona. Four people report to Brian. Neither Fiona nor Brian reports to one another, but they both report to Clive. Clive reports to Sybil. Sybil reports to the Board of Directors and they report to the Managing Director.

Questions

1 Using a pyramid shape, draw the business structure. (8 marks)
2 Comment on the structure in terms of the layers of management, hierarchies and spans of control. (9 marks)

Key elements of organisational structure (2)

LEARNING
OBJECTIVES
▶ Workloads
▶ Job allocation
▶ Delegation
▶ Communication flows

Workloads

A difficult part of deciding on the organisational structure of a business is deciding how to adequately spread the workload that will be placed on individual employees or groups of employees. Many businesses will allocate additional employees, or at least sufficient employees, in areas that directly generate sales revenue. They will usually keep employee levels relatively low in cost areas. This can often be a false economy, as unequal workloads put unnecessary and unworkable pressure on certain parts of the business and can cause systems to break down and communication channels to fail, and can ultimately result in higher than average **labour turnover**.

⊙━ *For more on motivation and empowerment see* Developing an effective workforce: motivating employees *on pp. 196–207.*

KEY TERMS

Empower – to give responsibility and authority to subordinates lower down in a hierarchy.

Labour turnover – a measurement, usually as a percentage, of the number of employees joining and leaving a business. The higher the percentage, the higher the turnover of employees in that period.

Job allocation

For very small businesses, responsibilities for particular jobs or routine duties are usually blurred. However if a business has job descriptions then there will be a clear indication of the responsibilities and duties assigned to each employee.

Job allocation involves assigning duties and responsibilities to specific job roles or to teams, departments, sections or groups of employees. Responsibility, for example, for banking cheques received from customers will be an integral part of an accounts department's work. It is unlikely that this type of job would be allocated to a member of the warehouse staff.

Job allocation has close association with workload, as the range of duties and responsibilities allocated to each job role will have a bearing on the workload involved.

Delegation

Delegation means giving authority and responsibility to subordinates in order to complete a task. It is important for the manager or supervisor to give both authority and responsibility, as this **empowers** the subordinate to actually do the work. Without authority, decisions are unlikely to be implemented. Delegation involves recognition of the talents and skills of the subordinates and this trust can be very effective in giving them job satisfaction and keeping them motivated.

In order to ensure that delegation works, a business needs to ensure:

- that the nature of the tasks to be carried out is clearly outlined;
- that staff are capable and willing to undertake the tasks;
- that expected results and timings are both realistic and clear;
- that sufficient authority is delegated for the member of staff to deal with a task;
- that those who need to know and will work with the person are informed;
- that the person who has delegated the tasks still has the ultimate responsibility, and that the delegate should always report to them and obtain advice as required.

There are many limits to delegation in terms of its effectiveness, as follows:

- Some businesses choose not to delegate because they believe that the costs in time, resources and outcome do not warrant it.
- By delegating to a range of individuals, not all are able to cope with new responsibilities.
- Smaller businesses tend to delegate small tasks or delegate too much, which can cause difficulties.
- Certain tasks cannot be delegated due to the special knowledge required to carry them out.

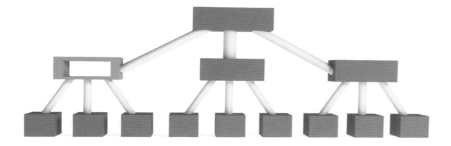

Communication flows

As we will see when we look at the motivation of employees, delegation can be seen as a key motivating technique that gives empowerment to employees and allows them to experience decision-making and problem-solving at a level beyond their current job role. For the business itself it allows them to look at the longer-term prospects of a particular employee, to see if they are suited to roles with greater responsibility in the future.

A business needs to have efficient channels of communication up and down the structure. Information and instructions have to be routinely passed on, so that those who could benefit from it, or are affected by it, become aware of the situation as soon as possible.

The more layers of management in a business, the more difficult it may be for this information to pass up and down the levels in an efficient manner. Channels of communication are often referred to as chains of command.

Typically, a chain of command will begin with the managing director, passing through successive layers of managers and supervisors, until it reaches the employees at the bottom of the organisational structure.

In very strict and complicated pyramids the chains of command, or channels of communication, can be very complex and problematic. The major problem is that senior management is distanced from the daily tasks and duties carried out by the bulk of employees at the bottom of the structure.

CASE STUDY PIGOTT PASTRIES

Phyllis Pigott is the managing director of Pigott Pastries. The company supplies cafés and petrol stations with a range of savoury pastry products. The business has grown rapidly over the last three years, from half a dozen employees to nearly 100. To keep up with demand the factory needs to operate 24 hours a day with three eight-hour shifts. During the day an administration manager and a food purchasing manager, as well as the day shift food production manager assist Phyllis. A deputy manager and a shift supervisor assist the day-shift food production manager. The same three-level model is also used for the evening and the night shifts. Not everything is working as efficiently as Phyllis would hope.

Questions

1 An advisor from Business Link has suggested to Phyllis that the role of deputy manager be removed and that the shift manager and supervisor could share responsibility. Comment on the effect on the hierarchy and other possible benefits. (6 marks)
2 Using the above suggestion, explain what you understand by the terms 'de-layering', 'delegation' and 'span of control'. (6 marks)
3 Is there a necessity for either Phyllis, the administration manager or the food purchasing manager to be on the premises for 24 hours a day? (4 marks)

Workforce roles

Directors

The terms 'directors', 'owners' and 'shareholders' are often interchangeable. All of these people will have some kind of financial stake in a business. All of them will own shares or be outright owners of the business. The directors and the owners will make day-to-day decisions that affect the future of the business. Shareholders look to these people to make the right decisions so that they receive a share of the profits. Shareholders literally own a share of the business. The value of those shares will go up or down, depending on the success or failure of the business. Shareholders will look to receive their part of the profits as a dividend.

Although shareholders legally control a limited company, they rarely take day-to-day control of the business, particularly when there might be thousands of shareholders in a public limited company. Each year the shareholders elect directors at the Annual General Meeting. The directors represent the wishes of the shareholders.

The directors cannot, of course, do everything in a business, so they use managers to run the company for them. The Board of Directors begins by appointing a Managing Director. Directors on the Board of Directors with day-to-day responsibilities are called Executive Directors because they execute, or carry out, the wishes of the Board of Directors.

For smaller businesses it is often the case that the same people are the shareholders, the managers and the directors of the company. As far as the law is concerned they are shareholders and directors, but because they are involved in the day-to-day running of the business they are also managers.

Managers

Managers at different levels of the organisation are ultimately responsible for the decisions that affect the success or failure of the organisation. In making the correct decisions and improving profitability, managers are often rewarded with higher salaries and **bonuses**. They may also enjoy additional benefits, such as private healthcare and company cars.

Managers, at various levels of a business, are responsible for the day-to-day decision-making. It is their role to translate objectives into tasks and activities that will be carried out by their **subordinates**. At the top of the organisation, objectives are vague; they become clearer further down the pyramid where tasks are more concrete.

Managers will try to make sure that employees:

- understand the nature of tasks they undertake
- perform tasks within the timescale needed
- have the resources available to do the job
- know the expected results of their tasks

A manager will, therefore, work in the middle ground, between the main decision-makers of a business and the people who will actually do the work. A manager's role is therefore:

- to communicate in an effective way
- to give clear instructions
- to allocate time for tasks
- to provide resources
- to explain what the end result of the task should be
- to monitor the progress of the task
- to judge whether the task could be done any better next time

KEY TERMS

Bonuses – additional pay made to directors, managers and employees as a reward for their efforts in ensuring that the business meets its objectives and targets.

Subordinates – employees working in a business who report to a manager, team leader or supervisor.

Team leaders

In many businesses, employees are expected to work as part of a team and to contribute to the activities and success of that team. Teams are created for a variety of reasons, but they often have the following objectives:

- to help the business solve particular problems
- to help the business make particular improvements
- to help individual team members learn and develop
- to help encourage a feeling of team spirit within the business
- to encourage employees to be creative
- to encourage employees to exchange ideas

- to encourage employees to work together in a constructive manner
- to develop the individual team members' skills
- to develop the skills of the team as a whole.

Teams can be created to carry out a variety of different tasks or for a series of short- or long-term jobs. A business's customer service provision is a good example of the way a business would use a team.

The term team leader can often be interchanged with that of a manager: the main difference is that the team leader is usually more 'hands on' and works closely with the team, directing their activities, unlike a manager who may distance themselves from the day-to-day work.

Supervisors

A supervisor is often considered to be on the lowest tier of management and will have a degree of authority over team members, but will be expected to carry out very similar duties to the rest of the employees. A supervisor is the first line of management responsible for work groups. Sometimes, supervisors are referred to as foremen, charge hands or superintendents.

Changes in working practices have meant that many supervisors are actually referred to as team leaders. They direct and guide others in the performance of their tasks. In some cases, they do not perform the tasks themselves, but in most they have very similar duties to those in the work group.

CASE STUDY THE CHANGING ROLE OF THE SUPERVISOR

New technology has reduced the need for supervisors to plan and control the pace of work. In certain areas the rate of change is now so rapid that supervisors may have little knowledge of the technology actually used in the working process. In some cases the members of the supervisor's team may be better qualified than their immediate supervisor to solve technical problems that arise.

Changes in working practices, notably through productivity and flexibility agreements, have reduced some traditional demarcations in organisations and led to employees who are skilled in more than one activity.

Harmonisation of staff terms and conditions of employment has further diluted the status of the supervisor, while supervisors' pay differentials over those

they manage have also been undermined in certain cases by overtime and bonus earnings. In addition legislation has increased the responsibilities of supervisors in relation to recruitment and dismissal, and health and safety.

Source adapted from ACAS

Questions

1 What might be meant by the term 'working practices'? (4 marks)
2 What is productivity? (2 marks)
3 What might be meant by 'traditional demarcations'? (4 marks)
4 What is a pay differential? (2 marks)

Case studies, questions and exam practice

CASE STUDY THE PERFECT ORGANISATION

Structure is concerned with the co-ordination of different roles into appropriate groups.

Guidelines for good practice include:

- flat structures, avoiding one-to-one relationships
- manageable spans of control (span often depends on work type)
- short chains of control/direction
- no overlaps of role, or gaps between accountabilities
- planning and control should not be separated from the 'doing' activity
- each work group should be responsible for planning, evaluating and improving the quality of its own work

Spans of control can increase with process clarity and automation. In other words, in well-defined processes, with high degrees of automation, fewer managers are needed. Smaller spans mean higher overhead costs. Hierarchy can be justified only by competency, or specialist knowledge advantage.

There are a number of possible options for grouping roles, and many organisations will need to consider one or more, in combination:

Organisation option	Description	Example
Function	The conventional way of grouping similar roles within organisations, focused around specialist technical divisions of tasks	e.g. Marketing, Research and development, Human resources, Finance
Process	Roles are focused on the end-to-end operation of a single process	e.g. a manufacturing process from raw materials to end product
Location	Roles are grouped according to geographic location where the work is performed	e.g. a branch, office or site
Customer	Roles are focused on meeting the various needs of discrete customers	e.g. all transactions required by a given type of customer
Project	Roles are focused on a time-based set of activities, leading to a given objective	e.g. short-term or long-term projects with specific milestones and results

Source: adapted from Ad Esse Consulting

Questions

1 What might be meant by 'a chain of control'? (2 marks)
2 Comment on the view that 'Hierarchy can only be justified by competency or specialist knowledge advantage'? (6 marks)
3 Which, if any, of the organisation options may require regular reorganisation and why? (10 marks)

SHORT-ANSWER QUESTIONS

1 What is the standard shape of an organisational structure?

2 Define the term 'span of control'.

3 Why might most business organisations be hierarchies?

4 What do you understand by the term 'delegation'?

5 What key elements are required for successful delegation?

6 How might a business fairly allocate workload?

7 What is the role of a director in a business?

8 Distinguish between a team leader and a supervisor.

9 What is a flat structure?

10 What is empowerment?

CASE STUDY MODERN COMMUNICATION

Modern communication systems focus on empowerment, and multi-flow communications. These communication systems include team briefings, discussions and meetings, informal talks, emails and discussion boards.

There are different types of communication flows in an organisation: downward communication involves the passing down of instructions from higher levels of the hierarchy to the lower levels. Upward communication is the feeding back of ideas from the lower levels of the organisation to the higher levels. This involves a consultation process with employees and should allow managers to get some good ideas from the employees carrying out day-to-day work.

Sideways communication is the exchange of information and ideas from those at similar levels of the organisation, perhaps working in different functional areas of the business. Multi-channel communication involves a wide range of different communication flows using technology and networking.

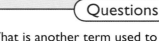

Questions

1 What is another term used to describe downward communication? (2 marks)
2 What might be the positive impact on the business in encouraging upward communication? (6 marks)
3 How might modern technology have enhanced communications in an organisation? (8 marks)

Methods of measuring workforce performance

LEARNING OBJECTIVES

▶ Labour productivity
▶ Absenteeism
▶ Labour turnover
▶ Waste levels

Labour productivity

Labour productivity is one of the most important measurements of employee effectiveness. It is designed to compare the number of employees with the output of products or services that they are creating. The following formula is used:

$$\text{labour productivity} = \frac{\text{output (over a particular period of time)}}{\text{number of employees (over a particular period of time)}}$$

FOR EXAMPLE

A building contractor has eight bricklayers. In a normal 20-day month they will lay 120,000 bricks. To work out the productivity per worker per month:

$$\frac{120,000}{8} = 15,000 \text{ bricks laid per employee per month}$$

If the business wanted to then calculate the daily rate of output per worker they would divide the figure again by 20 to give an average of 750 bricks laid per worker per day.

The higher the productivity of the workforce, the better the workforce is performing. Increases show improvements in efficiency. Productivity rates are often looked at in relation to the labour costs per unit. This allows the business to calculate the cost of labour compared to the revenue the business is receiving for carrying out the work for the customer.

Absenteeism

Another way of measuring performance is to work out the percentage of employees that have missed work for some reason. The formula used is:

$$\text{absenteeism} = \frac{\text{number of absent staff}}{\text{total number of staff}} \times 100$$

FOR EXAMPLE

A business employs 38 people and on one particular day three are absent from work. The absentee rate is:

$$\frac{3}{38} \times 100 = 7.89\%$$

An alternative way of working out lost productivity due to absences is to consider the number of days lost.

FOR EXAMPLE

If on average employees work for 47 weeks a year and work a five-day week, then the total number of days worked per year per employee is 235. If the business has 38 workers then the total number of working days is 8,930. If the total number of absences over a given year were 612 then the absentee rate for the year would be

$$\frac{612}{8,930} \times 100 = 6.85\%$$

For reasons why employees may be absent from work see Developing and retaining an effective workforce: motivating employees *on pp. 208–21.*

SELF-PERFORMANCE EVALUATION

ANNUAL

Factor	Well Above (8)

Performance Factors

1   **Quality of Work**: Ability to provide neat, accurate and thorough quality work at an appropriate level based on understanding gained through experience, education and training. Adherence to policies and procedures including safety

2   **Quantity of Work**: Ability to produce required volume of work in a timely manner

3   **Initiative**: Competency to start and complete assignments without specific directions; recognize problems and apply or suggest viable solutions; engage in professional

Labour turnover

Labour turnover measures the changes in a business's workforce. A high labour turnover may show that employees are dissatisfied with the business or their work. In some cases there may be external reasons, such as better vacancies arising in other businesses or improved transportation, enabling employees to look further afield for more suitable work. It is more likely that there are internal reasons for high labour turnover, such as poor recruitment and selection, low levels of motivation or, perhaps, wage or salary levels that are no longer competitive. The formula used for labour turnover is:

$$\frac{\text{number of staff leaving per year}}{\text{average number of staff}} \times 100$$

FOR EXAMPLE

If a business has 38 employees, and if, in the past year, six members of staff have left, then:

$$\frac{6}{38} \times 100 = 15.78\%$$

= 15.78% labour turnover

It is important not to consider labour turnover figures in isolation. They need to be compared with previous years in order to make any judgement about whether labour turnover is increasing or decreasing, as well as to identify whether similar circumstances apply to high turnover periods, or whether it is an escalating trend.

Waste levels

The waste levels produced by a business are a good indication of the efficiency of the workforce. Businesses will attempt to keep the level of wastage down, as this directly affects not only the output of the business but also the prospect of having products returned as faulty by customers. Both of these factors have a direct impact on the profitability of a business.

The formula used in order to calculate waste levels is:

$$\frac{\text{quantity of waste materials}}{\text{total production}} \times 100$$

FOR EXAMPLE

If on average a business produces 128,000 units per year and has to reject 800 units as faulty then the waste level is:

$$\frac{800}{128,000} \times 100 = 0.625\%$$

Again waste levels should be compared with similar periods in order to make a judgement about whether waste levels are increasing or decreasing. Only then can investigations be made in order to discover the key reasons behind trends in levels of waste generated, or why wastage rates are increasing.

There are many costs associated with waste:

- The business has to pay the cost of the unused or scrapped materials
- The business may have to try to reuse the scrap materials, using more labour

- If a high proportion of faulty products is sent out to customers then there is the likelihood that the business will have a reputation for faults
- If a high level of wastage causes a hold-up in the delivery of products to customers then customers may look elsewhere for a more reliable supplier.

Usually, high waste levels are as a result of poorly trained employees. Poorly trained employees are more likely to make mistakes. Another major reason is the layout of the business premises. The more products have to be moved around, the greater the likelihood that they will be damaged as they are moved from one part of the factory to another. The final main reason links back to motivation and commitment from the employees. If they feel undervalued and underpaid they are far more likely to be careless in their work and make more mistakes.

Questions

1 What are the likely costs of high absenteeism? (6 marks)
2 What additional costs might be incurred by a business with high labour turnover? (4 marks)
3 How might working out labour productivity as an average not be a true reflection of the output of individual employees? (6 marks)

Case studies, questions and exam practice

CASE STUDY EFFICIENCY

A business has compiled the following data in order to work out the ratios on employee performance:

Measure	2008	2009	2010
Output	68,000	74,000	79,000
Wastage	723	855	879
Average workforce	56	62	61
Employees who left	6	8	10
Total working days per employee	234	234	234
Working days lost to illness	807	885	762
Average number of staff absent	5	5	7

Questions

1 Work out the following ratios:
  • Labour productivity (3 marks)
  • Absenteeism (3 marks)
  • Labour turnover (3 marks)
  • Waste levels (3 marks)
2 What might the business have learned from working out these ratios? (15 marks)

SHORT-ANSWER QUESTIONS

1 What is labour turnover?

2 What is labour productivity?

3 What is absenteeism?

4 What is the significance of waste levels?

5 What might be the internal reasons for a high labour turnover?

6 What might be the external reasons for a high labour turnover?

7 How can labour productivity help a business assess its earnings to cost on a particular job or contract with a customer?

8 Give three reasons for high wastage levels.

9 What are the likely consequences of high labour turnover for a business?

10 Are measurement ratios on employee performance useful indicators for a business?

CASE STUDY COMPARING BRANCHES

Norglenn Double Glazing operates in a highly competitive and sales-orientated market, selling double glazing products, conservatories and replacement doors direct to the public by cold-calling on the telephone or in person.

The business has four branches scattered around the outskirts of Cardiff in Wales.

The managing director has compiled the following data on the four branches and she is concerned that the figures suggest that the branches' performances are very different. In her mind, there may be a major problem with human resources and something needs to be done.

Measure	Branch A	Branch B	Branch C	Branch D
Full-time staff	12	10	10	14
Labour turnover	20%	25%	150%	10%
Absence rate	5%	6%	24%	12%
Average sales revenue generated per employee	£120,000	£110,000	£77,000	£89,000

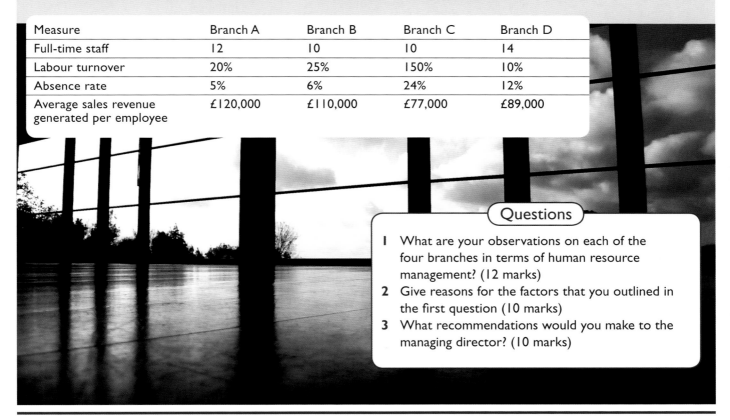

Questions

1 What are your observations on each of the four branches in terms of human resource management? (12 marks)
2 Give reasons for the factors that you outlined in the first question (10 marks)
3 What recommendations would you make to the managing director? (10 marks)

The recruitment process

LEARNING OBJECTIVES
▶ The selection process
▶ Application forms
▶ CVs and letters of application
▶ Assessing applications

The selection process

Once a business has identified the fact that it has a vacancy, it will begin by preparing a job description. The job description will provide a list of duties and responsibilities for that particular job and will include:

- Job title
- Job grade
- To whom the person reports
- Day-to-day tasks
- Job responsibilities

Once the job description has been completed, a person specification can be created. This process attempts to match the essential and desirable skills, qualifications or experience required to carry out the tasks and duties. This will be very useful in the selection process, as applications can be compared against the essential and desirable lists. Once these two documents have been completed the business will choose the way in which it wishes to advertise the post. It will hope to receive a number of applications from suitable candidates.

The job description, along with details about the business, will be included in any information pack sent out with a job application form. The business will then give a date by which the applications have to be returned.

As the applications arrive, the business will compare the information on the application forms with the person specification they have prepared. Likely candidates will be set aside and considered for short-listing. Those without the right qualities will be rejected at this stage.

Application forms

Many businesses use their own standard type of application forms. They will contain a number of sections, including:

- Name, address and other contact details
- Date of birth, gender and marital status
- Education
- Work experience
- Qualifications
- Skills, aptitudes and qualities
- Statement in support of application
- Names and contact details of two to four referees

Usually it will be sufficient for a candidate simply to return the application form without a covering letter. The business will have sent a job description and details of its business along with the application form. It is vitally important for applicants to read this additional information, as it may have a bearing on the completion of the application form.

CVs and letters of application

Not all businesses require applicants to complete application forms. Some ask for direct contact by telephone or email, or for a visit to the office. Other businesses ask for letters of application and curricula vitae and use these to compare against person specifications.

A curriculum vitae (CV) is a condensed history of your life. It contains various sections and should be as short, but as complete as possible. The main information required is:

- Full name
- Address
- Date of birth
- Marital status
- Education and qualifications
- Employment and work experience
- Hobbies and interests
- Statement about good personal qualities or achievements
- Names and contact details of at least two referees

It is important for CVs to be kept up-to-date. They may need to be adapted for different job applications.

Curriculum vitae

Personal profile
I am an enthusiastic and motivated profession: have experience of working in a rang areas including communic motivating. I wa colle

Assessing applications

Some job advertisements ask the applicants for a letter of application along with a CV. Some businesses like letters of application to be handwritten.

Letters of application should include the following:

- An opening paragraph that states where the applicant saw the advertisement
- Why the job appeals to the applicant
- Why they are applying for the job
- A summary of the applicant's main strengths, stressing their suitability for the job
- Enthusiasm
- A statement of when the applicant would be available for interview and when they could start the job

The letter of application should be short and to the point and in a standard business-letter format. The letter of application gives the candidate the opportunity to stress the key points in their CV or in their application form. For the business it gives an opportunity to see a candidate's real writing skills and, in the case of handwritten work, they may decide to analyse the handwriting.

When the deadline for applications has passed, the human resources department, along with the direct line manager will meet to discuss the applicants. They will have to decide how many applicants they are going to invite in to be interviewed. Normally they will want a reasonable number so that no more than a day or two is set aside for the interview process.

The business will look for a number of things on an application form, including:

- Legibility and neatness
- Relevance of a candidate's skills, experience and qualifications
- No unexplained gaps in education or work experience

Sometimes a business may judge a candidate on factors that they should not take into account, such as marital status, gender or even how far the candidate lives from the business location.

One of the major problems with CVs is that there is no commonly adopted format. They can appear in all kinds of designs and length and there is little agreement even as to the order of the sections or their headings.

It is therefore difficult to compare CVs because there might not be much information that they have in common. CVs are nearly always typed or word-processed. This makes it difficult for the business to assess the communication skills of the applicant. Unless instructed otherwise by an advertising business, a CV should never be sent alone – letter of application should always accompany it.

The short-list process aims to objectively compare the applications from candidates with the person specifications and job descriptions prepared by the business at the beginning of the recruitment process. Those candidates with either the exact, better or potential skills, experience and education are chosen to be called for interview.

KEY TERMS

Letter of application – a brief introductory letter, explaining why the candidate wants the job and how their skills and experience match the post.

Curriculum vitae (CV) – a summary of an individual's education, qualifications, experience and skills.

Questions

1 What is a job description? (2 marks)
2 What is a person specification? (2 marks)
3 What is the purpose of a letter of application? (2 marks)

Internal and external recruitment

Internal recruitment

Internal recruitment refers to the filling of vacancies from within the business or organisation. In other words, existing employees are either encouraged to apply or are selected for a vacancy that has arisen for whatever reason.

The business may choose to take this course of action, as managers may believe that they already have employees working for the organisation with the right skills for the job. Those employees will already have adopted the ways in which the business operates and may have already undergone training and development programmes.

Internal recruitment is achieved in a number of different ways:

- The vacancy may be advertised on a staff noticeboard
- Details of the vacancy may be placed on the organisation's Intranet
- Details may be included in the organisation's in-house magazine or newsletter
- The vacancy may be announced at a staff meeting

There are a number of key advantages in using internal recruitment, and these include:

- Existing employees have greater opportunities to advance their careers and gain promotion and additional skills and experience
- Restricting the vacancy to internal candidates can also help retain employees who might otherwise have left the organisation
- The employer will know much more about the aptitudes and abilities of the internal candidates, thus reducing the chance of selecting an inappropriate candidate for the post
- Internal recruitment tends to be a far more rapid process than external recruitment and, of course, is far cheaper

The principle disadvantages of internal recruitment are:

- The number of potential candidates for the post is limited to those from within the organisation
- There may be far better external candidates who have more experience and better qualifications
- If an internal candidate is selected to fill a vacancy, a new vacancy instantly arises
- In using internal recruitment, existing employees, whether competent or not, will feel that they have an automatic right to be given a more senior post
- The business may become stagnant, as in using internal recruitment no new ideas, attitudes and perspectives are brought into the organisation by new, external members of staff

External sources of recruitment

External recruitment means filling the job vacancies with individuals from outside the organisation. This can be achieved in a number of different ways and an organisation may choose to do it themselves by advertising a vacancy and then carrying out the selection process. Or it may outsource this to a specialist organisation.

Most businesses tend to use external recruitment agencies on a regular basis. Sometimes it is a necessary feature of recruitment and selection, as a great many organisations have a high staff turnover. This means that a large proportion of the employees are constantly leaving the organisation for opportunities elsewhere. Therefore, to take the strain from the organisation's human resources, external agencies are used as a constant rolling source of new employees.

There are, of course, a number of different types of organisation that will undertake the recruitment and selection process on behalf of an organisation. One of the most common is the employment or recruitment agency. Many of these organisations specialise in recruitment in specific sectors, such as finance, administration or travel. Individuals have registered with these agencies and the agency can scan the registered candidates and come up with a shortlist of

suitable individuals who match the specification of the vacancy. The agencies can provide both permanent employees and temporary staff. The agencies are highly specialised organisations, used to dealing with specific human resources requirements. They will invariably have a ready supply of potential candidates and can significantly reduce the administrative burden on the recruiting organisation.

In most cases employment or recruitment agencies will charge up to 30% of the first year wage to the recruiting organisation. In other words, for a vacancy attracting a salary of £20,000, the recruiting organisation would pay the agency £6,000.

In more specialist and senior posts organisations can turn to **head-hunters** or recruitment consultants. They too have lists of registered applicants and some of these individuals have not made it clear to their existing employers that they wish to move jobs. The recruitment consultants will systematically match their registered applicants against the requirements of the vacancy. They will use sophisticated filtering methods to produce a precise shortlist of potential candidates. The cost of using head-hunters or recruitments consultants is considerably higher than using a recruitment agency.

For the majority of posts that become available in organisations, the government-run agency known as the Job Centre is an ideal starting point for identifying local candidates. It also has the main advantage of providing a free service to employers. Generally it is used for clerical, manual and semi-skilled posts. Candidates, who may or may not be unemployed, register with the Job Centre. It is the Job Centre's role to match the skills and experience of the registered applicants with jobs that are placed with them by recruiting organisations.

External recruitment is probably the most common method of recruitment. By advertising the post the recruiting organisation hopes to attract the widest possible audience, including some suitable candidates. Both the recruiting organisation and consultancies, agencies and Job Centres working on their behalf, will use advertising.

Dependent upon the nature of the vacancy, organisations will choose specialist magazines, local, regional or national newspapers or the Internet to advertise their vacancies.

KEY TERM

Head-hunters – specialist recruiters who actively seek to lure key employees away from one organisation to place them in another.

Cost and time considerations of external sourcing

Recent research has shown that recruitment can take up to 20% of a manager's day. The manager will have to write advertisements, and organise having them placed in newspapers. Once the potential applicants start getting in touch with the organisation there could be hours spent on the telephone, the preparation of information packs and application forms. After that the actual applicants need to be screened, checked, short-listed and then interviewed. Even at the end of this process the organisation may not have found a suitable candidate.

Placing an advertisement in a national newspaper can cost as much as £6,000. It is not unknown for agencies or consultants to charge between 20% and 40% of the advertised salary. Both options, therefore, involve both time and cost considerations. Certainly, as there are fewer potential candidates, as employment is high, it is even harder to find suitable candidates.

Questions

1 Why might a business choose to use an external organisation to carry out the bulk of its recruitment? (4 marks)
2 Why is external recruitment the most common form of recruitment? (4 marks)

Selecting the best employee

Interviews

Face-to-face selection interviews are, perhaps, the most traditional way of assessing potential candidates. However, organisations use different types of face-to-face interviewing, including one-to-one interviews, serial interviews, sequential, panel and group interviews. We will look at each of these in the following table.

Face-to-face interview type	How it works
One-to-one	A single, senior individual in the organisation gives a unique, personal interview to every candidate. This can give the employer a much better understanding of whether the candidate will fit into the organisation.
Serial	The candidates are passed from one interviewer to another throughout the course of the day. Specialist interviewers will examine different aspects of the candidate's experience, personality and attributes. Gradually the field of candidates will be cut down until a final interview takes place at the end of the day.
Sequential	The candidates again meet with one or more interviewers on a one-to-one basis. This process can happen over the course of several days or weeks. Each time the interview is designed to move the candidate progressively closer to learning more details about the position and ultimately the offer of a job.
Panel	A committee or panel of interviewers is assembled and candidates are evaluated on interpersonal skills, qualifications and their ability to think on their feet. This can be one of the most intimidating of all interview types.
Group	Several candidates are interviewed at the same time. The idea is to find out about a candidate's leadership potential, style, and strength of argument and persuasion skills. Candidates may also be required to solve problems together, during which they will be observed.

An organisation will almost certainly have allowed those on the interview panel to meet beforehand and to frame the nature of the interviews. They will have a set of agreed questions and each interviewer will probably be given a checklist. Many of the panels have a chairperson in order to control the direction of the interview and to make sure that it does not overrun. Particular attributes and behaviours of applicants will be assigned to members of the interview panel.

The interview protocol is usually split into three main sections, these are:

- Activities carried out by the interview panel prior to the interviews
- Behaviour, processes and procedures during the interview
- Procedures and processes after the interview

Assessment criteria

The interview panel will have been working on the assumption that all of the applicants match, to a greater or lesser extent, the person specification outlined in the job description. Not all candidates are necessarily the same, even if they are of similar age and background. Some will come across better at interview stage, while some who appeared good on paper will not perform as well at interview.

The panel will have its interview checklist and will have made notes about the suitability of candidates as they have seen them throughout the day. Normally key criteria, such as abilities, aptitude and experience, will be noted on a checklist and an assessment will be made on the spot by each of the panel members. In addition to this the interviewers will have made notes on each of the applicants and will have their own views as to the suitability of each of them.

The discussions are aimed to culminate in a positive and majority decision as to the most suitable candidate. This will be a mix of matching essential and desirable abilities and aptitudes along with the impressions of each of the panel members from their experience in the interview room.

Tests

Organisations will use a variety of methods to assess applicants. This is in addition to the use of application forms, letters of application, interviews, group discussions and even practical exercises. As a screening method they may use written tests and exercises. But an increasingly popular method is to require candidates to complete tasks and tests.

One of the most common are the aptitude tests, which are structured ways of looking at how applicants perform tasks or react in different situations. They have standardised methods of scoring, which allow the organisation to compare how other applicants have managed. Increasingly a computer administers them.

Aptitude, ability and intelligence tests tend to have similar characteristics. These are:

- They are administered under timed examination conditions and are designed to test logical reasoning. They tend to become more difficult and usually take the form of multiple-choice answers, with right and wrong answers included.
- Applicants are not necessarily required to complete the entire test. An applicant's score relates to their performance compared to similar individuals with the same aptitude, ability and intelligence.
- The score can be used in a number of different ways. Some tests have a pass mark and by achieving that mark the candidate is automatically offered a job. Alternatively, individuals with marks in certain bands are offered interviews.

Personality questionnaires can be used as a means by which the organisation can determine an applicant's typical reactions and attitudes in different situations. The tests are designed to see how the candidate responds to others and how their normal reactions are changed in stressful situations. These questionnaires do not have right or wrong answers and are usually presented as personality profiles. There are trick questions, or repeated questions, in order to identify whether the applicant is lying.

Psychometric tests are in effect programmed aptitude tests. They measure an individual's aptitude for learning. The questions appear meaningless on their own, but together they provide a way in which the individual can be assessed and graded. Some take the form of multiple-choice questions, others are simple maths or word puzzles and others are designed primarily to test language skills.

Questions

1 Why might a business use tests as part of its selection process? (10 marks)
2 Distinguish between the five main types of interview. (10 marks)
3 Give two examples of key assessment criteria. (2 marks)

How recruitment and selection can improve a workforce

Some problems and issues

Around 80% of small- to medium-sized businesses prefer to recruit from outside the company rather than promote internally, according to new research from Peninsula Business Wise (PBW). However, the business consulting firm found that 77% of employees believed that they were adequately qualified and experienced for a promotion. Peter Done, managing director at PBW, said that the findings are a concern, not only for employees, but for managers as well, as continually hiring in new starters rather than promoting existing staff is 'incredibly expensive'. Done went on to state:

'This is because an external recruit necessitates in the most part a large amount of training and bringing up to speed upon joining the company. This extensive training not only ties up key members of staff during its duration but also costs, and as the majority of SMEs cannot afford to spend money they don't need to, it could often be seen as a misallocation of funding. The vast majority of employees feel that they themselves are capable and serious concerns are raised if bosses are automatically bypassing them during the recruitment and promotion process.'

Internal v external

As we have seen, recruitment is the process of employing someone up to the point at which applications have arrived at the organisation. The selection procedure begins when the business starts choosing a suitable candidate from amongst the applicants.

Filling particular posts within a business can be done either internally by recruitment within the organisation, or externally by recruiting people from outside. Internal recruitment can be significantly cheaper than external, and candidates with an inside knowledge of how a business works will need shorter periods of training and time for fitting in. At the same time, the internal promotions can often act as an incentive to employees to work harder and the business will already have a clear idea about the strengths and weaknesses of the candidates. Internal recruitment also avoids the danger of picking an external candidate who looks good on paper, but in practice is not quite as good.

The business will have to replace any person that is given an internal promotion, and promoting one person in favour of another will mean that other candidates could be angry and confused that they were not selected. Another problem with internal recruitment is that fresh ideas are not brought into the business. External candidates will be experiencing the policies and procedures of the business for the first time and will make critical judgements about them that could lead to positive improvements.

External recruitment makes it possible for the business to be able to draw upon a wider range of talent. It also provides the opportunity to bring new experience and ideas into the business. External recruitment is more expensive, and the business could find itself with an individual who is far less effective in practice than they appeared on paper.

Improving the workforce

There are ongoing skills shortages and changes in the labour market which means that recruitment is becoming more difficult for all job roles. As a result, more sophisticated recruitment strategies are being developed. These need to be consistent with a long-term workforce plan. Usually, this means that a business will integrate recruitment with training and development and staff retention measures.

Recent studies on the factors that influence commitment, loyalty and staff retention show that the following issues need to be addressed in terms of recruiting and retaining key members of staff:

- Supportive line managers and senior management
- Opportunities for learning, improvement and personal growth
- A positive working environment, where individuals feel supported by the team
- Similarities in the values of the individual and the organisation

- Better working conditions and flexibility to fit with personal commitments
- Mutual expectations of the business and the employees

Some of these issues can be addressed as part of the recruitment process. Candidates can be given information that reassures them about the organisation and gives them the chance to test out the business (such as job trials).

Improvements in the workforce can bring the organisation a number of benefits:

- The promotion of internal candidates offers a greater incentive to existing employees who will work harder and see their role in the business as important and potentially a career-long commitment.
- Retaining key employees by offering internal promotion opportunities allows a business to make sure that its key members of staff and their skills are not lost to competitors.
- Attracting suitable external candidates for advertised posts means that a business has the opportunity to refresh the workforce with new talent, ideas and experience.
- New employees are more likely to work harder in the initial period of their employment and offer suggestions for improvements in the processes and systems used by the business.
- Productivity should be improved if the business is able to identify, through its recruitment process, the ideal candidates for posts (those that have the necessary skills and expertise, as well as drive, to do the work).

CASE STUDY DEPARTMENT FOR TRANSPORT

The Department for Transport uses a competency-based selection process for both promotions and external recruitment. This ensures that applicants are able to draw on their experiences from within work and in their private lives in order to demonstrate the required competencies.

For some postings, the Department uses assessment centres, which are known to be one of the most accurate predictors of performance of all selection techniques. The Department regularly reviews the assessment centres to ensure equality and fairness.

Anyone involved within the selection of promotion (and external recruitment) must have completed specific training in order to be an approved interviewer or assessor.

Source adapted from www.dft.gov.uk

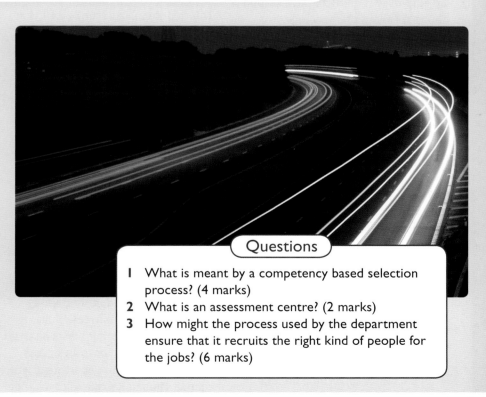

Questions

1 What is meant by a competency based selection process? (4 marks)
2 What is an assessment centre? (2 marks)
3 How might the process used by the department ensure that it recruits the right kind of people for the jobs? (6 marks)

Methods of training

Induction

A new job means a new start. It also means having to learn about the new business, the policies and practices and how to do the new job. Good employers organise well-planned induction sessions for new employees. The induction sessions are designed to be an introductory training programme to help new employees become familiar with the business and how it operates. The induction programme is important because it can often take a long time and cost a great deal of money to find the ideal employees. The main idea behind the induction is to help new employees settle into the business as quickly as possible. It is definitely the case that if an employee is going to have second thoughts about the new jobs, it is going to happen in the first few days. The induction programme can ease any doubts.

Typical programmes would include:

- A welcome meeting on the first day
- A guided tour of the organisation
- Copies of, or the opportunity to see and read business documentation, including departmental manuals, health and safety documents and staff handbooks
- Accompanied introduction to new work colleagues
- Initial introductions, training or the promise of training for any new software, hardware or machinery not known to the new employee
- An opportunity to sit in on team meetings and a general opportunity to become familiar with the working environment

Induction programmes can last for anything from a single day to several weeks. Their nature will depend on the job itself and the challenges ahead for the new employee. Usually additional training and a review, to see how well the new employee is fitting in to the working environment, will follow up the induction programme.

Training opportunities

An induction programme is just the first of the training and development opportunities that could be offered to new employees. Increasingly jobs are becoming more complicated and require a broader range of skills. This is particularly true of jobs that involve information technology. It is in the best interests of the business to train their employees to the highest possible standard in order for them to do their jobs with the highest level of performance.

Untrained or badly trained employees can make mistakes. At worst they can be a danger to themselves and those around them. They can also cause customers and suppliers to become dissatisfied.

It is the responsibility of the human resources department to make sure that all employees attend basic training sessions. After that specific departments will identify training needs for their employees. This is a process called **training needs analysis**.

Once the need for training has been identified, the department will contact Human Resources to arrange

the necessary details. It can then be decided whether several employees would benefit from this training or whether this is training specific to that individual employee.

It is one thing for an organisation to provide or to pay for training and development, but it also needs to be assured that it is effective. Once training needs have been identified, processes need to be put in place in order for the business to be informed of the value of the training. The business will want to review the training given, usually through feedback from those undertaking the training.

The review and feedback should provide enough information for the business to see whether the training was adequate and positive. Managers will want to find out whether the employees actually achieved or learned what they had set out to discover.

There is always competition for the money available for training in a business. Managers will want to secure as much of this money as possible for their own staff.

Staff development

In most organisations staff development needs are identified in a process known as appraisal. Every six months or a year an employee will meet with their manager or supervisor. The purpose of the meeting is to discuss their performance over the previous time period, since the last appraisal. During the appraisal meeting, the strengths and weaknesses of the employee will be discussed in a positive way. The process aims to identify any training or development needs the employee may have that could improve their performance.

By assisting them in obtaining training or development opportunities, the business will make an investment in their employees. This not only improves the employees' performance but also cements the relationship between employer and employees.

Development opportunities and new skills open doors to employees. The employer would hope that those doors remain within the organisation and not with another business. A business would hope to obtain a commitment from an employee to remain with the business, in return for funding additional staff development.

KEY TERM

Training needs analysis – a process by which the business identifies the training requirements of its employees.

In-house training

In-house training simply means carrying out a training programme specifically designed for the business. These are still very common and are used to help update employees on policies and procedures. The problem is that they may have no practical value to the employee should they change their place of work.

In-house training could be provided by:

- Human resources
- Project leaders
- Management or supervisors
- External specialists

On-the-job training

This is training that takes place in the working environment. Typical forms of on-the-job training include:

- Shadowing or following around an experienced employee to learn from them
- Mentoring of a new employee by an experienced employee
- Coaching of a new employee to learn new tasks

The purposes of these types of training are, in turn:

- When the new employee has lots of different things to learn
- When the new employee would benefit from reassurance in the first few weeks
- When the new employee might need to know about new equipment or machinery

External training

A wide range of different training organisations including colleges, specialist training providers and training agencies, can provide external training. One of the big advantages of external training is that it comes with a certificate. Many of the training programmes are ongoing and employees can be given the necessary time to attend a course. The vast majority of the training programmes are not organisation-specific, but are based around particular skills, abilities or knowledge. Examples could include health and safety or new software training.

Off-the-job training involves attending training courses outside the working environment. Typically it includes:

- Management training
- Sales and customer-service training
- Health and safety training

Questions

1 Distinguish between on-the-job and off-the-job training. (4 marks)
2 What is meant by the term training needs analysis? (2 marks)
3 What is the purpose of an induction programme? (4 marks)

Case studies, questions and exam practice

CASE STUDY POOR SPELLING

A survey has found that more than three-quarters of employers would be put off a job candidate by poor spelling or grammar.

A study by Hertfordshire University in 2005 of 515 companies found that bad English alienated 77% of firms surveyed.

The biggest draw for potential employers was relevant work experience, mentioned by 46%, followed by a 'good work ethic' (43%).

Just a quarter (24%) of employers said they were interested in a candidate's class of degree and 14% in the reputation of the university they had attended.

Research from the CBI indicated that 42% are unhappy with the basic skills of those applying for jobs. Employers report that graduates are writing illiterate memos and are in need of constant supervision.

Source: adapted from www.herts.ac.uk

52 Main road
Conlington
4th Febuary

Dear Sir/Madam

I was very interested to see you're advertisment in the local paper for a Comunications Executive. I am enclosing a copy my CV in support of my application for this post.

You will see that Ive several year's experience working in this area, and got excelent copy-writing skillls. I am looking for an opportunity to move into a more higher level role, with more responsiblities, and this job looks like a grate opportunity.

I will hope to here from yo

Yours f

Tom Vir

Questions

1 What is meant by the term 'good work ethic'? (2 marks)
2 What is the CBI and who does it represent? (4 marks)
3 Why is it of vital importance to check everything you have written before sending it to a potential employer? (6 marks)

SHORT-ANSWER QUESTIONS

1 What is meant by 'training needs analysis'?

2 Distinguish between a job description and a person specification.

3 What is short-listing?

4 Outline the different types of interview that may be used by a business during the interview stage of recruitment.

5 Distinguish between internal and external recruitment.

6 What are the potential benefits to a business in encouraging internal applications?

7 What is an appraisal?

8 Outline the common types of tests used as part of the recruitment and selection process.

9 What is a CV?

10 What do you understand by the term interview protocol?

CASE STUDY LINK COMMUNICATION

Link Communication is Britain's largest network of field marketing personnel, promotion staff, models, leafleting teams and commercial actors. It creates and executes innovative and effective campaigns.

The company not only carries out marketing campaigns, but is also active in assisting clients to recruit suitable employees. The following outlines one such campaign for STA Travel in Edinburgh.

CLIENT: Sky Recruitment

AGENCY: Youth Media

CAMPAIGN: Sky Recruitment campaign

BRIEF: To recruit new members of staff for Sky's main business centre in Edinburgh.

TARGET AUDIENCE: Over 55s

CAMPAIGN DESCRIPTION: Link Communication provided promotion staff outside every major bingo hall in Edinburgh as crowds exited after the main mid-week, day-time gaming session. Staff outlined core job benefits to each recipient and left them with a leaflet explaining how to apply.

RESULTS:
1. 12,000 leaflets distributed to core target audience group within seven days.
2. Client had unprecedented number of applications during the first week and then extended the activity for three further weeks, across a wider range of locations.
3. Client has built this activity as a core part of the over 55s recruitment targeting.

Questions

1. Why might the client have targeted the over 55s? (4 marks)
2. What is meant by core job benefits? (2 marks)
3. Why might STA Travel have opted for this form of recruitment and why might it have been necessary (6 marks)

Source: adapted from www.linkcommunication.co.uk

Using financial methods to motivate employees

LEARNING OBJECTIVES

▶ Bonuses
▶ Commission
▶ Performance related pay
▶ Fringe benefits
▶ Job satisfaction

Bonuses

Bonuses are often paid to employees for the following reasons:

- They have achieved a goal or objective set by the business
- The business itself, overall, has achieved particular goals or objectives

Bonuses are usually paid as a large, lump sum at a particular time of the year, sometimes just before Christmas. At other times they will be paid shortly before the end of the tax year. Alternatives to bonuses include awarding employees holidays, cars or other financial rewards.

Commission

Commission is usually paid to employees on relatively low hourly rates of pay. Commission is usually a small percentage of the total value of sales made by that employee. If, for example, an employee receives 2% commission, he or she will receive £2 in commission for every £100 of products or services sold. This commission is added to the employee's basic pay.

Performance related pay

Performance related payments are additional payments made to employees who manage to achieve specific goals. Usually these goals have been agreed in the following ways:

- In individual appraisals
- In team meetings
- In statements made to the employees across the whole organisation

In the wider sense, performance related pay is rather like a bonus, but the payment is very closely linked to actual achievements, such as:

- Increased efficiency
- Higher profits
- Lower numbers of complaints
- Dealing faster with customer queries

Individual employees could be awarded performance related pay for the following reasons:

- Achievement of goals
- Efficiency
- Helpfulness
- Good attendance

The system works by rewarding individual employees for meeting their agreed goals, which could give them a higher rate of pay than others doing similar work who have not met the goals. Many businesses use performance related pay linked to appraisals. They will grade each employee in the following manner:

- Unacceptable (U)
- Improvement needed (I)
- Good (G)
- High achievement (H)
- Outstanding (O)

If the employee can, over time, reach the outstanding category then they will be awarded a 5-10% pay increase. Those in category U do not receive a pay increase, not even to keep pace with inflation.

Performance related pay was one of the big new ideas of the 1980s, and just ten years later nearly 60% of businesses had adopted it. Some called it merit pay. By the late 1990s businesses were beginning to realise that it was not really effective in motivating staff. It was also expensive to run and could cause unhealthy rivalry between employees.

The main problems of performance related pay were shown to be:

- That the merit pay was often not generous enough to encourage employees
- That it was seen as being unfair
- That it damaged teamwork as one person wanted to take credit for success
- That it was actually unlikely that money alone would motivate employees

As far as employees are concerned, according to government research, less than 10% of employees believe that performance related or merit pay is the best way of improving motivation at work.

Fringe benefits and pensions

As an alternative to extra pay or higher rates of pay, a business may offer a range of fringe benefits instead. The correct term for fringe benefits is 'non-financial rewards'. They are also often called **incentives**. They include the following:

- **Subsidised** meals and drinks
- Free or subsidised travel
- Free pick-up or drop-off to work
- Free travel passes
- Travel loan schemes
- Company cars
- Essential car users' allowances (employees provided with car and credit card for fuel)
- Overseas travel and expenses for work
- Refund of travel expenses
- Discount on purchases made from the business
- Loans and mortgages at reduced rates (typical for bank employees)
- Health insurance

In addition to paying National Insurance contributions, there are two other forms of pension:

- Non-contributory pensions – the employer pays into the pension scheme.
- Contributory pensions – the employer and the employee pay into the pension scheme.

Pensions that feature a contribution from the employer are very attractive as a fringe benefit, as the pension will support the employee after they retire. Generally there are two different types of pension:

- A company pension scheme
- A personal pension scheme

The advantage of the personal pension scheme is that the pension is only related to the employee. When they move job to a different business the pension can move with them.

Job satisfaction

A business needs to try to motivate its employees. A motivated employee is far more likely to work harder. This can bring enormous benefits to the business both in terms of productivity, profits and quality. In order to be motivated, an employee needs to have a degree of job satisfaction (the amount of enjoyment or pleasure derived from work). The job satisfaction will come from the work itself not from any other source such as money or fringe benefits.

The motivation theorists discovered that financial and non-financial rewards only motivated employees up to a certain point, or for a certain length of time. After that, employees did not feel motivated as they had no job satisfaction. Maintaining job satisfaction, therefore, means continued motivation and a desire to continue to work to complete tasks.

KEY TERMS

Incentives – any kind of rewards or benefits to encourage employees.

Subsidised – partly paid for or offered at the price it costs the business to obtain it.

Questions

1 What might be the advantage of the fringe benefit of a company uniform? (2 marks)
2 Why might the fringe benefit of lower-cost loans and mortgages not be as attractive as it first appears? (4 marks)
3 Outline the key problems of performance related pay. (6 marks)

Improving job design

Job design

Most people would like to have interesting and challenging jobs, but many of them do boring and monotonous work. Businesses know that in order to reduce recruitment costs by retaining their best employees and motivating them to perform, they can generate higher profits.

It is widely believed that there are five factors of job design that typically contribute to people's enjoyment of a role:

- Skill variety – Increasing the number of skills that individuals use in their work
- Task identity – Enabling people to perform a whole job, from the start to the finish
- Task significance – Providing work that has a clear reason and purpose behind it as far the individual, the business and the stakeholders are concerned
- Autonomy – Increasing the degree of decision-making (the individual's freedom to choose how and when the work is carried out)
- Feedback – by increasing recognition of a good job done and feeding back to the employee, they feel valued and part of the process

Job enrichment is just one of the ways in which these factors can enhance the job's key elements and increase the employee's sense of fulfilment in their job role.

Job enrichment

A key part of job design is job enrichment. This is the practice of adding to, or enhancing a job in order to give greater responsibility and to make the job more rewarding and inspiring. Job enrichment expands the tasks that an individual does, giving them more stimulating work, greater variety and a challenge. It aims to vary the normal tasks done on a day-to-day basis. The major point of the exercise is to increase the depth of the work and to give the individual more control over it.

Typically, this would mean that the individual will be given tasks that would normally have been carried out by supervisors or team leaders. Employees will have greater influence over the planning, execution and evaluation of the work that they do. Individuals can complete whole activities and tasks which gives them greater freedom to assess and correct their performance. The key benefits of job enrichment are:

- Individuals have the ability to grow into their jobs
- They will be more satisfied with their work
- They tend to be better performers
- The organisation encourages greater motivation in the workforce
- There is less absenteeism, labour turnover and potential grievances
- The human resources of the business are fully utilised
- The business is more effective overall

Job enlargement

Job enlargement involves the individual being able to do a range of different tasks, rather than being restricted to a series of repetitive and boring tasks each day. It usually means that the individual is given more duties to vary their work. Job enlargement is usually referred to as horizontal loading, which infers that the broadening of the work is at the same level of skill or expertise and not of greater complexity or responsibility.

Job enlargement therefore addresses the breadth of the work, adding to the number of tasks that the employee performs. This can also be achieved by job rotation. Job enlargement differs from job enrichment in the sense that enrichment means adding to the depth of the work (more control, responsibility and discretion about the work), whereas job enlargement just gives the employee a greater variety of tasks.

The major differences between the two techniques can be seen in the diagram on the opposite page.

KEY TERMS

Grievances – potential disputes between employees and employers, usually as a result of poor or unfair treatment and limited access to opportunities.

Multi-skill – this involves providing learning opportunities for the workforce so that they are able to carry out a wide variety of job roles and tasks.

Job rotation

Job rotation involves moving employees from one job role to another, with the idea that it gives them greater variety of work and helps to multi-skill the workforce. In a factory, the employees can be moved around so that they work on different aspects of the production process, preventing them from being bored, while at the same time learning new skills. For the business, this encourages multi-skilling, so that employees have a wide variety of skills and competences so that they are able to carry out almost any work required in the business (or certainly in their overall area of work). This is particularly useful if the business has staff shortages in crucial areas of the organisation.

Job rotation is used to increase the efficiency and the abilities of the workforce. Some regard it as a motivational too, while others see it purely as an organisational tool. There is a confusing similarity between job enlargement and job rotation, enlargement is simply giving the individual more jobs at the same level of difficulty, while rotation means varying the type and the difficulty of the jobs.

Job rotation is seen as a solution to two major problems often faced by businesses:

- Skills shortages and skills gaps (not having suitability experienced individuals available either in the business or the local labour market).
- Employee motivation.

Skills shortages can often occur when there is a lack of skilled individuals in the organisation's workforce, whereas a skills gap occurs when it is difficult to find suitably skilled employees in an area (either from the unemployed or currently working for a competitor).

JOB ENRICHMENT AND JOB PERFORMANCE

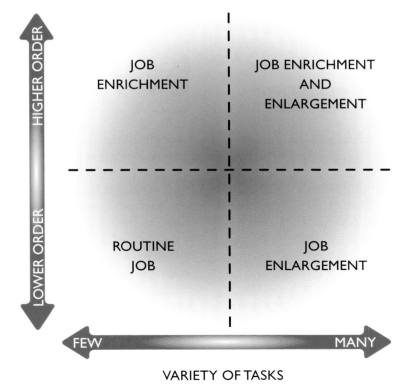

ACCENT ON NEEDS

HIGHER ORDER / LOWER ORDER

JOB ENRICHMENT

JOB ENRICHMENT AND ENLARGEMENT

ROUTINE JOB

JOB ENLARGEMENT

FEW — MANY

VARIETY OF TASKS

Questions

1 Distinguish between job rotation and job enlargement (6 marks)
2 What are the five factors that should be taken into account during job design? (5 marks)
3 What are the advantages of job enrichment? (5 marks)

Empowering employees

LEARNING OBJECTIVES

▶ What is empowerment?
▶ Main types of empowerment
▶ Empowerment, well-being and performance
▶ Appropriate use of empowerment
▶ Designing and implementing empowerment

What is empowerment?

Empowerment involves enhancing the involvement of employees in business processes and in decision-making. It is viewed to some extent as being democratic and promoting employee well-being, while using employee knowledge and ability to improve performance.

Many businesses recognise that they can achieve far more if they have able and empowered employees, but it is actually only used by a small minority of businesses. It is a far less common technique than more widespread initiatives, such as quality management, teamwork, supply chain partnerships and advanced stock control.

KEY TERM

Total quality management – often referred to as TQM, this is a focus on quality in all processes and systems throughout the organisation.

In the *Operations management section*, see Developing effective operations: quality on pp. 234–45.

For more on Taylor see Theories of motivation on pp. 216–17.

Main types of empowerment

The most direct form of empowerment is delegation. This aims to add responsibility to individual employees or teams so that they can manage their own tasks. The most common indirect form of empowerment is the encouragement of participation in decision-making.

We have already looked at some direct forms of empowerment, such as job enrichment. In the next section, when we consider teamwork we will look at another – self management.

Empowerment is also to be found in total quality management.

Many aspects of human resource management involve a degree of empowerment, particularly when considering job design and systems that encourage feedback, input and ideas directly from the workforce.

Empowerment, well-being and performance

Empowerment as a concept has been around for over 100 years and is often seen as a response to the work of management theorists, such as F W Taylor.

Taylor looked at work design and attempted to simplify jobs by breaking down work into a sequence of simple tasks that could be carried out by different employees. This would mean that each employee only needed a limited range of skills, as they were doing very narrowly defined jobs. They had little freedom

or responsibility in their work and for many this approach was described as disempowerment. The major problem with this approach was that most employees were doing repetitive and boring work, which caused dissatisfaction. It also affected the well-being of the employees: there were numerous disputes between employees and employers.

Empowerment takes an entirely different view, and through techniques such as job enrichment and the creation of self-managed work teams employees' attitudes to their jobs are improved, as well as their well-being. Despite this, many employees are still carrying out repetitive work which entirely disempowers them.

There is no clear-cut evidence that empowerment has a major beneficial effect on performance. Some management theorists claim that by simplifying work that is common on a production line, productivity is in fact high and the business can be very profitable. Empowerment at the very least has no negative impact on performance, but it does give employees broader and more responsible work roles.

Some recent studies suggest that businesses do benefit from empowerment, but the empowerment has to be brought in along with other initiatives, including total quality management. The problem is that by bringing in empowerment and allowing employees to take responsibility, costs could increase, as it becomes part of their role to fulfill support tasks, including administration and the management of equipment. These roles would previously have been carried out centrally and, arguably, more efficiently.

Empowerment can be seen to improve employees' effectiveness, certainly in terms of their initiative, knowledge and competence. But not all businesses recognise significant benefits.

Appropriate use of empowerment

For businesses with a regular, predictable and systematic level of work and required output, empowerment tends not to be very useful. In situations where there is a huge variety of work requirements, empowerment can be very effective. In these situations there will be frequent changes and work may have to be tailored to suit the needs of individual customers.

Businesses need to make considerable investments if they follow the empowerment route. Employees need to be trained and supported, they need to have access to information and be encouraged to take the initiative and make decisions in order to complete their work. This also means that empowerment tends to be more effective when a business has a stable workforce, with a low labour turnover. The business needs to make a considerable investment in empowerment and it will take time for the benefits to become apparent. This is only possible in businesses with low labour turnover; otherwise investment made in employees will be wasted.

Designing and implementing empowerment

Many businesses begin their empowerment processes by involving employees in the creation of new work practices and new job roles. Empowerment involves far more than simply giving additional responsibility to employees. Empowerment requires mutual trust between employees and the management and by involving employees at the outset this trust can be established. In fact, management support is of vital importance because as newly empowered employees begin taking on new responsibilities they will inevitably make mistakes. The business needs to view these as learning opportunities rather than errors. The management needs to react in a positive and supportive manner rather than apportioning blame.

Questions

1 Why might a business choose not to implement empowerment? (6 marks)
2 Why might empowerment be more appropriate in a retail environment rather than a food processing factory? (10 marks)
3 What is indirect empowerment? Give ONE example. (4 marks)

Working in teams

Teams

Teams are created for a variety of different reasons, but they tend to all have the following objectives:

- To help solve problems and make improvements
- To help team members learn and develop
- To try to create a true team spirit
- To encourage creativity and exchange ideas
- To work together in a constructive way
- To develop both the team's overall skills and the abilities of the team members
- To break down complex tasks into a series of simpler tasks

Teams can be set up by a business to cover a variety of different work. They can also be set up for a specific series of jobs or, indeed, long-term jobs to make the team responsible for certain work (such as a customer service team).

Functions of a team and roles of individual members

What do teams do? What is the purpose of a team? Why do many people prefer working in a team rather than working on their own? These are the key questions when we ask ourselves what are the functions of a team. The simple answers are that teams can do a variety of different tasks for a business, their purpose being to make sure that the tasks are carried out and, as far as individuals are concerned, it's about having close social relationships at work.

There have been many attempts to try to explain the exact nature or roles of teams. Before we look at the main functions of teams, here are some of the facts about them, clearly showing why businesses are so keen on developing them:

- Teams can mean that productivity (getting things done) can be increased by up to 80%
- The quality of work done increases in about 70% of cases
- Over 50% of teams reduce the amount of waste (in time and materials)
- Over 65% of team members say that teams gave them more job satisfaction
- Nearly 60% of teams managed to improve customer satisfaction

Many businesses have now re-organised themselves to take into account the fact that teams work and should be used. The diagram below shows how this can happen.

Team functions can be broken down into three main areas which take up the team's time and effort:

- Tasks – all time and effort which is put into the achievement of the team's objectives or goals. In effect this is the actual 'doing' of things.
- Interaction – this is the contact between the members of the team. To begin with the interaction will be all about setting out how things are to be done and sorting out conflict. Once the team is established, interaction between team members (talking to each other, etc.) will revolve around asking for support and help when it is needed.
- Self – this is about putting time and effort into making sure that you, as an individual, are doing what you need to do to support the team. It is also about being noticed and satisfying your own needs relating to the work you are carrying out.

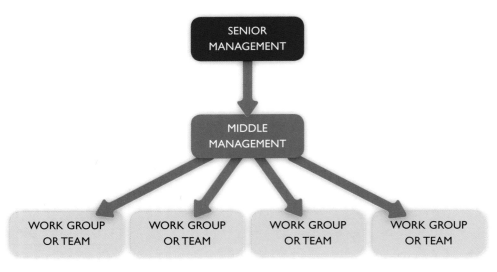

Roles in teams

Individual roles within the group are important and there needs to be a good mix of different types of people, with skills and abilities which support one another. Here are some ideas about the mix of people that would be ideal for teams to be efficient and effective:

TASK BASED
– getting the job done

- Initiators – these are people who set goals and suggest ways in which things can be done and ways of dealing with team problems
- Information or opinion givers – these people offer facts and suggestions
- Information seekers – these are people who need facts and figures to get their work done
- Elaborators – these people clear up confusion by giving examples and explaining things
- Summarisers – these people pull together various facts or ideas and help to tell the team where they are in a task
- Agreement testers – these people check to see if all of the team agrees with what and how jobs are being done

FUNCTION BASED
– enabling the work to be done

- Encouragers – these people accept others and are responsive and friendly to others
- Expressers – these people share their feelings with the team and help establish relationships
- Compromisers – these people want the team to work and will give way on things if it might cause a problem
- Harmonisers – these people try to deal with problems in the team and reduce tension
- Gate-keepers – these are the people who encourage some of the team to get involved and freeze out others that they do not want to get involved
- Standard-setters – these are the people who try to set the minimum standards of work and try to get everyone in the team to stick to these

The most famous attempt to explain the roles of individuals in teams was suggested by Dr. R. Meredith Belbin in the 1980s. The Belbin types, or roles, still remain one of the best ways of describing the various roles of individuals within a team.

Teams work best when there is a balance of primary types and when team members know their roles, work to their strengths and actively manage weaknesses.

Overall	Belbin type	Description
Doing/Acting	Implementer	• Well organised and predictable. • Takes basic ideas and makes them work in practice. • Can be slow.
	Shaper	• Lots of energy and action. • Challenges others to move forwards. • Can be insensitive.
	Completer/finisher	• Reliably sees things through to the end, ironing out wrinkles and ensuring everything works well. • Can worry too much and not trust others.
Thinking/Problem solving	Plant	• Solves difficult problems with original and creative ideas. • Can be a poor communicator and may ignore the details.
	Monitor/evaluator	• Sees the big picture. • Thinks carefully and accurately about things. • May lack energy or the ability to inspire others.
	Specialist	• Has expert knowledge and skills in key areas and will solve many problems. • Can be disinterested in all other areas.
People/Feelings	Coordinator	• Respected leader who helps everyone focus on their task. • Can be seen as too controlling.
	Team worker	• Cares for individuals and the team. • Good listener and works to resolve social problems. • Can have problems making difficult decisions.
	Resource/investigator	• Explores new ideas and possibility with energy and with others. • Good networker. • Can be too optimistic and lose energy after the first flush of it.

Questions

1 Why might a business choose to set up teams? (4 marks)
2 Why is it important to have a mix of different personality types in a team? (10 marks)

Theories of motivation

Motivation theory

All employees want to be happy in their work and have job satisfaction. It is important to always remember that people do not live to work but work to live. For some people work is a necessary evil that cannot be avoided. Hating work is all too common and in these cases the employer tends not to get the best out of the employee. They may be bored, overworked, lacking in promotion opportunities and poorly paid. Motivation theory is about turning this around and looking at employees' reasons for working. These reasons are often described as motives, hence the phrase motivation theory.

Abraham Maslow

Back in 1943 Abraham Maslow wrote about the five basic needs of human beings and the fact that they were hierarchical in nature. In other words, the higher level needs could not be achieved without the basic needs having already been met. Maslow visualised the five needs as a pyramid, with each layer building on top of the previous one, until the individual had reached their potential.

Maslow's theory has become known as the hierarchy of needs. The stages in work terms mean:

- Physiological or basic needs –sufficient wages to cover the costs of food, clothing and shelter. Maslow realised that pay was not a great motivator for the well paid.
- Safety – a good pension scheme, health insurance and a lack of fear

LEARNING OBJECTIVES
- ▶ Motivation theory
- ▶ Abraham Maslow
- ▶ Douglas McGregor
- ▶ Elton Mayo
- ▶ Frederick Herzberg
- ▶ FW Taylor

KEY TERM

Hawthorne Effect – when people are observed, their behaviour or performance temporarily changes.

of redundancy or being sacked.
- Belonging or social – to feel a part of a big family at work and a member of a team.
- Esteem or respect – recognition of an employee's ability by promotion. The offer of training and feeling that their special skills are valued.
- Self-actualisation or ambition fulfilment – that whatever goal the employee sets themselves has become a reality, a chance to make their own decisions or be recognised as a key employee or authority in a particular area.

Some people believe that Maslow missed out some important parts of peoples' needs. They would insert the need to know and understand between esteem and self-actualisation. Another thing to insert between esteem and self-actualisation is the ability to help others achieve their potential. This factor is possible once the individual has reached their full potential and they realise that they can help others to achieve their goals.

Douglas McGregor

Douglas McGregor came up with the concept of Theory X and Theory Y. He borrowed many of the ideas of Maslow and moulded them into his Theory Y.

His Theory X takes the view that all employees are lazy and will avoid work if they possibly can. This means that they have to be closely supervised. He therefore believed that managers who follow a Theory X view have to be quite authoritarian and force their employees to work.

Theory Y managers accept that people are ambitious and self-motivated. All the manager has to do is to provide the right conditions for them to flourish.

Another theorist called William Ouchi came up with Theory Z. He believed that the way forward was for businesses to offer job security, which in turn would lead to high productivity and job satisfaction for which the employees could be well rewarded with high pay.

Elton Mayo

Elton Mayo was an Australian but he spent most of his career working in America. He was fascinated by the way in which people behaved at work. His most famous study became known as the Hawthorne Effect.

Over the course of two-and-a-half years Mayo watched employees working at a light bulb factory near Chicago. He was trying to work out exactly what motivated employees, but actually found out how to increase productivity. He tried plenty of experiments, such as changing the lighting, lengthening the working day and then shortening it. He experimented with the tea breaks, the pay and even the heating.

Every time he made a change the productivity went up. Every time he changed it back to the way it used to be productivity went up. It finally dawned on Mayo that people were responding to him and not what he was doing. Because he and his research team were wandering around the factory with clipboards the employees had got the impression that they were being treated as special.

Although you may think that Mayo's whole study was worthless because people did not seem to respond to any changes he made, he did find that motivation and productivity increased if people felt important. He could summarise his findings in four ways:

- People always act as a group; because they work as part of a team they behave as a team
- Money and good working conditions are actually less important than being a member of a team
- Friendships outside the workplace have a strong influence on the behaviour of teams
- Managers need to be aware of the need that people have to be part of a team and encourage teamwork in order to get the best out of them

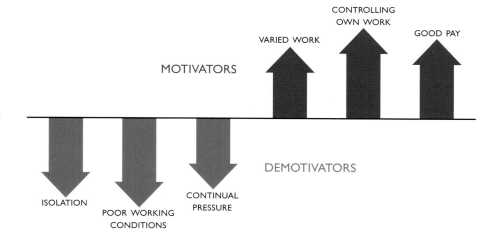

Frederick Herzberg

Herzberg originally came up with his Two Factor Theory in the late 1950s:

- He believed that satisfaction came from motivating factors that helped increase satisfaction
- Dissatisfaction came as a result of hygiene factors. If these factors were absent then employees would be dissatisfied with their work

His motivators were:

- Achievement
- Recognition
- The work itself
- Responsibility
- Promotion
- Growth

His hygiene factors were:

- Pay and benefits
- The business's policy and administration
- Relationships with people at work
- The working conditions
- Supervision
- The status of the employee
- Job security

FW Taylor

Taylor is known as the Father of Scientific Management. He was involved in analysing work and is best known for developing the Time and Motion Study. This study involved breaking down a particular task into minute parts, in other words every action or movement required by the employee to do it. His most famous study involved the use of spades and he worked out exactly what the most efficient load on a spade should be and designed spades so that each time they would scoop up that weight.

Taylor believed that the best way forward for businesses was to have a trained and qualified management and employees who were encouraged to come up with good ideas. He believed that it was possible to train and develops every employee to do their job to the maximum efficiency, and that managers should apply scientific principles to the planning of work and the planning of every task.

Questions

1 Herzberg suggested that businesses should focus on dealing with demotivated employees and rearrange work in a way that would allow motivating factors to take effect. What are the three common ways of doing this? (6 marks)
2 What was the vital addition made to McGregor's theory by Ouchi? (2 marks)

Organisational structure and motivational techniques

LEARNING OBJECTIVES
▶ Flat structures
▶ Centralised and decentralised structures
▶ Cooperation

Flat structures

Compared to a tall organisation, a flat organisation will have relatively few layers or just a single layer of management. The chain of command will be short and the span of control wide. In a motivational sense, this can have a number of advantages and disadvantages:

Advantages of flat organisations	Disadvantages of flat organisations
There is greater communication between employees and management.	Employees can have more than one manager, which could cause confusion.
There tends to be a better team spirit.	The growth of the organisation could be held back.
Decision-making is easier and there is less bureaucracy.	The structure tends to be limited to smaller businesses as it is difficult for it to work with larger organisations.
The costs are lower, as there are fewer managers and the pay differentials between employees and managers is less marked.	The functions of each department or area are blurred, and responsibility for certain areas of work may not be clear.

Centralised and decentralised structures

In a centralised organisation, the head office, comprising a number of senior managers, will retain most of the power and responsibility. In a decentralised structure, the responsibility is more widely spread and managers and team leaders at lower levels will have responsibility for decision-making.

Organisations can have a combination of centralisation and decentralisation. Accounting and purchasing may be centralised (in order to cut costs), but functions such as recruitment may be decentralised as the individual departments or branches have a clearer understanding of the type of employee they need to fulfil a specific role.

Some organisations implement vertical decentralisation. In these cases, they give the power to make decisions in certain areas to lower levels of management: the idea is that that this form of decentralisation helps to increase productivity by allowing individuals at lower levels of the hierarchy to make decisions regarding production and output.

Other organisations opt for horizontal decentralisation with the aim of spreading responsibility across the organisation. This is particularly true when new technologies are introduced to the organisation. It is advantageous for information technology specialists to implement the installation, training, monitoring and support of a new computer system rather than put it in the hands of the purchasing department (which may have authorised and paid for the system).

FOR EXAMPLE

The supermarket giant Tesco has a decentralised structure. Each supermarket has a store manager that can make certain decisions concerning the store. Ultimately, the store manager is responsible to a regional manager who encourages decisions to be made at store level as the store manager has greater hands-on experience of the needs of the local market.

Advantages of centralised structure for organisations	Advantages of decentralised structure for organisations
Senior managers control all organisational decisions.

Standardised procedures tend to cut costs.

Decisions may tend to benefit the organisation as a whole, rather than a part of the organisation.

Decision-making is in the hands of experienced, senior managers who are less likely to make mistakes.

Strong centralised leadership ensures that different parts of an organisation are moving in the same direction and that there are no competing factions that might cause the organisation to lose its way. | Senior management can concentrate on strategic decision-making, leaving lower level decisions to lower level management.

Sharing decision-making is a form of empowerment, this increases motivation and could mean that staff output increases.

Employees lower down the hierarchy can acquire a better understanding of the environment in which they work. This new range of knowledge and skills makes them more effective decision-makers than the more remote senior management.

Empowerment will enable departments and employees to respond faster to changes and new challenges. Senior managers may take longer to appreciate that business needs have changed.

Empowerment makes it easier for people to accept and cope with more responsibility. |

KEY TERM

Bureaucracy – an organisation that has a high level of rules, regulations and procedures that must be followed by all parts of the organisation at all times.

Cooperation

Teamwork relies on cooperation, as each member of the team relies on the others in order to do their work. Cooperation means being helpful, available and open to suggestions. This means that in order for the team to have cooperative members, the following has to occur:

- The members should be more concerned about the needs of the rest of the team than themselves
- The members of the team should try to work in a friendly and sociable atmosphere
- The team should try to avoid conflict (arguments)
- The members should not be too competitive with one another
- The team members should feel that they are part of a close-knit group
- The members of the team need to follow the rules of the group
- The members of the team need to begin, from the start, to trust one another
- Each of the members' points of view should be respected

- Any of the members' own expectations of the others should be fulfilled by the group (if possible)

Team members must learn that in order to achieve tasks, they need one another. This means that the team has what are known as mutual goals. In other words, they are all striving to achieve the same thing, which can only be achieved if they all work together, cooperatively. In addition to this, the team has to share resources and fulfil any role which has been given to them.

Questions

1 Why might it be difficult for a large organisation to have a flat structure? (4 marks)
2 Distinguish between a centralised and a decentralised structure. (6 marks)
3 Distinguish between horizontal and vertical decentralisation. (4 marks)
4 Why might a decentralised structure encourage empowerment? (6 marks)

Case studies, questions and exam practice

CASE STUDY ON THE MOVE

Jess and Eve set up their IT training agency in the centre of London eight years ago. They have come under enormous pressure from competitors that have more staff and can offer a wider range of training courses. While they have continued to be successful, Eve and Jess have found it difficult to convince businesses to let them put on training programmes for their staff.

The 50% increase in the rent for their offices was the final straw. It did not mean that they would not make a profit, but it just added to the pressure. For some years they had both wanted to relocate to Suffolk, where they had both enjoyed holidays and had a number of friends. Between them they decided that they would move in five months and now had the problem of telling their employees.

Frank, Evelyn and Roger were all full-time members of staff. They carried out all the administration work, accounts and marketing, and liaised with businesses, as well as trainers. They all live in London and would probably be reluctant to move. Eve and Jess knew that they needed Frank and Evelyn because they were key members of staff. They could replace Roger.

All the other employees were taken on when a training programme was up and running with a customer. They used a pool of about 20 different trainers dotted around the country. Moving to Suffolk, therefore, would not cause problems for the majority of the trainers.

Questions

1 How should they handle telling their three full-time members of staff about their plans and their desire for two of them to move to Suffolk? (4 marks)
2 What should they tell their trainers? (4 marks)
3 What should they do about their current customers in London? (4 marks)
4 What should they do to find out whether there is a need for a training company in Suffolk? (4 marks)
5 What is the order in which they should do things? (6 marks)

SHORT-ANSWER QUESTIONS

1 What is meant by job design?

2 What is meant by job enlargement?

3 What is meant by job enrichment?

4 Give three examples of financial rewards that can motivate employees.

5 What is empowerment?

6 Who created Theory X?

7 What are the advantages of teamwork?

8 How might commission be a motivator?

8 What is performance related pay?

10 Give three examples of fringe benefits.

CASE STUDY JOB ROTATION IN RENFREWSHIRE

The council set up a programme that provides financial support to a business to employ an unemployed Renfrewshire resident for six months. This will allow them to release up to four staff for training, which will contribute to the growth of the business.

Businesses employing fewer than 250 staff and which have a permanent base within the Renfrewshire Council area can apply. Retail businesses are not eligible for support under this programme.

The following financial support is available.

- Subsidy of up to 45% of the salary of the job rotation trainee or £78.00 a week, whichever is lower.
- Training support of up to £750 or 50% of the costs, whichever is lower, for each job rotation trainee
- Training support of up to £750 or 50% of the costs, whichever is the lower, for up to four members of staff

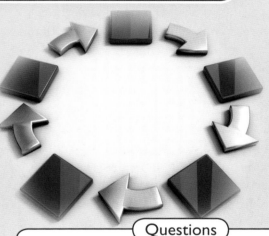

Questions

1 What are the potential benefits for the business of this scheme? (6 marks)

2 What are the potential benefits to the area of this scheme? (6 marks)

TOPIC 3 OPERATIONS MANAGEMENT

Introduction

This is the third of the four core themes for *Managing a business*. Even if you have not come across the term 'operations management' before, some of the concepts will be familiar, including quality management, customer service, relationships with suppliers and the use of technology.

Operational decisions are important in all types of business, regardless of whether they are in the primary, secondary or tertiary sectors. You will be looking at how operations management can assist a business to be more effective and how, more often than not, technology plays an important role in this aspect of an organisation's work.

Many operational decisions begin with the setting of targets and then the management of the organisation's activities in order to achieve those targets. For businesses in the secondary sector in particular this can be a complex issue, requiring a high level of management input and control.

The management of quality is also vital and you will be introduced to the concept of total quality management. This is the implementation of exacting quality standards over every aspect of a business's production process, its suppliers and all other aspects of its work.

Customer service is an equally important consideration and often seen to be a key determining factor when customers are faced with a choice of potential suppliers offering broadly the same products and services. The meeting of customer expectations, the continual improvement of customer service and the business's willingness to maintain high standards can be vital in a highly competitive market.

Suppliers play an important role in most organisations' activities. Increasingly they are becoming partners rather than suppliers and the relationship between supplier and customer is close and mutually reliant.

Finally, technology – from robotics and automation to more common communication technology – has brought about cost reduction, increases in quality, the reduction of waste and, above all, increased productivity.

Operational targets

LEARNING OBJECTIVES

► Operational targets
► Capacity utilisation
► Costs
► Calculation and interpretation of unit costs
► Quality

Operational targets

The exact nature of an operational target will depend on the type of business involved. Typically, targets could include service hours, availability, response times, capacity management, or performance measurement.

Operational targets are set as objectives to be reached or to be exceeded by the business and there could be major consequences to the business if they are not achieved. Having a particular level of output as an operational target means the business is focusing on levels of productivity. If operational targets are related to customer service, and not reached, customers are likely to be dissatisfied. A general inability to meet targets could lead to a loss of business or a loss of market share.

Capacity utilisation

Capacity utilisation is a key element of operational targets. It is the proportion of the maximum possible output of a business that is currently being used. A business may be capable of producing 100,000 units per week, but at present it produces 70,000 units, which means that it has a capacity utilisation of 70%. As we will see, capacity utilisation is linked to many other aspects of a business's operations.

See Calculating and managing capacity utilisation *on pp. 226–7.*

Costs

Businesses need to be aware of the fact that they have fixed costs, which have no direct relationship to the current production levels, or indeed to the capacity utilisation. Fixed costs will always remain the same whether the business has a capacity utilisation of 100% or 70%. What is important is that fixed costs are apportioned to each unit produced, therefore the contribution made by each unit is higher when capacity utilisation is low. The higher the capacity utilisation, the lower the contribution necessary per unit.

It is also important to consider the fact that every unit produced has its own costs. These may be costs related to components and raw materials used, or direct costs, such as labour. There will also be variable costs to add to this, which could include increased utility bills due to machines being used more frequently.

Calculation and interpretation of unit costs

It is important to be able to calculate and interpret unit costs, as well as to appreciate the potentially heavy burden of fixed costs on each unit produced. To begin with, there are the direct costs related to each unit of production. It is usually the case that the fewer units produced the higher the direct costs, both in terms of components, raw materials and labour, as the business is likely to be purchasing limited amounts from suppliers, and may well be using expensive direct labour.

FOR EXAMPLE

A business has a total capacity of 10,000 units per week. It currently produces 5,000 units, which gives it a capacity utilisation of 50%. At a production rate of 5,000, direct material costs are £3.50 per unit and direct labour costs are £4.80 per unit, giving a total of £8.30 per unit. If production were increased to 7,500 units per week, increased discounts from suppliers would mean that direct material costs would fall to £3.25 per unit. Additional investment in streamlining production could reduce direct labour costs to £4.20 per unit, now giving a direct cost per unit of £7.45. This would result in a saving per unit of £0.85. This could significantly add to the business's profit, giving the potential for reinvestment or for a portion of the savings to be passed on to customers to stimulate increased demand.

Quality

Fixed costs can be handled in a very similar way. Obviously with a low level of output the contribution towards fixed costs per unit is high. Businesses with outputs of tens or hundreds of thousands of units are able to spread the contribution per unit to fixed overheads far more thinly across their output levels.

The maintenance of high-quality standards is vital to an organisation, whether it is producing products or providing services. It is also concerned with levels of quality, whether it is producing 10 units per week or 10 million. Clearly there could be quality concerns if capacity utilisation is increased and nears full capacity. Machinery and the workforce will be working at maximum output. Unless systems are implemented to check quality and to aim to reduce faults and wastage, then there is a danger that quality standards could drop as capacity increases.

Quality standards, regardless of capacity utilisation, are often a separate but integrated part of an operational target. A business will expect that a certain number of products prove to be faulty, perhaps due to a component malfunction or a production mistake. An acceptable level could be up to 5%, but if capacity is increased then measures need to be put in place to ensure that this maximum acceptable fault level is not exceeded.

FOR EXAMPLE

If the same business producing 5,000 units had overheads of £5,000 then each unit would be shouldering £1 worth of contribution towards fixed overheads. By increasing production to 7,500 units, the contribution per unit would fall to £0.66.

Questions

1. A business is manufacturing and selling 12,000 units per month. This represents a capacity utilisation of 60%. What is the business's maximum output? (4 marks)

2. What is meant by the phrase '100% capacity utilisation'? (3 marks)

3. At what level of capacity utilisation will fixed costs per unit be the lowest? Explain your answer. (4 marks)

4. A business wishes to calculate its profit per week at capacity utilisation of 50%, 75% and 100%. It has a maximum capacity of 1,200 units per week. It has variable costs per unit of £180, total fixed costs per week of £150,000 and a selling price per unit of £430. Calculate the profit per week at the three levels of capacity utilisation. (12 marks)

Calculating and managing capacity utilisation

LEARNING
OBJECTIVES
▶ Calculating capacity utilisation
▶ Full capacity
▶ Low capacity
▶ Changing capacity

Calculating capacity utilisation

As we have seen, capacity utilisation is measured by comparing current output with the maximum possible output. The formula used is:

$$\frac{\text{Current output}}{\text{Maximum output}} \times 100$$

The maximum possible output will depend on the machinery, buildings and labour potentially available to the business. Maximum output refers to the output when the business is making full use of these resources. When making full use of the resources and working at full capacity, it is said that the business is working at 100% capacity utilisation. In actual fact it is relatively rare for a business to be working at 100% capacity utilisation and current output often falls well below that level.

FOR EXAMPLE

If a business has a maximum possible output of 150,000 units per week and is currently producing 120,000 units per week then:

$$\frac{120,000}{150,000} \times 100 = 80\%$$

This means that the business has a capacity utilisation of 80%. It is operating 20% under full capacity.

Full capacity

In not achieving 100% capacity utilisation the business is under-utilising its possible resources. It may in fact be shouldering costs such as wages and payments on machinery and factory space, which it currently does not need. Obviously, a business needs to try to match its production of units in line with the demand for those units. There is little point in operating at 100% capacity utilisation if the demand for those units means that only 60 or 70% of them would be sold.

In order to try to make demand match full capacity utilisation then something has to be done to increase demand. Typically this would be achieved by price cutting, additional spending on marketing and promotions or attempting to find new markets to sell the products.

The key advantages and disadvantages of a business working at full capacity are shown in the following table:

Advantages	Disadvantages
By working at full capacity the fixed costs per unit are at their lowest level. The business is spreading the fixed costs across the maximum number of units it can produce.	If demand exceeds full capacity then some customers will not be able to be supplied. At best, customers will have to wait for their products to be delivered to them.
The business is using its fixed assets to their full potential.	Employees and management may feel under stress and overworked.
Fixed assets are purchased in order to generate profit and at full capacity profits will be at their highest.	There is little time for the business to deal with mistakes, so all production planning needs to be accurate and on target.
A business that is working at full capacity is seen to be successful, with high demand for its products. The workforce will have job security, and customers will see the high demand for the products as a good indication that the products are of good quality.	The business's machinery will be working at full capacity. This means that routine maintenance is difficult, as the machines will have to be closed down for a period. This could cause the machinery to break down, leading to a loss in production.

For more information on Matching production and demand see *pp. 230–1*.

Low capacity

While many businesses will attempt to operate at close to full capacity, many face the prospect of being capable of producing more units than they can possibly sell. One approach to this is to actually cut maximum capacity, perhaps by changing the shift patterns of the employees, moving to smaller premises, or selling off unused machinery.

Fixed costs will be cut, but the business will not be in a strong position to suddenly increase production should demand recover.

Businesses will take the decision to work at low capacity or to cut capacity on the basis of the underlying reasons for their low-capacity utilisation. If the business believes that low demand is only a temporary phenomenon, such as a seasonal trend, then it may temporarily cut capacity with a view to being able to reinstate full capacity at a later date. If it appears that demand will remain low due to longer-term effects, such as a recession, then the business may have to take the decision to cut capacity on a more permanent basis.

By continuing to work at low capacity without cutting fixed costs, enormous economic pressure will be brought to bear on the business and may even threaten its survival.

KEY TERMS

Recession – a period in which demand is either stagnant or growing more slowly than previously. Businesses will find that they are probably selling less than they had budgeted for.

Changing capacity

If demand for products slows down and is perceived as being a longer-term trend, then a business will have to deal with the problem of excess capacity. It will look to find ways in which to reduce capacity and make savings. This often means going through a process of rationalisation. Rationalisation usually means cutting capacity but increasing efficiency, so that the business increases its percentage utilisation. It will usually involve reducing fixed costs by cutting down on machinery, buildings and labour. A business may choose to sell off machinery or, instead of purchasing new machinery, rent it instead. This would enable the business to dispose of the machinery when it needs to reduce capacity. Employees might be made redundant, which is an expensive and complicated procedure. In other cases employees may find that their working hours are cut or they are transferred to other shifts.

Questions

1   How might a business increase its capacity utilisation without increasing its output? (3 marks)
2   At what level of capacity utilisation are fixed costs per unit the lowest? Explain your answer (4 marks)
3   What are the major disadvantages to a business working at full capacity? (4 marks)

Dealing with non-standard orders

Non-standard orders

In a factory environment there are generally three different ways in which production is carried out, but only two are really suitable for dealing with non-standard orders. A non-standard order means that the products required by the customer have essential differences from the usual production units that are created by the business. They may differ in quality, size, colour or even function. The three key types of production are:

- Job production – this is when a business, such as a restaurant or hairdresser, produces goods according to the specific requirements of each individual customer. Non-standard orders can easily be accommodated.
- Batch production – a group of products is produced each time and each batch goes through one stage of the production process before being moved on to the next stage.

This is how a baker or a fish-and-chip shop would operate. Specific non-standard orders could be accommodated within each batch.
- Flow production – this is essentially mass production, with each unit being produced, moving from one stage of the production process to the next, almost non-stop. A wine bottling plant, which is probably fully mechanised, is a good example, as is a factory that produces chocolate bars or cans of baked beans. It is difficult to accommodate non-standard orders in flow production.

Non-standard orders have the unfortunate ability to adversely affect production rates. Switching over to the production of non-standard orders may necessitate a change in machinery or tools used by the business. This **downtime** impacts on the potential capacity that the business can achieve.

Capital-intensive production

Capital-intensive production means that a business relies very heavily on machinery, equipment and vehicles in order to make its products or provide its services. Capital-intensive businesses have made a high level of capital investment compared to their labour costs. They tend to be highly automated, use flow production and produce products on a large scale. In order for them to maximise their capital investment, businesses need to work at full capacity and increase their efficiency wherever possible. It is difficult for such businesses to increase or decrease their scale of production.

KEY TERM

Downtime – a period when machinery is not being used, either as a result of maintenance or when parts of the machinery have to be adapted to produce a slightly different unit of production.

Minimum efficient scale – the smallest output that a business can produce while making sure that its average costs are minimised.

BOOK RESEARCH

Greasley, Andrew. *Operations Management.* John Wiley & Sons. 2005.

Labour-intensive production

The complete opposite to a capital-intensive business is a labour-intensive one, which relies on employees to carry out most of its processes. It will tend to have a relatively low investment in capital or fixed assets, but will have high labour costs. These types of business are far more likely to be producing products or providing services on a smaller scale, as they have the ability to produce either personalised or non-standard products, specifically made-to-order for their customers. They will make considerable investment in their wage costs, but also in their recruitment procedures and their

ongoing employee training.

Many of these businesses have a degree of flexibility in terms of their capacity, and at times of high demand will use temporary staff or overtime in order to step up production. These types of operation will tend to use job production techniques, as the reliance will be far more on the skills of their workforces rather than the machinery. A typical example would be a business that makes bespoke kitchens or bedroom furniture.

Economies of scale

Economies of scale usually occur in larger businesses, as a result of the scale of their operations. They can lower unit costs and obtain production efficiency once they reach a certain size. They will have made a minimum level of investment which economists call a **minimum efficient scale**.

Businesses can obtain internal economies of scale by focusing on the following:

- Purchasing – the ability to bulk buy by buying direct from manufacturers, reducing transport costs and the use of wholesalers.
- Technical – an investment in the most advanced production machinery and information technology.
- Managerial – to have specialist managers for each different function, such as production, marketing and finance.
- Specialisation – employees have precise sets of skills and expertise to match the requirements of particular jobs.
- Financial – seen as low risk by finance providers, which reduces the costs of borrowing.
- Spreading risk – producing a wide range of products so that a downturn in demand for one product does not adversely affect the whole business.

These larger businesses will also enjoy external economies of scale. Suppliers are more likely to locate close to them so that they can supply the business in an efficient manner. As the business is likely to be a major employer, local authorities will invest in infrastructure and there may be better telecommunications. The business will also attract a pool of skilled labour.

Large businesses can suffer from diseconomies of scale as they increase in size. Essentially, these are inefficiencies. Managers may not have good relationships with the bulk of employees, which could cause a fall in productivity. Equally there may be poor communication within the business, and certain parts of the organisation may either not be properly informed, or may misunderstand instructions. Above all, a large business needs to be well organised, as coordination can be difficult and each new layer of management adds to the costs and can cause problems in communication.

Questions

1 Distinguish between capital-intensive and labour-intensive production. (6 marks)
2 Outline the key differences between job, batch and flow production. (8 marks)
3 Give THREE reasons why a large business may suffer from diseconomies of scale. (3 marks)

Matching production and demand

LEARNING OBJECTIVES

▶ Dealing with high-capacity utilisation
▶ Dealing with low-capacity utilisation
▶ Causes of under-utilisation

Dealing with high-capacity utilisation

Most businesses will generally feel that the situation is acceptable if they have achieved 80% to 90% capacity utilisation. At this point, fixed costs per unit are comparatively low. At the same time the business can accommodate new orders from customers, as there is still some spare capacity and it can afford to have limited downtime for maintenance of machinery, or for employee training.

Businesses do not expect to be in a position where they can achieve 80% to 90% capacity utilisation immediately, but make investment in new facilities in the anticipation that growth in demand will allow them to achieve good utilisation in the near future.

There are situations when businesses do struggle to keep up with demand. There are several different ways in which the business could cope with this increased demand:

• Additional shifts and overtime – essentially this means using additional labour. By adding a night shift, machinery can be used 24-hours a day, but this is often only a short-term solution. It does mean an increase in labour costs and other fixed costs (such as heating and lighting). It also means that maintenance and training become a problem. The business could also have a negative impact on the local community, where residents will be subjected to noise and traffic at night or over the weekends.

• Seasonal workers – some businesses, such as retail in the run-up to Christmas, or the leisure industry and farming in the summer, need temporary workers in order to meet demand. The major problem is to find suitably skilled workers willing to work for a relatively limited period of time.

• Outsourcing and subcontracting – if a business finds it impossible to increase its own capacity it could consider contracting another business to carry out part of the production on its behalf. Many vehicle manufacturers routinely use subcontractors to produce components, or even whole parts of vehicles, leaving the business itself to concentrate on the assembly and finishing of the vehicles. The business may discover that the outsource operation is very efficient and can strike up a longer-term relationship.

• Expansion – this is a longer-term approach as it will require the acquisition of larger premises, more machinery and additional employees. It is an option usually only taken if the business believes that there is steady and sustainable growth in demand.

FOR EXAMPLE

The vacuum-cleaner manufacturer Dyson, in order to cope with increased demand, outsourced manufacture to partners in Korea, while Apple, the manufacturer of the iPod, outsourced manufacture to China.

Dealing with low-capacity utilisation

If a business cannot sell enough units it will find that those units produced suffer a heavy burden of fixed costs. There are various solutions that can be adopted, including:

- Search for new customers – the business may have to invest in marketing and try to find either new customers in existing markets or new markets to sell into.
- Rationalisation and downsizing – this is one attempt to reduce overheads. It can mean either the closure or the selling off of part of the business, leading to redundancy and longer-term negative effects on the business's prospects.
- Reduction in working hours – again staff may have to be made redundant. Alternatively overtime may be banned: a shift may be abandoned and working hours reduced.
- Wage rates may have to be reduced.

Causes of under-utilisation

A business should not suddenly realise that it has low-capacity utilisation. There will be a steady decline, which should alert the business to the fact that action needs to be taken in order to reverse the trend. Usually there are root causes behind under-utilisation, some of which may be long-term problems:

- A new competitor, perhaps from abroad, may have seized a portion of the business's market share by offering better quality or better priced products or services.
- New competitors, with their own ability to produce a certain level of products or services, may have caused over-supply in the market. This means that there are now more products or services being produced than the market actually demands. All businesses would see that there is now a mismatch between the production levels that they had established and the new level of demand.
- There may be a fall in demand in the market due to changes in tastes or fashions. Customers may periodically change their purchasing habits and demand newer or more technologically advanced versions of the same product or service.
- Poor use of the marketing mix – if a business fails to construct a marketing campaign that focuses on messages that the market will be receptive to and respond to then any anticipated increase in demand as a result of the marketing may be unfounded.
- Seasonal demands – the tourist industry in particular suffers from fluctuations in demand as a result of the time of year. Hotels and theme parks are often at full capacity during the summer but at other times of the year may be virtually empty. Theme parks adjust to this by closing between October and March each year, when demand is traditionally very low.

More on the marketing mix can be found in Designing an effective marketing mix *on pp. 274–9.*

Questions

1 Suggest THREE problems that could arise as the result of low-capacity utilisation. (3 marks)
2 Give THREE benefits of low-capacity utilisation (3 marks)
3 How might a hotel in a tourist resort seek to improve its capacity utilisation out of season? (6 marks)

Case studies, questions and exam practice

CASE STUDY MUGS4U LTD

Mugs4ULtd was founded 110 years ago, as Harold Watson China Ltd. It is based near Great Yarmouth and is a manufacturer of pottery and porcelain kitchen and dining products. Until the 1990s they supplied retailers directly, but since then they have seen a fall in the number of retail customers. They now supply wholesalers in a chain of high street printers, with blank mugs ready for logos and pictures to be applied. The company changed its name five years ago in the hope it would appear more modern and forward-looking. At present the business manufactures and sells 18,000 mugs per month.

The managing director, the great-great-great-grandson of Harold Watson, Harold Ernest Watson, has prepared the costings shown in the table.

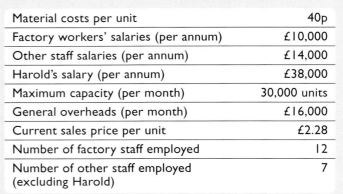

Material costs per unit	40p
Factory workers' salaries (per annum)	£10,000
Other staff salaries (per annum)	£14,000
Harold's salary (per annum)	£38,000
Maximum capacity (per month)	30,000 units
General overheads (per month)	£16,000
Current sales price per unit	£2.28
Number of factory staff employed	12
Number of other staff employed (excluding Harold)	7

Harold is concerned about the business's future and he has called together the workforce to present them with two main options:

1 To make half of the factory workers redundant, as well as two of the other staff. This would limit production to a maximum of 12,000 units per month.
2 To sign an exclusive contract with the distributor to manufacture 20,000 mugs per month at a price of £1.98 per unit. This would be a five-year contract.

Questions

1 What is Mugs4U Ltd's monthly profit, as things stand at the moment? (5 marks)
2 What would be the monthly profit if Option 1 were adopted? (10 marks)
3 What would be the monthly profit if Option 2 were adopted? (10 marks)
4 Which of the two options would you choose and why? Is there any other information that is necessary before a decision is made? (5 marks)

SHORT-ANSWER QUESTIONS

1 What do you understand by the term 'operational target'?

2 Outline the information required to calculate unit costs.

3 What is meant by the term '100% capacity utilisation'?

4 Outline THREE advantages and THREE disadvantages of a business operating at full capacity.

5 What do you understand by the word 'rationalisation'?

6 Define the term 'economies of scale'.

7 List FIVE possible internal economies of scale.

8 Suggest FOUR reasons why a business may be suffering from under-utilisation of capacity.

9 Distinguish between capital and labour-intensive production.

10 Why might a business outsource or subcontract part or all of its production?

CASE STUDY HECTOR'S PLEASURE BEACH

On open days the pleasure beach attracts 12,000 visitors each day. The cost for unlimited rides is £25 per adult and £14 per child. The split is approximately 40% adult and 60% children. When the park is open, overhead costs, including staff, are £42,000 per day. When the park is closed this drops to £4,800 but includes permanent staff and ongoing repairs and maintenance. The park is open for 225 days a year. Potentially the business could cope with 15,000 customers per day and could also open for an additional eight weekends in the year.

Questions

1 What is the capacity utilisation of the park on an open day? (2 marks)

2 What is the profit made by the park on each open day? (4 marks)

3 What is the overall profit made by the park each year? (8 marks)

4 What would be the likely additional profit per year if it were open the extra weekends? (4 marks)

5 How might the park attract more customers and increase capacity utilisation to 100% on open days? (4 marks)

The meaning of quality

LEARNING OBJECTIVES

▶ What is quality?
▶ Quality and specifications
▶ Quality and the law

What is quality?

Businesses know that quality can often be the determining factor in a customer's choice when making a buying decision between a number of similar potential suppliers. Increasingly it has become the main ingredient of a purchasing decision. There is always a trade-off between price and quality, but there is always a minimum acceptable level of quality. This is often referred to as the product being fit for use or purpose. Below this minimum quality standard the majority of customers would be unwilling to purchase the product. Customers will also expect a higher level of quality if the price charged for a product by a business is higher than the average price of products offered by competitors.

Quality is actually quite difficult to define. It implies a certain specification or standard. Many believe that notions of quality are actually always defined by the customer, as ultimately it is the customer who will make the decision about whether a particular product is worth the price being demanded by the business and equally, how it compares to the quality and price offered by competitors.

In a highly competitive market, customers will demand that a business's products are at least equal to, or better than, the competitors' in quality terms.

Quality does not necessarily have to be intrinsic in the product: there are other factors that together make the business and the product of a sufficiently high quality to be attractive. A local corner shop cannot possibly compete on price grounds alone with major supermarkets. It may offer identical products, but the quality issues are likely to be related to customer service and/or convenience.

Quality and specifications

With quality usually defined by the customer, businesses need to ensure that they maintain quality standards. Most businesses rely on suppliers for raw materials, components and finished products. In order to ensure that minimum standards are maintained they will impose quality standards on their suppliers. The larger the business, the more power it has to force its suppliers to conform to its notion of quality levels.

KEY TERMS

Ombudsmen – commonly known as watchdogs: independent organisations that police specific industries and investigate complaints on behalf of customers.

After-sales service – support, advice and information about a product or service given to customers once they have made a purchase.

FOR EXAMPLE

The government and local authorities are large purchasers of products and services from a wide range of businesses. In this dominant position these bodies are able to demand consistently high standards from their suppliers. Roads are checked once subcontractors have completed their work. If the quality standards have not been reached then the contractor will have to re-lay the road. Businesses such as Marks and Spencer Plc demand that their own high-quality standards are met by all their suppliers, otherwise they will seek alternative suppliers that are able and willing to meet their exacting standards.

Quality and the law

In certain situations, when businesses supply products and services to customers, quality standards may be set by legislation. Food products have to show sell-by and use-by dates, a list of exact ingredients and the sources of those ingredients. Electrical goods must be sold with a plug already fitted; takeaways must conform to various health and safety minimum quality standards.

In order to police the minimum quality standards, local authorities use Trading Standards Departments to periodically check businesses to ensure that minimum standards are being delivered. They also investigate customer complaints about quality issues. Many industries themselves have their own trading standards, set by trade associations, in order to ensure that all registered businesses within that industry conform to the same levels of basic minimum quality. Other industries have **ombudsmen**, which are industry regulators, to ensure that minimum quality standards are maintained.

Some businesses also demand that their suppliers have obtained a British Standards Institute (BSI) certification, which guarantees by law a minimum quality standard.

Many businesses recognise that quality requires them to meet customer expectations. Customers require their products to be of a consistently high level. This is beyond the actual reliability of the product itself. They require high-quality **after-sales service** and every aspect of their dealings with the business needs to be of a consistently high quality. The major problem that always faces businesses is that a customer's expectations of quality standards are always increasing. What may have been an acceptable level of quality in the past may no longer be acceptable to the majority of customers. Each time the business improves its quality standards, the expectations of customers rises and future expectations will be even higher.

Additional information on BSI quality standards can be found in Quality standards *in this section on pp. 240–1.*

INTERNET RESEARCH

For more on British Standards, go to www.bsiglobal.com.

For more on ombudsmen, go to www.bioa.org.uk.

CASE STUDY LEXUS CAR RECALL

In November 2007 almost 4,000 Lexus cars sold in Britain were recalled as a result of concerns regarding faulty fuel pipes. Worldwide, this recall affected 264,000 vehicles. The vehicles were manufactured between September 2004 and December 2005. The potentially faulty fuel pipe design could lead to fuel leaks. Lexus claimed that there were no incidents of fuel pipe problems in Britain and that the recall was a precautionary measure. They also assured customers that fuel pipe replacements would be free of charge.

Source: adapted from www.motortrader.com.

Questions

1 In the same year Lexus car dealers were rated the best dealers in Britain by an *Auto Express* survey. How might news of the recall have affected Lexus's reputation?
(4 marks)

2 In July 2007 Lexus dealers were named in a survey for having the best sales and after-sales service. 80% of Lexus owners were very satisfied when they made their purchase and 79% rated service and repair very highly. How might the recall be seen to be part of Lexus's determination to maintain customer satisfaction? (4 marks)

Quality control and quality assurance

LEARNING
    OBJECTIVES
▶ Why is quality control important?
▶ Quality control problems
▶ Controlling quality

Why is quality control important?

As we have seen, quality can be a major determinant in ensuring that customers make a purchasing decision in favour of the business. In this way quality is an important competitive factor. However quality levels and the importance of quality will depend on how competitive the market is and how much quality plays a part in a purchasing decision.

Having a strong reputation for high-quality products is advantageous for the following reasons:

• It will be easier to establish a new product in the market
• Customers are more likely to make repeat purchases
• The product will have a longer **product lifecycle**
• It will allow the business to build up a range of products or **brands**
• It will allow the business to charge a higher price for the product, thus generating higher profits
• Stockists are more likely to want to purchase the product
• There should be some savings in advertising costs

For more on product lifecycles and brands see Using the marketing mix: product *on pp. 280–9.*

If a business, product or service is tainted with negative views on quality then there could be severe implications for the business:

• The business may see a loss of sales and reputation
• It may have to discount the products
• The poor-quality image may impact on other products and services offered by the same business
• Retailers may be unwilling to stock the products
• Customers would be less likely to make repeat purchases
• If the business has to recall the products then they will have to be reworked, leading to higher costs in labour and materials

KEY TERMS

Product lifecycle – the stages through which all products pass, from their development stage to their final decline and withdrawal from sale.

Brands – recognisable names or logos (such as those shown below) that are legally protected by a business. A brand name helps customers instantly recognise and differentiate a product from its competitors.

Quality-control problems

Quality control, therefore, means that a minimum quality level needs to be established and maintained by the business. As we will see there are ways in which the business can control quality.

The first problem, however, is to recognise where quality issues could emerge and to intercept them before the products or services reach the customer:

• The traditional method is to inspect finished goods before they are sent out to customers. It may not be possible to inspect every single product, but a sample of products can be test-inspected.
• Some businesses use self-inspection by employees who have manufactured the product. This is seen as an important and effective way of carrying out quality control, as it reinforces the importance of quality to all employees.
• Machine checking of quality standards can also be established, particularly in factories where flow production is used. Machinery can be set to measure particular specifications and to alert the operators if a particular product either exceeds or does not meet the specification standards required.

Controlling quality

If quality control has failed, and products of insufficient quality do reach the market, then it is usually feedback from customers, via complaints and returned goods, that will alert the business to the fact that it has a quality-control problem. It is important that any specific fault or problem with a batch of products is fed back to the manufacturer, so that additional quality-control checks can be brought in to prevent a recurrence.

Businesses may also use market research to establish whether customers have the perception that there are quality problems with a particular product or service. The business can also check customers' views of competitors' products and services and ascertain whether there are any major differences.

For most businesses, quality control is not only about the product itself, but also about any service aspects related to that product. This means that it is no longer possible to use mechanical fault checking alone, as this may only pick up on product faults and not service faults. Most businesses have a broader view of quality control, which falls into four major stages, as can be seen in the following table:

Quality-control stage	Explanation
Prevention	This initial stage obviously tries to avoid problems happening in the first place. Even when a product is designed it will be checked for its reliability, and steps will be taken to ensure that the way it is to be produced is unlikely to give rise to a high percentage of production errors.
Detection	This means checking that there are no quality problems before the product reaches the customer. Businesses have tended to make detection of quality problems the responsibility of all employees, backed up by computer-aided statistical analysis and other tools to help detect faults.
Correction	A business will want to know why there is a particular problem and what steps need to be taken in order to ensure that the faults do not recur. Obviously this goes beyond simply repairing known faults to recalling products that have already been distributed.
Improvement	As we have seen, customers have a continually increasing expectation regarding the quality levels of products and services that they purchase. Businesses will at least wish to remain ahead of customer expectations. Often they wish to delight or surprise customers by their level of quality, so that it exceeds the customers' expectations.

Questions

1 List SIX possible implications for a business with a poor product or service quality. (6 marks)
2 Why might self-inspection motivate employees? (2 marks)
3 What are the FOUR stages in quality control? (4 marks)

Systems of quality assurance

Total Quality Management (TQM)

Total Quality Management was introduced by W Edwards Deming in the 1980s. Deming worked with Japanese manufacturers and saw TQM as a philosophy and a way of dealing with quality issues. TQM requires every part of the business and all its employees to have a total commitment to quality control, from design through to after-sales. One of the phrases that most closely describes TQM is the idea of building-in quality, rather than inspecting it out.

Every employee is encouraged to think about how customers need to be satisfied. Major British businesses, such as Tesco, have focused on TQM for many years. The idea is to delight customers with higher than expected levels of quality. One of the hopes is that delighted customers become the best advertisement for the business.

Quality circles

Quality circles are an integral part of the TQM process, as their focus is on the increasing participation of employees in quality issues. A quality circle is a group of employees who meet on a regular basis to identify any problems and recommend solutions to the working or production process. The group is involved in continuous development, quality control and improvement. Its aim is to contribute to the improvement and development of all projects, and focus on ensuring that human input into quality is as broad as possible.

Quality circles' effectiveness can be measured in three different ways:

- Quality improvements – a reduction in defects or faults, wastage and customer complaints and returns.
- Cost reductions – a drop in the overall cost of manufacture, failure costs and cost of sales.
- Employee attitudes – a reduction in labour turnover, absentee rates, accidents and employee grievances.

Benchmarking

Benchmarking involves comparing the business against best practice as exhibited by competitors, or at least leading businesses from other, similar industries. The purpose of benchmarking is to:

- discover how well the business is performing in comparison to other, similar businesses
- to set a standard for the business that at least matches, or preferably exceeds, the best identified competitor or other business
- to discover new ideas and ways of doing things that can then be put into practice by the business

Benchmarking can bring benefits to a business, as it can identify areas that require improvement and efficiency. It can also save the business money and time, as potential problems can be systematically identified and dealt with. It also allows the business to set itself clear targets.

Not everyone believes that benchmarking is the ideal answer, as businesses may be reluctant to release information that could be of value to their own competitors. Some believe that benchmarking merely encourages a business to copy what competitors are already doing, rather than to innovate. Others suggest that benchmarking is just a paper exercise: by identifying a problem it does not necessarily follow that the business will be able or willing to do anything about it.

FOR EXAMPLE

In order to build its reputation in the photocopier market, Xerox pioneered the use of benchmarking in the production of its photocopiers. It looked at each stage of production, as well as the quality of the servicing it offered to customers. This gave it a huge advantage over its competitors in the market.

Continuous improvement

The Japanese call continuous improvement 'Kaizen'. It suggests that all employees should be involved in constant, ongoing improvements. A business needs to give employees the ability to use their talents to identify ways in which to maximise quality, at the lowest possible cost. The idea is to encourage employees to become involved and to create a culture of quality.

FOR EXAMPLE

The Japanese vehicle manufacturer Toyota receives nearly three-quarters of a million suggestions on improving quality each year. Around 99% of the ideas are incorporated. Toyota rewards employees who have made suitable suggestions by paying them anything from £2.50 to £1,000.

CASE STUDY DEMING

Much of Japan had been levelled by allied bombing during World War Two. It needed to rebuild its industry. In 1950 W Edwards Deming visited Japan and lectured on quality issues. Before Deming, businesses believed that inspection was the key to quality and that quality control cost money. Regardless of quality, businesses would buy from the cheapest supplier and in order to get the best deals would play suppliers off against one another. Deming believed differently: he suggested that if a business produced defect-free products, then inspection would no longer be necessary. Rather than considering quality control as a cost, it should be seen to increase profits. He also believed that businesses should always work with their suppliers and only buy from those committed to quality. Above all he did not believe that high quality came from quality control. Instead it came from the commitment of all management.

W Edwards Deming

It is not just Japanese businesses that have incorporated Deming's ideas. British car manufacturers use TQM and encourage quality circles. A quality circle will select a problem, analyse it and then suggest a solution. It will then present its ideas to relevant managers who will make a decision about whether to implement the solution.

Questions

1 Compare and contrast the traditional approach towards quality and the Deming approach. (10 marks)
2 What are the THREE main areas in which the effectiveness of a quality circle programme could be measured? (6 marks)
3 Why might it have been easier for Japan to implement this new approach to quality than for European or American manufacturers? (6 marks)

Quality standards

LEARNING OBJECTIVES

▶ Training
▶ British Standards
▶ The five Ss
▶ Poka-Yoka

Training

Any business will find it difficult to produce products or services of a consistently high standard if it does not invest in its employees. Employees need a broad range of skills and qualities, which can be achieved through an effective training and development programme. Training also needs to be forward-looking. The workforce will have a level of skills and capabilities, but these may not be sufficient for the business to be able to meet its objectives or maintain and eventually improve its quality standards in the future.

We have already seen that continuous improvement (Kaizen) demands gradual steps by a business to improve its quality standards. Training can be used to achieve this, particularly if employees are empowered to make their own decisions as members of teams. They can be encouraged to problem-solve and to tackle quality issues.

Clearly training is not a quick-fix solution to bringing in high-quality standards across a business. It takes time for employees to adapt to their new work roles and to recognise that quality standards can be achieved gradually, by coming up with a solution to each problem as it arises.

INTERNET RESEARCH 🔍

For more on British Standards go to www.bsi-global.com.

British Standards

A standard is an agreed and repeatable way of doing something. It may be a technical specification, guideline, rule or definition. Standards are there to simplify matters and to increase the reliability and effectiveness of processes, products and services.

Standards themselves are voluntary and are not regulations. But there are certain laws and regulations that lay down minimum standards and require businesses to comply with them. The British Standards is Britain's national standards body. It was the world's first standards body and it operates across manufacturing, services, governments and consumers. Currently it has 27,000 standards, covering every type of product or service, from accounting to camera lenses.

The most popular standard in the world is the ISO 9001 Quality Management Systems Requirements. It is used by over 670,000 organisations in 154 countries.

There are clear benefits in adopting BSI standards, as they can assure customers, demonstrate leadership in the market place, give the business a competitive advantage and support the development and the maintenance of best practice. In effect the standards are a badge of quality, which has been awarded by independent verification. Businesses earn the certification mark after rigorous examination.

The five Ss

Some British businesses have adopted Japanese approaches to quality. These underpin the quality standards within the organisation, one of which, known as the five Ss, is central to quality and to production. The five Ss aim to communicate targets, measurement, analysis and achievement to management and employees.

Central to the system is the Andon system. This is a sign board that can be activated by any employee to stop production when a quality or process problem has been encountered. It is one of the principal elements of the Jidoka system, which is also known as Autonomation.

The five Ss are:

- Seiri – the proper arrangement of work. This encourages employees to sort through what they need and discard the unnecessary.
- Seiton – orderliness. Employees are encouraged to put their most-used items in a particular order so they always know where they can be found.
- Seiso – cleanliness. All equipment, tools and the workplace itself should be kept clean.
- Seiketsu – employees should clean up after themselves and particularly at the end of a shift.
- Shitsuke – discipline. Employees should stick to the rules and make them a habit.

raising sta

Standards

We provide org
all sectors with
solutions and s
represent and
needs of busin
in the UK and v

Read more...

Assessm

Poka-Yoka

Poka-Yoka dates back to the 1960s when Shigeo Shingo, a Japanese industrial designer working for Toyota, visited an electric company. There were consistent problems in production with employees forgetting to add simple components to the products they were making. Shingo suggested the creation of a checklist and a standardised way of arranging the materials and components that each employee would need to carry out their work. Central to the idea was the concept of mistake-proofing a particular product or process. Shingo suggested designing processes and products so that errors could not be made. If this were impossible then the product or process should be designed in such a way that if there were a defect it would be immediately obvious and be immediately rectified.

BOOK RESEARCH

Scotchmer, Andrew.
5S Kaizen in 90 Minutes.
Management Books 2000
Ltd. 2008.

CASE STUDY QUALITY IN BUSINESS

The BS En ISO 9001 is a standard that British businesses can adopt for improving quality in all their systems. Employees benefit from better working conditions, increased job satisfaction and improved health and safety. The owners or investors of the business will see increased return on investment, improved operational results, an increased market share and profit. Customers and users of the products and services will be assured that what they are buying conforms to the requirements; are dependable and reliable; available when needed and that the quality is always maintained. Society in general benefits, as the products, services and processes comply with legal or regulatory requirements. There is a reduced environmental impact, as well as improved health and safety features.

Increasingly, the pressure is from major customers for businesses to receive British Standard registration. This assists the customer in ensuring that the quality of products and services purchased from suppliers is of a consistently high standard. For many businesses it means reduced errors, faults, a shortening of delays on deliveries and more responsive suppliers, willing to work alongside the customers.

Questions

1. What is BS En ISO 9001? (3 marks)
2. Why might a business want to achieve this accreditation? (4 marks)
3. What might be the benefits to a stationery supplier dealing with business customers of achieving this accreditation? (4 marks)

Introducing and managing quality systems

Quality initiatives

Quality issues can apply to products, services and processes, from the development of a new product or service through to the after-sales service provided to customers. Introducing quality systems within a business is not a straightforward process; neither should it be expected to bring immediate results. It requires the commitment of both management and employees to establish quality-control measures, as well as inspection. It may also mean major changes in the culture of the organisation.

Clearly, bringing in quality initiatives is going to cost money and it will also take time. The business needs to be assured that these costs and the potential disruption to production will bring positive benefits in the future. As we have seen, there are various different ways in which quality systems can be configured, and businesses will adopt one or more initiatives in order to tackle any quality problems.

The key options are shown in the table on the right.

KEY TERM

Ad hoc group – one that has been set up to deal with a specific problem rather than broader issues.

Problems with quality initiatives

Undoubtedly businesses do benefit from the introduction of quality initiatives. However these initiatives are not without problems. The first major concern that often inhibits a business in introducing quality initiatives is cost. Before, during and after the quality system has been introduced, the cost of inspection, either internally or by independent inspectors, could represent a significant expense or could potentially disrupt production. Once a quality system has been chosen, there are training cost implications for both management and other employees. The business may also have to consider switching suppliers and purchasing higher-quality raw materials, components or finished goods. Many of the systems also need enhanced computer technology

Quality initiative	Explanation
Total Quality Management	TQM needs to be seen as a philosophy rather than a management tool. The whole organisation needs to be committed to introducing and managing the system. Every part of the business will consider quality issues, from design through to after-sales. This is, perhaps, one of the most difficult of all of the quality systems to introduce and manage.
Continuous improvement	This is another Japanese technique, requiring the whole organisation to be committed to making small, gradual changes to improve the quality of products, employees, processes and services. Again this needs to be an organisation-wide approach, but can be considered to be rather more gradual than TQM.
Benchmarking	Finding a suitable or relevant business to compare is, perhaps, the first difficult task. The business needs to have a clear understanding of the best practices used by the organisation it is benchmarking itself against. The business may discover that it is difficult to replicate systems and procedures, particularly if the benchmarking business is not operating in the same industry.
Cross-functional improvement groups	These are ad hoc groups, which are set up to investigate how relationships and interactions between departments can be improved. Their principal aim is to look at quality issues, improve efficiency and reduce costs. In order for them to be successful they need to be given the power and the authority to investigate, implement and monitor initiatives.
Quality accreditation	In order to achieve BSI accreditation a business needs to subject itself to an independent inspection and examination. Prior to this it needs to have a documented quality assurance system. The business will need to ensure that it extends across the whole of the business and, if relevant, encompasses the activities carried out on its behalf by subcontractors, as well as suppliers.

or even improved production machinery. As the business transfers from one way of carrying out the production process to another, production can be interrupted, or at best disrupted, which could cost the business output and profit.

Quality initiatives take time to work and results may not be immediately apparent. For a time the whole business will be affected by the introduction of the quality system and the results of the training may not be clear until all management and employees have passed through the training programmes.

Businesses, particularly those that have shareholders, will be under pressure to show short-term results from the expenditure in bringing in the quality systems. Shareholders are notoriously impatient and often cannot see beyond the short-term, even though the quality initiatives require a longer-term view.

The investment in the quality systems will mean a cost today, but the benefits may be two, three or even five years down the line. Even when the benefits show themselves in the business's financial performance they may be difficult to measure or to attribute to the quality initiative.

Quality initiative	Explanation
Quality circles	Rather like cross-functional improvement groups, quality circles are groups of employees whose role is to identify problems and recommend improvements to processes. They focus on quality issues and try to identify the best practice to improve quality. A business will usually have a major advantage in setting up these quality circles, as it will be tapping into the knowledge and experience of individuals involved in every stage of a production process. Again the quality circle needs to have the necessary power and authority to persuade management to incorporate its recommendations.
Training	Businesses can take two different views on training, effectively adopting either a micro or a macro approach to quality issues. On the micro level, specific job-related training for new and existing employees should focus on quality issues as an integral part of the programme. On a macro basis, specific quality training programmes can be rolled out to the whole workforce. New employees need to be quickly adapted to the quality culture of the business and given a clear explanation as to how this matches the key objectives of the organisation.
Zero defects	Like TQM, this is a philosophy that requires organisation-wide commitment. Every employee needs to be part of the quality assurance system. The key aim is to produce products and services that have no faults or that present no particular problems. This may mean redesign, or a fresh look at the production process or any other aspect that could be detrimental to the quality of the products or services delivered.

Questions

1 Which quality initiatives are perhaps easier to introduce and manage, and why? (6 marks)
2 Why might a business not see an immediate improvement after the introduction of a quality system? (4 marks)

Case studies, questions and exam practice

CASE STUDY HAMILTON COMPUTERS

Hamilton Computers assemble, install and service IT systems for businesses in the Bedfordshire area. They have many competitors, local, national and international. The business is seeing a slowing of sales and is worried about quality control. Recent market data has suggested that Hamilton Computers has a 9% defect rate compared to an industry standard of between 6% and 7%. It may not seem much, but the business is aware that its computers have a growing reputation for not being as reliable as the competition.

The sales and marketing manager is adamant that the slowing of sales has nothing to do with the effectiveness of her sales force. She blames production for the problems. After a stormy board meeting the production director resigned and his assistant was promoted. Immediately the new temporary director suggested that the factory should be closed for a week so that a complete reorganisation could be carried out. He argued for a £750,000 equipment investment and a training programme for all production staff. Equally importantly, he also identified the fact that the business was using inferior components from China,

rather than South Korea, which was the source of most of the components the competitors were using. He felt the cheaper components were one of the main reasons for the higher defect rate. He went on to suggest that employees and managers from across the organisation be put into teams to investigate problems and suggest solutions. The board was astounded by the wide-reaching suggestions and more than a little concerned about the potential costs.

Questions

1 Give TWO reasons why Hamilton might be experiencing quality problems (2 marks)
2 What are the advantages of getting managers and employees to look at problems? (4 marks)
3 How might Hamilton bring in quality initiatives and manage the system? (10 marks)
4 What might be the implications if the initiatives are not adopted? (6 marks)
5 What are the advantages and disadvantages of the suggestions made by the new production director? (8 marks)

SHORT-ANSWER QUESTIONS

1 Why is quality control important to a business?

2 How might a business control quality?

3 What is TQM?

4 What are the five Ss?

5 What is the purpose of the British Standards?

6 What do you understand by the term 'zero defects'?

7 What are the problems associated with benchmarking?

8 Distinguish between a quality circle and a cross-functional improvement group.

9 What is Kaizen better known as, and what does it involve?

10 What are the FOUR key stages of quality control?

CASE STUDY TREVOR'S TOYLAND

Trevor and his brother Gary have been running a toyshop in a small market town for the past 25 years. They are now in their late fifties and are seriously considering selling the business and retiring. Until recently the brothers worked in the shop only three days a week each as the store was run by their longstanding friend Alf. Alf then retired, after working for them for 24 years. There is a very high turnover of staff and the brothers are finding it increasingly difficult to find part-time workers. The brothers have seen the turnover and profits drop, particularly after a large chain store opened a branch in a bigger town only 15 miles away. They have seen a rising number of complaints from customers, particularly about items not being in stock and delays in delivery. The brothers have always tried to make sure that the shop has sufficient stocks of basic items and have had good relationships with suppliers. Many of the suppliers seem to have had delivery problems of their own in recent months: orders have been short and late, and often products that the brothers had not ordered have been delivered, causing extra problems with customers. None of this seemed to happen when Alf was in charge of the store.

Questions

1 Suggest what the brothers could do to improve the quality issues that seem to be arising in the business. (10 marks)

2 Why might the brothers find it difficult to sell the business and retire as they had planned? (6 marks)

Methods of meeting customer expectations

LEARNING OBJECTIVES

▶ What is customer service?
▶ Customer expectations
▶ Using market research
▶ Training employees
▶ Using quality assurance, control and quality standards

What is customer service?

Customer relations have three main parts. The first task is to identify customers; the second is to develop a relationship with those customers. Thirdly, the organisation must then try to hold on to those customers, in order to sell products and services to them over a long period of time. More broadly, we can see that customer relations involve a number of different aspects:

- Identifying customers who could be interested in the business's products or services
- Giving customers good service
- Allowing customers to buy products in ways that suit them (online or using credit or instalments)
- Making sure customers have all the information they need

- Supporting customers and reassuring them that any objections or queries they may have are answered
- Closing sales efficiently and effectively
- Following up sales with service and support
- Contacting existing customers to achieve additional sales

Customer relations is a new word for a very old concept in business. Businesses have always known that high-quality customer service means that customers will inevitably come back to them for future purchases. There is a saying that suggests that 80% of a business's total profits come from their most loyal 20% of customers. In effect, a business is always interested in customers who can provide them with the greatest level of profit.

INTERNET RESEARCH

For more information on the work of customer services and how businesses investigate customer expectations, visit the website of the Institute of Customer Service at www.instituteof customerservice.com.

Customer expectations

Customer needs and expectations are constantly changing. Awareness of new technology, consumer legislation and what competitors have to offer creates new demands. It is vital for a business to be able to constantly improve its range of products and services and the ways these are supported and sold in order to satisfy customer needs and wants.

Customers need reliable products and services that they can trust, at the price they want to pay, and for these to be available when and where they want them. These are the basic demands of customers, but they require far more than this and the business needs to be aware of this. Customer expectations revolve around what is known as customer satisfaction. This means that the business needs to be aware of a customer's needs and expectations and provide products and services in such a way that will meet these demands.

KEY TERMS

Qualitative – a market research method that uses a relatively small sample of customers who are canvassed for their views and attitudes.

Quantitative – a market research method that uses statistical information in order to identify trends, usually linked to sales figures, market share and customer complaints figures.

USP (unique selling point or unique selling proposition) – a feature or series of features of a product or service that makes it superior to competing products or services.

Using market research

Many businesses use periodic or ongoing market research to establish customer perceptions and expectations of products and services. The market research can help identify the key expectations of customers in relation to the business's own products and services, as well as making vital comparisons with key competitors.

Market research in this respect tends to focus on **qualitative** research. This research focuses on the views and opinions of customers and can be distinguished from **quantitative** research, which tends to look at broader facts and figures, usually related to sales figures or numbers of customer complaints. In investigating the views and attitudes of customers, provided the sample used is representative of the overall customer base, the business can not only gauge current attitudes but can also seek to anticipate future expectations.

FOR EXAMPLE

The British School of Motoring offers training for drivers to teach learners essential driving skills in order for them to pass the DVLA tests. Over the years the BSM has established itself as a high-quality organisation with an impressive pass rate. Customers are attracted to driving instructors who have been trained by BSM or are BSM approved. This gives them a distinct advantage over the competition and goes a long way to meet customer expectations of the service.

Training employees

When the subject of customer service is considered, it is important to remember that there are both internal and external customers receiving service from a business. Many departments within a large organisation provide a range of services to other parts of the organisation, such as Human Resources providing personnel services; and Accounts providing payment to employees and dealing with invoices from suppliers on behalf of the purchasing department. It is therefore important that any customer service training undertaken by the business encompasses the broadest possible range of employees: not just those who have contact with external customers. Clearly these individuals are the external face of the business as far as customers are concerned. But customer service also needs to address the internal customer service requirements.

Training, therefore, needs to involve the broadest possible range of employees. The expectations of internal customers are equally as important as those of the external customers who provide the income and profit generation for the business.

Using quality assurance, control and quality standards

In a highly competitive market there is often little to distinguish between various competing businesses offering similar products and services. A key distinguishing factor, or **USP**, can be quality assurance or a quality standards guarantee made by the business. The most convincing and potentially effective forms of guarantees are those that have been awarded to the business as a result of external and independent inspection, such as those carried out by the BSI.

There is also an increasing trend for many industries or trades to promote their members as approved or recommended suppliers. More recently there has also been a trend for general service websites to recommend tradespeople who have undergone rigorous inspection.

Once quality assurance or quality standards have been established by a business it needs to focus on the maintenance, support and improvement of that customer service, in order to ensure that customer service expectations are met both now and in the future.

For more information about quality assurance, control and standards see Developing effective operations: quality on pp. 234–45.

Questions

1 How might market research assist a business in identifying customer expectations? (4 marks)
2 Distinguish between internal and external customers. (4 marks)
3 Why might customer service training programmes be applied to all areas of an organisation? (4 marks)

Monitoring and improving customer service

LEARNING OBJECTIVES
▶ Monitoring customer service
▶ Evaluating and improving customer service

Monitoring customer service

Many organisations set up their customer service provision as a direct result of experiences they have had in the past with customers. They can only base their systems on what they know, and cater for the most common problems that customers may present to them. They also need to make sure that the customer service provision not only maintains its high standards but also is adaptable and can be improved on a number of different levels as and when required.

The first aspect of ensuring that customer service remains efficient and effective is to set up monitoring systems. The purpose of the monitoring systems is to pick up problems, as well as customer perceptions of the customer service provision.

The first and perhaps least efficient way of doing this is to rely on informal customer feedback. This means taking note of comments that customers make in relation to the customer service they receive. This is not a terribly good way of obtaining objective information about the customer service, as only the most vocal customers will make comment.

A more structured way of collecting information is to use customer questionnaires and comment cards. These are now widely used and certain customer service questions are even included on **guarantees** and **warranties**. They will ask customers various questions concerning customer services, such as the politeness of staff, their helpfulness and whether a situation was resolved to their satisfaction. The only problem with this type of questionnaire and comment cards is the number of them completed by customers. They will also need to be looked at in some detail and the results collated to be of any particular use to the business.

Staff can also provide useful feedback for monitoring and evaluating customer service. They can identify problem areas and the most common complaints from customers. If taken together with customer feedback, questionnaires or comment cards, these can provide a good indication of how the customer service provision is working in practice.

Some businesses use 'mystery customers'. These are individuals unknown to the business and its employees. They will test the customer service provision by pretending to be customers with specific customer service problems. They will provide a report on how they were treated and whether they were satisfied with the level of help they received. This can prove to be a useful double check for the business, particularly if it has just changed the way in which it provides customer service.

The final way of monitoring and evaluating customer service is to examine the number and nature of complaints or compliments received, either verbally or in writing from customers. Many businesses pin up their compliment letters, but are at pains to hide complaints.

The complaints or compliments will probably contain detailed information about the transaction and use of customer service. How these were responded to can provide the business with useful case study material with which to train its staff.

KEY TERMS

Guarantees – official reassurances given free of charge by the manufacturer of a product to the customer that if the product proves faulty within a specified period their money will be refunded.

Warranties – similar to guarantees, but normally the customer pays for the extra protection. They are often known as extended warranties or insurance policies against repair and replacement costs.

Evaluating and improving customer service

There are several different ways in which a business can evaluate its customer service provision. These are in addition to the regular feedback, comments and other information gained from actually carrying out customer service. A business might evaluate its customer service using some of the following methods:

- Level of sales – a steady or increasing level of sales would indicate that customers are happy with the overall customer service they are receiving from the business. Businesses would also take account of the number of products that have been returned faulty, compared with the number of those products sold.
- Repeat customers – as we have already seen in this unit, repeat customers are of enormous importance to a business. Loyal customers provide the bulk of the profits for the business and keeping these customers increases not only sales, but also profitability.

- New customers – there are a number of different ways in which new customers could come to the organisation. Perhaps they are responding to advertising, but many purchase from the business for the first time as a result of recommendations. Once these customers have made their first purchase the business will want to ensure that they become repeat customers.
- Level of complaints/compliments – businesses want to minimise the number of complaints while increasing the number of compliments. It is rare for businesses to receive many written complaints or compliments, so for the most part these are not a great way of evaluating customer service.
- Staff turnover – experienced and reliable staff are of great importance to any business. Continued problems with customers can force employees to look for work elsewhere. Employees become tired and frustrated if they are constantly dealing with complaints and problems from customers.

By continually monitoring and evaluating customer service, a business will hope to make steady improvements. It will try to ensure that levels of service and products and services remain good value for money and that the overall package provides a reliable service to customers.

By improving customer service, a business will:

- retain existing customers
- retain its experienced and most valued members of staff
- attract new customers
- sell more products and services, increasing turnover
- become more profitable and almost certainly employ more staff
- respond quickly to legal obligations and exceed the requirements of law
- increase staff, turnover and profitability and thus maximise the opportunity to continue to improve.

> ## Questions
>
> 1 What is informal customer feedback? (2 marks)
> 2 What is the difference between a guarantee and a warranty? (4 marks)
> 3 What is a repeat customer? (2 marks)
> 4 If a business were suffering from a falling level of sales, what might be wrong with its customer service provision? (6 marks)

Benefits of high levels of customer service

LEARNING OBJECTIVES

▶ Customer satisfaction
▶ Customer confidence
▶ Reputation
▶ Profits, health and safety and security
▶ Customers, the business and employees

Customer satisfaction

Research shows that a 5% increase in customer loyalty can boost profits by 25% to 85%. Research has also revealed that satisfied clients lead to greater profitability and growth. To excel in today's competitive market place, organisations must create positive experiences for customers with each and every interaction.

There is a general acceptance in today's business environment that customer service and customer satisfaction are key elements for success. Customers are promised great service by advertising campaigns, so expectations are high.

Customer confidence

Customer satisfaction has many key advantages, both to the business and to the customers. If a business can establish a reputation for high levels of customer service then it can hope to ensure that customers are not merely satisfied, but delighted by the level of service they receive from the business.

A business will always strive to exceed its customers' expectations in ways such as having a no-quibble refund policy (Marks and Spencer) or trying to source Fair Trade products from abroad as standard (the Co-Op).

Although providing high levels of customer service is important, it is always expensive. Customer service staff need to be employed, though they are not directly selling products and services – sales may, of course, rise if customers are pleased with the service. This is all an added

cost to the business at a time when customers are demanding ever increasing value for money.

Businesses now realise that they have to have a major and recognisable reason for not charging the same or less than their competitors. Great customer service can be one of these reasons, but for the most part, customers will tend to buy from an organisation that offers products and services at the lowest possible price or at least a competitive one.

Reputation

As a business builds up its customer base, the hope is that it will begin to achieve a reputation for high-quality products, services, staff and customer service. A business stands and falls on its reputation and the last thing it wants is to be associated with poor-quality service. The worst examples of poor service can be seen on BBC Watchdog, but customers have daily problems with organisations and report them to local Trading Standards (run by the local government to investigate customer complaints). As far as a business is concerned, good news travels fast, but bad news travels faster. They cannot afford for it to be known that they provide poor-quality service: if they fail to sort out a problem, then their reputation will suffer.

Profits, health and safety, and security

One of the greatest problems relating to customer service is measuring its impact on the profitability of the business. One of the first things that a business will do when setting up a customer service provision is to set a series of targets in dealing with customer complaints and problems. They will have a recommended, maximum waiting time for customers; they may have clear instructions to their staff about the exchange of products or the refund of money paid.

With businesses increasingly using customer loyalty cards or store debit cards, they are able to see whether a customer problem has led to a decrease in that customer's spending with the business. This would infer that they were not happy with the customer service. Or they could detect whether the customer was happy with the provision and continued to shop with the business.

Although there is legislation to protect customers from hazards when they visit a business's premises, many businesses in fact take this far further than is legally required. Customers cannot be exposed to dangers and simple hazards, such as slippery floors, fumes, trailing wire or a host of other potential problems. These must be monitored and dealt with by health and safety representatives in a business. Above all, customers want a safe and secure shopping environment and cameras, security staff and special training for shop floor staff are all designed to assist this, in addition to stopping shoplifting and theft.

Customers, the business and employees

Businesses want to respond to customer needs. They also want to encourage new customers. It is vital that the business has a good image as far as existing customers and potential customers are concerned. Obviously, businesses do not just have customer services for the benefits of their customers. They know that good customer service will benefit them. The first key benefit to good customer service is increased sales. A company needs to generate enough money to pay its staff, to buy equipment and stock (a benefit to the business, employees and customers) and to make a profit, which will benefit the owners of the organisation.

Another key benefit to an organisation of having effective customer service provision is that customers will be happy. If they are happy they will continue to use the business and buy products and services from them. This is known as repeat business. The organisation wants the customers to keep coming back and to recommend them to their friends and family.

Many businesses spend a huge amount of money on advertising in order not only to tell customers about their products and services, but also to put across a positive and strong public image. They want customers to believe that their products and services are reliable, are value for money, and are safe, healthy and a host of other features. Every business is in competition with hundreds, thousands, or tens of thousands of others. As we have seen, having a good level of customer service can give a business an advantage over the competition. So a business has to build up and then maintain a reputation for having excellent customer service. A dissatisfied customer is a lost customer and that customer, once lost, will tell others of their bad experience.

CASE STUDY PLUMBERS 'WORST VALUE FOR MONEY'

According to the website www.propertyfinder.com, plumbers are the worst value for money and provide the worst overall quality of service of any tradesmen. Builders are seen to be the second worst group at offering value for money and they are also regarded as the worst timekeepers, followed by plumbers.

Builders were rated as providing the second worst overall service, after plumbers, with electricians in third place, followed by painters and decorators. At the other end of the scale locksmiths were seen as providing the best service, with 48% of people rating them as good or excellent for all three categories of value for money, quality of service and timekeeping.

Questions

1 What could a local plumber do to explain to potential customers that their service offered is good value for money? (6 marks)
2 What other professions do you think offer poor value for money and why might this be the case? (4 marks)

Case studies, questions and exam practice

CASE STUDY GOOD CHOICE – ICELAND

During over 600 face-to-face interviews, consumers were asked what they would do to improve their health. While these findings are limited in that they do not provide information about what the consumers were already doing, they are valuable in that they offer an indication of consumers' current awareness of health promotion messages, and where further work is needed to communicate these messages. Fat emerges as the main constituent people want to remove from their diet; 34% would choose low-fat versions of food. Recognition of the importance of exercise is clear. Many consumers have made changes to their diet and see exercise as the next solution.

The challenge for frozen-food store, Iceland, was to develop a healthy-eating range that followed Government nutrition guidelines, met customer demand and was still competitive within the market place. The 'Good Choice' range was developed following a carefully written technical policy. In addition to the overall Brand Policy of allowing no GM ingredients, artificial colours or flavours, the policy takes into account Government advice on nutrition content, nutrition labelling, etc., and customer feedback derived from research. To ensure that the nutrition content was appropriate, expert bodies such as Consensus Action on Salt and Hypertension (CASH) were consulted. Sodium/salt limits were set for individual product areas, taking into account the expected consumption of that product in a day.

To ensure that nutrition labelling was clear and informative, customer research was carried out to identify what information customers wanted to see and how it should be displayed. Government guidance on nutrition claims, such as those that could be considered misleading, was followed and incorporated into the technical policy. The customer research resulted in the design of a nutrition panel showing the fat and salt figures highlighted and the fat and calories per portion detailed in a summary line. The percentage of fat in the product is prominently displayed on the front of packaging.

The resulting 'Good Choice' range was launched as Iceland's healthy eating option. The entire range has been specially developed to be lower in fat and with controlled salt levels. Other nutrients, such as fibre and sugar, become criteria for the 'Good Choice' range if appropriate – for example, fibre would also be criteria in breakfast cereals. The 'Good Choice' range is the most successful Iceland sub-brand sold to date. The range has doubled in size, and was redeveloped and re-launched to ensure that enthusiasm and awareness of the need for healthy eating is maintained.

Post-launch customer research indicated that the nutrition labelling was understood and that the 'Good Choice' brand was trusted. The need for more vegetarian products within the range was identified and these suggestions were incorporated into the re-launch design brief. In summary, the 'Good Choice' range has been successful in terms of developing a profitable, healthier range of products that meets customer needs.

Source: adapted from www.iceland.co.uk

Questions

1 Where would you find information on the government nutrition guidelines? (2 marks)
2 What is meant by 'brand policy'? (4 marks)
3 Why might customers be especially interested in the labelling? (4 marks)
4 What is a re-launch design brief? (4 marks)

SHORT-ANSWER QUESTIONS

1 What is meant by customer service?

2 How might market research help a business meet the expectations of its customers?

3 How might a business monitor its customer service provision?

4 How can a business improve its customer service provision?

5 What are the major benefits to a business of having high customer service levels?

6 How might a business's reputation be improved by ensuring that customer service provision is high?

7 How can customer confidence be affected by the level of customer service offered by a business?

8 How can customer loyalty cards be used to gauge customer satisfaction?

9 How might quality standards be useful in dealing with customer expectations?

10 What are the major advantages to a business of having loyal customers?

CASE STUDY CUSTOMER NEEDS

AstraZeneca is one of the world's leading pharmaceutical companies. It is clear about its commitment to matching customer needs in this statement:

Supply and manufacturing
One of our top priorities is to provide our customers with a fast, flexible and cost-effective supply of our products wherever they are required. To meet that challenge, we have around 15,000 people at 30 manufacturing sites in 20 countries dedicated to ensuring that we can deliver a reliable flow of all the products in our range worldwide. We also continue to invest for the future in new facilities to support the launch of new medicines and meet the increasing demand for the products in our range. Ensuring patient safety is a core priority, as is our commitment to high safety, health and environmental standards at all of our facilities.

Product strategy and licensing
Our product strategy and licensing organisation, working closely with our R&D community and major marketing companies, leads the commercial aspects of drug development and co-ordinates global product marketing strategy. This includes selecting the right products and projects for investment, developing effective marketing platforms in time for new product launches, and directing the creation and delivery of product marketing strategies that successfully align global and national plans.

Sales and marketing
Active in over 100 countries, we have an extensive, high-quality sales and marketing network worldwide, structured to anticipate and respond to local market needs. We sell mostly through our own local marketing companies, and our products are marketed mainly to physicians and other healthcare professionals. We also explain the economic as well as the therapeutic advantages of our products to governments and healthcare buying groups, such as managed care organisations in the US. In the marketing of our medicines, we are committed to ethical behaviour and aim to ensure that we communicate information about our products effectively and in a proper manner.

Source: adapted from www.astrazeneca.com

Questions

1 What is meant by the term 'cost-effective'? (2 marks)
2 What is 'R&D'? (2 marks)
3 Why might the way in which the business operates in the UK differ from its operation in a developing African country? (6 marks)
4 What is meant by 'we also explain the economic as well as the therapeutic advantages of our products?' (4 marks)

Choosing effective suppliers

LEARNING OBJECTIVES

- ▶ Choosing a supplier
- ▶ Targeting potential suppliers
- ▶ Key qualities of good suppliers
- ▶ Identifying good suppliers
- ▶ Drawing up a shortlist of suppliers
- ▶ Comparing potential suppliers

Choosing a supplier

Picking the right supplier is a far more involved process than looking at price lists. There is a broad range of factors that need to be taken into account, including liability, service, value for money and quality. These factors also need to be considered in relation to the business's priorities and strategies.

Targeting potential suppliers

Many businesses make the mistake of having too broad a range of suppliers and far more than they actually need. This is especially the case when buying from a relatively small number of suppliers could bring the following benefits:

- It is easier to control the suppliers
- The business is more important to them because it is spending more
- They may be able to offer deals that will give the business a competitive advantage

If a handful of suppliers is used, they are more likely to be receptive if the customer is spending a reasonable amount with them each month, rather than spreading their spending across several suppliers. However, using only one supplier can be a dangerous strategy, particularly if the supplier lets the business down or goes out of business. Using a single supplier may lead to that company becoming complacent, and there may be a drop in quality standards, or conversely it could lead to better customer service.

Key qualities of a good supplier

The following table outlines some of the key considerations when looking at suppliers:

Quality	Implication
Reliability	It is important to remember that if a supplier lets the business down, the business will have to let its own customers down.
Quality	Supplies need to be consistent. A business's customers will associate poor quality with their supplier, not with the business's supplier.
Value for money	The lowest price is not necessarily the best value for money. It needs to be a combination of reliability, quality and payment terms.
Good customer service and communications	A supplier needs to deliver on time and to be upfront if it is likely to be late in delivering products or services. Suppliers should maintain a regular dialogue, discover the needs of their own customers and look for ways to provide a better service.
Financial security	Many businesses run a credit check on suppliers before they commit to them just to make sure that they will not go out of business when they are most needed. A supplier will need a relatively strong cash flow to deliver products and services when the customer wants them.
Partnership approach	A strong relationship will benefit both supplier and customer. Customers want to know that they are important to the supplier and that every effort is being made to provide them with the best service. This needs to be a two-way process.

Identifying good suppliers

It is possible to spend days hunting for suitable suppliers, but most businesses will begin by drawing up a shortlist using a combination of different sources, which are outlined in the following table:

INTERNET RESEARCH

For information on different supplier exhibitions visit www.tsnn.co.uk

BOOK RESEARCH

For a full listing of trade magazines use either *BRAD* or *Willings Press Guide*, both of which can be found in reference libraries.

Source of information	Explanation
Recommendations	Existing business partners are likely to give an honest assessment of a supplier's strengths and weaknesses, as they may already have used their services.
Directories	A reasonably complete listing of local or regional suppliers can be found in directories such as *Yellow Pages* and *Thomson*, although this is no guarantee of their reliability.
Trade associations	If a business's needs are specific to a particular trade or industry there will undoubtedly be a trade association that can assist in finding suitable suppliers.
Business advisors	Organisations such as Business Link, Chambers of Commerce or Enterprise agencies can recommend or provide lists of potential suppliers. They may have already had dealings with these suppliers.
Exhibitions	Trade exhibitions are a valuable opportunity to talk to a range of potential suppliers in one location at the same time.
Trade press	Many different trades and industries have their own magazines or newspapers, which feature advertisements and articles on different businesses.

Drawing up a shortlist of suppliers

Once the business has identified potential suppliers a shortlist can be drawn up. The following questions should be asked:

- Can they deliver what is needed when it is needed?
- Are they financially secure?
- How long have they been established?
- Does anyone know who has used them and can recommend them?
- Are they on any approved supplier list (such as a trade association or government)?

Ideally, after the research the business should trim the list down to around four or five potential suppliers.

Comparing potential suppliers

The business will then approach each supplier for a quotation for particular products and services. In some cases the quality of their products and services may be the most important consideration. Price may not be the sole determining factor, as poorer-quality products and services may not be cost-effective.

It is also important to consider whether the supplier is actually providing the product or service themselves, or whether they have outsourced the work to subcontractors. Businesses usually like to have a face-to-face meeting with potential suppliers and perhaps to tour their premises to see how they operate. Increasingly businesses are also concerned with the labour practices of their suppliers, as some businesses' reputations are judged on the basis of the activities of their suppliers.

FOR EXAMPLE

The clothing retailer GAP, while having an ethical trading policy and strict guidelines for suppliers, was found on a number of occasions to have used suppliers that employed children in less than acceptable conditions in countries such as India. Their reputation was affected by the practices of their suppliers.

Questions

1 Why might price alone not be the key determinant in choosing a supplier? (4 marks)
2 How might a business draw up a shortlist of potential suppliers? (6 marks)

Suppliers' role in improving operational performance

LEARNING OBJECTIVES
▶ Managing suppliers
▶ Quality service
▶ Specific needs of a business
▶ Building good relationships with suppliers
▶ Helping key suppliers
▶ Using technology
▶ Reviewing suppliers' performance

Managing suppliers

The role and relationship of a supplier begins with the way in which the business negotiates terms. The terms are usually based on:

- The way in which the business pays their supplier (overdrafts, foreign currency or commercial bills paid for by bank)
- Potential costs, including administration, taxes and transport
- Possible risks, such as late payment to suppliers or faulty, late or undelivered goods

Quality service

As we have seen, there are a number of national and international certification bodies, such as the ISO or BSI standards. Many of them are used and recognised worldwide. They aim to guarantee that suppliers will not only provide consistently high-quality products and services, but will also help improve the operation and performance of the business.

Specific needs

Businesses need to choose suppliers that can meet specific needs, such as fast turnaround. One way in which this can be achieved is to draw up a service level agreement. These define the service that the supplier provides, the level of service that is expected and their responsibilities and priorities. Many of these agreements are contractual obligations and built into contracts, and some of them are complex documents that need to be well defined. They will cover problem management, warranties, and remedies, dealing with disputes, compensation and legal compliance.

Building good relations with suppliers

Businesses often invest time in building good relationships with their key suppliers. This can lead to quality improvements, as well as cost savings. In dealing with suppliers and discovering what role they could play in the future of the business the following may be undertaken:

- The business will have face-to-face meetings with the supplier to understand how they work and how they can benefit the business.
- The business's account managers should be met, and steps taken to ensure that they can be easily contacted.
- Any suppliers' plans for development or expansion that might affect the products and services provided, should be considered.
- Suppliers need to receive orders in good time and be given clear instructions about deadlines.
- The business should also consider passing on new business opportunities to the supplier, as this will improve the relationship.

Helping key suppliers

In order for the business to benefit in the long-term in their relationship with their supplier, there are ways in which the business's activities can be coordinated with the supplier's:

- The business's production schedules should be discussed with suppliers so that their supply to the business can be coordinated with specific needs.
- Ways in which to reduce overall costs through the size or timing of orders should be examined.
- The business should ask whether additional products or services could be provided.
- Any major changes or new products planned should be discussed with suppliers, in order to help them adapt to meet these needs.
- An analysis of sales forecasts can be shared with suppliers to help coordinate deliveries and schedules.
- The use of a purchase order system to control and monitor the purchase of products and services can help prevent misunderstandings at the suppliers' end.
- Finally, suppliers should be paid promptly in order to ensure that their continued cooperation is assured.

Using technology

Broadband connection allows businesses to collaborate closely with their suppliers, and share data, forecasts and plans. This makes it easier to analyse sales, orders and trends and then react to them. This should improve efficiency and particularly required stock levels. It is known as e-collaboration and can be straightforward using email and spreadsheets. Many businesses have actually taken this a stage further and share information in real time:

- Inventory planning – allows stock control records to be used to forecast market demand.
- Analytical processing – sales performances can be analysed and forecasts compared.
- Enterprise resource planning – can assist in planning and scheduling the whole business by effectively connecting the order and purchasing system with the supplier. Orders can then be placed and tracked.

For more on the types of technology used in operations management see Using technology in operations on pp. 260–5.

Reviewing suppliers' performance

At regular intervals businesses will review their suppliers' performance, often comparing the requirements of a service level agreement with actual performance. In order to make sure that the supplier continues to contribute towards the improvement of operational performance the following questions will often be asked:

- Is the business getting the best price, and does the supplier offer bulk discounts or other favourable terms?
- Is the business generally satisfied with the quality of the products or services supplied?
- Do suppliers regularly update the business about new products and services that could make improvements?
- Do supplies arrive in good condition and on time?
- Do the suppliers respond quickly to orders and queries?
- Have the suppliers met their obligations with regard to service level agreements?

If suppliers are not performing, then, rather than immediately seeking alternatives, a face-to-face meeting could be arranged to help iron out any difficulties or deficiencies in the service. It is important to remember that a supplier's performance directly affects the operational activities of the business they are supplying. However, this is a two-way relationship, as suppliers are unlikely to maintain high standards if they are consistently having to chase a business for payment.

> **Questions**
>
> 1 What is a service level agreement? (4 marks)
> 2 How might a supplier assist a business in improving its own operational performance? (6 marks)
> 3 How might a business review the performance of its suppliers? (6 marks)

Case studies, questions and exam practice

CASE STUDY ROS LEE

Ros Lee is Administration Director for contract publishing company McMillan-Scott. When she joined the business, one of her first challenges was to rethink the way suppliers were managed. A thorough review and cost analysis led to a new purchasing policy and significant savings.

'When we started our supplier review, the company didn't have an official purchasing policy. Like many businesses, we had grown significantly but purchasing systems hadn't caught up. Staff were still ordering supplies on an ad hoc basis. The first thing we did was to list all our suppliers and calculate the current spend on everything from stationery to company cars. Once we had all the information in a central database, we could look at areas for improvement. It was clear that there was scope to cut costs by centralising all purchasing, rationalising our supplier base and negotiating better deals with key suppliers. The next step was to consult with existing suppliers and investigate alternatives. Even where there were cheaper options, we didn't dismiss existing suppliers out of hand. We talked to them face-to-face to explain our new purchasing policy. We wanted to give them a chance to compete with the other suppliers we were considering. We also made sure new suppliers understood our needs and that we understood the way they operated. Developing good relationships from the outset is important. If you help your suppliers, they'll be more willing to help you. It was essential to put an end to ad hoc buying, so the new policy was immediately circulated to all staff. There was some initial resistance, but by talking to them and listening to their concerns we overcame it. One major staff worry was that product quality would decline, making their jobs harder. We were careful to provide a product sample for testing whenever a substitution was planned. Some savings are apparent straight away. For example, changing our stationery supplier resulted in an immediate 20 per cent cost reduction, while limiting supplier choice for company cars led to an average 15 per cent discount on prices. We also undertook a formal annual review of our purchasing policy. We compared costs year on year and assessed product quality and service performance across all our suppliers. Staff feedback was taken into account and key findings were communicated to suppliers where appropriate. The ultimate goal of a purchasing policy is to control costs, but good supplier relationships are based on more than just money. We learnt a few lessons in the early days. For example, we switched telephone suppliers to gain a huge cost saving. But the service levels didn't meet our needs and the business suffered temporarily. Before long, we reverted to our original supplier. Now, every decision we make to retain a supplier or take on a new one involves careful analysis of service levels.'

Source: adapted from Business Link

Questions

1 What does Ros mean when she says that people were ordering on an 'ad hoc basis'? (2 marks)
2 What steps were taken to rationalise and centralise purchasing? (6 marks)
3 What was the purpose of the annual reviews and what did they achieve? (6 makrs)
4 What is meant by the statement 'every decision we make to retain a supplier or take on a new one involves careful analysis of service levels'? (6 marks)

SHORT-ANSWER QUESTIONS

1 List **SIX** key factors that a business should look for in a supplier.

2 How might a business draw up a shortlist of suppliers?

3 Why might a business's reputation be affected by the practices of its suppliers?

4 Why are the terms that are initially negotiated with a supplier important?

5 What do you understand by the term 'service level agreement'?

6 How might a business aim to build a good relationship with its supplier?

7 How might a business assist key suppliers?

8 Outline how improved communications technology can improve the efficiency of a business and a supplier.

9 How might a business review a supplier's performance?

10 Why might price not be the sole determining factor in choosing a supplier?

CASE STUDY E-PROCUREMENT

AtoZ Accord is a major stationery supplier to Essex County Council. AtoZ knew that the local authority was looking at automating its buying and selling processes. The business wanted to make sure that it was part of the authority's new e-procurement system, and set up AtoZ Direct, which has an electronic catalogue. The head of the new business, Karen Payne, said:

'The biggest investment has been time. If you want to do it, you are working to deadlines all the time. It's new and we did not have people employed to do it but at the end of the day we can see what the benefits will be. The fact that we are e-enabled means there will be a growth in our business. There will be cost reductions because it's all systems-based.'

The orders are now received from the Council by email and the business then follows its normal distribution and fulfilment. Many small and medium-sized businesses have not adopted e-procurement services, but it is a trend that is being implemented by many councils, as Adrian Gibson,

the Procurement Manager for Essex County Council said:

'E-procurement generates a lot of improvements. It takes all the paper away. From our desktops we can just click on an icon and do what used to take days in a matter of minutes.'

Businesses that have joined the electronic marketplace, where councils invite quotes for orders, have entered a new area of business opportunity.

Questions

1 What do you understand by the term 'e-procurement'? (3 marks)

2 What might be meant by the term 'e-enabled'? (2 marks)

3 What are the main advantages of a small to medium-sized business adopting an e-procurement service? (6 marks)

Types of technology in operations management

LEARNING OBJECTIVES

▶ Robotics
▶ Automation
▶ Stock control
▶ Communications
▶ Design technology
▶ Flexible production

Robotics

Robotics are an important part of modern production technology. Robots on the production line are automatically controlled: some are programmed by keying in instructions. Others are taught to copy movements made by a human operator. New-generation robots used on the production line are also able to check progress and pick up errors.

Modern factories use robots when employees can be replaced in repetitive work situations, where no real intelligence is required to carry out the tasks. Robots can also be used where the working conditions are either dangerous or difficult for humans such as in cramped conditions or with heavy or hot materials.

Though robots are expensive to purchase, programme and install, they become very economical to run once this investment has been made.

Automation

Many assembly lines have elements of automation, particularly in the car industry and in the production of pharmaceuticals. Automation ranges from stand-alone special-purpose machines to fully integrated assembly lines. They also range from the assembly and handling of small components to larger, automated robot systems that can handle whole vehicles in the car industry.

Automated systems reduce labour costs, increase output and eliminate many health and safety problems. Automated systems can be as complex as required, from simple automated tests to fully automated production line systems. Many of the automated systems are modular so that they can be configured to match the requirements of the business and the available space in the factory.

Once the system has been set up, the processes can be continually monitored and should produce zero defect output, as the automated system simply repeats precisely the same actions at each point along the production line. The equipment can be either automatic or semi-automatic, with the latter requiring some employee input.

Stock control

Many retailers have introduced electronic point-of-sale (EPOS) technology. This technology allows businesses to monitor their sales and stock levels. At the cash till a laser scans the barcode of each product being sold. Not only do the product details appear on the point-of-sale display, the information is also passed on to a database holding the stock information. The number of products being purchased is automatically subtracted from the existing stock level to give the new stock level. The business can set re-order levels,

which are triggered when the stock falls below a certain level.

Electronic Data Interchange (EDI) is an Internet-based system that allows the business to create an integrated production process. It links the various parts of the business (such as factories, head office or branches) and the business's suppliers. As stock, such as components, raw materials or finished goods, is used or despatched by the business, the EDI system can automatically trigger a re-order from suppliers. This has been particularly useful for businesses that have adopted a Just In Time (JIT) production system.

Communications

Various relatively new technologies have transformed the way in which businesses communicate with themselves, with their suppliers and with their customers. The development of laptops, the Internet, email and mobile phones allow work to be carried out, and communication to be made almost anywhere in the world. This has had an impact on the way in which some employees work and many of them now have the capacity to work from home (teleworking).

Instant communication through email allows the immediate transfer of documents and images across the world. Even meetings have been transformed by new communications technology. Videoconferencing uses the Internet to transfer real-time voices and images so that meetings can take place with each person 'present' at the meeting in a different location thus reducing the need for expensive and time-consuming travel for face-to-face meetings.

Design technology

There have been two major developments in design technology that have revolutionised the way in which products are created, tested and manufactured. Computer-aided Design (CAD) uses three-dimensional technology to create drawings, which can be altered and viewed with a single click. They can be produced precisely and computer-tested to ensure that they meet specific criteria.

As a continuation of the CAD system, businesses can also use Computer-aided Manufacture (CAM). This uses computer technology to plan and control the whole manufacturing process. The business can link up the CAD designs to the computer-controlled machines, in order to create an automated production process. The CAM system is very accurate and is used by businesses to create specific products to meet the needs of different customers.

Flexible production

The types of technology and production systems used by a business will depend on the type of market that they serve. Businesses that make standardised products in large volume will probably use a flow production system, which is likely to be automated. However there are still many businesses that produce tailor-made products for each customer, and while technology may be useful in improving the efficiency, each job is different and still requires the input of skilled employees.

Businesses look for the cost advantages that they can enjoy from making large-volume, standardised products, but with the flexibility to be able to produce different products for different markets. Smaller businesses often have flexibility in design and the capacity to make one-off products for different customers, whereas larger businesses, with either robot-operated or automated production lines, do not tend to have this flexibility.

KEY TERM

Just In Time (JIT) – a system where a manufacturer only holds sufficient stock for its immediate needs. In effect suppliers hold buffer stock for the manufacturer and deliver on demand.

Questions

1 How might new stock control systems aid a large supermarket? (4 marks)
2 What are the limitations of robotics and automation? (4 marks)
3 Distinguish between CAD and CAM systems. (4 marks)

Issues in introducing and updating technology

LEARNING OBJECTIVES

- ▶ Technological change and managing change
- ▶ Products and materials
- ▶ Processes and systems
- ▶ Technological change, advantages and disadvantages

Technological change and managing change

Few businesses can afford to ignore technological changes, as they may discover that the products and services they offer and the processes they use to make or deliver them no longer match the expectations of customers. New ideas are being developed almost on a daily basis, either by new inventions being created or innovations that develop the new ideas into profitable products and services.

Businesses have seen technological change in almost every industry: some have had an impact across a number of industries, including the Internet, digital technology and genetic modification. Technological change can affect raw materials and components used to create products; the production process itself; or the business systems that either support the sale of products or allow services to be delivered.

The introduction of new technology by businesses can threaten to undermine the workforce: employees may feel at risk of being replaced by machinery, automated systems or direct services provided via the Internet. Businesses need to try to ensure that any threats presented by

new technology are minimised, while the advantages are maximised. A business will tend to develop and test any new equipment or processes before it takes the decision to begin using them. It will also need to make sure that the new ways in which it either processes products or delivers services match the needs of its customers.

When new technology is introduced it may adversely disrupt the smooth running of a business: there will certainly be a period of transition. In order to avoid problems with the workforce, the business needs to make sure that it is involved in the process of change. Inevitably, new technology will change the way in which people work. This means that a business will have to invest in training and staff development so that the management and employees can adapt to the new processes and acquire the necessary skills.

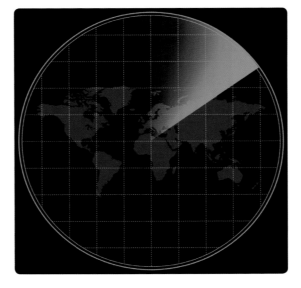

Products and materials

Businesses that come up with a truly new form of technology and are able to innovate by launching a new product or service have a distinct advantage over the competition. If a business manages to achieve this it can easily become a market leader, as it has the advantage of being the first to offer a product or service of its kind. This means that if the marketing and promotion of the product is successful, it can enjoy good sales and profitability before the competitors catch up.

In recent years there have been a number of product developments across a wide range of primarily consumer products and services. The mobile phone has seen the development of mobile communications technologies. This has extended into handheld computer technology (either laptops or palmtops). Digital technology has brought in digital rather than analogue television and radio. The Internet has meant that an increase in percentage of music sales is achieved by downloads rather than through sales of traditional CDs. Banks have offset the closure of many branches by developing Internet banking. In the medical world new vaccines have been developed, as has cloning.

Many new products rely on new materials, which can either transform the production process or the way in which a product is presented to customers. Genetically modified food aims to increase the quality and the quantity of food production, from milk to tomatoes. New packaging materials mean that packaging is stronger and cheaper, and an increasing percentage of it is biodegradable. Silicon chips have revolutionised computer technology, allowing miniaturisation to take place, with smaller and more powerful laptop and palmtop computers being developed.

Processes and systems

It is in the field of computer technology that the greatest changes to production methods and manufacturing have taken place. Computer-integrated manufacturing uses computer technology to integrate each stage of the production process. Manufacturing resource planning (MRPii) provides software that enables a business to plan the production process and to test the impact of different decisions.

We have already seen that electronic data interchange has enabled the linking of a worldwide business and its suppliers, while computer aided design and computer aided manufacture enable the creation and manufacture of products to be fully integrated.

Different parts of organisations have found new systems that can assist them in becoming more efficient and effective. In marketing, websites have been developed, and the Internet in general can be used as a direct means of communication between a business and its customers. Internet shopping has opened up new markets and cut costs. Consumers are able to compare prices at the click of their mouse, and products can be researched both by businesses and by customers. Stock control and purchasing have been transformed by systems such as EPOS, while accounts departments have become reliant on the use of computer spreadsheet software, such as Excel, and specialist accounting software, such as Sage. These allow them to manage their payrolls, analyse financial information, and check budgets, cash flow and variances. In Human Resource departments, databases can be used to manage skills and training, as well as holding information on each employee and their payments.

Technological change, advantages and disadvantages

While technological change is a complex issue that affects businesses in different ways, the following table seeks to summarise some of the key advantages and disadvantages:

Advantages	Disadvantages
Cost reduction – technology increases efficiency, speeds up design and manufacture, increases output and reduces the need for humans.	*New risks* – anything that has not been tried and tested could fail. A business committing itself to new technology may be prone to delays or breakdowns or other major problems.
New markets – new markets can be opened up using advanced technology such as the Internet, extending a business's access to customers across the world.	*Initial investment costs* – new technology costs a considerable amount of money, not just for the initial purchase but for maintenance and for the training of employees. In five years' time the new technology may not be new at all and may have to be replaced.
Improved communication – this is quicker and easier and allows the rapid exchange of information.	*Information overload* – with access to all information a business may simply have too much information, which could cause it to have problems in decision-making.
Better quality – new materials and new production processes bring more reliable and better-quality products and a greater choice.	*Job losses* – robots and automation mean fewer jobs, bringing potential problems to the wider society. In a business it may bring conflict between management and the workforce.
Employee benefits – robots and automated systems can take over boring tasks, giving employees more opportunity to come up with ideas. The workplace is also safer and cleaner.	*Resistance to change* – technology causes insecurity, and challenges the traditional ways in which products and services are delivered. It can also make a set of skills obsolete. People affected may resist the implementation of the new technologies.

Questions

1 If invention means generating new ideas, what does innovation mean? (2 marks)
2 Why might customers be reluctant to use genetically modified foods? (4 marks)

Case studies, questions and exam practice

CASE STUDY CHEESE SLICER

There are many examples of successful automation in the food industry. In the cheese industry on the curdling and shaping lines, a fully automated curd-slicing operation has been developed. The Staubli RX 170 robot allows a large choice of automated and specific slicing tools depending on the recipe of the cheese being manufactured.

After every slicing cycle, the tools are rinsed in a wash module, which eliminates any contamination from one bowl to another and ensures a perfect cut on every operation. An automatic wash of the tools can also be carried out at the end of the recipe. This solution offers the possibility of complex cutting profiles and speeds compared to existing mechanisms. The robot provides a high precision of slicing, contributing to improvement of both the quality and productivity for the cheese maker.

The major advantages are:

- Elimination of difficult work in a wet environment
- High-precision slicing
- Increased revenue through improved quality and productivity
- Optimal food hygiene
- Higher flexibility of the manufacturing process

Source: adapted from www.staublirobotics.com

Questions

1 What are the implications to a business customer of the five major advantages listed? (10 marks)
2 Why might automation be important in the food industry? (6 marks)

SHORT-ANSWER QUESTIONS

1 What is automation?

2 How can new technology assist stock control?

3 Distinguish between **CAD** and **CAM**.

4 How have new communications technologies transformed employees' work life?

5 What do you understand by the term 'electronic data interchange'?

6 What is **MRPii**?

7 List **FIVE** advantages and **FIVE** disadvantages of technological change.

8 How might a business that has managed to develop and launch a new product ahead of the competition be at a distinct advantage?

9 How has the Internet affected marketing?

10 What is teleworking?

CASE STUDY AUTOMATION AND THE THEATRE

Automation is the use of electrical, hydraulic or pneumatic power to move stage machinery, staging, performers or scenery. The effectiveness of any automation system depends entirely on the quality of its underlying electrical, mechanical and control engineering. As computers have changed all aspects of the entertainment industry so the advances have revolutionised automation, making sophisticated effects ever more widely available.

Both in a performance environment and as part of the supporting infrastructure, the uses and advantages of automation are enormous. Automation facilitates:

- Moving heavier loads
- Positioning accurately
- Moving very fast/slowly
- Accurately controlling acceleration/deceleration
- Simultaneously moving multiple pieces or performers

The advantages are:

- Absolute control of speed and position
- Repeatability of moves
- Coordination of multiple piece moves
- Offline editing and simulation
- Movement of pieces in complicated paths
- Reduced manual handling
- Indefinite repetition of moves
- Automatic safety checking
- Improved efficiency
- Safe movement of a single piece controlled by several motors
- Movement in confined spaces

Automation is relevant in any situation where scenic elements (or other equipment) are required to move or performers to fly. This may be in a permanent installation or for a temporary venue or production.

Source adapted from a www.stagetech.com

Feature of Automation	Uses
Power flying	Automating systems, primarily for theatres and concert halls, using winches and point hoists to vertically lift loads.
Counterweight-assist	Automating counterweights by using winches rather than people to haul the weights.
Performer flying	Allowing people to fly in one, two or three dimensions and following complicated pre-determined paths in space.
Revolves	To move turntables accurately, allowing multiple rotations stopping at pre-determined positions.
Trucks/wagons	To move stage trucks or wagons, travelling in tracks or freely on stage.
Additional show effects	Providing scenic effects that require accurate control, particularly those requiring synchronisation with other effects.
Under-stage machinery	To provide orchestra, stage and performance lifts, particularly where large weights or high speeds are required or in places with poor access.
Venue specific	To move seats, walls, drapes or overhead bridges to alter the shape or size of a performance space.

Questions

1 The business works closely with its customers to provide for their specific needs and expectations. Why is this an important aspect of the relationship? (4 marks)
2 What are the major features of the product or service that could appeal to their target customers? (6 marks)
3 Identify the type of customer supplied by the business. (6 marks)

TOPIC 4 MARKETING AND THE COMPETITIVE ENVIRONMENT

Introduction

This is the last of the four core themes for *Managing a business*. You will discover the importance of marketing, both to other businesses and to consumers, and how marketing can give a competitive edge to a business. One of the primary focuses will be on using the results of market research to develop an appropriate marketing programme.

Effective marketing begins by understanding the needs and expectations of the customer and then addressing those needs by providing appropriate products and services; establishing the price; preparing appropriate advertising and promotion; and ensuring that distribution is in place so that the widest range of customers can gain access to the product or service.

Collectively these elements are known as the marketing mix and they have an impact on brand names, promotions, sales technique, pricing, distribution, and even the creation and development of products and services.

Businesses in different markets use different types of marketing. Some face strong competition and need to have effective marketing in order to ensure that potential customers are aware of the features and benefits of their products.

You will be introduced to concepts such as product portfolio analysis, which looks at the broadest range of products and services offered by a business and at how the business can configure them to match the needs of different markets. You will also see that products and services have a definite lifespan – known as a product lifecycle – and that businesses need to use different marketing techniques as a product grows, matures and then begins to decline in popularity and sales.

The competitiveness of a business can be improved by marketing, and can be further enhanced by a range of other factors, such as quality, cost and employee training.

FOCUS ON EFFECTIVE MARKETING

FOCUS ON DESIGNING AN EFFECTIVE MARKETING MIX

FOCUS ON USING THE MARKETING MIX: PRODUCT

FOCUS ON USING THE MARKETING MIX: PROMOTION

FOCUS ON USING THE MARKETING MIX: PRICING

FOCUS ON USING THE MARKETING MIX: PLACE

FOCUS ON MARKETING AND COMPETITIVENESS

The purpose of marketing

LEARNING OBJECTIVES

▶ What is marketing?
▶ Consumer marketing
▶ Business-to-business marketing

What is marketing?

Marketing is all about identifying, anticipating and satisfying customer needs and expectations. Ideally this means viewing everything that a business does from the customer's point of view. As we will see, it also involves using the correct **marketing mix**, which means having the right product in the right place, at the right time, at the right price.

Many businesses confuse marketing with what are, in effect, sales techniques, such as printing brochures, offering promotions in a retail store, sponsoring a television programme or a football team, using a famous name to endorse products or services, or sending email offers. These are ways in which businesses market their products and services, but are only part of what marketing is all about.

Businesses need to keep and create customers, and marketing plays an important role in this, essentially attracting and retaining customers at a profit.

Many businesses believe that marketing should be at the heart of everything the organisation does and not just left to the specialists in the marketing department. Marketing is recognised as being a key business function: research is carried out, communications made with customers, new products developed and pricing decisions made.

Consumer marketing

Businesses have specific target markets. These are profiles of the typical customer who would purchase a particular product or service. For **consumer** markets this is usually broken down by looking at the consumer's age, gender, class and income. This process is known as market segmentation. It seeks to identify common characteristics of consumers and then create appropriate products, services and marketing messages to appeal to them.

Strictly speaking, consumer marketing looks at creating and delivering products to satisfy consumers. Consumers can be households, individuals, or even organisations that purchase products and services.

A business will try to create a profile of its consumers and build a range of products or services that will directly appeal to them and, importantly, match their demands and expectations. The business will use elements of the marketing mix, matching these elements against the profiles of the consumers.

FOR EXAMPLE

In the not-so-recent past, Disney saw itself as a film-maker and focused entirely on making and promoting films. The organisation then realised that its business was far broader than this, and expanded into the leisure and retail industries. The theme parks provide leisure facilities and the Disney stores offer an opportunity for customers to buy Disney products direct.

KEY TERM

Marketing mix – a combination of four key elements used by businesses to implement their marketing strategy.

Consumer – the end-user of a product or service (not to be confused with the customer, which is likely to be a retail store or wholesaler).

FOR EXAMPLE

Marks and Spencer's products and services appeal to relatively affluent, predominantly female customers. They do not necessarily compete on price, their products are available nationwide through their chain of retail outlets, their packaging is easily identifiable, their products have a reputation for reliability and quality and it has only been in the past two or three years that they have begun advertising on television.

MARKETING

Business-to-business marketing

Industrial or business-to-business (b2b) marketing is focused on satisfying the needs of other businesses. Industrial markets are different from consumer markets and it is not always the case that the four elements of the marketing mix are enough. Businesses want more from their suppliers. They want their suppliers to not only match their requirements, but also to provide solutions to problems.

Suppliers in business-to-business situations tend to work far more closely with their customers than businesses that provide products and services to the consumer market. Suppliers are considered to be trusted partners, rather than simply suppliers of components, raw materials and finished goods. The relationships are often closer and rely upon close contact between sales representatives and buyers. Above all, the key aspect of marketing in industrial markets is to be flexible and to precisely cater for the needs of the limited number of customers.

A comparison between consumer marketing and business marketing techniques can be seen in the table below left.

The differences extend to the way in which contact is made during the sales process, which is an integral part of marketing. Businesses selling to other businesses tend to use a direct sales force or distributors. They may rely on wholesalers, agents that are paid a percentage of sales, catalogues or, increasingly, the Internet.

Businesses selling to consumer markets, on the other hand, often use retailers. They are re-sellers and will often use complex distribution chains, where the products pass through several wholesalers or distributors before they reach the end-user of the product. Again the Internet is becoming more important, cutting out many of the ways in which products and services have traditionally been made available to consumers.

Types of marketing	Business-to-business	Consumer
Advertising	Normally focussed on trade journals and magazines, not TV.	Often used, including TV, Radio and mass circulation print advertising.
Direct mail	Smaller markets may make this difficult.	Sometimes not used due to the large numbers and the low value of each sale.
Face-to-face sales	Very suitable.	Rarely suitable, except in retail situations.
Corporate hospitality	Very suitable because of often high business value per decision-maker.	Not often used for consumers.
Editorial space in the media	Very suitable in targeted print media.	Sometimes suitable.
Publicity	Suitable.	Suitable.
Customer loyalty schemes	Rarely suitable as there is often a buyer working for the purchasing business.	Often suitable. Decision-maker and person making payment are often the same person.
Discounting	Often to reward volume customers.	Discount sales are often used for sales promotion.
Exhibitions and trade shows	Often used for high-value and lower-value items.	Mainly suitable for higher-value items.
Point-of-sale materials	Not often used except where distribution involves trade counters.	Extensive use.

Questions

1 Define marketing. (4 marks)
2 Distinguish between consumer and business-to-business marketing. (10 marks)
3 Briefly describe FOUR suitable ways in which business-to-business marketing could be achieved. (4 marks)

Niche and mass marketing

Niche marketing

A niche market is a small segment of a larger market. Niche marketing aims to provide specialist products and services that meet the specific needs of that niche. In order for niche marketing to be successful, the business has to be able to make profit from a relatively low level of sales. This means that the business's overheads cannot be spread over a high output. Fixed costs per unit are relatively high, so to be successful in a niche market, high prices need to be charged.

Businesses identify niche markets in a number of different ways:

- Many potential ideas come from customers themselves who comment on the benefits and drawbacks of currently available products and services. They give valuable ideas that help the creation of new niche products and services.
- Many small businesses are run by specialists, enthusiasts, hobbyists or those with expert knowledge in a particular area. They will be catering for a niche market, based on their own experience as a consumer. A prime example of this was James Dyson, who designed the bag-less vacuum cleaner in response to his own frustration over models that were currently available.
- Retail loyalty cards have also begun to give valuable insight into the creation of niche products. They not only show the purchasing trends of particular customers, but also give valuable insights into the types of products and services they would buy if they were made available.

Niche markets need to be sufficiently recognisable or differentiated from other markets. They are usually characterised by customers who are prepared to pay premium prices for products. The sales are of relatively low volume and the products or services offered are significantly different from mainstream products and services. Above all, the business that provides them should have an advantage, as it will be relatively difficult for larger competitors to replicate the expertise and skills used in delivering them.

Promotion needs to be very specific and targeted, so it is important for the business to understand how the customers in that niche market can be reached and the kinds of message that need to be conveyed to them. Ideally the customers need to be accessible and the niche needs to be growing. Above all it must be a market that is not already being serviced by an established competitor.

Mass marketing

Mass marketing is the opposite to niche marketing, as it focuses on high sales volume and comparatively low prices. Rather than targeting particular types of customer, mass marketing aims to provide products and services that will appeal to the whole market. Ideally the products and services should appeal to customers regardless of age, gender, income or location.

Many mass-market products have become household names, having built a **brand** that is instantly recognisable by customers. Sometimes brands even become the name that is used for a product category, such as Hoover, Bacardi or Coke.

KEY TERM

Brand – a recognisable product or service name, with associated packaging that is instantly recognised by the customer.

Mass marketing dates back at least 100 years; the first major business to use mass marketing was the vehicle manufacturer Ford. The company built a standardised product from standardised parts, offered vehicles at low cost and cut its prices continually, in order to cater for the ever-increasing demand and market size. In fact, between 1909 and 1916, Ford sales increased by a staggering 4,594%.

Mass marketing can be very profitable, but it does not have to mean that the price has to be low.

Businesses such as Calvin Klein manufacture products such as fragrances for the mass market, but their prices are comparatively high. They chose a different distribution policy to reach the mass market, selling their products through record stores instead of traditional department stores.

Many businesses, such as Sony, Levi, McDonald's and Coca-Cola, offer standardised products, available through a wide range of outlets. They promote their products heavily in all types of media. The price is comparatively low and the sales volume extremely high.

Other businesses try a different approach to mass marketing and focus on price. This is known as cost leadership, where prices are forced as low as possible in order to capture as much market share as possible, leaving little room for competitors. In this way the undifferentiated products offered by these businesses fight off the competition that could otherwise offer very similar products and services, but not match them for price.

CASE STUDY FRENCH CONNECTION

French Connection was founded in 1969, as a niche market retailer selling clothes and accessories. In April 1997 it re-branded itself as FCUK, and adopted a distinctly mass-market approach, aiming to open stores worldwide. The new branding sparked off hundreds of complaints about their advertising and their range of T-shirts using the FCUK logo. After continuing to use the logo to promote the business, the company finally replaced it in 2006 with a new advertising campaign. During the late 1990s and the early part of the twenty-first century, FCUK had seen record profits and rapid expansion. However, by 2004 sales began to slow, hence the reason for replacing the FCUK slogan.

French Connection managed to re-invent itself, from being a relatively small retailer with a handful of outlets, an exclusive image and premium pricing, to a mass-market organisation that uses aggressive marketing and has expanded rapidly to most major high streets. Despite the controversy over the FCUK logo, the move catapulted the business into a business with over £240m turnover and stores in more than thirty countries around the world.

Questions

1 What aspects of the French Connection business before 1997 lead you to believe that it was a niche-market business? (6 marks)
2 Why might the business have made the decision to transform itself from a niche-market to a mass-market operation? (4 marks)
3 Why might French Connection's FCUK advertising be seen as aggressive? (2 marks)

Case studies, questions and exam practice

CASE STUDY IS HE RIGHT?

'We are moving from a world of mass marketing, global advertising and brand awareness to a world of one-to-one relationships – one in which customers will interact with what they want to and suppliers will survive only by their knowledge of their customers and of their preferences and intentions. The very concepts of broadcasting and of the practice of mass advertising that underpin much of our industry today may be on their way out.'

Miles Flint, President, Sony Broadcast & Professional Europe.

When the managing director of Bentham's, the national electrical goods retailer, read this in the newspaper, he shivered at the prospect. Frank Bentham had built his business on the 'pile them high; sell them cheap' philosophy, and had been using traditional advertising on television and in national newspapers since the business was launched 12 years before.

It worked. Bentham's was quite big, quite profitable, but always under threat. Frank could never understand why someone would walk into a smaller competitor and buy something for 20% more than he was charging. It didn't make sense. He knew there were problems at Bentham's – the low rates of pay meant there was a high turnover of staff. He also knew that the business had a higher than average rate of returns, but Frank put that down to the suppliers sending him useless stock because he had forced such big discounts with them.

Frank could cope with the big boys in the high streets and the retail parks, like Tesco or Curry's, but the Internet worried him. Bentham's had only a basic site and customers couldn't buy online because it wasn't Frank's way – he wanted his customers in the store and to sell them extended warranties for the televisions. The specialist stores concerned him too; he'd love staff like that, but he wasn't prepared to pay for them.

Questions

1 Why might Bentham's be described as a mass-market operation? (3 marks)

2 Why was Frank so concerned about the newspaper article he read? (6 marks)

3 How might Bentham's learn from the competitors and improve its customer service and marketing? (10 marks)

SHORT-ANSWER QUESTIONS

1 What do you understand by the term 'marketing'?

2 Distinguish between consumer marketing and business marketing.

3 How do the ways in which businesses market their products and services differ between consumer markets and business markets?

4 What is a niche market?

5 Give an example of a niche marketing technique.

6 Give **THREE** examples of businesses that provide mass-market products.

7 What is a brand?

8 How might a business supplying a niche market be able to compete with a business that caters for the mass market?

9 What is cost leadership?

10 Distinguish between differentiated and undifferentiated markets.

CASE STUDY Wii RULE?

Nintendo, the gaming giant, was forced to pull ads for its Wii console in the run-up to Christmas 2007 as demand was already too high. The campaign for Wii, created by Karmarama, was replaced by ads for its hand-held console, Nintendo DS. The company said that it was forced to pull the ads because retailers had been running out of consoles so it would be irresponsible to continue with the campaign.

A Nintendo spokesman said: 'We have been running the campaign all year round, but we want to take a responsible stance this Christmas and not fuel demand.'

Nintendo added that, as the campaign was not seasonally themed, it could be put back to the New Year when the Christmas rush was over. One ad industry insider said: 'You can tell what has been happening. They have a lot of spots on TV, but I am seeing more ads for the DS than I am for the Wii, so you can draw your own conclusions.'

Although production was stepped up to 1.8 million units a month, Nintendo said that it had not been able to meet the demand. The game company increased its forecast of the number of units it expected to sell in the year to March 2008 from 14 million to 17.5 million. But why has the Wii been so popular? Just over a year before,

everyone assumed that Sony's Playstation 3 would be the dominant console around the world.

By the end of September 2007, Sony had shipped just 5.6 million PS3 consoles. Sony has struggled with its PS3 console because it put its corporate agenda above the consumer one. Sony was keen to create an advanced console product, it also wanted to do something else – win the larger corporate battle over future storage disc formats. It decided to use its proprietary Blu-Ray system in the PS3 in an attempt to give it the edge over the Toshiba-backed HD DVD disc. But this strategy meant that the console had to be delayed in its European launch, missing the 2006 Christmas season. The Blu-Ray inclusion also pushed the PS3 price beyond that of its competitors. Sony still loses money on each console sold due to component costs.

Questions

1 Why was Nintendo right to pull the advertising for the Wii? (4 marks)

2 Why might Ninetendo be right about the customer needs and not Sony? (4 marks)

3 How can Sony afford to sell PS3s at a loss? (4 marks)

Influences on the marketing mix

LEARNING OBJECTIVES

▶ What is the marketing mix?
▶ Influences on the marketing mix
▶ Different mixes

What is the marketing mix?

In order for marketing to be effective, businesses need to look carefully at the combination of four factors: product, price, place and promotion. They need to find a balance that not only ensures information about the products or services reaches the target market, but that the market can easily make a purchase.

The business also needs to balance costs and effectiveness. If the mix is wrong then a good product could fail because of a poor pricing strategy. If the distribution is wrong then any money spent on advertising the product will be wasted. Ideally, a successful mix will achieve the marketing objectives of the business while giving customer satisfaction.

The aim of the marketing mix is to position the product or service in the market in a way that makes it attractive to target customers. It needs to be able to assure customers that the product can satisfy their demands far better than any competing products.

For more about pricing strategies see Using the marketing mix: pricing on pp. 298–305. For further information about distribution see Using the marketing mix: place on pp. 306–11.

Influences on the marketing mix

There are three key influences on the marketing mix which impact on a business's ability to manipulate the four factors to best effect:

• Market research – this involves examining the needs, demands and expectations of the potential market and then trying to create or offer products and services to match these requirements. A business will usually carry out routine market research in order to discover trends and changes and to gauge reaction to existing products and products in the planning phase. Market research will also identify the key characteristics of the target market and indicate ways in which the market can be reached, both by marketing messages and by an appropriate distribution system for the product or service. Clearly the more information the business has before launching the product or service, the more likely it is to succeed in establishing it in the market place.

• Finance – a business may need to make a considerable investment in a product or service before it even launches it onto the market. The development phase of new products and services is expensive and not offset by income from sales. Many new products and services fail at the early stages of development, either because the business does not feel that it can provide sufficient returns in the future or that there is a fundamental flaw in them. Finance also determines the type of

marketing that the business will be able to afford. Mass marketing through advertising is, perhaps, the most expensive form of marketing. Cheaper alternatives are possible, particularly with the advent of the Internet, where targeted email campaigns can be run at relatively low cost.

- Technology – as far as marketing is concerned, technology directly affects the options open to a business in terms of how it promotes and distributes its products and services. There is a wide range of different promotional opportunities, from conventional television and newspaper advertising to digital advertising in the form of banner advertising on websites and direct mail emails. Technology also has an impact on distribution. Many services, such as banking, can now be delivered via the Internet. Other more conventional products can be ordered via the Internet, telephone or interactive television.

Different mixes

Businesses will use different combinations of the marketing mix, depending on the type of customer they are aiming their products and services at and the size of those markets. The marketing mix for industrial markets needs to not only focus on awareness but also cost, quality, reliability and availability. Much of this is achieved through direct contact with potential customers. Industrial markets incorporate materials, components, capital goods such as machinery and vehicles, distribution, insurance and banking.

Tackling a consumer market offers a different series of opportunities as far as the marketing mix is concerned. Most purchases in the consumer market fall into two main categories: either convenience goods, which are bought fairly frequently and tend to be **non-durable**, or shopping goods, which tend to be durable and customers take longer to decide before they make a purchase.

The marketing mix can also be influenced by the type of customer or how they are categorised or segmented. Some businesses will categorise their customers by their spending power. Higher income customers will expect to see products they wish to purchase in exclusive stores, while lower income households will look for products that they can buy in most high-street stores.

Age is another determinant. Toys are promoted on commercial television during children's programmes, while sportswear, alcohol and cars may be promoted on sports channels.

Gender also affects the marketing mix. The type of product, its packaging and its promotion are aimed specifically at either men or women. Products can be modified, such as Lynx being targeted at men, while Impulse is targeted at women: essentially they are the same product.

It is important to remember that each part of the marketing mix is of equal relevance and that each segment of the market will respond to its own blend of the marketing mix. The fashion industry tends to focus either on quality and exclusivity or on cheap products that are available in a wide variety of outlets.

KEY TERMS

Non-durable – perishable goods or products that are used up very quickly, such as most products bought from supermarkets, including food, cleaning products and soft drinks.

Questions

1 What are the four elements of the marketing mix? (4 marks)
2 Distinguish between convenience goods and shopping goods. (4 marks)
3 Give TWO examples of shopping goods. (2 marks)

The importance of an integrated marketing mix

Marketing orientation

Marketing orientation refers to a belief that success can be achieved by focusing entirely on satisfying customer demands and expectations. Businesses with this belief are often referred to as being either consumer-centred or consumer-driven.

While most businesses have a marketing department that focuses on research, the analysis of competitors, strategy and promotion, a marketing-orientated business takes this one stage further and examines the ways in which it can continue to provide products and services that respond to any changing needs, wants or demands of its customers. It will heavily invest in product development and in communicating with its customers.

FOR EXAMPLE

Levi, the jeans manufacturer, brought out its hipster jeans when market research showed that female customers tended to wear their jeans lower than male customers. A new line of products was created specifically to cater for women wanting to wear their jeans on their hips rather than their waists.

Product, production and sales orientation

Businesses with a product orientation tend to stress the product's features and use their technical strengths and expertise, rather than the demands of the market. The major problem is that a product-orientated business may find that there is not a demand, regardless of how good its product or service may be, as it has not identified consumer demands before launching the product.

FOR EXAMPLE

Until relatively recently in the music industry the primary way of selling music was by manufacturing CDs. But consumers actually want to consume or purchase music and they are not particularly concerned about the way in which this music is delivered to them. The market has moved from vinyl records through cassette tapes to CDs. Now many music consumers purchase downloadable music, which places CD manufacturers under threat as they are product-orientated.

Production orientation refers to businesses that use efficiencies that they have built up in their factories to produce low-cost products in high volumes. The problem arises when

either supply exceeds demand – in which case prices have to be dropped even further to encourage sales – or demand exceeds supply – in which case there may be no additional capacity to produce extra products and take advantage of increased sales.

Businesses may also have a sales orientation. This focuses on the needs of the seller rather than the needs of the buyer. The focus is therefore to try to convince a potential buyer that they really need to buy the product or service. This is often the method of operation for businesses selling products or services that consumers would not normally think of buying.

FOR EXAMPLE

There is a nationwide chain of independent distributors of Betterware products, which are predominantly plastic kitchen equipment and labour-saving devices. Customers are unlikely to see these products in high-street stores, and sales are generated through the distribution of catalogues by door-to-door agents.

The different market orientations suggest that different businesses have a different focus, each offering specific benefits, but each with its own distinct disadvantages too, as can be seen in the table on page 277.

Orientation	Focus on	Benefits to the business	Disadvantages of the orientation
Marketing	The consumer and their demands and expectations	Turnover and profit by providing products or services demanded by consumers	High potential costs before product launch
Product	The features of the product	High-quality products	Research may not have identified demand for the product
Production	Products or services that can be produced cheaply and efficiently	Low unit costs	Production may not match consumer demand, and costs determine the price, not demand
Sales	Income generation and number of products sold	Meeting of sales targets and healthy cash flow	High-pressure sales techniques may put customers off

Asset-led marketing

Asset-led marketing combines a marketing-led approach with a focus on the strengths of the business itself. The business aims to use its skills, experience and knowledge of the market to develop new products and services that will appeal to consumers.

The strengths of the business can be in distribution, its manufacturing, the brand names it has, its image or its employees.

An asset is something that the business has: not necessarily a tangible asset, such as a factory or assembly line. It can be an intangible asset, such as its reputation or its highly trained staff. Asset-led marketing means using whatever assets the business has to help deliver products and services that meet customer needs.

The key differences between market-led and asset-led orientation is that asset-led businesses face a lower level of risk, as they are focusing on their own strengths. It may also mean less investment and a shorter payback period before the product or service becomes successful and profitable.

FOR EXAMPLE

Confectionery manufacturers have built on their success to break into the ice cream market. Businesses such as Cadbury, Nestlé and Mars have successfully launched high sales volume ice cream products.

CASE STUDY WAITING TO BUY

What is an airport? Just a place to wait before the aircraft takes off or arrives? No, think again, it's a sales opportunity. Research has shown the following:

- Almost all passengers interviewed said that they like to feel that they can shop if they choose to.
- Passengers said they would feel 'cheated' if there was a poor selection of shops.
- Premium passengers also want easy access to the shops. It is not always the best solution to give premium passengers fast-track security directly into the business lounge.
- Eighty-five per cent of passengers want shops easily accessible from the departures lounge.
- Ninety-five per cent of passengers agreed that 'shops add colour and atmosphere to the terminal'.
- Over 60 per cent of passengers plan, in advance, to use shops and/or cafés at the airport.

Questions

1 Should airports consider maximising waiting time in order for passengers to spend? (4 marks)
2 What other options may be open to airports? (4 marks)
3 What kind of orientation may be used by airports and why? (4 marks)

Case studies, questions and exam practice

CASE STUDY JJB SPORTS

JJB Sports plc was created in 1971. By 1994 it had grown to a chain of 120 stores. When JJB acquired Sports Division in 1998, it became the largest sports retailer in the UK, with 430 stores nationwide. JJB also currently operates a chain of combined health clubs/superstores together with a number of soccer centres.

The brand is mainstream and value-based with an emphasis on fashion. Its image is more 'find it yourself' bargain hunting than considered expert service; despite this it remains very popular. The stores tend to be in large modern units with high ceilings and you are welcomed with promotional price-led placards. The majority of the range (two-thirds) is given over to sports fashion and the remaining third to sports equipment. The stores are bright and easy to navigate with leading fashion items (e.g. replica shirts) closest to the entrance. The service is mixed depending on when you visit (we visited a store mid-week when it was quiet and got good service, but at weekends service can be variable). The staff, although willing, struggled with more complex requests on the availability of items and with technical advice on higher-ticket items.

The product range is focused on big-selling, mass-market, heavily branded items that everyone can recognise and therefore trust (Nike, Adidas, Puma). It does not extend much into specialist brands.

The JJB brand is very much about accessibility to the latest must-have item at low prices. The shop gives the customer a confidence that if JJB stocks the item you are looking for, you are unlikely to find it cheaper elsewhere. All the brands stocked are major labels and you feel assured that you are getting a good deal.

JJB has a mixture of store locations (both town centre and out-of-town). Its value-for-money feel, and need to stock extensive ranges/larger items (bikes, gym equipment) lends itself to larger out-of-town units. However, its fashion-led proposition (despite being a sports store) lends itself to high street locations.

JJB Sports does however have a number of potential problems. There is a danger of becoming too fashion orientated (replica kit, casual wear), there are lots of fashionwear competitors and not many sportswear competitors. The employees in store seem to lack detailed product knowledge, so customer service and product knowledge should be training priorities.

Source adapted from Marketing Week

Questions

1 Indentify the marketing orientation of JJB Sports and give reasons for your suggestion. (8 marks)
2 Outline the ways in which the business attracts customers and whether it is niche or mass market. (6 marks)
3 How might the potential problems facing the business be dealt with? (6 marks)

SHORT-ANSWER QUESTIONS

1 What is the marketing mix?

2 Why might a business in the **B2B** market have a different marketing mix than one in the consumer market?

3 What is the purpose of market research?

4 How might technology affect a business's marketing mix?

5 Which of the four elements of the marketing mix is most important and why?

6 What is marketing orientation?

7 Distinguish between product and production orientation.

8 What problems may face a business with a sales orientation?

9 What is asset-led marketing?

10 Distinguish between asset-led marketing and market orientation.

CASE STUDY THORNTON'S

Thornton's has become the UK's number one retail confectionery brand. It dominates its niche in the high street with over 400 stores. The Thornton's brand has high awareness and the product is currently being rolled out into supermarkets in order to gain a higher percentage of market share.

Product pricing and information is well presented but clearer signage of product sections would be of benefit. However, while the offer may once have been considered a luxury, Thornton's stores have become more of a corner sweetshop than the place for that special present 'to die for'. The offer has become mass market.

The majority of stores have a traditional feel, with browns and beiges dominating the decor. The stores exude a feeling of authority within the confectionery market and interiors are well organised making the most of the wall space, especially in the more compact outlets.

Thornton's is the only major chain within the luxury confectionery market; the main competition comes from supermarkets and smaller specialists (including mail order and the Internet). The store is seen as a destination and not for browsing, which poses a problem – would customers rather buy chocolate while doing their weekly shop, or make a special trip to Thornton's? Customers also need to feel as though they are indulging themselves when they buy a luxury item, and this is not effectively communicated within the store.

Source adapted from *Pragma*

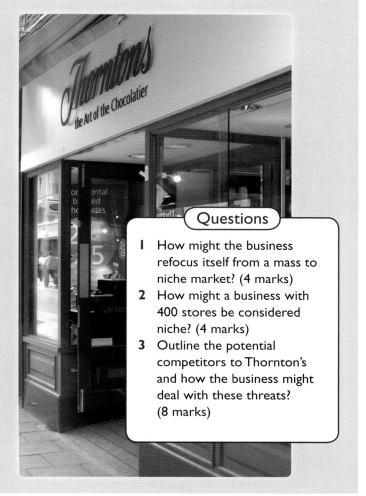

Questions

1 How might the business refocus itself from a mass to niche market? (4 marks)

2 How might a business with 400 stores be considered niche? (4 marks)

3 Outline the potential competitors to Thornton's and how the business might deal with these threats? (8 marks)

Influences on the development of new goods and services

The product development process

Decisions made about the type of products and services that a business will develop will establish not only the range offered, but also many other aspects of the business's marketing mix.

Product development needs to be viewed as an investment rather than a risk. Many businesses, such as Black & Decker, Sony, Polaroid and 3M have invested billions of pounds in product development. Each of them tends to use a number of stages:

- Creativity – coming up with an initial idea, perhaps to develop new ways of dealing with problems, then moving on to assessing the ideas and deciding which ones are worth investing in, in terms of both time and money.
- Defining the concept – this involves turning an idea into a business opportunity and assessing whether the necessary investment will be outweighed by the expected returns. The business will look at the market potential: whether it is technically feasible to provide the product or service, the timescales, how the launch will affect existing products and how the competition will react.
- Developing the concept – this begins by looking at specific customer requirements and then creating a prototype of the product or service to test whether it will provide a solution

to customer needs. The design and development of the product continues into the stages that follow until it is finally released into the market.

- Testing and finalising the concept – some businesses refer to this as alpha and beta testing. They are controlled releases of the product so that the customer, manufacturing and distribution can test their systems and the product can still be modified. The business may discover that there is no market because the concept was wrong and the product will be pulled before more expense is incurred in releasing it into the market.
- Product launch – this is the most expensive and risky stage. The market needs to be developed, the sales and distribution channels created, advertising needs to be organised and the business needs to gear up for providing the product or service and supporting it.
- Managing the lifecycle – the product may not sell for an indefinite period of time. Periodically it needs to be supported by additional marketing initiatives. The business should also be actively seeking to develop its successor and not wait until the existing product shows signs of decline in falling sales.

Technology

Many of the businesses already mentioned, such as Sony and Polaroid, could not possibly have created their revolutionary new products without considerable investment in technology. Less than ten years ago businesses could not have anticipated that an increasing percentage of their sales would be achieved via the Internet rather than by traditional retailing methods. If a business can develop a product that is genuinely technologically more advanced than its competitors, then it has a major advantage for as long as it takes the competitors to catch up and copy the technology.

This means that products and services that rely on new technology are closely guarded secrets. Their existence needs to remain unknown to the market and to the competition until the last possible moment, in order to avoid 'me too' copies of the product being launched by the competition at the same time.

The competition

Businesses can often be described as market leaders or market followers. Truly innovative businesses that launch new products have, as we have seen, a distinct advantage. Offset against this is the costs that they face in the investments they have made in the product development. Providing they can

 *For detail on the product lifecycle see pp. 286–7.*

remain ahead of the competition the investment can be recouped.

Other businesses are more content on lessening their risk by waiting to see what the competitors are planning and then creating their own version of that product or service. While this is less risky in terms of investment, it does mean that they are always somewhat behind the market leaders.

Skills of managers and owners

Ultimately investment decisions in new product development rest with the management or the owners of a business. They will want to be assured that any potential investment in new product development can provide a payback to the business in the future, in terms of sales and profits.

Businesses may carry out a cost benefit analysis, which aims to examine the precise costs of the product development and compare these costs to the expected returns should the product prove to be moderately or very successful. They will also seek to identify the impact on the business if the investment is made but the product is a failure.

CASE STUDY SWATCH

The development of the Swatch is a prime example of a business launching a radically new product. SMH was an established Swiss watchmaker facing fierce competition from lower-cost producers abroad. The company wanted to create a new product: part watch and part fashion accessory. It came up with the name Swatch by bringing together the words 'Swiss' and 'watch'. The Swatch was to become the most successful wristwatch of all time and in the first few years, up to 1996, it had sold over 200m units and had transformed SMH into one of the largest watch companies in the world.

Questions

1 What influenced the development of the Swatch? (8 marks)
2 SMH's market research suggested that what was needed was a fashion accessory that told the time, rather than a technically superior watch. SMH acted accordingly. What kind of orientation is this and why? (4 marks)
3 SMH diversified and went into a joint venture with Daimler Benz to create the Smart car range. What do you understand by the terms 'diversified' and 'joint venture'? (6 marks)

USPs

LEARNING
OBJECTIVES

▶ What is a USP?
▶ Do USPs exist?
▶ How to work out a USP

What is a USP?

A USP is either a unique selling point or a unique selling proposition. It is one of the basics of effective marketing. A USP is designed to help customers save time when they are choosing a product or service because it simply and clearly explains why the product or service is different from the competition.

A USP can be attached to almost every product or service, or it can be applied to a feature of the business, such as its customer service. Every business does need a USP, as it helps it to be noticed in highly competitive markets.

A USP helps the business to focus on the key benefits that help it sell its products or services, and will ultimately contribute towards its profits. A USP needs to be able to be conveyed in a few words and explain why the business is different and what customers can expect when they purchase products or services from that business.

In order for a USP to really work the business must make a specific proposition to customers and promise them that if they buy the product or service, they will get a particular range of specific

benefits. Ideally, the proposition needs to be unique: in other words something that the competitors do not currently offer or will not be able to offer.

The ultimate test of a USP is that it is strong enough and attractive enough to bring in new customers.

A USP assists a business in establishing its product or service differentiation. It may also differentiate the business itself from its competitors. It is a way of comparing the business, product or service to that of the competitors operating in the same market. USPs are an integral part of branding: they outline attributes or benefits that a customer can identify with that brand and provide the business with a shorthand means of communicating the benefits to customers.

Do USPs exist?

It is arguable whether many products or services actually have genuine USPs. The pizza delivery chain, Domino's, has a thirty-minute guarantee, meaning that it will not charge the customer if the delivery is late. But it is not the only pizza delivery chain to pledge this to customers, in the same way that Head and Shoulders is not the only shampoo on the market that is designed to combat dandruff, and Ronseal claims that its products do 'exactly what it says on the tin'. This could be claimed to be a USP, but it is in fact clever advertising and, as most products do what their packaging claims, this is probably not a USP.

A USP can, in the case of Head and Shoulders and Domino's Pizzas, be considered as original, as they were the first to make that claim. As the market leaders in their specific areas the USP may not be technically unique, but it remains a USP as far as customers are concerned.

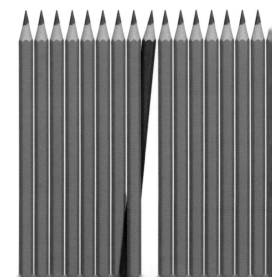

How to work out a USP

Before a business can create a USP it needs to establish the features of the product or service that it wishes to promote. It also needs to know how and why customers use the product or service. Finally it needs to compare its own products and services with those of the competitors.

Ideas to help create a USP can be gleaned from market research, either focusing on customers, distributors or retailers. Businesses will use the following steps to try to define a USP:

- They will focus on a product or service that has the greatest potential or provides the largest contribution to their profits.
- They will then list the main features that help describe what the product or service does, including delivery, price, quality, service and functional/technical characteristics.
- They will then convert these features into benefits, as each feature of the product should deliver a benefit to the customer.
- Some of the benefits will be more important to customers than others, so the business will then rank them in priority order.
- Next each benefit will be looked at in turn. Those that provide similar benefits to the competition can be discarded. But those that are different or special to the product are highlighted, as they are prospective USPs.
- The business will then look at how the benefits compare to the competition. This should identify which benefits mark the biggest difference between the product or service and those offered by the competition.
- Finally the business needs to consider how they will promote these newly discovered USPs.

Another way of identifying USPs is to look at the marketing carried out by the competition. It should be relatively straightforward to spot what they see to be their USPs and how they are communicating these to their target audience.

It is important to remember that a USP will not last forever. At some point all the competitors will be able to match the benefits and at that point the USP simply becomes a standard across the industry. By this stage, of course, the business will have had to develop a brand new product or service that has a new range of genuine USPs in order to stay ahead.

Questions

1 What might be the potential danger of not identifying a USP? (4 marks)
2 'A USP often boils down to simply being cheaper or better.' To what extent do you think this statement is true? (10 marks)
3 How might a USP ensure that customers remain loyal to the product or service? (6 marks)

Product portfolio analysis

LEARNING OBJECTIVES

▶ The Boston Growth Matrix
▶ General Electric Screen Matrix
▶ Ansoff Matrix

The Boston Growth Matrix

The theory underlying the Boston Matrix is the product lifecycle concept, which states that business opportunities move through lifecycle phases of introduction, growth, maturity and decline. The Boston classification, or BCG, matrix is a classification developed by the Boston Consulting Group to analyse products and businesses by market share and market growth. In this, cash cow refers to a product or business with high market share and low market growth; dog refers to one with a low market share and low growth; problem child (or question mark or wild cat) has low market share and high growth, and a star has high growth and high market share.

These phases are typically represented by an anti-clockwise movement around the Boston Matrix quadrants in the following order:

- From a market entry position as a question-mark product. Products are usually launched into high-growth markets, but suffer from a low market share.
- To a star position as sales and market share are increased. If the investment necessary to build sales and market share is successfully made, then the product's position will move towards the star position of high growth/high market share.
- To a cash cow position as the market growth rate slows and market leadership is achieved. As the impact of the product lifecycle takes effect and the market growth rate slows, the product will move from the star position of high growth to the cash cow position of low growth/high share.
- Finally to a dog position as investment is minimised as the product ages and loses market share.

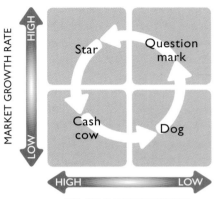

More about product lifecycle can be found on pp. 286–7.

THE ANTI-CLOCKWISE MOVEMENT AROUND THE BOSTON MATRIX

At each position within the matrix there are a number of opportunities open to the business. For example, at the cash cow stage the options are either to invest to maintain market share, or to minimise investment in the product, maximise the cash returns and grow market dominance with other products.

General Electric Screen Matrix

The General Electric (GE) Screen Matrix is essentially a derivation of the Boston Consulting Group Matrix. It was developed by McKinsey and Co for General Electric. It has been recognised that the Boston Consulting Group Matrix was not flexible enough to take into account broader issues.

The GE Matrix cross-references market attractiveness and business position using three criteria for each – high, medium and low. The market attractiveness considers variables relating to the market itself,

LINK BETWEEN THE PRODUCT LIFECYCLE AND THE BOSTON MATRIX

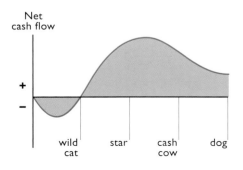

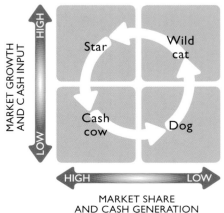

MARKET SHARE
AND CASH GENERATION

including the rate of market growth, market size, potential barriers to entering the market, the number and size of competitors, the actual profit margins currently enjoyed and the technological implications of involvement in the market. The business position criteria look at the business's strengths and weaknesses in a variety of fields. These include their relative position to competitors, the business's ability to handle product research, development and ultimate production. It also considers how well-placed the management is to deploy these resources.

The matrix differs in its complexity compared to the Boston Matrix. Superimposed on the basic diagram are a number of circles. These circles are of variable size. The size of each represents the size of each market. Within each circle is a clearly defined segment which represents the business's market share within that market. The larger the circle, the larger the market, and the larger the segment, the larger the market share.

BUSINESS POSITION

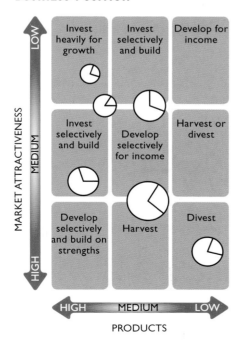

Source: General Electric (GE) Matrix

Ansoff Matrix

The Ansoff Matrix is one of a number of classical marketing concepts that looks at the future vision of the business.

The matrix examines the potential strategies available to a business in four areas, cross-referenced as new or existing markets and new or existing products. The matrix suggests the marketing strategies available to the business in each of these areas:

- Market Penetration – Existing Products into Existing Markets. Management seeks to increase its market share with the current product range. This is considered to be the least risky strategy of all the options available. Existing customers are encouraged to buy more products and services, those at present buying a competing brand are persuaded to switch, and non-buyers are convinced to begin to make purchases. Any readily recognisable weaknesses in the portfolio of the business need to be addressed and strengthened.
- Market Development – Existing Products into New Markets. Systematic market research should reveal new potential markets for the existing products. Clearly stated segments are then targeted individually, either through existing marketing and distribution channels or through

new ones set up to service the new segments. As the business is moving into new markets, it needs to be aware of the potential differences in reactions, expectations and other factors.
- Product Development – New Products into Existing Markets. Assuming the business has sufficient resources, new products, or developments in existing products, can be brought into the market. Provided the business has closely matched the new products with the requirements of its existing markets, risks are minimised. The major concern is 'time to market', which means the length of time it will take to develop the new products, and whether it is possible to defray the development costs quickly.
- Diversification – New Products into New Markets. This is considered to be the highest risk of all the strategies. Essentially, there are two options available to a business; the first is diversification which relies on the business being able to harness its existing product and market knowledge (production processes, channels of distribution, etc.). The other option is that the business departs from its existing product and market knowledge. This form of diversification is often achieved by merging with or taking over a business operating in another unrelated area.

Questions

1 What is a product in the maturity stage of the product lifecycle classed as in the Boston Matrix? (2 marks)
2 What do the circles represent in the General Electric Screen Matrix? (2 marks)

285

Product lifecycle

Product lifecycle

The product lifecycle is a widely accepted model which describes the stages through which a product or service, or indeed a category of product, passes through from its introduction to its final removal from the market. The model suggests that in the introduction stage, or launch, of the product, it sells in small numbers, and marketing activities are expensive. It also suggests that if the first stage is successful, it will be superseded by three other stages. The growth stage is characterised by higher sales and greater profitability, but crucially, more competition. At the maturity stage, if a product has managed to survive, stable sales and a higher level of profitability are enjoyed. The final stage, known as the decline stage, shows that the product is finally declining in terms of demand and associated profits. Optionally, it is possible to insert a further stage between maturity and decline, denoting a period of the product's lifecycle when competition has reached a stage which makes it difficult to sustain the original product. Indeed, it may be the case that the product is already growing stale. This saturation period marks a slight downturn, which can be adjusted by a re-launch or a repackaging of the product; otherwise it will begin its inevitable slip into the decline stage.

At the decline stage, the business needs to carefully consider its policy towards the product or service, as it is not merely a question of letting the item fade away over a period of time (perhaps when stocks are finally exhausted). An abandonment policy must be put in place which takes into account the ramifications in terms of its impact on staffing levels, and deployment of human and other resources, as well as its impact on the market, suppliers and distributors.

BOOK RESEARCH

Shaw, John J., *Product Lifecycles and Product Management.* Greenwood Press, 1989.

Rink D. and Swan J. (1979) Product lifecycle research: A Literature review. *Journal of business Research,* Vol. 40, pp. 219–43.

The standard product lifecycle graph showing the phases of the lifecycle and the association between profits and sales over the cycle.

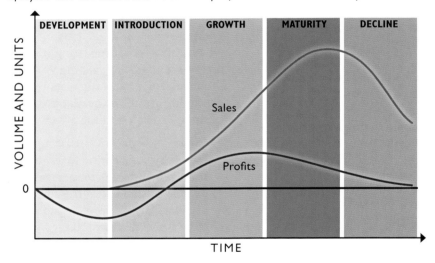

This is a more complex view of the product lifecycle which illustrates the dangers often faced by product innovators in developing new product ideas only to lose the potential of sales as a result of the actions of competitors.

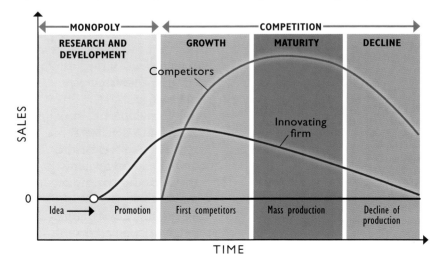

The stages of the lifecycle

The key stages of the product lifecycle are outlined in the table on the right.

Saturation

If a product is selling consistently well then it will encourage competitors to bring out similar products to take some of the sales. Eventually there will be a great deal of choice for customers and the danger is that the older product might begin to decline in popularity. The sales may begin to fall, and at this stage the business really needs to make a decision about the product's future. It can either try to stop the fall in sales or it can allow the sales to slowly disappear and eventually let the product die.

Product lifecycle management

Rink & Swan (1979) present product lifecycle patterns (see right), which afford an opportunity to consider whether a business is able to influence or manage the shape of the curve.

Specifically, the ideas of the various shapes offer the following opportunities:

1 The most critical problem for a multi-product business is to determine how its limited resources will be allocated to various products in the most optimum way. In this respect, the product lifecycle concept is an ideal basis for optimising the allocation of the resources.
2 The multidimensional approach is useful in conceptualising the product lifecycle of future products.
3 The use of product lifecycles is ideal when brought into the equation as far as business planning is concerned.

Stage	Explanation
Introduction/launch	This is one of the first stages of the product lifecycle. In the birth or introduction stage, the business hopes to build product awareness and develop a market for the product. Significant amounts are spent on advertising and promotion to tell all potential customers that the product is available.
Growth	This is the next stage of the product lifecycle. In the growth stage, the business seeks to build brand preference and increase market share. There is continued high spending on marketing to establish the product in the market.
Maturity	This is the third stage of the product lifecycle. At maturity, the strong growth in sales slows down. Competition may appear with similar products. Marketing efforts now switch to defending market share while maximising profit. There is steady and continued support, with occasional promotions to maintain interest in the product.
Decline	This is the final stage of the standard product lifecycle. As sales decline, the business has several options: • Maintain the product, possibly by adding new features and finding new uses. • Try to reduce costs and continue to offer it, possibly to a loyal market segment. • Discontinue the product, selling off any remaining stock (if it is a product) or selling it to another business that is willing to continue the product. There may be little or no marketing support, although the business would wish to clear the stocks of the product before it ceases producing it.

PRODUCT LIFECYCLE PATTERNS
(Rink & Swan 1979)

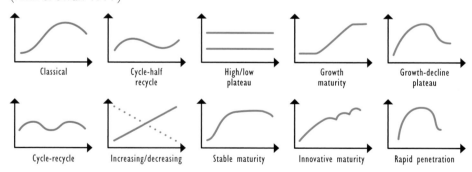

Classical Cycle-half recycle High/low plateau Growth maturity Growth-decline plateau

Cycle-recycle Increasing/decreasing Stable maturity Innovative maturity Rapid penetration

Extension strategies

A business will do everything in its power to maintain sales, particularly at the product maturity stage, where sales are the strongest. In order to reduce the risk of the product going into decline, the business will continue to support it with advertising and promotion. It may give the product a facelift by changing a feature of it, such as its size, design or even its name.

Questions

1 What might happen to the product lifecycle if the product shows very little growth, and sales begin to tail off? (6 marks)
2 Why might a product need a large amount spent on advertising and promotion at its launch stage? (4 marks)

Case studies, questions and exam practice

CASE STUDY WHICH STAGE?

Products and services are at various stages of their lifecycle, e-conferencing is at the introduction stage, portable DVD players are in the growth stage, personal computers have reached maturity, and typewriters are in decline.

Other examples of products and services at various lifecycle stages include:

- Email
- Faxes
- Third generation mobile phones
- Breathable synthetic fabrics
- Handwritten letters
- Shell suits
- Cotton T-shirts
- Personal identity cards
- Smart cards
- Credit cards
- Cheque books
- Racing skin suits

Questions

1 Copy the following table and place the 12 products or services in the appropriate columns. (12 marks)

Introduction	Growth	Maturity	Decline

2 If handwritten letters are in decline, list four types of business that could be affected by the permanent downturn in sales and explain why they might be affected. (8 marks)

SHORT-ANSWER QUESTIONS

1 What are the **FOUR** main stages of the product lifecycle?

2 Briefly explain the purpose of the Boston Matrix.

3 What are the key differences between the Boston Matrix and the General Electric Matrix?

4 What is the Ansoff Matrix and what does it show?

5 What is a USP?

6 What are the main stages involved in product development?

7 What is 'problem child'?

8 What is diversification?

9 What do you understand by the term 'market penetration'?

10 What is an extension strategy?

CASE STUDY KITKAT

This product was developed as a four-finger wafer crisp, initially launched in London and the South East in September 1935 as 'Rowntree's Chocolate Crisp' and re-named two years later as KitKat Chocolate Crisp. It became KitKat after the Second World War.

Within two years of launch, KitKat was established as Rowntree's leading product, a position that it has maintained ever since. During the war, KitKat was portrayed as a valuable wartime food with advertising described the brand as 'What active people need'.

For most of its life, KitKat has appeared in a red and white wrapper. It did, however, change to a blue wrapper in 1945, when it was produced with a plain chocolate covering due to shortages of milk after the war.

KitKat was first advertised on TV back in 1957 and had its first colour advert in 1967. Famous adverts include the 'Dancing Panda' in 1987 and the 'Have a Break' adverts in the 1990s. KitKat is produced at the Nestlé Rowntree Factory, and in 2004 a massive 39,000 tonnes of KitKat were sold – 107 tonnes a day.

Over the years, the four-finger KitKat has appeared in orange and mint variants, and in 2004 Nestlé Rowntree released a lemon and yogurt flavour, as well as a Halloween variant, Blood Orange, and Lime. A Caramac variant was launched in 2005 and has proved to be the most successful variant to date.

In 2005 there were over 800 million two-finger KitKats sold in the UK. In 2005, some 73 million KitKat Chunkys were sold. The 1997 Guinness Book of Records states that 13.2 billion fingers were sold worldwide in 1995 and that every second, 418 KitKat fingers are consumed across the world.

Adapted from Nestlé

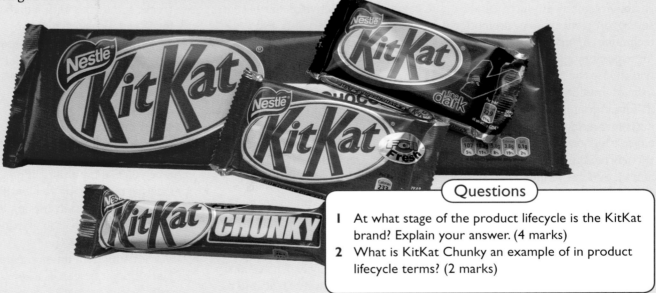

Questions

1 At what stage of the product lifecycle is the KitKat brand? Explain your answer. (4 marks)
2 What is KitKat Chunky an example of in product lifecycle terms? (2 marks)

Elements of the promotional mix: above-the-line

LEARNING OBJECTIVES

▶ What is promotion?
▶ Above-the-line
▶ Advertising
▶ Pull and push strategies

What is promotion?

Promotion is often referred to as marketing communication, as this is the element of the marketing mix that passes on information to potential customers to encourage them to buy a product, or indeed change their attitudes and behaviours about purchasing. Businesses use a wide variety of different methods to communicate with their target markets.

Broadly, they can be described as either above- or below-the-line, as we will see. But collectively they aim to provide information, pass on a particular message, or seek to influence potential customers. Promotion aims to encourage customers to buy products. Often several different types of promotional techniques are used simultaneously for maximum effect. A business will choose the most appropriate form of promotion in order to reach its target groups. This could mean mass-marketing exercises, such as advertising, or promotional methods that encourage repeat purchases or aim to reinforce brand loyalty.

Promotion can cover a wide range of different techniques, from packaging, vouchers and special offers to advertising on television, radio, billboards, the Internet or even on the sides of lorries.

Above-the-line

Any form of advertising for which a commission or fee is payable to a recognised advertising agency operating on behalf of its client(s) is known as 'above-the-line'. The 'line' is an imaginary boundary between those advertising media that pay commission to advertising agencies and those that do not – the latter being below-the-line media. Directories, yearbooks and point-of-sale materials are below-the-line. Typically, above-the-line is associated with advertising, but in reality the description is a broader term.

Over the past decade or so, the division between above- and below-the-line activities has become increasingly blurred. It is also possible to associate below-the-line activities with direct marketing, whereas above-the-line activities are more associated with mainstream advertising such as television or radio advertising campaigns.

Typical above-the-line marketing techniques include the following:

- Press advertising – including newspapers and magazines. The advertisements can be very detailed.
- Television advertising – short, simple, relatively expensive but with the potential of reaching large audiences.
- Radio advertising – through national, regional and local, independent or commercial radio stations. Ideal for targeting specific groups or geographical areas.
- Cinema advertising – often used to test advertisements that will be later screened on television. This is a market that has seen some growth in recent years.
- Posters and billboards – usually sited at road junctions, near shops and travel hubs, where there is a large amount of passing 'traffic'.
- Internet – primarily using banner advertising, which allows a single click for the user to be sent to the business's home page or shopping facility on its website.
- Mobile advertising – a growing category that not only includes trucks and lorries with names, logos and websites, but also specific vehicles with billboards. This category also now includes text messages sent to mobile phone users.

Advertising

Advertising is the paid, public and non-personal announcement of a persuasive message by an identified sponsor. In essence, advertising is the promotion of a product to existing or potential customers.

Advertising is an integral part of marketing; it is seen as a key element in the promotion of products and services to customers (either consumers or businesses). Advertising seeks to create a desire to purchase and influence the needs and wants of potential customers. Advertising, having succeeded in this role, allows a business to satisfy those needs and

BOOK RESEARCH

Caples, John and Hahn, Fred E., *Tested Advertising Methods*, fifth edition. Prentice Hall Trade, July 1998.

For more about below-the-line activities see pp. 292–3.

wants by selling its products and services.

Advertising needs to convince the potential customer that there are benefits to be derived from the purchasing of the product or the service. False or inflated benefits only result in the customer being dissatisfied with the product or service, making repeat purchases unlikely. Advertising is strictly controlled in this respect throughout the world and monitored by organisations such as the Advertising Standards Authority (ASA).

Pull and push strategies

Pull strategy is a term which is simultaneously related to both distribution and advertising. Literally, as the term implies, advertising and marketing aims to motivate end users to demand a product or service. They then approach the retailer, who is then persuaded to stock the products and services.

An alternative to pull strategy, or perhaps used in conjunction with it, is a push strategy, which aims to provide encouragement to distributors to stock and therefore make available products and services to end users. The principle objective of a push strategy is to offer incentives, usually through personal selling techniques to distributors to encourage them to stock and display products and services, thus achieving the goal of pushing the products and services through the distribution channel to the end user.

As can be seen in the diagram below, pull and push strategy can be used simultaneously to force products and services through distributors to the end users.

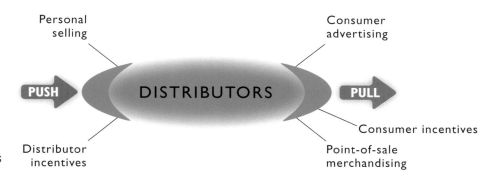

PUSH — Personal selling / Distributor incentives → **DISTRIBUTORS** ← PULL — Consumer advertising / Consumer incentives / Point-of-sale merchandising

---

CASE STUDY HOMEBASE

In 2005 Homebase launched a large-scale, in-store campaign to coincide with its new-look press and TV adverts. For the first time, the home enhancement and DIY retailer tied Point of Purchase (POP) advertising into its press activity, to create a consistent brand message across above-the-line and below-the-line media. The new approach utilises the 'orange dot' from the Homebase logo, providing instant recognition for all future POP material. Ajay Kavan, Homebase Marketing Director, says: 'The new campaign is a totally different direction for us and, as such, it is essential that all promotional media consistently and clearly communicate the new Homebase brand identity and proposition. The orange dot campaign is effective across TV, press, direct mail and in-store media. This is important as although many retailers use POP as a tactical, promotional tool, to us it is one of the most important ways in which our customers link our brand promise and actual brand experience.'

New retail media will be rolled out to all 286 Homebase stores nationwide and will include everything from promotional posters and headers to shelf strips and hanging signs.

Questions

1 What is meant by the term 'point of purchase'? (2 marks)
2 What might be meant by the term 'tactical promotional tool'? (2 marks)
3 Why might Homebase have chosen to organise its marketing campaign in this way? (6 marks)

Elements of the promotional mix: below-the-line

LEARNING
OBJECTIVES

► Below-the-line
► Public relations
► Branding
► Merchandising
► Sales promotion
► Direct selling
► Packaging

BOOK RESEARCH

Point of Purchase Advertising Institute. *Point of purchase design annual.* Hearst Books International, 2002.

Below-the-line

Below-the-line marketing activities are often confused with sales promotions, but they actually represent a large range of different activities, which include direct selling and direct mail, merchandising and point-of-sale materials, branding and public relations.

Public relations

The basic function of public relations is to establish and maintain a mutual understanding between a business and its publics. Typically, public relations activities will include the preparation of press kits, seminars, making charitable donations and sponsorships, community relations and lobbying.

Broadly, public relations have the following objectives:

• Establish and maintain the prestige and reputation of the business
• Support the promotion of products and services
• Deal with arising issues and opportunities
• Establish and maintain goodwill with customers, employees, government, suppliers and distributors
• Deal promptly with unfavourable publicity

In effect, public relations seeks to transfer a negative or null opinion of the business into knowledge or a positive attitude. Public relations can be seen as distinctly different from advertising, as can be seen in the following table:

Public relations	Advertising
Informative	Informative and persuasive
Subdued messages	Immediate impact
No repetition	Repetition
Credibility	Less credible
Newsworthy	Not necessary
Low-cost	High-cost

Branding

Branding is the adoption of values, image, awareness, recognition, quality, features, benefits and name onto a product. In effect, branding is the intangible value created by a badge of reassurance that simultaneously differentiates the product from its competitors.

Businesses will brand their products primarily for differentiation, but branding is a hook upon which to hang the advertising and promotion of the product. Coupled with this, branding also encourages customers to accept and recognise the product, helping them with their buying

decisions. Above all, it reduces the need for the business to compete with other businesses purely on the basis of price.

There are several different types of brand or branding solutions:

• Individual brand (e.g. KitKat, Clio)
• Blanket family brand name for all products (e.g. Dyson, Heinz)
• Separate family names for different product divisions (e.g. Nescafé and Rowntree)
• The company trade name combined with an individual product name (e.g. Ford Focus, Microsoft Age of Empires)

Merchandising

The area of a retail outlet known as 'merchandising' or 'point of sale' is the area immediately surrounding the cash register. It is an area where additional items can be offered, to tempt customers into impulse-buying while they are in the purchasing queue. This area is sometimes alternatively called 'point of purchase', but 'point of purchase' is also used to mean the wider point of purchase, ie the retail outlet itself, and therefore 'point of purchase' advertising can mean outdoor signage, window displays, counter pieces, display racks, self-service containers and banners.

Sales promotion

Sales promotion is taken to mean any marketing activity that involves the promotion of sales, excluding advertising. It has close connections with merchandising and is more commonly known as below-the-line. More commonly, sales promotion is also associated with the shorter term techniques employed by a business, such as special offers or price reductions.

Direct selling

Direct selling, or telemarketing, is an alternative term used to describe telephone sales. Telemarketing uses the telephone as its primary means of contacting potential customers. Clearly, the purpose is to obtain orders from the customer without the need to visit the customer or their premises personally. Telemarketing has become an increasingly valuable tool and an integral part of direct marketing. It enables a business to streamline its distribution channels in order to cut out the intermediaries upon which it formerly relied to provide products and services to the end users.

Increasingly sophisticated technology is being employed in order to assist telemarketing exercises, such as software, that can flag recommended intervals between sales contact with a customer, as well as storing aged data on all transactions, conversations, complaints and queries associated with that customer.

Packaging

Packaging entails the development of a product's container, label, design and overall identity. The packaging of a product is considered to be a very important consideration as it is the first impression that a customer receives from the product prior to purchase.

Packaging needs to fulfil a number of different functions, including, of course, protection for the product while it is within the distribution channel, in storage, or waiting on a retailer's shelves prior to purchase. In this respect there are a number of prerequisites, including ensuring that the product contents do not part company with the packaging prior to purchase (spillage, or damage to the product). In the past, packaging merely involved the printing of a trader's name or the product's name on a relatively functional or plain packaging material. Packaging now includes identifiable logos, slogans and names. Packaging reinforces advertising campaigns by allowing the customer to recognise the image that has been portrayed and also assists point-of-sale merchandising and brand image.

Increasingly, there have been concerns regarding the environmental and recycling issues affecting packaging. Green packaging, which involves the use of recycled material, the opportunity to recycle, or more biodegradable materials, has begun to be used extensively.

Questions

1 How can packaging support an advertising campaign? (2 marks)
2 Give THREE examples of merchandising. (3 marks)
3 Why do businesses decide to brand their products? (4 marks)
4 What is the purpose of public relations? (4 marks)

Influences on the choice of promotional mix

LEARNING OBJECTIVES

▶ Promotion
▶ Promotional mix
▶ Promotional budget
▶ Other key influences on promotion

Promotion

Promotion incorporates a number of different marketing techniques, including advertising, personal selling, public relations and sales promotion. In essence, promotion incorporates any communications between the business and customers and potential customers.

Promotion is also an integral part of the marketing mix. There are several associated factors that influence the selection of promotional methods. These are:

- Promotional objectives
- Cultural and legal constraints
- Infrastructure available to support the promotional effort (within the organisation or its agents)
- The development of the market (in terms of accessibility and sophistication)
- Distribution infrastructure
- Availability of suitable media
- Activities and intentions of the competition.

Method	Description
Affordable approach	This approach is essentially a production-oriented method. The business calculates gross margins, determines its required net profit and then deducts all other costs and expenses. The remainder can be allocated to the promotional budget.
Objective and task approach	This approach looks at the objectives and calculates the funds that are required to meet them. It is often difficult to build unexpected eventualities into the budget.
Competitive parity approach	This budgeting technique uses the competitors as a benchmark and requires the business to spend as much, if not more, than competitors.
Percentage-of-sales approach	Based on either historical or predicted sales figures, an agreed percentage per sale is allocated to advertising.
Historical approach	This approach is based on what has been spent in the past and is ideal for a stable market. It does not take into account what may or may not need to be spent and may often lead to the business spending more than is necessary.
Experiment and testing approach	Different levels of expenditure are allocated to each test market. Awareness and sales can then be measured and compared. This is a far more scientific approach to the allocation of the budget.
Modelling and simulation approach	This approach employs mathematical techniques to build models to help forecast performance against different media plans and advertising expenditure. This is, perhaps, the most scientific approach, as it takes into account the relationship between cost and response.

Promotional mix

The term 'promotional mix' describes the combination of two or more elements, which may include advertising, personal selling, public relations or sales promotion. These four elements are very much the traditional components of the promotional mix. In addition to these, other techniques are now increasingly added to it, including:

- Branding
- Corporate image
- Customer service
- Direct marketing
- Email/Internet
- Exhibitions
- Internal marketing
- Merchandising
- Packaging
- Sponsorship
- Word of mouth

Promotional budget

A promotional budget is the total amount of financial resources allocated by a business to promotions over a period of time. There are a number of different ways in which a business allocates or estimates its promotional budget, as listed in the table on the left.

BOOK RESEARCH

Soares, Eric J. *Promotional feats: The role of planned events in the marketing communications mix.* Greenwood Press, 1991.

PROMOTIONAL **FEATS**

THE ROLE OF PLANNED EVENTS IN THE MARKETING COMMUNICATIONS MIX

ERIC J. SOARES

Other key influences on promotion

The way in which a business chooses to promote its products or services, and the amount of money it wishes to spend, may well be dependent on just how competitive the relevant markets are. Where there are few competitors, customers will have very little choice, so less will be spent on persuading customers to make a purchase.

If the product is in short supply there will also be little reason for the business to promote the product (as with the Nintendo Wii in the run-up to Christmas 2007). Where there are several products available and supply exceeds demand, promotional spending may need to be comparatively high.

If the product can be easily differentiated from that of the competition then there will be little need to promote those differences, as the customers will already be aware of them.

Finally, promotional spending and choice will depend on the stage that the product has reached in its lifecycle. In the early stages, products and services need considerable support. At the very least the product or service needs to be announced to potential customers and then they need to be persuaded to try it. Each time there is a change in the product or service a promotion may be necessary to inform customers of the changes. Even when a product has reached maturity it still needs a degree of continued support in order to ensure that sales remain buoyant. If sales dip, the business obviously needs to make a key decision about whether to re-launch the product or to let it fade away.

CASE STUDY ONLINE ADVERTISING

In 2006, Internet advertising spending broke through the £2bn barrier, while television revenues fell, and newspaper spending barely moved. The £2bn represents 11.4% of total British advertising revenue. Britain has 31 million Internet users. It is a huge growth area. Commercial radio saw its revenues down by 3%, national newspapers saw a rise of just 0.2% and television advertising saw a fall of 4.7%.

The bulk of Internet advertising spending comes from search advertising, worth £1.2bn or 57.8% of the online market. Online classified advertising made up 18.8%. Pop-ups have been falling and are now only worth 0.7% of all online advertising.

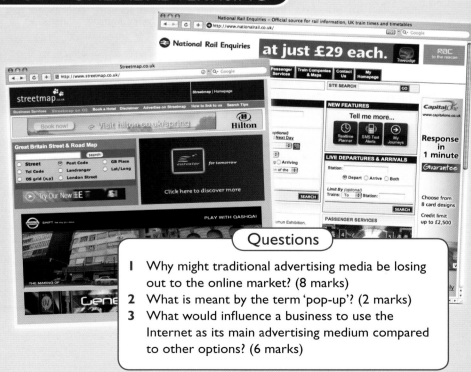

Questions

1 Why might traditional advertising media be losing out to the online market? (8 marks)
2 What is meant by the term 'pop-up'? (2 marks)
3 What would influence a business to use the Internet as its main advertising medium compared to other options? (6 marks)

Case studies, questions and exam practice

CASE STUDY XFM

Trinity Mobile and GCap Media have worked together over the past three months to bring mobile ticketing to XFM and Capital Radio listeners across the capital.

As part of XFM's 10th Birthday celebrations in 2007, the station put on a series of 10 concerts, featuring some of the biggest names in music. Tickets for the concerts have been, and still are, available to winners of competitions run on air. Winners simply gave their mobile phone number to the DJ and were then sent a pair of mobile tickets directly to their mobile phone on the day of the concert. Winners then turned up at the venue – venues included London Astoria, The Scala, Barfly, Buffalo Bar and 229 – and had their ticket scanned by a portable handheld scanner, linked via a wireless network into a live ticket database. Once tickets were redeemed, winners could enter the venue and enjoy a great night in front of some of the best-known bands in the world in a small, private, exclusive venue.

To date, over 1,000 winners and thousands of VIP and Guest List invitees have attended these exclusive events using mobile tickets. A 100% scan rate has been recorded at every event, with a complete elimination of touting or fraudulent use of any ticket. VIP and Guest List management has become a simple and efficient process using the system, with all the usual paper lists and manual checking a thing of the past.

Capital FM has also used the mobile ticketing system for a number of CapitaLive events, including concerts by David Gray, Hard-Fi and Rhianna. It was also used for a James Blunt gig on 5 November 2007 at The Park Club.

GCap says it now intends to offer mobile ticketing for all its events across the group's radio stations, both the distribution of free and competition winner tickets for in-house and promotional events, and also for purchased tickets for some of the bigger events the group runs.

'This service has completely changed the way we run ticketed events internally,' said GCap Head of Mobile, Beth Wilderspin. 'I am able to set up, launch, manage and report on events in minutes using the Easy Ticket software provided by Trinity Mobile. It makes it so easy. I then have event teams out on site running the ticket redemption using the FoneScan barcode scanners, reading barcodes directly off the phone screen, enabling us to redeem hundreds of tickets in minutes, making for efficient and reliable entry to a venue.

'It has been a pleasure working with Trinity, who have helped us every step of the way with advice, help and support so that I am now at a point where I can run all our ticketing events in-house without any external support or providers, other than the software sitting on my PC and the scanners we keep for events.'

Trinity Mobile Commercial Director Rob Clegg added:

'Working with GCap has been a great experience as they have adopted this market-leading service with such enthusiasm – hopefully that has been based on the ease of use, reliability and quality of the services we have supplied. The mobile ticketing service is ideally suited to radio, as it allows tickets to be won or purchased with a very simple call to action and no need for PCs, the Internet, paper or the post – a true "anywhere, anytime" service just like radio.'

Source adapted from www.mobilemarketingmagazine.co.uk

Questions

1 What type of promotion has XFM run and how was the promotion communicated to its customer base? (6 marks)
2 What is the purpose of a promotion such as this, which generates income only from the cost of the calls made to the radio station by competition entrants? (6 marks)
3 What are the names of all of the partner businesses involved in this promotion and what is their role? (10 marks)

SHORT-ANSWER QUESTIONS

1 Why is promotion an important part of the marketing mix?

2 Distinguish between above-the-line and below-the-line promotions.

3 What is the fastest-growing form of advertising?

4 What is the purpose of public relations?

5 What is POP?

6 What do you understand by the term 'branding'?

7 What are push and pull strategies?

8 What do you understand by the term 'promotional mix'?

9 Give FOUR examples of sales promotions.

10 What is the most common form of direct selling technique used by businesses?

Pricing strategies

Price

Price is one of the four original Ps of the marketing mix. Effectively price covers the money charged for a product or service, or, more explicitly, the sum of money that customers are prepared to pay for a product, based on their own valuation of the benefits they will receive. Price is an integral element of the marketing mix and there are a number of determining factors, which can be categorised into three areas:

- Cost – including the variable costs, fixed costs and proposed mark-up.
- Competition – the number of direct competitors, lower-priced segments in the market or substitutes available from other industries.
- Customers – past prices, just or fair prices, perceptions of quality and price expectations.

Pricing strategies

There are innumerable pricing strategies that can be adopted by businesses in order to fulfil specific marketing objectives. The most common are summarised in the following table:

Pricing strategy	Explanation
Market penetration pricing	Low prices, particularly when a product is first launched, in order to obtain a significant penetration into the market.
Market skimming	High prices to support heavy advertising and sales promotion. Involves a higher than usual profit margin on each unit sold.
Average price	Basing pricing on the average for the industry.
Product mix	A pricing strategy associated with setting prices along a product line, which successively offers more features or higher quality for a higher price.
Optional	The practice of setting price according to optional or accessory products which are offered together with the main product.
Captive	Setting a premium price on products that must be used with a popular main product.
Product bundle	Combining several products and offering the whole bundle at a discounted or reduced price.
Discount	Offering a variation in price for those who settle their account quickly, or seasonal discounts to encourage customers to buy at times when demand is low.
Discriminatory	Setting the price within a set of parameters, negotiated with each individual customer, dependent upon quantity purchased, location, timescales or product type.
Psychological	Setting prices that appear to be fundamentally better or more appealing to the customer.
Promotional	Offering temporary pricing structures to increase short-term sales, such as loss leaders or prices attached to special events, cash discounts for frequent purchasing or reduced prices for local stockists, where delivery is not a particular concern.
Cost Plus	Setting the price at a set proportion or percentage above the cost of production and all other associated costs.

Price skimming

Price skimming is a pricing strategy that is the direct opposite of penetration pricing. Price skimming is a situation that allows a business to set a high price for its products and services; a price that may be acceptable to only a proportion of its customers. Specifically, these customers are the ones who value the product highly and, importantly, have the means to continue purchasing it.

The diagram on the right shows that at P1, the skim price, quantity sold is comparatively low. If the business reduces its price to P2, then Q2 sales can be included into the overall equation. Having maintained a skim price at P1 for a period of time before reducing to P2, the total revenue enjoyed by the business is the sum of A, B and C, as shown on the diagram.

Penetration pricing

Penetration pricing is an aggressive form of pricing strategy. A business sets the prices on its products and services deliberately low enough to attract as many customers as possible in the shortest period of time. The sole purpose of penetration pricing is to undermine the pricing structure of competitors and to wrestle as much market share from them as is practicable in the shortest period of time. Having established a viable market share by adopting this policy, a business would then review its pricing strategies and may well revert to a more traditional pricing structure. Penetration pricing can be seen as the direct opposite of price skimming.

Price leaders and takers

As the term implies, a price leader is a business that sets the market price for particular products and services. It is likely to be the most dominant

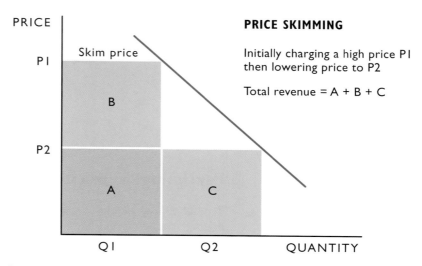

PRICE SKIMMING

Initially charging a high price P1 then lowering price to P2

Total revenue = A + B + C

business in a particular market and, therefore, has the power and ability to dictate the level of pricing. It will have set the price on the basis of its own objectives and criteria, such as sales levels and profitability. Because of its dominant position the other businesses in the same market may be forced to match the market price, whether they can afford to or not.

The other businesses are known as market takers, as they have to accept that in order to make any sales and to retain their market share they need to match the market price set by the price leader.

As we will see in the next spread on pricing tactics, there are ways in which this situation can be temporarily put out of balance by a business choosing a specific pricing tactic that will give it an edge until the other businesses choose to follow suit.

Another way of dealing with the price leader or, indeed, establishing the position of being price leader is to adopt predatory pricing.

Predatory pricing

Predatory pricing is a pricing strategy adopted by some businesses in order to inflict financial damage on competitors by forcing them to cut their profit margins and match the unfeasibly low prices

the business is offering. This is an extremely aggressive and often short-term policy, used to drive competitors out of a market. Invariably it is adopted by businesses that already have a substantial market share and enjoy considerable economies of scale, allowing them to temporarily offer products and services at prices well below the market norm. In recent years predatory pricing has become a feature in a number of areas, particularly with regard to supermarkets, where prices of basic stock items, such as bread, baked beans and tinned tomatoes, have been offered at virtually cost price. Extreme cases of predatory pricing do in fact aim to drive competitors out of business. If this purpose is revealed and proven, the strategy is deemed illegal.

Questions

1 What do you understand by the term 'price skimming'? (2 marks)
2 Distinguish between a price leader and a price taker. (4 marks)
3 Why might a business adopt penetration pricing? (2 marks)

Price tactics

Price tactics

Price tactics are an integral part of pricing strategies and can often be seen as part of the strategy, used by a business for a short period of time to have the maximum effect. They are then abandoned or changed as circumstances dictate. There are many different price tactics, the most common of which are explored below.

Loss leaders

Loss leader is a term associated with pricing policy and is a strategy that offers a product or service at a considerable discount. Although the discounting reduces profits in the short term, the strategy aims to attract additional customers who will hopefully remain loyal for the longer term. It is, therefore, a strategy that is often adopted by a business launching a product or service into a market for the first time. Loss leaders are used to introduce new customers to the product or service and the strategy is supported by other marketing activities, which aim to build a longer-term relationship with these customers.

Psychological pricing

Psychological pricing is a general pricing strategy term which encompasses all techniques that attempt to elicit a certain reaction from consumers, based on the price. Psychological pricing includes prestige pricing and odd-even pricing.

Prestige pricing

Prestige pricing is a pricing strategy which relies on the business, through marketing, having established a perception in the minds of customers that the product or service has notably superior levels of quality, exclusivity or service. Prestige pricing may also be referred to as premium pricing, as products or services have a pricing structure, often somewhat different from the competitors. The business trades and relies heavily on the continued and engrained customer perceptions of the product, for which it is prepared to pay a considerably higher price than other alternatives available.

Odd-even pricing

Odd-even pricing may be part of a business's pricing strategies that attempt to influence a buyer's perception of the price. There is considerable debate as to how customers perceive specific prices and in many respects odd-even pricing is very much akin to psychological pricing. Some businesses may opt for odd pricing, typically £19.99 or £99.99. This is based on the assumption that customers perceive the price as 9 rather than 10. Other businesses have recognised the value of even pricing and set their price points at £5, £10, £15 or £20. The inference here, and the consequent buyer perception, is that the business is not trying to fool them and that they are recognising the customers' intelligence in not being fooled.

Price bundling

Price or product bundling is the sale of two or more separate products in a single package. Price bundling is the sale of two or more separate products in a package at a discount, where there is no attempt to integrate the two products. The bundling does not create added value to the consumer as the two products are not directly associated. This is why a discount is offered to motivate consumers to buy the bundle.

In 1988 Microsoft began bundling several software programs under the title Microsoft Office. Until this time customers had been able to purchase Word, Excel, Access and PowerPoint as separate products. They may not have necessarily required or desired all of these products. However, at a discount compared to the individually priced items, they were now able to purchase all the software at a discounted rate. The result was that Microsoft enjoyed an enormous sales increase and moved towards market dominance.

Product bundling can be differentiated from price bundling in the sense that two or more separate products are integrated in some way, which implies that the Microsoft experiment was both a price bundling and a product bundling exercise. Other examples of product bundling tend to add value to the consumer's purchase, such as integrated stereo systems, which offer compactness.

Off-peak pricing

Off-peak pricing is another pricing strategy that attempts to stimulate demand by price reduction during periods when demand is traditionally low. Off-peak pricing is also referred to as seasonal pricing. It is not to be confused with discounting, which means running sales, for limited periods of time, to reduce stock levels.

Bait pricing

This is a product or service offered by a business at an unrealistically low price in order to lure customers. Once the customers have been successfully attracted, the business then attempts to sell more highly priced products and services. Bait pricing is considered to be a highly unethical means of promoting a product or service.

The technique is closely associated with bait advertising which promotes the low-priced products and services, which in fact, are in low stock or not in stock at all. Having specifically made the decision to make a purchase, customers are then offered alternatives to the low-priced items. The customers are considered to be more vulnerable to sales pitches under these circumstances. The process of offering lower-priced products and services, and then attempting to sell higher-priced ones is known as bait and switch pricing or selling.

Competitive pricing

Competitive pricing policy relates to a pricing strategy that takes into account periodic or permanent movements in the prices charged by competitors for similar products and services offered in the market. A business will systematically monitor the pricing structures of the major competitors and, if necessary, bring its prices into line with them. The competitive pricing strategy approach is often closely allied to the overall competitive strategy of the business, linked to the stage the product or service has reached in the lifecycle.

Cost plus pricing

Cost plus pricing methodology is one of the most common forms of pricing policy, and it is also one of the more straightforward. The pricing methodology simply involves adding a predetermined percentage or gross figure to the costs of production or purchase, thereby creating a price point for the product or service. This basic form of pricing does not individually take into account current market conditions and is in many cases considered to be too prescriptive in its structure for standard use. Despite this, many base prices are calculated in this cost plus assumption.

Differential pricing

Differential pricing is a pricing policy that offers different pricing levels and structures to different markets or customer groups for the same products and services. An example of this would be to offer a different scale of charges for products and services to full-time students or the unemployed, and standard pricing to other customers.

Questions

1 Why might a business choose to adopt a loss-leader pricing tactic? (2 marks)
2 Give TWO examples of a business that could adopt prestige pricing. (2 marks)
3 Which pricing tactic is probably the most commonly used by businesses and why? (4 marks)

Influences on pricing decisions

LEARNING OBJECTIVES
▶ Influences on pricing decisions
▶ Price sensitivity
▶ Price elasticity of demand
▶ Non-price competition

Influences on pricing decisions

Pricing plays an important role in not only the marketing mix, but also the long-term health of a business. If a business makes incorrect decisions on pricing then it stands to lose customers because to a large extent customers have a reasonably good idea of what they should be paying for products and services. In losing customers the business loses revenue and this ultimately leads to lost profits.

As we will see, there needs to be a balance between sales and revenue, and in order to appreciate this, businesses may look at the price elasticity of demand to assist them in their pricing decisions.

Price sensitivity

Price sensitivity is a measure of how customers may react to changes in the costs of the products and services they purchase. Price sensitivity is a term closely associated with price elasticity and it is largely determined by a difference in the perceived value of a product or service or the number of competitors in a market.

Not only do customers have an idea of the correct price for a particular product or service, they also make their decisions based on other criteria:

- They will consider the features and the benefits of the product or service, paying more for something that is precisely what they want.
- Customers will also consider quality. The higher the perceived quality of a product or service the higher the price premium (this is known as perceived quality).
- Customers will also be prepared to pay more if they want the product or service more. If it is absolutely essential or desirable then they will be more willing to pay a higher price.
- Customers' income is also important and the product or service needs to be within their income range. Customers with more disposable income have fewer concerns about price.
- Availability – scarcity can remove some barriers to price, but in reality most products and services are available from a number of different sources, so if the customer cannot easily find a product or service at the right price in one outlet, then they will simply look elsewhere.
- Another consideration is whether or not the item is available when the customer requires it. Often customers will pay more for an item if they can possess it within their own timescale.

Price elasticity of demand

In an ideal world, as far as a business is concerned it would want to charge the highest possible price without affecting the demand for that product or service. What is often an unknown quantity, however, is how much demand will be affected by a price rise.

A business can get a clue as to the possible impact by calculating the price elasticity of demand. Businesses know that price increase will affect demand: it is a question of how much, and this is what price elasticity of demand measures. It can explain the effect of a price cut as well as a price rise, and it shows how responsive demand is to a change in price.

Clearly some products and services are far more sensitive to price changes than others. Some products may see huge changes in demand by even a slight price

change. Newspapers have tried this tactic by slashing their cover prices, particularly on Sunday editions, and have seen demand vastly increase.

In order to calculate price elasticity the following formula is used:

$$\text{Price elasticity} = \frac{\text{percentage change in quantity demanded}}{\text{percentage change in price}}$$

FOR EXAMPLE

A business increases its prices by 5% and sees a 10% fall in demand:

$$\frac{10\%}{5\%} = 2$$

It is important to be able to read the results of the formula correctly. Strictly speaking, price elasticity is nearly always negative because price increase will always push demand down, and a price drop should always push demand up. This means that the percentage change in quantity demanded should always have a + or a − to show in which direction the demand is moving and the percentage price is increasing or decreasing.

Although you will not have to calculate price elasticity on the examination paper, you do need to be aware of what it means, and of the relationship between price and demand.

Non-price competition

Non-price competition is competition based on factors other than price. The primary task is to initially establish differentiating criteria that mark the product or service as being sufficiently unlike those offered by competitors. Normally, non-price competition would imply convenience, taste or a degree of prestige. Businesses have recognised that in the medium term to long term, pricing-based competition does little to benefit the organisations involved. Competition based on pricing can temporarily increase market share, but in the longer term customers begin to expect lower prices, and then alternative measures need to be sought in order to maintain market share. All that price-cutting achieves is a cut in the contribution of each unit and it may detrimentally affect profitability.

Non-price competition has, therefore, become the important battlefield for many markets. It usually involves adding a degree of value to whatever the business is offering its customers. Typically this might include some or all of the following:

- Customer loyalty cards
- Additional services
- Home delivery systems
- Discounts in allied product areas
- Extended opening hours
- Customer self-scanning of products
- Incentives for purchasing off-peak or out of season
- Internet shopping

Questions

1 List THREE possible influences on pricing. (3 marks)
2 What do you understand by 'price sensitivity'? (2 marks)
3 If the price of a product is decreased, what is the likely effect on demand, and why? (4 marks)
4 Give FOUR examples of non-price competition. (4 marks)

Case studies, questions and exam practice

CASE STUDY THE £2 CHICKEN

When Asda slashed the price of its chickens in September 2007 to just £2 each, the price war between Asda and Tesco was finally at an end. Tesco had decided to put up its prices and end loss-leading cheap foods. Sir Terry Leahy, Tesco's Chief Executive, said:

'For decades, food has been a falling proportion of total consumer spending and as a business we have contributed to this by cutting prices to help people spend less. That won't change, but the long-term trend of declining spend on food has stopped.'

Tesco declared that it would be selling the same size bird at £3.39. This was partly in response to the problems that farmers were having in trying to produce safe, healthy chickens at low prices.

Asda had been named in 2007 as Britain's cheapest supermarket by the trade magazine *The Grocer*. It was the tenth year running that it had won this award and it immediately brought in price cuts on 10,000 items, worth £250m.

Tesco had tried to prove that it was winning the price war and followed with £270m of price cuts on more than 3,000 products.

Asda was also in the news in 2007 when it launched a complete school uniform for less than £10. It had also had long-running public arguments with Bloomsbury, the publisher of JK Rowling's Harry Potter series. The publisher recommended a price of £17.99 but Asda was selling Harry Potter's final adventure for just £5, after having promised the publisher that it would not offer the book as a loss leader.

Questions

1 What is meant by the term 'loss leader' and why would Asda and Tesco adopt this approach? (10 marks)
2 Both Asda and Tesco could claim that they were price leaders and that the other was a price taker. Explain what you understand by these two terms. (6 marks)
3 Customers clearly benefit from price wars such as this. But what part of the distribution chain is most likely to be adversely affected and why? (6 marks)

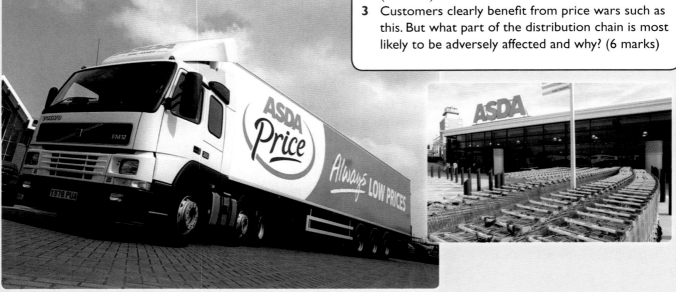

SHORT-ANSWER QUESTIONS

1 Distinguish between price skimming and price penetration.

2 What is predatory pricing?

3 What do you understand by the term 'psychological pricing' and give an example.

4 What is odd-even pricing?

5 What is price bundling and give an example.

6 Why might a business use bait pricing?

7 What is the relationship between price and demand?

8 Why might customers show signs of price sensitivity?

9 Give **FOUR** examples of non-price competition.

10 Distinguish between a price leader and a price taker.

CASE STUDY THE PRICE IS WRONG

In 2006 the computer manufacturer Dell announced that it was bringing in a major pricing initiative, primarily aimed at consumers and small business customers. Some 85% of Dell's customers are small businesses, but it has always wanted to expand its presence among home users. Dell has tried various tactics to get its computer customers to purchase its other electronic equipment, such as televisions and printers, but has always had mixed success.

When Dell was established, it enjoyed rapid growth, but in the past few years its growth has been slower and its projected revenue far lower than expected. The Chief Executive, Kevin Rollins, blamed much of the shortfall in revenue on the unprofitable low end of the computer market, because the company had to be focused on maintaining its market share.

Hewlett Packard was proving to be a major competitor to Dell. In addition to this Dell was receiving a higher than average number of service complaints, forcing it to invest heavily in technical support.

In 2006 Dell had cut its prices on a number of key desktop and laptop computers, while its partner, Intel, cut its prices on chip sets.

Questions

1 What pricing strategies would be appropriate to Dell in trying to maintain its market share? (6 marks)

2 What elements of Dell's operations could be considered non-price competition? (4 marks)

3 Why would Dell want to encourage customers to purchase its other electronic equipment and why might this not have been successful? (6 marks)

Choosing appropriate outlets and distributors

Place

This final part of the marketing mix is all about the availability of products and services. It incorporates physical location in which the products or services can be purchased, and the timing of their availability.

Businesses will spend much time considering the best ways in which they can ensure that products and services reach their potential customers. They may well need to convince retail outlets to stock the products and they will also have to consider how to physically transport products from their factories and warehouses, as well as importers or suppliers to retailers, wholesalers and distributors.

Trying to persuade other businesses to stock products is never a simple matter. In retail outlets in particular, shelf space is always scarce and probably full of products supplied by competitors. A retailer will have to take a risk in limiting the shelf space of stock that it knows already sells, in order to make room for a product that may not sell. It may also mean that some stock will have to be run down and not offered to customers any more, which could lead to lost sales for the retailer.

Another consideration is the type of product involved. Clearly there will need to be different distribution channels used depending on whether the product is enormous, like a tractor, delicate and perishable, like strawberries, or with a short period of popularity, such as a CD single.

Distribution

Distribution is the physical movement of products and services from the producer to the end user and often involves the transfer of ownership through intermediaries between the producer and the end user. A distribution channel ends when an individual or a business buys a product or service without the intention of immediate resale.

Part of the distribution channel involves organisations such as storage and transport companies and banks. These are integral parts of the distribution process, but they are outside of it in the sense that they never take ownership of the product or service, but merely aid the channel.

A business faces several different options when setting up the distribution system for its products and services. The key determinants of how this distribution channel is organised usually depends on the following:

- A determination of the role of distribution and how it will help achieve the marketing objectives.
- The selection of the type of channel and whether intermediaries are required.
- An assessment of the intensity of the distribution which allows the business to assess how many intermediaries will be needed at each level and in each area.
- The choosing of specific channel members that most closely match criteria set by the business.

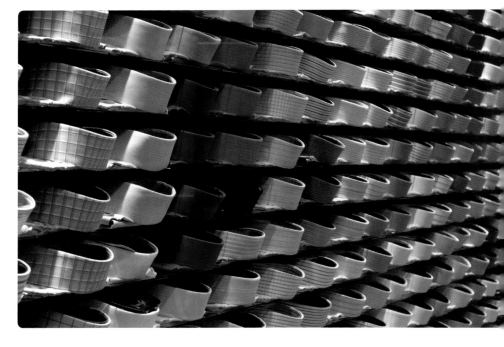

Direct distribution

A direct channel is essentially a direct distribution system in which products and services are delivered straight to the end user, without the use of an intermediary. Notable direct channels include direct sales and, in some cases, standard mail order.

Indirect distribution

Indirect distribution involves the inclusion of at least one intermediary between the producer and the end user. The exact nature of the distribution channel in indirect distribution very much depends upon the types of product and service being delivered and, more especially, to which type of market. In effect, there are three different models of indirect distribution, which are: consumer goods, business-to-business goods, and services. The key indirect channel choices can be seen in the table below.

Multiple distribution

Multiple distribution channels are used by a business either to avoid dependence on a single channel, or to reach two or more target markets that could not be served by a single distribution channel. Multiple distribution channels tend to be used when a business is essentially selling the same product to other businesses or direct to consumers. Multiple distribution channels are also widely used by multinational businesses and specifically those that have a broad portfolio of different products and services. In these cases it would be inappropriate to use the same distribution channel to supply products and services. Other businesses use multiple distribution channels to reach different segments within a single market, such as an airline selling direct to larger business while using travel agents to supply smaller businesses and consumers. One of the most common reasons for the use of multiple distributions is when products are being sold into a market that has a wide geographical spread. It is, therefore, necessary to use a wide variety of different intermediaries in order to service this market.

Distribution research

Distribution research is concerned with the investigation of data related to the distribution process. Different businesses adopt different policies depending on the depth of their distribution research. The data analysed includes:

- the number of calls made in a given time
- the number of sales compared to the number of calls
- the average sales revenue per call
- the average profit per call
- the sales revenue per customer
- the profit per customer
- the average order value
- sales expenses compared to sales revenue
- sales expenses compared to profit per customer
- the number of new accounts as a percentage of the total number of accounts
- the actual performance compared to the forecasted figures

INDIRECT DISTRIBUTION

Consumer goods	Business-to-business	Services
Producer to consumer or door-to-door	Producer to user	Producer to consumer
Producer to retailer to consumer	Producer to industrial distributor to user	Producer to agent to consumer
Producer to wholesaler to retailer to consumer	Producer to industrial distributor to reseller to user	
Producer to agent to retailer to consumer	Producer to agent to user	
	Producer to agent to industrial distributor to user	

Questions

1 Distinguish between direct and indirect distribution channels. (4 marks)
2 Why might a business use a multiple distribution channel? (2 marks)
3 Why might a retailer's willingness to stock a product be directly linked to the demand for that product? (4 marks)

Types of distribution channels

LEARNING OBJECTIVES

▶ Channels of distribution
▶ Using retailers
▶ Using wholesalers
▶ Using agents
▶ Choosing the right channel
▶ Elements of distribution

Channels of distribution

The channel of distribution is the link that brings together the manufacturer of a product and its end user, or consumer. The way in which this is organised will depend on the type of product and the market itself. For many businesses the decision has been made to either concentrate on one channel of distribution, or to make its products available through as many channels as possible.

As we will see, there are a number of different options open to a business, but broadly they can be typified as:

- Traditional – where manufacturers send their stock to a wholesaler, who in turn sells it to retailers for onward sale to consumers.
- Modern – where many large businesses do not buy from wholesalers but buy direct from the manufacturers and organise their own distribution to their own outlets.
- Direct – where the manufacturer has direct contact with the final consumer, either via the Internet, catalogues or telesales.

When there is another business in the channel of distribution, between the producer and the consumer, these businesses are called intermediaries and the channel of distribution is indirect. When the producer sells directly to the consumer then there are no intermediaries and the channel of distribution is direct.

Using retailers

Some retailers are actually owned by the producer, such as the Lush shops or the mobile phone company Vodafone. Other retailers stock products from many different producers, such as Tesco or HMV. In these cases the producer has to convince the retailer to stock the products. The producer will need a sales force to communicate with the retailer's buyers.

Using wholesalers

Many smaller retailers do not deal with producers directly, as their orders may not be big enough. Instead they buy their stock from wholesalers. Wholesalers act as intermediaries, buying products from producers, and then selling them to retailers. This is a slightly more expensive way of buying the products for the retailer, as the wholesaler will want to make a profit out of each sale.

FOR EXAMPLE

Books are a prime example of products that pass through multiple channels of distribution. It is possible to buy a book direct from the publisher. You can buy books in shops, such as Waterstones (a retailer), or you can buy online via the publisher or large businesses such as Amazon.

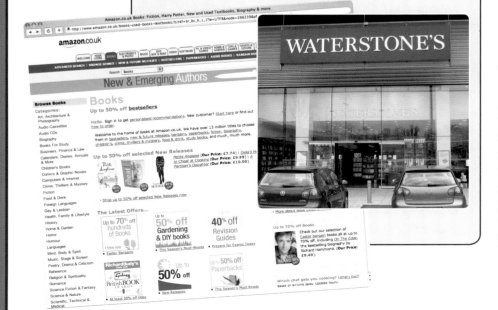

Using agents

Producers often use agents to sell their products in overseas markets. The agent has a sales team that contacts wholesalers and retailers in the overseas market to convince them to stock the producer's products. The agents receive **commission** on the sales they generate. Some agents act as wholesalers, stocking the product for the producer in the overseas country and then selling it on to retailers.

Choosing the right channel

There are three main considerations when a business seeks to discover the right kind of channel of distribution for its products. The first may be the product itself. A product that needs to get from the producer to the consumer very quickly needs a fast and efficient distribution channel. This is typical of food products. They need to be harvested, cleaned and packed and then shipped to wholesalers or retailers, so that they can be sold on to consumers.

Large and heavy products will require expensive transportation and usually these will move straight from the producer to the consumer. Other products are ideal for a long chain of distribution, because they are either **non-perishable**, or strong enough to cope with handling and storage.

The market is also another consideration. Mass-market products, which are sold in their thousands or millions, are usually sold via wholesalers and large retailers. These businesses buy the products in enormous numbers and it is much more efficient for the producer to deal with them.

Products that are sold into smaller markets, known as niche markets, tend to be sold either directly by the producer or through a handful of selected retailers.

Elements of distribution

Most of the products and services we buy are from retailers. Many of them are chains, such as Marks and Spencer, Tesco or Woolworths. Others are small, independent retailers, with only one or a handful of shops.

Ideally, producers of products want to sell them in bulk. This makes it difficult for them to sell either to small retailers or direct to the consumer. At the same time producers want to make sure that the consumer finds it as convenient as possible to find and buy their products. This is why they tend to carry out a lot of their business via large retailers, or through wholesalers. Both of them act as a 'bulk breaker'. In other words, they make a bulk order and then they sell individual products to their customers.

Retailers are particularly useful, as they hold stock of products that they have bought, either in bulk from the producer or in smaller quantities from a wholesaler. Their stock should be sufficient to cover immediate demand for the product.

KEY WORDS

Commission – a percentage of the value of each sale paid to an agent by the producer.

Non-perishable – a product that does not spoil when kept for a long time, such as a can of soft drink or a piece of furniture.

Questions

1 Some agents actually sell direct to consumers by visiting homes and holding parties. Give TWO examples of this in Britain. (2 marks)

2 Why might it not be in the interests of a producer to deal with hundreds of small orders from retailers, but to sell through wholesalers instead? (4 marks)

3 Some wholesalers are known as cash and carry warehouses. What does this mean? Think of an example of who might use them. (3 marks)

4 Some retailers are called specialist multiples and others are called variety chain stores. What do these two terms mean and give an example of each. (4 marks)

Case studies, questions and exam practice

CASE STUDY BULLET BOY

*B*ullet Boy was a low-budget, independent feature film starring British rapper Ashley Walters as Ricky, newly released from prison, but unable to distance himself from the cycle of gang violence that has become an everyday feature in some parts of inner-city London. The film describes the effects of Ricky's life on his mother and, especially, his younger brother.

Following festival screenings at the end of 2004, the film quickly gathered a reputation as the first film to tackle the difficult subject of contemporary gang and gun crime in Britain's inner cities. In Hackney, where the film is set, local people saw the film contributing, in one way or another, to the ongoing debate. By the time the film was released, it had accumulated both word-of-mouth and press coverage in the news pages.

The release of *Bullet Boy* was handled by Verve Pictures. Verve Pictures saw the potential of the film in the wider market, especially with a young black audience drawn by the presence of Ashley Walters (of So Solid Crew) to seek out the film in key urban multiplex sites. In order to broaden the theatrical release of the film, Verve applied successfully for funds from the UK Film Council's Fund.

The film was released on 8 April 2005, opening on 75 prints UK wide, in a combination of established independent cinemas and multiplexes concentrated in greater London and other major urban centres. The poster design aims to convey the look, subject and tone of the film, supported by key press quotes.

The ad campaign aimed for diverse audiences, interested in film and music, urban black and white. The campaign included advertising in all of the national daily newspapers that allocate significant space to film reviews, plus two tabloids, newspapers with a black perspective, a selective London Underground campaign and extensive use of radio stations with a concentration on R 'n' B and Garage, the musical forms with which Walters is associated.

Towards the end of its first six months of theatrical release, the film had grossed an impressive £450,000 at the UK box office, most of this achieved in carefully selected urban multiplexes rather than specialised cinemas. It was anticipated that the substantial audiences and awareness generated for the theatrical release would ensure success for the DVD release of the film, six months after the theatrical opening.

Source: adapted from Verve Pictures

Questions

1 Film distribution is complex and controlled by a handful of major cinema chains. Why did Verve go to independent cinemas for the distribution of this film? (4 marks)
2 Why was it important for Verve to ensure that the largest possible audience could view this film? (4 marks)
3 What promotional techniques were used, and why were they chosen? (8 marks)

SHORT-ANSWER QUESTIONS

1 What is distribution research?

2 What is multiple distribution and why might it be used?

3 Give THREE examples of indirect distribution relevant to consumer goods.

4 Give THREE examples of indirect distribution relevant to business-to-business distribution.

5 Why might a business use an indirect distribution channel?

6 Briefly distinguish between traditional,

modern and direct distribution channels.

7 Why is place an important part of the marketing mix?

8 Why might an existing manufacturer have more success in convincing retailers to stock its products than a new manufacturer?

9 How can multiple distribution channels assist a business in reaching different segments of a market?

10 What is an intermediary?

CASE STUDY CARGO EXPRESS

In the spring of 2006 Cargo Express successfully tendered for the UK distribution of awnings and sun blinds for a German manufacturer. The awnings are made to individual specification and designs can be over seven metres long and 150kg in weight. This makes them very difficult to handle through conventional distribution networks. The previous European and UK distributors had consistently delivered the product damaged. The high cost of damaging a unique product was not the only problem. Specialist installation teams scheduled to fit the awnings had to be rescheduled at extra cost. Demonstrating their commitment to customer service and their ability to distribute goods with the minimum handling was the key to Cargo Express winning the business.

Source: adapted from Cargo Express

Questions

1 What might be meant by a 'conventional distribution network'? Give an example. (4 marks)

2 Why might the manufacturer have made the changing of the distribution method a major priority? (2 marks)

3 What other options of distribution may have been available to the manufacturer? (6 marks)

Possible impacts of market conditions and degree of competition

Competitive environment

The most important aspect of a business's external environmental factors is its competitive environment. Clearly each different industry has its own characteristics, but in more complex organisations, involved in a number of different markets, or a number of different overseas environments, the complexity of dealing with the competitive environment becomes all the more crucial.

It is widely believed that in order to assess the industry or competitive environment, a business has to consider seven key issues. These are:

- The nature of the industry's dominant features, specifically the economic features
- The nature and strength of the competition
- Change factors that are impacting on the industry's competitive structure and general environment
- An identification of the major competitors and their relative competitive strength
- An anticipation of any strategic initiatives that competitors are likely to make
- An identification of any key factors that will determine competitive success
- The attractiveness of the industry in terms of drawing in new competitors and the ability of the business to attain a reasonable (sustainable) level of profitability.

Direct competitors and rivalry

Typically, any form of competitive analysis will begin with an investigation of the rivalry amongst existing businesses. In this respect the rivalry concerns direct competition and perhaps this is the most important of all of the five forces. Specifics regarding the rivalry include the following:

- The rate of market or industry growth – in fast-growing markets, businesses may not be overtly competitive, as there is sufficient demand for all. However, should a market be in decline, or be experiencing slow growth, it is inevitable that the businesses in that market will seek to seize market share from their competitors.
- The existence of capacity surplus – in many cases, while businesses

are forced to fund their fixed costs, or are reluctant to leave a market due to the high exit barrier costs, they are in a position where they have excess capacity. This clearly means that supply exceeds demand. In these cases the price expected for products and services is depressed and consequently a business's profits suffer.
- The size and number of competitors – when business competitors in a market are broadly

LEARNING OBJECTIVES

- ▶ Competitive environment
- ▶ Direct competitors and rivalry
- ▶ New competitors and substitute products and services
- ▶ Strength of suppliers
- ▶ The buyers

equal in terms of their capabilities and size, there is a tendency for competition to increase. Customers will also switch from one supplier to another when there are sufficient numbers of options available to them. In these cases rivalry is at a high level.

- New competitors – this aspect of examining the competitive environment deals with what may be known as either diverse or relatively new competitors. In effect, these new competitors challenge one another, and the existing businesses, as they may have different ideas regarding competition.
- Standardisation of products and services – it is clearly the case that the more similar products and services appear, the greater differentiation needs to be in order to retain customers.
- High exit barriers – if it is particularly difficult for a business to leave an industry or market due to the high costs of exit, it is left with one simple option. This option is to compete and, perhaps, compete on a more extreme basis than it had done before. This represents the only key to the company's continued survival.

New competitors and substitute products and services

New entrants tend to be successful and represent a considerable competition risk if they can create a synergy with their existing lines of business. Equally, they are a threatening prospect if they have access to considerable financial resources, alternative technology, and government assistance, or can penetrate the distribution channels.

Substitute products or services are also a concern in terms of competition. In strict terms these substitute products may either be existing or new products and services. A prime example is e-mail, which has become an effective substitute for postal services. New products or services are, strictly, those that did not necessarily exist before and that represent a major improvement on the products and services that were originally available. Prime examples from the past include the almost total replacement of typewriters by computers or word processors, and electronic watches replacing traditional mechanical watches. In recent years music and film, for example, have seen a number of major changes. Traditional acetate records were gradually replaced by cassette tapes, which in turn were replaced by CDs, which are now in the process of being replaced themselves by Internet music files.

Strength of the suppliers

The other major consideration in terms of the competitive environment is the strength of the suppliers to that market. This refers to suppliers that supply the businesses operating in a given market. Some suppliers are more powerful and can dictate the course or fortunes of the competition within the market, usually under the following circumstances:

- They are strong when there are few suppliers and demand for their products or services is high.
- They are also strong when they have a large number of customers and a choice of who to sell to, and at what price.
- Strength can also be found in cases where suppliers produce unique products or services that are otherwise difficult to obtain.
- Strength can be derived from circumstances when the suppliers have access to greater financial resources than the businesses operating within the market.
- The final consideration regarding supplier strength is that they could decide to engage in forward integration.

The buyers

The final factor in assessing the competitive environment is the buyers themselves. Buyers can either be other businesses or consumers, and in cases where buyers have numerous available sources for buying products, they have a relatively strong position. They are also significant in cases where there are actually very few buyers and demand is considerably less than supply. In cases where buyers can easily substitute one product or service for another, they have relative strength, assuming that the products and services are not particularly differentiated. The final major consideration for buyers is the fear that they may decide to engage in backward integration.

Questions

1 What are the seven key issues that a business needs to look at to assess the competitive environment? (7 marks)
2 What is meant by a high exit barrier? (2 marks)

Determinants of competitiveness

LEARNING OBJECTIVES

▶ Determinants of competitiveness
▶ Competitive advantage
▶ Porter's four generic competitive strategies
▶ Market share

Determinants of competitiveness

An analytical framework can be created which assumes that overall innovation and competitiveness is determined by industry-specific determinants:

- Technology
- The characteristics of the markets
- Corporate strategies
- Organisation of transactions

The technological component refers to the tools available in producing the services and then transferring them to the end user. Market-induced competitiveness refers to the economic performance, which results from the structural characteristics of the market and the strategies of the businesses. The relationships can be seen in the diagram below.

PRIVATE INCENTIVES

competition legislation; subsidies; promotion; taxation

PUBLIC INPUTS

education; infrastructure investment; research and development; social capital

ORGANISATIONAL COMPETITIVENESS

efficiency of communications and management; utilisation of resources; incentive schemes; use of capital and human assets

MARKET INDUCED COMPETITIVENESS

competitive strategies; control; market entry; cooperation; globalisation factors

TECHNOLOGICAL COMPETITIVENESS

technological infrastructure; IT; communications; automation

OVERALL INDUSTRY COMPETITIVENESS

Competitive advantage

The term competitive advantage refers to a situation where a business has a commercial advantage over the competition by being able to offer consumers better value, quality or service. Normally, a competitive advantage would be measured in terms of lower prices or, in the case of more benefits and greater quality, sometimes higher prices as a result of the competitive advantage enjoyed.

Porter's four generic competitive strategies

Porter's initial argument with regard to competitive strategies suggests that organisations have two basic decisions to make in order to establish a competitive advantage. These are:

- Whether to compete on price, or differentiation which justifies higher prices
- Whether to target a narrow or broad market

He suggests that the decision behind these two choices leads to four generic competitive strategies, although there is a fifth, which he does not mention. In essence the choices of strategy are those listed in the table on the opposite page.

BOOK RESEARCH

Porter, Michael, *Competitive advantage: Creating and sustaining superior performance.* New York: Simon & Schuster, 1998.

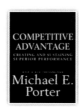

Porter, Michael, *Competitive strategy: Techniques for analyzing industries and competitors.* New York: Simon & Schuster, 1998.

Strategy	Description
Overall price or cost leadership	Theoretically this strategy seeks to appeal to the widest possible market, as products and services are offered at the lowest price. This form of strategy requires ongoing efforts to reduce costs without detrimentally affecting the product or service offered to the consumer. This tends to be an attractive strategy if the products generally on offer in the industry are much the same, or if the market is dominated by price competition. It is also the case that this is a good way forward in cases when product differentiation is difficult and most buyers purchase through the same channels.
Differentiation	This strategy rests on being able to offer differentiating features to the consumer, who is then prepared to pay premium prices, based on concepts such as quality, prestige, superior technology or special features. Ultimately any sustainable differentiation is derived from the core competencies of the organisation. The organisation has to have unique resources or capabilities, or some form of better management of their value-chain activities. Differentiation tends to take place when there are many ways in which products and services can be differentiated and the uses or needs of the consumers are diverse. It is also the case that differentiation is useful when competitors are not using this strategy and the market, or industry, is one which experiences rapid technological change or product innovation.
Price or cost focus	This is essentially a market niche strategy which aims to sell into a comparatively narrow segment of the competition, where lower prices are attractive to the consumer. This form of strategy tends to be used when the business lacks either resources, or the capabilities to offer their products or services to a wider market. It is ideal in situations when the consumers' needs are diverse and there are multiple niches, or segments, within the market. To some extent this is a trial and error strategy as each of the segments will differ in size, growth, intensity and profitability. It is also true that major industry leaders will not see the niche as being critical to their success and will therefore not focus upon it. Generally the strategy works only if few competitors are targeting the same segment.
Differentiation focus	In essence this is a variant form of market niche strategy, but instead of highlighting low prices as a key feature, the organisation concentrates on creating differentiating features.
Best cost provider	Theoretically at least this strategy gives consumers a blend of cost and value, as the organisation is offering them products or services which have relatively high characteristics and quality at a lower cost than most of the competitors. In essence this strategy has two elements – low cost and differentiation – and can be successfully used to target value-conscious buyers. Normally businesses operating this form of strategy do not target the broader market, but niches larger than segments. In order to be successful with this strategy, the business has to have sufficient resources and capabilities and must have the facility to be able to scale up its production and their fulfilment while maintaining lower costs.

Market share

Sales figures do not necessarily indicate how a business is performing in relation to its competitors. Changes in sales may simply reflect changes in the market size or changes in economic conditions. The business's performance relative to competitors can be measured by the proportion of the market that the firm is able to capture. This proportion is referred to as the business's market share and is calculated as follows:

$$\text{Market share} = \frac{\text{business's sales}}{\text{total market sales}}$$

Sales may be determined on a value basis (sales price multiplied by volume) or on a unit basis (number of units shipped or number of customers served).

While the business's own sales figures are readily available, total market sales are more difficult to

determine. Usually, this information is available from trade associations and market research firms.

> ### Questions
>
> 1 Briefly explain Porter's competitive strategies. (10 marks)
> 2 How might a business achieve a competitive or commercial advantage? (4 marks)

Methods of improving competitiveness

LEARNING OBJECTIVES

▶ Improving competitiveness
▶ SWOT analysis
▶ Performance importance grid
▶ Macro environment
▶ Competitive intelligence
▶ Competitive strategies

Improving competitiveness

There are many ways in which a business can seek to improve its competitiveness in the market place. In this section we focus on both marketing and non-marketing methods.

A business may attempt to reduce costs, improve quality or improve the way in which its staff are trained, leading to benefits in customer relations (customer service and after-sales service). Before a business can hope to improve its competitiveness it must assess its existing position through an internal and external audit. One way in which this can be done is by using a SWOT analysis, which identifies key strengths and weaknesses within the business, and opportunities and threats outside the business.

SWOT ANALYSIS

SWOT Analysis

Swot analysis is a very useful technique for looking at the overall future of a business, for example when considering the launch of a new marketing activity. SWOT analysis covers the following aspects:

* Strengths – what is the business good at? What are its key advantages over the competition in terms of its products and services, facilities, customer service and employee expertise
* Weaknesses – what is the business not good at? Where does it fall down in terms of the ways it does things? Are its products and services good enough? Is its marketing good enough?
* Opportunities – what is happening *outside* the business that could create an opportunity for it? For example, has the transport system in the area been improved, or has a major competitor closed down?
* Threats – what is happening *outside* the business that presents a threat to it? For example, are there more competitors?

On the left is a common SWOT-analysis grid, which helps to place all these considerations in the right place. A business needs to consider all these strengths, weakness, opportunities and threats before it makes any major marketing decisions.

Performance importance grid

A performance importance grid can be used by a business to identify its priorities, and its current strengths and weaknesses. In effect, the performance importance grid is a variant form of a SWOT analysis. Its direct application is to identify current priorities and current success in specific areas of the business's operations. It enables the business to identify the ideal strategies in relation to these two criteria, which are categorised as being high or low.

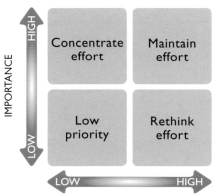

Macro environment

The term macro environment refers to all the external activities or influences that may have an impact on the operations of a business. Some do not have a direct impact, but may influence how the business operates over a period of time. In the vast majority of cases, businesses have little or no influence over these macro environmental factors.

Typically, the macro environment includes: society in general, politics, economics, socio-political change, technological developments, or socio-cultural changes and trends.

A business assesses and anlyses the macro environment in order to identify strategic issues that may have an impact on its operations. Typically, it will aim to:

- identify the issues that will have an impact on the business
- determine the trends of each of those issues
- classify the issues in terms of opportunities or threats
- evaluate the importance of the issues as opportunities or threats

Once the opportunities and threats have been prioritised, the business can identify their strategic impact.

Competitive intelligence

Competitive Intelligence (CI) is increasingly seen as an important task in the competitive environment, providing input into a whole range of decision-making processes. There are four stages in monitoring competitors, known as the four Cs:

1 Collecting information
2 Converting information into intelligence (CIA: collate and catalogue; interpret; analyse)
3 Communicating the intelligence
4 Countering any adverse competitor actions

Competitive strategies

Competitive strategies include all the activities of a business that are aimed at maintaining their competitive edge in the market. The following table summarises the overall options of competitive strategy:

Characteristics	Introduction	Growth	Maturity	Decline
Sales	Low	Rapidly rising	Peak	Declining
Costs	High per customer	Average per customer	Low per customer	Low per customer
Profitability	Negative	Rising profits	High profits	Declining profits
Customers	Innovators	Early adopters	Middle majority	Laggards
Competitors	Few	Growing number	Stable, but beginning to decline	Declining numbers
Marketing objectives	Create product awareness and trials	Increase market share	Maximise profits and defend market share	Milk brands and reduce costs
Competitive strategies				
Product	Basic product	Product extensions	Diversification	Eliminate weaker products
Price	Cost plus	Penetration	Competitive or matching the competition	Price reductions
Place	Selective	Intensive	More intensive	Eliminate unprofitable areas of the distribution
Advertising	Build product awareness among early adopters and dealers	Build product awareness and interest in the mass market	Focus on brand differences and benefits	Reduce to level needed to retain loyal customers
Sales promotion	Heavy use to encourage trials	Reduce as mass market begins to make purchases	Increase to encourage and discourage brand switching	Reduce to minimum

Questions

1 What are the four components of SWOT analysis and their relevance? (8 marks)
2 How might a business use a performance importance grid? (4 marks)

3 Explain how competitive strategies can be applied to the product lifecycle at each of the four major stages, giving a brief example in each case. (12 marks)

4 If the macro environment examines the external activities and influences on the operations of a business, what might the micro environment investigate? Give examples. (6 marks)

Case studies, questions and exam practice

CASE STUDY BIG FOUR

There are major concerns about the dominance of the big four supermarket chains and their influence over customers and suppliers. The market research group TNS Worldpanel have revealed that Tesco, Asda, Sainsbury's and Morrisons control 74.4% of the grocery market between them.

Tesco is the number one supermarket and now takes £1 of every £8 spent by consumers in Britain. The grocery market in Britain is worth more than the combined economies of Switzerland and the Republic of Ireland (at £250bn).

The All Party Parliamentary Small Shops Group has discovered that around half of Britain's 278,630 shops are owned and managed by sole traders. Most of these shops are now losing out to the supermarkets and in the twelve months to June 2006 alone, some 2,000 independent stores were forced to close, as supermarkets moved into their areas.

The criticisms of the situation seem to focus on the market leader, Tesco, which has a 30.2% share of the market, ahead of Asda (16.6%) and Sainsbury (16.2%).

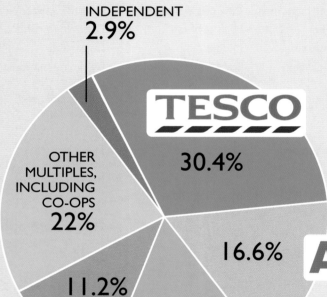

INDEPENDENT
2.9%

OTHER
MULTIPLES,
INCLUDING
CO-OPS
22%

TESCO
30.4%

16.6% **ASDA**

11.2%

16.2%

MORRISONS

Sainsbury's

Questions

1 What is Tesco's cash share of the grocery market? (4 marks)
2 What is meant by the term 'market leader'? (2 marks)
3 How might smaller retailers compete on a non-price basis with the big four? (6 marks)

SHORT-ANSWER QUESTIONS

1 What is a substitute product and give an example.

2 What is an exit barrier?

3 What are the **FOUR** key determinants of competitiveness?

4 What are Porter's four competitive strategies?

5 What do you understand by the term 'market share' and how is it calculated?

6 What is **SWOT** analysis?

7 Which of the two aspects of **SWOT** analysis examine the external environment?

8 What is the purpose of a performance improvement grid?

9 Distinguish between the micro and the macro environment.

10 What competitive strategies may be open to a business during the growth stage of a product or service in its product lifecycle?

CASE STUDY BSKYB

BSkyB owns 17.9% of ITV's shares and should be forced to sell some of its stake as far as the Competition Commission is concerned (December 2007). The regulator suggested that BSkyB cut its shares to just 7.5% of the total.

Virgin Media had tried to buy ITV, but BSkyB ownership of the shares had blocked this move. The Competition Commission believed:

- BSkyB's stake in ITV 'would limit ITV's strategic options', for example its ability to raise funds.
- This would have an effect on programming: 'Given its interests as a competitor and despite its interests as a shareholder, we believed that BSkyB would have the incentive to reduce ITV's investment in content.'

BSkyB responded by stating: 'The next phase of this process lies with the Secretary of State. We will be making representations to him in due course.' They clearly disagreed with the findings.

ITV said: 'ITV welcomes the publication of the Competition Commission's report today and awaits a final decision by the Secretary of State in due course.'

Virgin Media was quoted as saying: 'We're pleased that the Competition Commission has acknowledged the serious problems raised by Sky's stake in ITV and, in particular, its potential to distort the competitive landscape.'

It had cost BSkyB some £940m to acquire the 17.9% of the shares, claiming they had made the purchase because the shares were cheap. The Competition Commission disagreed and said:

'We thought it unlikely that that BSkyB would have chosen to invest in ITV purely as an investment vehicle.'

BSkyB had bought the shares for 135p each, but by the end of December 2007, they had dropped to 83p. Sir Richard Branson, head of Virgin, claimed that the purchase was 'a blatant attempt to distort competition'.

Questions

1 Why did Branson claim that the share purchase was 'a blatant attempt to distort competition'? What did he mean? (6 marks)
2 What is a regulator? (2 marks)
3 Why might BSkyB be forced to sell the shares and what are the financial implications for the business? (6 marks)

CHECKLIST AND REVISION

CHECKLIST

- [ ] Benefits and drawbacks of using budgets
- [ ] Calculation and interpretation of favourable and adverse variables
- [ ] Using variance analysis to inform decision-making
- [ ] Causes of cash-flow problems
- [ ] Methods of improving cash flow
- [ ] Calculation and understanding of net profit margins
- [ ] Calculation and understanding of return on capital
- [ ] Methods of improving profits and profitability
- [ ] The distinction between cash and profit
- [ ] Key elements of organisational structure – hierarchy and spans of control
- [ ] Key elements of organisational structure – workloads, job allocation, delegation and communication flows
- [ ] Workforce roles
- [ ] Methods of measuring workforce performance
- [ ] The recruitment process
- [ ] Internal and external recruitment
- [ ] Selecting the best employees
- [ ] How recruitment and selection can improve a workforce

- [ ] Methods of training
- [ ] Using financial methods to motivate employees
- [ ] Improving job design
- [ ] Empowering employees
- [ ] Working in teams
- [ ] Theories of motivation
- [ ] Organisational structure and motivational techniques
- [ ] Operational targets
- [ ] Calculating and managing capacity utilisation
- [ ] Dealing with non-standard orders
- [ ] Matching production and demand
- [ ] The meaning of quality
- [ ] Quality control and quality assurance
- [ ] Systems of quality assurance
- [ ] Quality standards
- [ ] Introducing and managing quality systems
- [ ] Methods of meeting customer expectations
- [ ] Monitoring and improving customer service
- [ ] Benefits of high levels of customer service
- [ ] Choosing effective suppliers
- [ ] Roles suppliers play in improving operational performance
- [ ] Types of technology in operations management

- [ ] Issues in introducing and updating technology
- [ ] The purpose of marketing
- [ ] Niche and mass marketing
- [ ] Influences on the marketing mix
- [ ] The importance of an integrated marketing mix
- [ ] Influences on the development of new goods and services
- [ ] USPs
- [ ] Product portfolio analysis
- [ ] Product lifecycle
- [ ] Elements of the promotional mix – above-the-line
- [ ] Elements of the promotional mix – below-the-line
- [ ] Influences on the choice of promotional mix
- [ ] Pricing strategies
- [ ] Price tactics
- [ ] Influences on pricing decisions
- [ ] Choosing appropriate outlets and distributors
- [ ] Types of distribution channels
- [ ] Possible impacts of market conditions and degree of competition
- [ ] Determinants of competitiveness
- [ ] Methods of improving competitiveness

FRANCO'S ICES

'Third generation Italian and second generation ice cream maker,' was Franco Desoto's boast on all of his advertisements and plastered across the sides of his eight ice cream vans. It was prominent on the two ice cream parlours as well.

Sales were up. Income was 20% more than last year at £340,000. Franco had reckoned on hitting £350,000 but he wasn't that disappointed. Profits ... well that was different. Franco had earned big and spent big too. The new van had cost him nearly £40,000 and a refit in one of the parlours close to £20,000. It seemed his suppliers were more expensive too – something to look at next year. The profits had dropped £35,000 to £55,000.

Last year's budgeted profit was £98,000 and this year Franco had hoped to top £110,000, but there was always next year. Franco had called in an advertising agency to have a look at his marketing. He thought he had a USP in that he was Italian, and was mentioning it in the advertising, but the agency pointed out that three out of the four ice cream van operations in the area were run by Italian families. They reckoned that the regional market for ice cream was worth over £2m, so that meant Franco was probably not the biggest anymore.

Questions

I (a) (i) What is the percentage difference between the budgeted sales income and the actual sales income? (2 marks)
(ii) What is the profit variance for this year and the previous year? State whether it is favourable or adverse. (6 marks)
(b) Franco tends to use internal recruitment for his vans and parlour managers. Analyse two advantages of using this type of recruitment. (8 marks)
(c) To what extent do you agree with the advertising agency that Franco's current advertising line is not working? (11 marks)
(d) What steps should Franco take to try to improve his profitability? (13 marks)

Harold Clifton's business is in trouble. The supermarkets have moved in, with Tesco two miles away and an Asda barely 500 yards from the front door. Clifton's had a reputation once, a good one; they were THE department store in the region. You could get anything there from a cashmere coat to cream crackers and everything in-between. Sales were disappointing, down nearly 35% at £1.4m, and the profits after tax were down to £105,000.

Competition was fierce everywhere. Since Harold shifted to a discount store format rather than a prestige store, he'd seen a change in the type of customer through the door. He missed the affluent customers who bought big and demanded the best. Nowadays, he was lucky if the average customer spent £10 – they probably stole more than that on the way out of the door.

Big flashy adverts in the local press, with 'Every Day is a Sale Day' across them had worked for the store for years. Harold couldn't afford television ads; he'd tried posters and wasn't convinced. He kept his shop open from 9am–9pm every day except Sundays, and he'd do the same then if it weren't for the law.

He didn't have a Human Resources department, didn't believe in one. He personally interviewed everyone who wanted a job and if he liked the look of them, he'd find them something to do. Not that anyone stayed with the business long, but that gave someone else the chance, someone better, hopefully.

Harold was disappointed with the sales of the cheap products he imported from the Far East, they didn't cost much, but he couldn't charge much for them either, everyone had them, so nothing seemed special anymore and that was a worry.

Questions

I (a) What is meant by the term net profit margin? Give an example from the case study. (4 marks)
(b) Why might quality be more important to the business than pricing? (9 marks)
(c) What is the marketing mix used by the business and why has it decided on this combination? (12 marks)
(d) The business refuses to spend very much on training and prefers to replace employees with better quality employees as the opportunity presents itself. To what extent do you agree with this policy? (15 marks)

PICTURE CREDITS

The publishers would like to thank the following for permission to reproduce images in this book.

p. 1 (t): © Tatiana–FOTOLIA; p. 1 (ctr): © Dmitry Mordolff–FOTOLIA; p. 1 (b): © Emilia Stasiak–FOTOLIA; p. 2: © Tatiana–FOTOLIA; p. 4: © Andres Rodriguez–FOTOLIA; p. 6: © Andy Dean–FOTOLIA; p. 7: © Linda Hewell–FOTOLIA; p. 8: © Junial Enterprises–FOTOLIA; p. 9 PA Photos; p. 11 (x2): Dyson Limited; p. 11 (r): © Stephen Finn–FOTOLIA; p. 12 (ctr): © webdata–FOTOLIA; p. 14: Connexion2 Limited; p. 16 (t): courtesy of Apple Inc.; p. 16: © Goran Bogicevic–FOTOLIA; p. 16 (b): Microsoft product shot reprinted with permission from Microsoft Corporation; p. 17: © air–FOTOLIA; p. 18: The Saga Group; p. 19: © Onidji–FOTOLIA; p. 20: Benetton Group; p. 20: The Body Shop International plc; p. 20: McDonald's Corporation; p. 21 (x2): Domino's Pizza Group Ltd; p. 23: PA Photos; p. 24: Street Advertising Services; p. 25: Chipsworld Limited; p. 27: © Vladislav Gajic–FOTOLIA; p. 28 (l to r): © mark smith–FOTOLIA, © Adam Borkowski–FOTOLIA, © Anette Linnea Rasmussen–FOTOLIA, © Clivia–FOTOLIA, © Graham Lumsden–FOTOLIA, © Jacques PALUT–FOTOLIA; p. 29 (tr): © Jane–FOTOLIA; p. 29 (tl): © Paul Murphy–FOTOLIA; p. 29 (b): © Mollypix–FOTOLIA; p. 30 (l to r): © Andrzej Tokarski–FOTOLIA, © Ruta Saulyte–FOTOLIA, © Feng Yu–FOTOLIA, © Irochka–FOTOLIA, © benoitphoto–FOTOLIA, © terex–FOTOLIA; p. 31: Corbis; p. 32 (l to r): © Sylvain Bilodeau–FOTOLIA, © amridesign–FOTOLIA, © Matty Symons–FOTOLIA, © Suprijono Suharjoto–FOTOLIA, © OlgaLIS–FOTOLIA; p. 33: © Christian Delbert–FOTOLIA; p. 35: © Com Evolution–FOTOLIA; p. 37: © Jun Dangoy–FOTOLIA; p. 38: © Chad McDermott–FOTOLIA; p. 39: Business Link; p. 40: © KonstantinosKokkinis–FOTOLIA; p. 42: © khz–FOTOLIA; p. 43: © Adrian Hillman–FOTOLIA; p. 44: © Designer_Andrea–FOTOLIA; p. 44 (b): © Nyberg–FOTOLIA; p. 48: © nsphotography–FOTOLIA; p. 50 (t to b): © RTimages–FOTOLIA, © Yuri Arcurs–FOTOLIA, © moodboard–FOTOLIA, © nyul–FOTOLIA, © Andres Rodriguez–FOTOLIA, © Marc Dietrich–FOTOLIA; p. 53: www.CartoonStock.com; p. 55: © Tatiana–FOTOLIA; p. 57 (b): © Dawn Hudson–FOTOLIA; p. 57 (l): © Dawn Hudson–FOTOLIA; p. 57 (r): © Mario–FOTOLIA; p. 58: © Radu Razvan–FOTOLIA; p. 59: © quayside–FOTOLIA; p. 60: © 3dweave.com–FOTOLIA; p. 61: © Elena Elisseeva–FOTOLIA; p. 62 (x5): Cadbury Schweppes Plc; p. 63: © Bram J. Meijer–FOTOLIA; p. 64: © Peter Galbraith–FOTOLIA; p. 66: © Andres Rodriguez–FOTOLIA; p. 67 (r): FreeFoto.com Ltd; p. 68: Google Inc.; p. 69 (l): Asda Group Limited; p. 69 (ctr): Patricia Briggs; p. 69 (r): www.PRshots.com; p. 70: © Jelena Popovic–FOTOLIA; p. 71: © Pavel Losevsky–FOTOLIA; p. 72 (t): © endostock–FOTOLIA; p. 72 (b): www.CartoonStock.com; p. 74: © Guillermo lobo–FOTOLIA; p. 75: © Lee Torrens–FOTOLIA; p. 76: © Douglas Freer–FOTOLIA; p. 77: © nycshooter–FOTOLIA; p. 78 (t): © Guy MASSARDIER–FOTOLIA; p. 78 (b): © nyul–FOTOLIA; p. 79: © mwproductions–FOTOLIA; p. 81: Patricia Briggs; p. 82: © Irochka–FOTOLIA; p. 83 (t): © pushkin–FOTOLIA; p. 83 (b): © Andres Rodriguez–FOTOLIA; p. 84: © Aloysius Patrimonio–FOTOLIA; p. 85: www.CartoonStock.com; p. 86: © Patrick Hermans–FOTOLIA; p. 87: 3i Group Plc; p. 87 (r): © Mike Thomas–FOTOLIA; p. 91: © nick pautrat–FOTOLIA; p. 94: © Vasiliy Yakobchuk–FOTOLIA; p. 96: © Danys83–FOTOLIA; p. 97: © nyul–FOTOLIA; p. 98: © Keith Frith–FOTOLIA; p. 99: © adam36–FOTOLIA; p. 101 (t): © diego cervo–FOTOLIA; p. 101 (b): © Charly–FOTOLIA; p. 103: © nyul–FOTOLIA; p. 106: © Julian Addington-Barker–FOTOLIA; p. 104: © Dmitry Mordolff–FOTOLIA; p. 107 (t): © Clivia–FOTOLIA; p. 107 (b): © David Mathieu–FOTOLIA; p. 108 (b): © Mykola Velychko–FOTOLIA; p. 108: © Chlorophylle–FOTOLIA; p. 109 (t): © Nikolai Sorokin–FOTOLIA; p. 109 (b): © Alex–FOTOLIA; p. 111: © Horticulture–FOTOLIA; p. 113: © Dušan Zidar–FOTOLIA; p. 115: © Radu Razvan–FOTOLIA; p. 116: © gajatz–FOTOLIA; p. 117: © Dmitry Mordolff–FOTOLIA; p. 118 (x4): Patricia Briggs; p. 119: © KonstantinosKokkinis–FOTOLIA; p. 120: © Joe Gough–FOTOLIA; p. 121: © poco_bw–FOTOLIA; p. 122: © Joe Gough–FOTOLIA; p. 123: © yong hong–FOTOLIA; p. 127: © Olesya Nosova–FOTOLIA; p. 128: © Stephen VanHorn–FOTOLIA; p. 129 (tr): © Roman Milert–FOTOLIA; p. 129 (tl): © Magdalena Kucova–FOTOLIA; p. 129 (b, l to r): © Margo Harrison–FOTOLIA, © Scott Williams–FOTOLIA, © Yang MingQi–FOTOLIA; p. 131: © Joe Gough–FOTOLIA; p. 134 (l): © Stephen Finn–FOTOLIA; p. 134 (r): © terex–FOTOLIA; p. 135: © Gentil Francois–FOTOLIA; p. 136: © Andrey Kiselev–FOTOLIA; p. 137: © Marcin Perkowski–FOTOLIA; p. 139: © Franck Boston–FOTOLIA; p. 141: © Chris Gardiner–FOTOLIA; p. 142 (l): www.CartoonStock.com; p. 142 (r): © drx–FOTOLIA; p. 143: © moodboard–FOTOLIA; p. 144 (x4): McDonald's Corporation; p. 145: © nyul–FOTOLIA; p. 147: © iofoto–FOTOLIA; p. 148: © Tjall–FOTOLIA; p. 149 (t to b): © Sean Gladwell–FOTOLIA; p. 149: © Iban Achutegui Tello–FOTOLIA; p. 149: © Lisa F. Young–FOTOLIA; p. 149: © broker–FOTOLIA; p. 151: © Linda Macpherson–FOTOLIA; p. 155 (t to b): © MarkFGD–FOTOLIA, © Lars Christensen–FOTOLIA, © mipan–FOTOLIA, © Shariff Che'Lah–FOTOLIA, © Emilia Stasiak–FOTOLIA; p. 156: © MarkFGD–FOTOLIA; p. 158: © istera–FOTOLIA; p. 159: © emily2k–FOTOLIA; p. 160 (l): © Andres Rodriguez–FOTOLIA; p. 160 (r): © Rozmaryna–FOTOLIA; p. 161: © krzysztof siekielski–FOTOLIA; p. 165: © endostock–FOTOLIA; p. 167 (t): © Yuri Arcurs–FOTOLIA; p. 168: © MarkFGD–FOTOLIA; p. 169 (l to r): © ellla–FOTOLIA; p. 169: © bluehoon–FOTOLIA; p. 169: © Lai Leng Yiap–FOTOLIA; p. 171: © Stu–FOTOLIA; p. 172: © Stephen Coburn–FOTOLIA; p. 174: © zts–FOTOLIA; p. 175 (l): © Christopher Nolan–FOTOLIA; p. 175 (r): © Dariusz Kopestynski–FOTOLIA; p. 177 (r): © Mikhail Tolstoy–FOTOLIA; p. 177 (l): © i9370–FOTOLIA; p. 178: © Johnny Lye–FOTOLIA; p. 179: © Andres Rodriguez–FOTOLIA; p. 180: © Freefly–FOTOLIA; p. 181: © Michel Bazin–FOTOLIA; p. 182: © Lars Christensen–FOTOLIA; p. 187 (t): © Peter Galbraith–FOTOLIA; p. 187 (b): © Brett Malcahy–FOTOLIA; p. 188: © Fotolial–FOTOLIA; p. 189: © mark huls–FOTOLIA; p. 191: © Fantasista–FOTOLIA; p. 192: © Mario Ragma Jr–FOTOLIA; p. 195: © Jacques PALUT–FOTOLIA; p. 199: © Lars Christensen–FOTOLIA; p. 200: © endostock–FOTOLIA; p. 201: © Anyka–FOTOLIA; p. 203: © David Winwood–FOTOLIA; p. 204: © pressmaster–FOTOLIA; p. 208: © msw–FOTOLIA; p. 209: © Sean Gladwell–FOTOLIA; p. 212: © bellemedia–FOTOLIA; p. 218: Tesco Plc; p. 219: © KonstantinosKokkinis–FOTOLIA; p. 220: © endostock–FOTOLIA; p. 221: © Kirill Roslyakov–FOTOLIA; p. 222: © mipan–FOTOLIA; p. 224: © Dan Bershing–FOTOLIA; p. 225: © Cristina Cazan–FOTOLIA; p. 227: © Mikhail Lavrenov–FOTOLIA; p. 228: © Kirill Zdorov–FOTOLIA; p. 229 (t): © Sergey Goruppa–FOTOLIA; p. 229 (b): © Natalia Bratslavsky–FOTOLIA; p. 230 (l): courtesy of Apple Inc.; p. 230: Dyson Limited; p. 231: © Graham Maddrell–FOTOLIA; p. 232: © rafalwit–FOTOLIA; p. 233: © Urbanhearts–FOTOLIA; p. 234: Marks & Spencer Group Plc; p. 235: Lexus (GB) Ltd; p. 236: BT Group Plc; p. 236: Skoda Auto UK; p. 236: Nike Inc.; p. 236: Volkswagen; p. 236: Virgin Group; p. 236: BBC; p. 237: Nokia; p. 237: © TimurD–FOTOLIA; p. 238: Xerox Corporation; p. 239 (x2): Toyota; p. 239: Corbis; p. 241: © Robyn Mackenzie–FOTOLIA; p. 243 (t): © Tjall–FOTOLIA; p. 243 (r): © Aloysius Patrimonio–FOTOLIA; p. 244: © Vieloryb–FOTOLIA; p. 245: © Andy Mac–FOTOLIA; p. 246: © Stephen Coburn–FOTOLIA; p. 247: © Steve Thompson–FOTOLIA; p. 248: © John Tomaselli–FOTOLIA; p. 249: © Dragan Trifunovic–FOTOLIA; p. 250 (x2): Fairtrade Foundation; p. 250: Marks & Spencer Group Plc; p. 251: © Lisa F. Young–FOTOLIA; p. 252: Patricia Briggs; p. 254: © Yuri Arcurs–FOTOLIA; p. 255: Patricia Briggs; p. 256: © pressmaster–FOTOLIA; p. 257 (tl): © drx–FOTOLIA; p. 257 (tr): © mipan–FOTOLIA; p. 260: Corbis; p. 261: © Nicholas Mcdonald–FOTOLIA; p. 262: © Eray Haciosmanoglu–FOTOLIA; p. 264: © Liz Van Steenburgh–FOTOLIA; p. 266: © Shariff Che'Lah–FOTOLIA; p. 268: Patricia Briggs; p. 269: © Norman Enke–FOTOLIA; p. 270: © memo–FOTOLIA; p. 271 (x2): www.PRshots.com; p. 272: © Milkos–FOTOLIA; p. 274: © alternative photo–FOTOLIA; p. 275: © Johnny Lye–FOTOLIA; p. 276 (l to r): Patricia Briggs; p. 276: © Vitalij Lang–FOTOLIA; p. 276: © Vincent Duprez–FOTOLIA; p. 277: © Udo Kroener–FOTOLIA; p. 278: Patricia Briggs; p. 279: Patricia Briggs; p. 281: PA Photos; p. 282 (t): © KonstantinosKokkinis–FOTOLIA; p. 282 (b): © Sylvie Thenard–FOTOLIA; p. 283: © Dmitry Sunagatov–FOTOLIA; p. 289: Patricia Briggs; p. 291: Patricia Briggs; p. 293: © Scott Maxwell–FOTOLIA; p. 296: PA Photos; p. 298: www.CartoonStock.com; p. 301: © ktsdesign–FOTOLIA; p. 302: © Aimohy–FOTOLIA; p. 303: © klikk–FOTOLIA; p. 304 (x2): Asda; p. 305: Dell Inc.; p. 306: © dotshock–FOTOLIA; p. 308 and p. 309 (x2): Patricia Briggs; p. 312: © Shariff Che'Lah–FOTOLIA